Examining the Vital Financial Role of SMEs in Achieving the Sustainable Development Goals

Dalila Taleb
University of Abou Bakr Belkaïd, Algeria

Mohammed El Amine Abdelli
University of Brest, France

Afef Khalil
University of Tunis, Carthage, Tunisia

Asma Sghaier
University of Sousse, Tunisia

A volume in the Advances in Logistics, Operations, and Management Science (ALOMS) Book Series

IGI Global
PUBLISHER of TIMELY KNOWLEDGE

Published in the United States of America by
IGI Global
Business Science Reference (an imprint of IGI Global)
701 E. Chocolate Avenue
Hershey PA, USA 17033
Tel: 717-533-8845
Fax: 717-533-8661
E-mail: cust@igi-global.com
Web site: http://www.igi-global.com

Library of Congress Cataloging-in-Publication Data

Names: Taleb, Dalila, editor.
Title: Examining the vital financial role of SMEs in achieving the sustainable development goals / Dalila Taleb, Mohammed El Amine Abdelli, Afef Khalil, and Asma Sghaier, editors.
Description: Hershey, PA : Business Science Reference, [2022] | Includes bibliographical references and index. | Summary: "This book provide theoretical and empirical frameworks and highlights the challenges and solutions with using the concepts of economic sustainability for the performance of SMEs in business activities to achieve financial sustainability in the business and economics sectors"-- Provided by publisher.
Identifiers: LCCN 2022013989 (print) | LCCN 2022013990 (ebook) | ISBN 9781668448342 (hardcover) | ISBN 9781668448359 (paperback) | ISBN 9781668448366 (ebook)
Subjects: LCSH: Small business--Environmental aspects. | Sustainable development.
Classification: LCC HD2341 .E93 2022 (print) | LCC HD2341 (ebook) | DDC 658.4/083--dc23/eng/20220325
LC record available at https://lccn.loc.gov/2022013989
LC ebook record available at https://lccn.loc.gov/2022013990

This book is published in the IGI Global book series Advances in Logistics, Operations, and Management Science (ALOMS) (ISSN: 2327-350X; eISSN: 2327-3518)

British Cataloguing in Publication Data
A Cataloguing in Publication record for this book is available from the British Library.

Advances in Logistics, Operations, and Management Science (ALOMS) Book Series

John Wang
Montclair State University, USA

ISSN:2327-350X
EISSN:2327-3518

MISSION

Operations research and management science continue to influence business processes, administration, and management information systems, particularly in covering the application methods for decision-making processes. New case studies and applications on management science, operations management, social sciences, and other behavioral sciences have been incorporated into business and organizations real-world objectives.

The **Advances in Logistics, Operations, and Management Science** (ALOMS) Book Series provides a collection of reference publications on the current trends, applications, theories, and practices in the management science field. Providing relevant and current research, this series and its individual publications would be useful for academics, researchers, scholars, and practitioners interested in improving decision making models and business functions.

COVERAGE

- Political Science
- Risk Management
- Finance
- Organizational Behavior
- Information Management
- Decision analysis and decision support
- Services management
- Networks
- Computing and information technologies
- Marketing engineering

IGI Global is currently accepting manuscripts for publication within this series. To submit a proposal for a volume in this series, please contact our Acquisition Editors at Acquisitions@igi-global.com or visit: http://www.igi-global.com/publish/.

The Advances in Logistics, Operations, and Management Science (ALOMS) Book Series (ISSN 2327-350X) is published by IGI Global, 701 E. Chocolate Avenue, Hershey, PA 17033-1240, USA, www.igi-global.com. This series is composed of titles available for purchase individually; each title is edited to be contextually exclusive from any other title within the series. For pricing and ordering information please visit http://www.igi-global.com/book-series/advances-logistics-operations-management-science/37170. Postmaster: Send all address changes to above address.

Titles in this Series

For a list of additional titles in this series, please visit: http://www.igi-global.com/book-series/

Futuristic Technology Perspectives on Entrepreneurship and Sustainable Innovation
Sanjay Misra (Ostfold University, Norway) Amit Jain (Amity University, India) Manju Kaushik (Amity University, India) and Chitreshh Banerjee (Amity University, India)
Business Science Reference • © 2023 • 300pp • H/C (ISBN: 9781668458716) • US $250.00

Cases on International Business Logistics in the Middle East
Islam Abdelbary (University of Plymouth, UK) Sandra Haddad (Arab Academy for Science, Technology and Maritime Transport, Egypt) and Ghada Elkady (Arab Academy for Science, Technology and Maritime Transport, Egypt)
Business Science Reference • © 2023 • 325pp • H/C (ISBN: 9781668446867) • US $240.00

Handbook of Research on Promoting Logistics and Supply Chain Resilience Through Digital Transformation
Ilyas Masudin (University of Muhammadiyah Malang, Indonesia) Mohammad Nabil Almunawar (Universiti Brunei Darussalam, Brunei) Dian Palupi Restuputri (University of Muhammadiyah Malang, Indonesia) and Ploy Sud-On (Mahidol University, Thailand)
Business Science Reference • © 2023 • 400pp • H/C (ISBN: 9781668458822) • US $315.00

Leadership and Workplace Culture in the Digital Era
Ebtihaj Al-A'ali (University of Bahrain, Bahrain) and Meryem Masmoudi (University of Bahrain, Bahrain)
Business Science Reference • © 2023 • 287pp • H/C (ISBN: 9781668458648) • US $240.00

Advanced Research and Real-World Applications of Industry 5.0
Mahmoud Numan Bakkar (Abu Dhabi Vocational Education and Training Institute (ADVETI), Institute of Applied Technology (IAT), UAE) and Elspeth McKay (Cogniware.com.au, Australia)
Business Science Reference • © 2023 • 315pp • H/C (ISBN: 9781799888055) • US $250.00

IGI Global
PUBLISHER of TIMELY KNOWLEDGE

701 East Chocolate Avenue, Hershey, PA 17033, USA
Tel: 717-533-8845 x100 • Fax: 717-533-8661
E-Mail: cust@igi-global.com • www.igi-global.com

Table of Contents

Preface xiv

Section 1
Sustainability and Financial Stability

Chapter 1
A Proposed Accounting Framework for Tax Accounting for Sustainable Development Activities in SMEs 1
Hesham Zakaria Mohamed, Higher Institute of Administrative Sciences in Janklees, Egypt
Khaled Mohamed Mahmoud, Faculty of Political Science, Economics, and Business Administration, May University, Cairo, Egypt
Mujeeb Saif Mohsen Al-Absy, College of Administrative and Financial Sciences, Gulf University, Bahrain
Hossam Osman, Zewail City of Science and Technology, Egypt

Chapter 2
Board of Directors' Characteristics and Financial Stability in Inslamic Banking 18
Afef Khalil, ISCAE, University of Manouba, Tunisia
Sabrine Chihi, Cresppa-GTM, UMR 7217, CNRS-University of Paris 8, France & University of Tunis, El Manar, Tunisia
Mohammed El Amine Abdelli, University of Western Brittany, France
Naima Bentouir, Ain Temouchent University, Algeria
Imen Ben Slimene, University of Upper Alsace, France

Chapter 3
The Influence of Shariah Supervisory Board on the Financial Stability of Islamic Banks: Do Religious Leaders, Women, and Skilled Shariah Members Matter? 33
Afef Khalil, ISCAE, University of Manouba, Tunisia
Sabrine Chihi, Cresppa-GTM, UMR 7217, CNRS-University of Paris 8, France & University of Tunis, El Manar, Tunisia
Mohammed El Amine Abdelli, University of Western Brittany, France
Imen Ben Slimene, University of Upper Alsace,France
Naima Bentouir, Ain Temouchent University, Algeria

Section 2
Case Studies

Chapter 4
How Can Small and Medium Enterprises in the Chinese Market Achieve Sustainable Development Goals Through Blockchain? 52
Poshan Yu, Soochow University, China & Australian Studies Centre, Shanghai University, China
Yao Ge, Independent Researcher, Suzhou, China
Kudzai Mandizvidza, Independent Researcher, Beijing, China
James Mulli, The European University of Luxembourg, Luxembourg

Chapter 5
Sustainability Within Italian SMEs and Its Effect on Their Financial Stability 86
Daniele Giordino, University of Turin, Italy
Cinzia Revello, University of Turin, Italy

Chapter 6
The Corporate Social Responsibility of the Family SMEs: A Descriptive Analysis in the Context of Tunisia 110
Zouhayer Mighri, ISIGK, Tunisia & LARTIGE, Tunisia
Sana Ben Ghodbane, IHEC Carthage, Tunisia & LARIMRAF, La Manouba, Tunisia
Mohamed Soufeljil, IHEC Sousse, Tunisia
Adel Redouane, Faculty of Economics, Commercial, and Management Sciences, Eloued University, Algeria

Chapter 7
Innovative Performance Management Practices for the Sustainable Development of Moroccan Construction SMEs 130
Abdelali Ezziadi, Polydisciplinary Faculty of Sidi Bennour, Chouaïb Doukkali University, Morocco
Mohamed Wadie Lahouirich, Polydisciplinary Faculty of Sidi Bennour, Chouaïb Doukkali University, Morocco
Aziza Chachdi, Polydisciplinary Faculty of Sidi Bennour, Chouaïb Doukkali University, Morocco

Chapter 8
Assessing the Impact of Financial Performance on the Entrepreneurship Dynamic for Social and Economic Development in Businesses: A Case Study of the Marrakech-Safi Region 149
Mohamed Wadie Lahouirich, Polydisciplinary Faculty of Sidi Bennour, Chouaïb Doukkali University, Morocco
Abdelali Ezziadi, Polydisciplinary Faculty of Sidi Bennour, Chouaïb Doukkali University, Morocco

Chapter 9
Can Industry 4.0 Technologies Offer a Solution for the Sustainability of SMEs? Case Studies From Turkey 179
Güzide Karakuş, Necmettin Erbakan University, Turkey

Compilation of References 207

Related References 240

About the Contributors 271

Index 274

Detailed Table of Contents

Preface xiv

Section 1
Sustainability and Financial Stability

Chapter 1
A Proposed Accounting Framework for Tax Accounting for Sustainable Development Activities in SMEs 1
Hesham Zakaria Mohamed, Higher Institute of Administrative Sciences in Janklees, Egypt
Khaled Mohamed Mahmoud, Faculty of Political Science, Economics, and Business Administration, May University, Cairo, Egypt
Mujeeb Saif Mohsen Al-Absy, College of Administrative and Financial Sciences, Gulf University, Bahrain
Hossam Osman, Zewail City of Science and Technology, Egypt

The chapter deals with determining the nature of sustainable development activities and their role in improving the performance of SMEs in the proposed accounting framework that works to clarify how to achieve tax accounting for the services and products provided by these projects. Without being exposed to the occurrence of the so-called tax pressure on their financial performance, which may hinder their development in the near future and increase their economic and financial value compared to other similar institutions operating in SMEs, and according to the latest statistic in 2021 received from the Central Agency for Mobilization and Statistics, SMEs in Egypt have about two million establishments in the private sector, in addition to what was reported by the Central Agency for Statistics. The need for an accounting framework comes with clear features of tax accounting for SMEs, as it will positively affect the performance of these projects by encouraging their continuity. The state should reduce unemployment and increase the informal economy.

Chapter 2
Board of Directors' Characteristics and Financial Stability in Inslamic Banking 18
Afef Khalil, ISCAE, University of Manouba, Tunisia
Sabrine Chihi, Cresppa-GTM, UMR 7217, CNRS-University of Paris 8, France & University of Tunis, El Manar, Tunisia
Mohammed El Amine Abdelli, University of Western Brittany, France
Naima Bentouir, Ain Temouchent University, Algeria
Imen Ben Slimene, University of Upper Alsace, France

In this study, the authors highlight some of the corporate governance mechanisms of Islamic banks, considering the board of directors, and empirically investigate its influence on the financial stability of Islamic banking. They employed regression analyses to test the effect of the board of directors' characteristics on the financial stability of Islamic banking, applying panel data consisting of 60 banks covering the period from 2015 to 2018. The main results indicate that the female director has a positive effect on the financial stability of Islamic banking. However, other dependent variables (the interlocked chairman with a shariah degree, the CEO duality, and the board of directors size) do not significantly affect banks' financial stability.

Chapter 3
The Influence of Shariah Supervisory Board on the Financial Stability of Islamic Banks: Do Religious Leaders, Women, and Skilled Shariah Members Matter? 33
Afef Khalil, ISCAE, University of Manouba, Tunisia
Sabrine Chihi, Cresppa-GTM, UMR 7217, CNRS-University of Paris 8, France & University of Tunis, El Manar, Tunisia
Mohammed El Amine Abdelli, University of Western Brittany, France
Imen Ben Slimene, University of Upper Alsace,France
Naima Bentouir, Ain Temouchent University, Algeria

The chapter studies the impact of the shariah board's characteristics on the financial stability of Islamic banks. Regression analysis is used to investigate the effect of the shariah board's characteristics on the financial stability of Islamic banks, employing a panel data set of 60 Islamic banking from 2015 to 2018. The findings show that a skilled shariah scholar and a female member have a negative effect on the financial stability of Islamic banks. However, the interlocked shariah scholars and foreigners positively influence the financial stability of banks. Plus, the results indicate that the religious leader (Mufti) and shariah board's size have no significant influence on the financial stability of Islamic banking. This study enhances the literature analysis on corporate governance frameworks and their effect on Islamic banking's financial stability.

Section 2
Case Studies

Chapter 4
How Can Small and Medium Enterprises in the Chinese Market Achieve Sustainable Development Goals Through Blockchain? 52
Poshan Yu, Soochow University, China & Australian Studies Centre, Shanghai University, China
Yao Ge, Independent Researcher, Suzhou, China
Kudzai Mandizvidza, Independent Researcher, Beijing, China
James Mulli, The European University of Luxembourg, Luxembourg

Blockchain is one of the most important innovative technologies developed in recent years. It has great potential and capacity to help SMEs prosper due to its decentralized public ledger, which provides a secure infrastructure for transactions between unfamiliar parties without any major influence from a central authority. The use of a decentralized public ledger also makes it possible for SMEs to get credit more easily, thus assisting them in achieving sustainable development. This chapter gives an overview of the functions and applications of blockchain, the situation of SMEs in the Chinese market, and sheds some light on how the Chinese policies on blockchain may affect SMEs. The chapter uses the case of WeBank to show how blockchain technology can accelerate the development of SMEs.

Chapter 5
Sustainability Within Italian SMEs and Its Effect on Their Financial Stability 86
Daniele Giordino, University of Turin, Italy
Cinzia Revello, University of Turin, Italy

This study attempts to investigate the relationship between sustainability innovation, firm performance, financial stability, and competitive advantage. In order to do so, the authors explore the effects that the implementation of a new business process which targets sustainability has on three small and medium sized businesses (SMEs) operating in Italy. Within the methodology section the authors have discussed the various criteria utilized to select an appropriate and adequate sample of SMEs. Semi-structured interviews were utilized to gather qualitative data so as to reflect the lived experiences of various members of SMEs' personnel. Data, charts, and various reports were utilized. The findings suggest the presence of a positive relationship between sustainability innovation and firm performance. Furthermore, the authors have gathered and analyzed evidence which supports the hypothesis that sustainability innovation has a positive correlation when it comes to financial stability.

Chapter 6
The Corporate Social Responsibility of the Family SMEs: A Descriptive Analysis in the Context of Tunisia 110
Zouhayer Mighri, ISIGK, Tunisia & LARTIGE, Tunisia
Sana Ben Ghodbane, IHEC Carthage, Tunisia & LARIMRAF, La Manouba, Tunisia
Mohamed Soufeljil, IHEC Sousse, Tunisia
Adel Redouane, Faculty of Economics, Commercial, and Management Sciences, Eloued University, Algeria

The social responsibility of business is a topical theme, which is of interest to both the researchers and the leaders of the companies. This paper aims to respond to the following problem: if the family companies adopt CSR then what about the social dimensions to their counterparts among non-family members? The study that the authors conducted with 141 enterprises shows that the adoption of the social responsibility of the small business family is progressive and slow. The authors find that the family SME is characterized by societal choices that differ from those of the non-family business. Our results have a considerable professional contribution. In this paper the authors provide to the manager an analysis of the behavior of leaders in a family SME around their CSR commitments. This paper is organized as follows: first, there is presented an introduction and review of literature and research hypotheses. The third section describes the study's sample and methodology choice where the authors briefly describe the main methods or treatments applied. The fourth section presents the discussion of results, and the last section concludes the study.

Chapter 7
Innovative Performance Management Practices for the Sustainable Development of Moroccan Construction SMEs 130
Abdelali Ezziadi, Polydisciplinary Faculty of Sidi Bennour, Chouaïb Doukkali University, Morocco
Mohamed Wadie Lahouirich, Polydisciplinary Faculty of Sidi Bennour, Chouaïb Doukkali University, Morocco
Aziza Chachdi, Polydisciplinary Faculty of Sidi Bennour, Chouaïb Doukkali University, Morocco

The construction industry plays a crucial role in the economic and social development of every country However, the construction sector uses 36% of total energy, 30% of raw materials, 39% of energy-related CO2 emissions, and 35% of solid waste production. In fact, the emergence of sustainable development has been accompanied by a profusion of research dealing with the impact of the integration of sustainability on managerial practices. In Morocco, the orientation to sustainable construction implies an evolution of construction project management practices to not only ensure that projects meet time, cost, and technical quality requirements, but also to guarantee that the construction project is sustainable. This paper aims to study the sustainable project management practices developed within Moroccan companies. For this purpose, the authors have used secondary data and activity reports from seven Moroccan companies in the construction sector. The results of this study show that the seven companies adopt very heterogeneous practices, ranging from continuous actions to specific actions

Chapter 8
Assessing the Impact of Financial Performance on the Entrepreneurship Dynamic for Social and Economic Development in Businesses: A Case Study of the Marrakech-Safi Region..149
Mohamed Wadie Lahouirich, Polydisciplinary Faculty of Sidi Bennour, Chouaïb Doukkali University, Morocco
Abdelali Ezziadi, Polydisciplinary Faculty of Sidi Bennour, Chouaïb Doukkali University, Morocco

Considering the weight of SMEs on an international scale, mainly in times of crisis, entrepreneurship becomes an important factor for achieving economic and social development that meets the demands of society. However, entrepreneurship requires motivations and implies objectives, and especially a financial performance, which will play the role of vector for entrepreneurship, and by extension for socio-economic development. In other words, it is about connecting 3 concepts: Financial performance, entrepreneurship, and socio-economic development. For that, this paper will first focus on the motivations and objectives of entrepreneurs, before developing in detail the concept of financial performance, its evolution to the sustainable development, as well as its importance in the entrepreneurial environment, as vector and objective.

Chapter 9
Can Industry 4.0 Technologies Offer a Solution for the Sustainability of SMEs? Case Studies From Turkey..179
Güzide Karakuş, Necmettin Erbakan University, Turkey

Digital transformation tools within the scope of the fourth industrial revolution continue to improve with changing needs and are an issue that maintains its importance. The fact that these technologies have an important place in the sustainability of businesses is a primary motivation of this study. Similarly, it is critical for SMEs, which have an important place in the national and global economy, to protect their assets in this process. In this study, semi-structured interviews were conducted with five SME managers in Turkey to understand whether SMEs, which are important actors of economic development, see Industry 4.0 technologies as an opportunity for their sustainability. In line with the findings obtained, it has been concluded that

SMEs see Industry 4.0 technologies as an opportunity in terms of their sustainability, ability to perform digital transformations in line with their own needs in business functions, and ability to prepare a roadmap for the future.

Compilation of References 207

Related References 240

About the Contributors 271

Index 274

Preface

Small and medium-sized businesses (SMEs) rely on banks and have opaque information. Because the scope and volume of complex data are constrained, banks mostly rely on soft information when lending to SMEs. SME survival relates to the number of years the company has existed, the presence of future plans, and the variety of products and services it offers. This model aids SMEs in better planning their support requirements as well as government and administrative entities at all levels and companies that provide support services in better comprehending SMEs' issues and support requirements. Although the importance of SMEs in these countries is acknowledged, several factors, A lack of appropriate technology, limited access to international markets, the existence of laws, regulations, and rules that impede sector development, weak institutional capacity, a lack of management skills and training, and, most importantly, a lack of financing severely limit their ability to grow. Therefore, SMEs have a significant role in the socioeconomic structure of any nation.

COVERAGE AND CONTENT OF THE BOOK

After double-blind refereeing, nine chapters were chosen that cover an important area of research for academics and professionals. These chapters examine the vital financial roles of SMEs in achieving sustainable development goals.

Chapter 1 defines sustainable development initiatives and how they might help SMEs operate better. According to the most recent statistics, the scale of projects reaching SMEs in Egypt has reportedly reached around two million private sector enterprises. Since it would enhance SMEs' performance, the requirement for an accounting framework comes with prominent tax accounting elements. In Chapter 2, the authors highlight a few of the board-related corporate governance practices of Islamic banks and empirically explore how they affect the financial stability of Islamic banking. In this study, Regression models were used to examine the impact of the board of directors' characteristics on the financial stability of Islamic banking. Panel data made up of 60 banks covering the years was used in the analysis. The third chapter aims to examine how the Shariah Board's qualities affect the stability of Islamic banks' finances using a panel data set of 60 Islamic banks from 2015 to 2018, and regression analysis is utilized to examine the impact of the Shariah Board's criteria on the financial stability of Islamic banks. Chapter 4 provides an overview of the roles and uses of blockchain, the state of SMEs in the Chinese market, and the potential effects of Chinese blockchain regulations on SMEs. The chapter concludes by demonstrating how blockchain technology might hasten the growth of SMEs by using the case of WeBank. Chapter 5 examines the connections between sustainability innovation, business success, financial security, and competitive advantage. To do this, the authors examine how three small and medium-sized enterprises (SMEs) operating in Italy are affected by implementing a new business process focusing on sustainability. The authors have covered the many factors for choosing an acceptable and sufficient sample of SMEs in the methodology section. Semi-structured interviews were used to collect qualitative information that reflects the lived experiences of various SME personnel members. There were graphs, reports, and data used. The authors of Chapter 6 used the survey of 141 firms, which reveal that small business families are gradually adopting social responsibility. The family SME differs from non-family enterprises in making different societal decisions. In Chapter 7, every nation's economic and social progress depends on the construction industry. However, the building industry uses energy, raw materials, CO_2 emissions, and solid waste production, accounting for 36% of overall energy use. A flurry of studies on the effects of integrating sustainability into managerial practices has accompanied the rise of sustainable development. The focus on sustainable building in Morocco necessitates evolving project management techniques to ensure that projects are completed on schedule, within budget, and with the required level of technical excellence. This chapter examines the sustainable project management methods used by Moroccan businesses. For Chapter 8, in times of crisis, entrepreneurship becomes an essential factor for achieving economic and social development that meets the demands of society. Entrepreneurship requires motivations and implies objectives, especially financial performance, which will play the role of a vector for entrepreneurship and, by extension, for socio-economic development. Finally, for Chapter 9, in the context of the fourth industrial revolution, digital transformation tools are a problem that maintains their importance while improving in response to changing needs. The main driving force behind this study is that these technologies play a significant role in the viability of organizations. Similarly, it is crucial for SMEs, who play an essential role in national and international economies, to safeguard their assets during this procedure. Five SME managers in Turkey were the subjects of semi-structured interviews as part of this study to learn whether SMEs, who play a crucial role in economic development, regard Industry 4.0 technologies as a chance to ensure their sustainability.

Dalila Taleb
University of Abou Bakr Belaid, Algeria

Mohammed El Amine Abdelli
University of Brest, France

Afef Khalil
University of Tunis, Carthage, Tunisia

Asma Sghaier
University of Sousse, Tunisia

Section 1

Sustainability and Financial Stability

Chapter 1
A Proposed Accounting Framework for Tax Accounting for Sustainable Development Activities in SMEs

Hesham Zakaria Mohamed
Higher Institute of Administrative Sciences in Janklees, Egypt

Khaled Mohamed Mahmoud
Faculty of Political Science, Economics, and Business Administration, May University, Cairo, Egypt

Mujeeb Saif Mohsen Al-Absy
College of Administrative and Financial Sciences, Gulf University, Bahrain

Hossam Osman
Zewail City of Science and Technology, Egypt

ABSTRACT

The chapter deals with determining the nature of sustainable development activities and their role in improving the performance of SMEs in the proposed accounting framework that works to clarify how to achieve tax accounting for the services and products provided by these projects. Without being exposed to the occurrence of the so-called tax pressure on their financial performance, which may hinder their development in the near future and increase their economic and financial value compared to other similar institutions operating in SMEs, and according to the latest statistic in 2021 received from the Central Agency for Mobilization and Statistics, SMEs in Egypt have about two million establishments in the private sector, in addition

DOI: 10.4018/978-1-6684-4834-2.ch001

to what was reported by the Central Agency for Statistics. The need for an accounting framework comes with clear features of tax accounting for SMEs, as it will positively affect the performance of these projects by encouraging their continuity. The state should reduce unemployment and increase the informal economy.

INTRODUCTION

SMEs play an important role in the economies of both developed and developing countries, making them the most powerful alternative for overcoming many economic problems, especially in current circumstances, because of the adoption of global thinking, the spread of the effects of economic globalization and increased global competition. Economic enterprises, in general, and SMEs, in particular (European Commission, 2022), have become active players in achieving sustainable development in the context of the classic enterprise concept and the adoption of the sustainable business idea, namely the environmentally friendly and socially responsible enterprise. This can only be achieved when SMEs, in their different activities, respect the concept of sustainable development; this goes back to the qualities of the latter, which enable it to reach the desired growth rate; however, it has not been possible to achieve balanced growth and sustainable development without the support and development of SMEs (Nnam Imaobong, et. al, 2022), which is why Egypt like other countries, seeks to promote the type of business, and this by adopting an integrated strategy and creating an appropriate legal environment through which it aims to guide the benefits of these companies, to serve sustainable development.

WHAT IS SUSTAINABLE DEVELOPMENT?

The beginning of interest in sustainable development in the seventies of the last century, as the Stockholm Conference of 1972 represents the initial beginnings of interest in the concept of sustainable development and the presentation of various discussions about the reality of environmental issues at the world level. Human life, taking into account the capabilities and capabilities of the ecosystem (Shobhalata, 2013), and the year 2002 is the real and global beginning to demonstrate the importance of sustainable development, specifically in the outcome of the World Summit in Johannesburg, South Africa (World Summit on Sustainable Development outcome; Biamrn Selin, 2013), and to determine what is sustainable development, the following can be addressed.

The Concept of Sustainable Development

Many opinions and scientific research have defined sustainable development as the decisions through which it is possible to increase the net gains from economic development while ensuring the preservation of natural resources without being negatively affected, but rather that their development is taken into account. In addition to this definition, sustainable development may be one of the alternatives to prosperity and progress in dealing with economic resources and their optimum utilization (Klarin, Tomislav, 2018). Taking into account the basic needs strategy and focusing on improving living conditions and taking care of the poor while maintaining sustainability in the economic and development fields and the available natural resources capable of development and renewal.

Therefore, sustainable development is defined as the compatibility between sustainable social and economic development and the preservation of the environment, and this is determined by the statement of the linkage and relationship between each of the economic, social and environmental dimensions, and taking into account future trends and needs in light of the current changes (Drexhage & Murphy, 2012)

The Importance of Adopting Sustainable Development

The theory of sustainable development depends on a set of aspects that, in turn, represent the importance of adopting sustainable development on the economic, social, environmental, political and other levels through the following (ICLEL, 2015):-

1. **Justice & equity** means that each individual in society receives a fair share of the society's wealth and energy to secure fair shares of growth for all social groups and for all countries.
2. **Control & empowerment** means that all individuals in society are allowed to participate fully in the decisions and mechanisms facing their lives and destinies.
3. **Welfare & poverty eradication** means that poverty is one of the most important social issues sustainable development seeks to reduce and eliminate.
4. **Democracy** is the vital principle of sustainable development, compatible with all economic, social, political, legal and other aspects. Without democracy, participation in the planning and decision-making processes is not achieved.

Sustainable Development and Its Accounting Perspective

The relationship between sustainable development and its accounting perspective, in general, can be demonstrated through two aspects. The first is if the concept of sustainable development is adopted in partial economic units such as companies. In this aspect, sustainable development considers the current and expected economic resources in the future to ensure the continuity and survival of any company. As for the second aspect, on the level of the macroeconomic unit (or national), sustainable development works to provide information that helps in measuring and evaluating the performance of the macroeconomic unit and allocating all responsibilities Concerned parties of all their internal and external categories (CIMA, 2020), while addressing the economic, environmental and social impacts, which demonstrates the accuracy and objectivity of the performance of economic units and the extent to which they are affected by expectations and forecasts. A picture of accounting information that helps all parties and groups.

Developments in the Axes of Sustainable Development

Sustainable development depends on a set of axes and dimensions that are not adopted and implemented in any country or unit, and they are as follows (Mensah, Ricart, 2019):-

1. **The economic axis of sustainable development** is determined through this axis to work on the optimal use of available economic resources, reducing disparities in income and wealth, and rational use of economic capabilities.
2. **The social axis,** the relationship is determined by taking into account the needs of the human society while striving to improve basic health and educational services and meet the minimum standards of safety and respect for human rights in the community.
3. **The technological axis,** represented in that sustainable development, aims to include the technical aspect in its various activities with the positive use of technology without negative impact on other elements, such as the use of technology in the industry and exposing the environment to pollution under the name of industrial-technological development.
4. **Environmental erasure,** the sustainable environment aims at observing the ecological limits of each ecosystem so that both consumption and depletion are taken into account, as the event of exceeding these limits leads to the deterioration of the environmental system, taking into account the relationship between consumption, population growth, pollution, bad production patterns and depletion resources.

UNPACKING THE SMALL EPISODE OF THE IMAGE

SMEs represent the mainstay on which any flexible economy depends because of their ability to start with costs and financing burdens that will reflect their returns on the owners of these projects. Perhaps the Asian model or values known as the Asian tigers have identified many aspects in this regard, specifically in the industrial field. And the manufacture of cars and vehicles, in particular, as the manufacture of cars vehicles, operates on complete production lines divided into small and medium projects until reaching the final product, which is the car or vehicle. Therefore, a unified scientific and practical framework contributes to the possibility of comparing them in terms of performance or growth or adopting more advanced and important aspects such as sustainable development. To clarify what is meant, the following points can be addressed.

Defining SMEs

There are many differences in the definition of SMEs, whether within one country or different countries, according to other concepts, including workers, capital, or providing products or services (Hashi, 2017), and given the multiple definitions and the difficulty resulting from the possibility of developing a specific and accurate definition of these projects. Therefore, it is necessary to draw attention to the structural nature of small and medium-sized enterprises, which have different environments and viewpoints, in addition to the various environmental, spatial or geographical criteria and standards, and to familiarize themselves with the commercial and economic laws regulating the set of special relations between SMEs on the one hand and between them and other projects in the national economy on the other.

Therefore, it is necessary for there to be public and private bodies and institutions that adopt the definitions of small and medium-sized enterprises through the adoption of unified standards when using. Among the definitions of small and medium-sized enterprises are the following:

a. The definition of the European Commission: "A small enterprise includes between 10 workers and 49 workers on its own."
b. The definition of the International Labor Organization: "SMEs are units that produce and distribute goods and services and consist mostly of independent producers. Unstable job opportunities, and this definition adds that it is an informal sector, meaning that it is an establishment that is not registered with government agencies or official statistics, often.
c. The definition of the American Economic Development Commission: "These projects are those that depend on the independence of management and that

the manager is the owner of the project and it consists of a group of individuals and a local origin so that the owners of the project reside in the project area."

d. The definition of the European Union: "SMEs are defined according to this union as follows: very small enterprises from 1-9 workers, small enterprises from 10 - 99 workers, and medium enterprises from 100-499 workers."

Characteristics and Advantages of SMEs

These industries have a significant role in building the national economy. Their importance appears through the exploitation of energies and capabilities and the development of expertise and skills, as they are considered one of the most important tributaries of the development process. Despite the controversy surrounding the age or modernity of small and medium industries, it has been found that these industries are old because they were the nucleus and the beginning of the industrialization movement. For example, the United Colors of Benetton Company, its owner, started working on one sewing machine at the entrance to the building that inhabited it. These projects have developed and expanded, and they are also new in terms of gaining the greatest attention from those interested in economic, social and development issues. Despite this discrepancy in the order of priority enjoyed by small and medium industries, they possess certain characteristics that distinguish them from other sectors, which are as follows:-

1. The facility's owner is its manager, as he undertakes the administrative and technical operations, and this characteristic predominates on these projects, as they are often family in nature.
2. In light of the low volume of savings for these investors in small and medium projects, the decrease in the absolute size of the capital required to establish small projects.
3. Reliance on primary local resources contributes to reducing production costs and thus leads to lower capital/labour coefficient levels.
4. Appropriate ownership patterns in terms of the size of the capital and its suitability for the owners of these projects, as the low capital increase the demand of those who are characterized by their low savings on such projects due to their low cost compared to large projects.
5. Low self-development and expansion capabilities due to neglect of research and development aspects and not being convinced of their importance and necessity.
6. Raising levels of savings and investment is a good source of private savings and capital mobilization.

7. Flexibility and the ability to spread due to its ability to adapt to various conditions on the one hand, which leads to achieving balance in the development process.
8. Complementary industries to large industries as well as feeding them.
9. Given the high cost of these operations, the difficulty of marketing and distribution operations, and their inability to bear such costs.
10. The lack of an administrative structure, as it is managed by one person who is administratively, financially and technically responsible.
11. The cost of creating job opportunities is low compared to its cost in large industries.

It is noted from the above that the characteristics of SMEs are negative, and some are positive. However, the negative aspects of these projects are not directly related to them as much as they are related to the problems they face. What must be emphasized here is that SMEs can continue for a long time without making profits, but they quickly collapse when faced with a critical financial push that does not accept the delay. Therefore, the direct cash flows of such projects are more important than the profit or investment returns volume.

The Role of SMEs in Achieving Economic Development

Given the great importance that these institutions occupy in the economies of countries, their position appears clearly and fundamentally (Holden & Banister, 2014), and this role can be limited to the following points:

1. **The economic role,** this role can be summarized in the following lines as follows (Howaida Mahmoud, 2021):
    a. Valuing the labour force: through the use of low-capital and labour-intensive technology.
    b. Mobilizing financial resources: by collecting funds from different sources, as these institutions can be established by families and families and consequently collect those funds, or for a person or skilled workers with a group of workers to form production units based on their savings, thus forming additional energies, enabling them To highlight their competencies and maintain their financial independence and unity.
    c. Raising worker productivity: embodying an effective and continuous control system to ensure the good progress of work, as well as controlling the workflow due to the small size of these institutions.
    d. Creating the Gross Domestic Product: We can see it through the private sector's contribution to a certain percentage of revenue in the gross domestic product.

e. The growth of foreign trade: These institutions, like other institutions, carry out all commercial exchanges, including export and import.
f. Providing the market requirements of goods and services and major institutions' requirements with raw materials.
g. Protecting the local industrial character: In light of the current developments and the face of the openness of global markets, liberalization of trade, lifting of customs control and the abolition of customs duties, there is external competition for products that affect local products, so these institutions work to protect their products through quality control and cost control. And trying to create a competitive advantage to counter that competition, and therefore if it can confront it, it can protect local products.

2. **The social role,** these institutions work to achieve regional balance and bring about developments at the social level. The social role of these institutions can be limited to the following points: eliminating unemployment by providing job opportunities and reducing the phenomenon of rural displacement through the establishment of some projects in rural areas or remote areas, thus bringing employment opportunities closer to the population of those rural areas. In this regard (Hesham Magd & Amina El Gareib, 2021), SMEs can eliminate social problems, improve the living standard in the countryside, optimise the utilization of material and human energies, and optimise the use of local resources.

THE EGYPTIAN EXPERIENCE IN THE FIELD OF FINANCING SMEs

Given the importance of SMEs and their effective contribution to the national economy, many developed and developing countries have worked to increase the effectiveness and efficiency of these projects, especially in the financing field (Nnam Imaobong et. al, Optic, 2022). Some of them were cooperation between the public and private sectors.

In Egypt, the Bank Credit Risk Guarantee Company for Small Enterprises was established as a public joint stock company, according to the Egyptian Companies Law No. 159 of 1981, with contributions from nine Egyptian banks with common ownership and an insurance company that was in 1991. The company aims to encourage and develop small projects in various production and service fields by facilitating the access of these projects to the bank credit necessary to establish the project, develop its performance (Daily News, 2021), or promote its activity, and all of this by providing a guarantee for the funds granted by banks. Its work is through an agreement signed with two Thirty banks in Egypt.

The company covers 50% of the value of the required financing, provided that the minimum guarantee value for a single facility is 10,000 pounds and the maximum is 700 thousand Egyptian pounds. Accordingly, the facility can obtain financing ranging from 20,000 to 1.4 million pounds. The warranty period is between six months and five years as a maximum, and it may be extended, and there may be a grace period. The company charges 1% of the balance of the loan or facility as administrative expenses annually. The company offers various guarantees, including guarantees for doctors, pharmacists, medical centres and analysis laboratories, and loans from the Social Fund, in addition to several other activities. The loan risk guarantee program implemented in this company was able to achieve great results during the first five years of its operation, as it was able to provide financing amounting to 697 million pounds, of which the company guaranteed 335 million pounds, and the average value of one loan is 143 thousand pounds for small and medium projects. The company's current policy requires not agreeing to guarantee any project unless it is self-financed at a rate of 30% to 50% of the total investment value (OECD, 2020).

Therefore, the government is counting on the micro SMEs to play a major role in the "sustainable development strategy" framework of "Egypt Vision 2030." Projects operating in an ongoing manner, according to an economic census event, where the Egyptian economy reached 6.99 percent of the total enterprises. Micro projects amounted to about 239,336.2 establishments, representing nearly 97 percent of the total projects operating in the sector. In comparison, the number of small projects reached About 398.64 establishments (7.2 percent), while the number of medium-sized enterprises amounted to 792.7 establishments (32.0%). The activity of small and medium-sized enterprises is mainly concentrated in the wholesale and retail trade and vehicle repair sector, where the number of small and medium-sized enterprises operating in this sector reached. The sector is about 57 percent of the total number of sector projects operating in the economy (Mahmoud Mohieldin, 2022). This percentage was distributed as follows: ultra-small 58 percent, small 3.24 percent, and medium 8.21 percent (www.amf.org.ae).

The MSMEs sector in Egypt benefits from an independent law regulating the sector represented in the Small Enterprises Development Law. There is also another law regulating the activity of micro-enterprises. Meanwhile, a new project organizing the sector's work is being prepared that includes micro and small projects, as well as work currently in previous laws, where the draft law is now being studied, as well as medium projects that were not covered by several ministries and agencies specialized in projects, including the Ministry of Trade and Industry. MSMEs (Doaa A. Moneim, 2021), the Central Bank of Egypt, and the Ministry of Justice. The sector also benefits from the government's approval of the movable guarantees law and its activation of the microfinance leasing formula decision.

The most important bodies regulating the work of the MSME sector are the MSMEs Development Agency, the Central Bank of Egypt, the Industrial Development Authority, the Ministry of Investment and International Cooperation, and the Financial Supervisory Authority. The most important source of local financing for SMEs and this is considered the banking sector, which consists of 38, in addition to several other sources of financing represented in companies, associations and civil institutions working in the field of microfinance, the development agency for medium, small and micro enterprises, financial leasing companies, and financing companies. Real estate companies, factoring companies, direct investment funds, business incubators and accelerators, and venture capital companies.

THE ROLE OF TAXES IN SUPPORTING THE SUSTAINABLE DEVELOPMENT OF SMEs

The Egyptian Tax System and Its Position on SMEs

The Egyptian Tax Authority has raised awareness for owners of SMEs about the facilities provided by the law for the development of medium, small and micro enterprises and the amendments to the value-added tax law (www.eta.gov.eg)., As follows:

i. **Tax treatment,** as stipulated in Law 152 of 2020, applies to owners of medium, small and micro enterprises. Still, the taxpayer has the right to use to be subject to the tax treatment prescribed in the Income Tax Law if the taxpayer estimates that he has made losses for the tax period in question. And if the taxpayer estimated that the tax due according to the simplified transaction system exceeded the tax due to him according to the Income Tax Law (Zeinab Abbas, Doaa Salman, 2020).
ii. **Tax benefits**, SMEs obtain the tax benefits stipulated in the law by registering with the Enterprise Development Authority to obtain a transaction certificate and a classification certificate for the project (Amer Bary, 2019).
iii. **Exceptions and tax exemptions,** an exception was issued from this condition, as it was agreed between each of the Medium, Small and Micro Enterprise Agency to submit the tax return for the year 2021 on the electronic system without registering with the Enterprise Authority and without obtaining a classification and treatment certificate, provided that these financiers are obligated to register after The tax returns season has ended. In addition, the Tax Authority will also be obligated to notify the Projects Authority of the

financiers who submitted tax returns, provided that the Authority registers them (Daily News, 2021).

iv. **Tax administrative procedures.** One window has been allocated to the SME Agency, with a tax officer and an employee to obtain the license and complete the documents so that he can open a tax file and enjoy the advantage of tax override following the regulations set by the law.

v. **The tax equation,** the tax on registered or registered micro-enterprises after the issuance of the law, is calculated according to the annual business volume for five years. For example, if a thousand does not exceed 500 thousand annually, the tax due is 2500 pounds annually. If the business volume is from 500 thousand and does not exceed one million, the tax due will be 5000 pounds annually (Daily News, 2021).

vi. **The criteria for determining the size of the business in SMEs,** the business volume is determined according to each of the data of the last final tax assessment for the financier registered with the Authority on the date that Law 152 of 2020, as well as the data of the previous tax return submitted by the financier, registered with the Authority and who was not taxed until the date of enforcement of the law Details of the declaration submitted by the taxpayer who is registered for tax after the date of enforcement of the law.

vii. **Due to tax,** the taxpayer has the right to apply to be subject to the tax treatment prescribed in the income tax law if the taxpayer estimates that he has made losses for the tax period under accounting and if the taxpayer assesses that the tax due according to the simplified treatment system exceeds the tax due on him following the income tax law, provided that he submits an application to the competent Tax Office on the form prepared for this purpose 30 days before the end of the tax period for which the provisions of the Income Tax Law are to be applied. Income tax on it.

The Egyptian Tax System and Its Position on Sustainable Development

The role of the tax system in general for the subject of economic and social development can be clarified as it works to provide support for economic units by directing investments towards specific activities and projects that, in turn, serve the economic and social vision and strategy set and drawn up by decision-makers and decision-makers in any country, as well as deepening trust between each of the parties to the system. taxpayers, financiers, and tax administration) to adopt the principle of transparency and credibility, and therefore the tax system and its position on sustainable development achieve an addition to a new party to the tax system, which is the future environmental dimension and the non-exhaustion of economic and social resources (Enterprise, 2019), even if this is reflected in the increase in tax resources of the state. That is, the tax system is used as an effective tool that limits the depletion of economic, social and environmental resources. Perhaps the Egyptian tax system has limited its stance to seeking to implement ecological taxes, which in other countries are called pollution (or carbon) taxes, which lead to an increase in the percentage of carbon dioxide pollution in the atmosphere.

PREPARING AND CREATING A PLATFORM FOR SMEs

In cooperation with the e-finance operating company, SMEs Development Agency has started developing a SMEs Platform. Special for small business owners, entrepreneurs and start-ups (FY22, 2021) (Noura Eissa, 2020), (European Bank, 2022).

i. The platform provides all the data and information needed to start or develop projects in a simplified manner.
ii. The Small Enterprises Platform contains all the financing, training, technical and marketing services provided by the various parties interested in SMEs.
iii. These services can be benefited electronically through the platform, which contributes to the support and development of this vital sector through the international information network and the services provided by the small project's platform.
iv. SMEs Platform includes the needs of entrepreneurs for information on service providers and guidance and direction in the field of entrepreneurship.
v. The platform provides services for preparing business plans, feasibility studies and the appropriate financing tools.
vi. The platform provides financing opportunities, business development services, marketing, administrative and financial services.
vii. The platform provides specialized technological and technical services in all economical sectors and value chains associated with each sector.
viii. SMEs Platform provides educational materials on "How to start, plan and grow your business", national programs and projects, and initiatives related to small, medium and micro enterprises.
ix. Platform development work includes adding new services; To support owners of SMEs and help them develop their projects through a set of sub-pages for banking and non-banking entities and through an electronic market that helps suppliers and agencies to provide trade exchange services. In addition, the platform presents new investment opportunities for the public and private sectors that owners can benefit from SMEs.

The platform includes the provision of a mobile application that ensures quick and easy access to information and services to users through their mobile devices.

THE EGYPTIAN ROLE IN SUPPORTING THE ACTIVITIES OF SMEs TO ACHIEVE SUSTAINABLE DEVELOPMENT

The Egyptian administration addressed many social problems and issues positively and effectively, including the issues of SMEs and the associated support for the national economy and the service of the Egyptian community, especially in the Egyptian state's endeavour to comprehensively account for the activities of the informal economy, so the matter called for several proposals to support projects Small and medium-sized and achieve sustainable development through the following, (Howaida Mahmoud, Optic, 20221), (African, 2022), (Reem El Saady, 2021), (DN, 2022): -

i. Activating the role of civil society institutions such as NGOs and businessmen associations and providing them with financing to re-lending them in light of their experience in dealing with small and micro projects using unconventional methods, in addition to their ability to follow up on their members.
ii. Expanding the spread of companies supporting SMEs and activating their roles, such as financial leasing companies, credit inquiries, guarantee companies and institutions.
iii. Establish a research body to explore new investment opportunities and conduct market studies in which the types of industries and projects with a gap and their locations are determined. Those wishing to establish projects are directed to these areas.
iv. Expanding the establishment of local and foreign exhibitions to help owners of SMEs to market products may be through the governorates, bearing a large part of the costs of that on behalf of the owners of the projects and with the help of businessmen out of social responsibility.
v. Searching for incentives and advantages to integrating the informal sector into the formal sector through simplified procedures for obtaining licenses with the provision of tax incentives with no retroactive tax accounting with the provision of technical and administrative support and financing to them.
vi. Attempting to apply the so-called protection method, which has been applied in some countries through allocating certain goods that are only produced through SMEs, in addition to the commitment of projects that receive government tenders to have a share in the inputs for owners of SMEs?
vii. That there should be a voluntary or obligatory ratio in the portfolios of all banks to finance small and medium-sized projects, and the ratio must reach a

level that is consistent with the importance of these projects and the need for their value because of their multi-axle positives.

viii. Paying attention to technical education and its development and vocational training centres in a way that contributes to raising the professional level of graduates.

Hence, the development of SMEs is one of the most important tributaries of the economic and social development process in Egypt, as it is a basic starting point for increasing production capacity on the one hand and contributing to addressing the problems of poverty and unemployment on the other hand. Therefore, Egypt has paid increasing attention to these projects, providing them with assistance in various ways and according to the available capabilities.

CONCLUSION

It can be concluded that the relationship between sustainable development and small and medium-sized enterprises is a direct relationship that each works to develop the other and that in the light of providing economic, social, financial, environmental and political information, it leads to the success of each in achieving and supporting the other, even if the tax accounting is through what it includes of the tools and means that are considered the main link in providing and creating accounting, economic, social, environmental and other information, as it is the initial step of the national accounting information, or in other words it is considered an input to the national ecological accounting system, which is regarded as one of its most important components of sustainable development in SMEs.

The future outlook for SMEs is represented in the challenges and opportunities, which are currently being followed by a national strategy for MSMEs to work on issuing a scientific and practical framework that, in turn, works to provide a suitable environment for MSMEs and entrepreneurs through several mechanisms, including upgrading the capabilities of micro-enterprises MSMEs, including preparing the Egyptian tax system to accommodate each of these projects in all its categories and indicate their effective role in achieving sustainable development, in addition to enabling MSMEs to transform the challenges they face into opportunities and to benefit from the growth opportunities of international markets.

The experience of the MSMEs sector indicates that there are several challenges facing the sector of MSMEs, the most important of which is the weak technical and administrative capabilities of project owners, the inability to prepare feasibility studies, appropriate work plans, and an administrative and organizational structure to obtain On the necessary financing, and the limited and high cost of non-financial services provided to these projects (advisory, financial, accounting, legal, ... etc.). Therefore, in addition to the reluctance of several banks to finance the SME sector due to the lack of capabilities and expertise, they have to deal with this category.

The challenge of having a number of these projects outside the official system adds to the challenges that prevent these projects from accessing financing in the absence of a documented credit or financial history, in addition to the weak ability to emerge projects to manage a percentage of self-resources acceptable to institutions of Finance.

REFERENCES

Abbas, Z., & Salman, D. (2020). *Egyptian small and medium sized enterprises' battle against COVID-19 pandemic: March–July 2020*. https://www.emerald.com/insight/content/doi/10.1108/JHASS-09-2020-0161/full/pdf

African. (2021). *The role of Small and Medium Enterprises (SMEs) in making Egypt self-sufficient.* African Association of Entrepreneurs. https://aaeafrica.org/home

Bary A. (2019). SMEs Sector: A Key Driver to The Egyptian Economic Development. https://www.researchgate.net/publication/331037085

CIMA. (2020). Accounting for sustainable development performance. *Research Executive Summaries Series, 2*(15). https://www.cimaglobal.com

Daily News. (2021a). *Egypt announces tax exemptions to boost economic growth.* https://dailynewsegypt.com/2021/12/13

Daily News. (2021b). *Simplified tax system could be applied to SMEs: Egypt's Finance Minister*. https://dailynewsegypt.com

DN. (2022). *EIB announces supporting Egypt's green, sustainable projects.* https://dailynewsegypt.com/2022/07/07/eib-announces-supporting-egypts-green-sustainable-projects/

Drexhage, J., & Murphy, D. (2012). *Sustainable Development: From Brundtland to Rio 2012*. International Institute for Sustainable Development (IISD), United Nations. https://www.e-education.psu.edu/emsc302/sites

Eissa, N. (2020). Egypt within the Sustainable Development Goals One and Two of the United Nations: Overview and Recommendations Thereof. *Research in World Economy*. https://www.researchgate.net/publication/344977238

El Saady, R. (2021). *The Role of SMEs in Mediterranean Economies: The Egyptian Experience*. https://www.iemed.org/wp-content/uploads/2021/02/The-Role-of-SMEs-in-Mediterranean-Economies-The-Egyptian-Experience.pdf

Enterprise. (2019). *Egypt gov't decides on tax reductions for SMEs*. https://enterprise.press/stories/2019/04/03/egypt-govt-decides-on-tax-reductions-for-smes

European Bank. (2022). *Egypt Country Strategy 2022-2027*. https://www.ebrd.com/documents/strategy-and-policy-coordination/egypt-country-strategy.pdf

European Commission. (2022). *Internal Market, Industry, Entrepreneurship and SMEs*. https://ec.europa.eu/growth/smes/sme-strategy/taxation-and-smes_en

FY22. (2021). *Unlocking Egypt's Potential for Poverty Reduction and Inclusive Growth*. https://documents1.worldbank.org/curated/en/407981634140851775

Hashi, S. (2017). *Role of Small & Medium Enterprises in Economic Development*. https://www.linkedin.com/pulse

Holden, E., Linnerud, K., & Banister, D. (2014). Sustainable development: Our Common Future revisited. *Global Environmental Change, 26*, 130–139. doi:10.1016/j.gloenvcha.2014.04.006

ICLEL. (2015). *The importance of all Sustainable Development Goals (SDGs) for cities and communities*. https://www.local2030.org/library/234

Imaobong, N., Felix, A., Linus, E., & Stella, O. (2022). Taxation Practices and the Survival of Small and Medium-Sized Enterprises (SMEs). *Universal Journal of Accounting and Finance, 10*(2), 399-410. https://www.hrpub.org/download/20220228/UJAF4-12225594.pdf

Inna, M., & Alex, P. (2017). The role of accounting in sustainable development. *Accounting and Financial Control, 1*(2). https://www.businessperspectives.org/index.php/journals?controller=pdfview&task=download&item_id=9472, 5/2/2022.

Klarin, T. (2018). The Concept of Sustainable Development: From its Beginning to the Contemporary Issues. *Zagreb International Review of Economics and Business, 21*(1), 67-94. https://www.researchgate.net/publication/326164068

Maged, H., & El Gareib, A. (2021). Entrepreneurship and SMEs Sustainable Development through Business Incubators: The case of Oman. *Scientific Journal for Financial and Commercial Studies and Researches, 2*(2). https://cfdj.journals.ekb.eg/article_146717_f954e2090a386a0118533a70313459eb.pdf

Mahmoud, H. (2021). *Sustainable Development Practices of Small and Medium-Sized Enterprises: A Case Study of Egypt* [PhD thesis]. Arab Academy for science, Technology & Maritime Transport (AASTMT). https://www.researchgate.net/publication/35406138

Mensah, J., & Ricart, S. (2022, March 2). 2019, "Sustainable development: Meaning, history, principles, pillars, and implications for human action: Literature review. *Cogent Social Sciences*, *5*(1), 1653531. doi:10.1080/23311886.2019.1653531

Mohieldin, M. (2022). Financing Sustainable Development in Egypt. In *Conference Management Section Economic and Social Commission for Western Asia (ESCWA)*. A League of Arab States Publication. https://mped.gov.eg/AdminPanel/sharedFiles/9d6b07e2-80fd-4f8a-b13a-8485a773f406

Moneim, D. A. (2021). *Egypt's central bank approves new facilities for MSMEs*. Ahram Online. https://english.ahram.org.eg/NewsContent/3/12/404632/Business/Economy/Egypt%E2%80%99s-central-bank-approves-new-facilities-for-M.aspx

OECD. (2020). OECD Investment Policy Reviews: Egypt 2020. *Assessment and Recommendations*. https://www.oecd-ilibrary.org/sites/9f9c589a-en

Ola, B., & Henrik, S. (2013). The United Nations Conference on Sustainable Development: Forty Years in the Making. *Environment and Planning C Government and Policy, 31*(6), 971-987. https://www.researchgate.net/publication/277683928 doi:10.1068/c12287

Shobhalata, U., & Sakkarnaikar, F. S. (2015). From Stockholm to Rio to Rio+20: Green Economy and the Road Ahead. *American International Journal of Research in Humanities, Arts and Social Sciences*. http://iasir.net/AIJRHASSpapers

ENDNOTES

http://www.eta.gov.eg
https://www.amf.org.ae/sites/default/files.

Chapter 2
Board of Directors' Characteristics and Financial Stability in Inslamic Banking

Afef Khalil
ISCAE, University of Manouba, Tunisia

Sabrine Chihi
Cresppa-GTM, UMR 7217, CNRS-University of Paris 8, France & University of Tunis, El Manar, Tunisia

Mohammed El Amine Abdelli
https://orcid.org/0000-0002-5784-4306
University of Western Brittany, France

Naima Bentouir
Ain Temouchent University, Algeria

Imen Ben Slimene
University of Upper Alsace, France

ABSTRACT

In this study, the authors highlight some of the corporate governance mechanisms of Islamic banks, considering the board of directors, and empirically investigate its influence on the financial stability of Islamic banking. They employed regression analyses to test the effect of the board of directors' characteristics on the financial stability of Islamic banking, applying panel data consisting of 60 banks covering the period from 2015 to 2018. The main results indicate that the female director has a positive effect on the financial stability of Islamic banking. However, other dependent variables (the interlocked chairman with a shariah degree, the CEO duality, and the board of directors size) do not significantly affect banks' financial stability.

DOI: 10.4018/978-1-6684-4834-2.ch002

INTRODUCTION

Islamic banking bases its operations on sharia Laws. Shariah became the centre of attention when something went wrong in banks (Khalil and Taktak, 2020). The Board of Directors has an important impact on the governance of Islamic banks (Alanazi, 2019; Khalil and Chihi, 2020c; Bakhouche et al., 2022). The shariah laws add responsibilities and expectations to the board of Islamic banks (Hakimi et al., 2018; Pranata and Laela, 2020; Khalil and Chihi, 2020b). Thus, the Broad Directors must apply shariah laws (Ullah et al., 2014; Hakimi et al., 2018; Khalil and Chihi, 2020d). In this context, the Director's Broads are responsible for the framework of the Islamic governance role and ensure that this framework is in accordant with nature and the Islamic financial institution size (IFI) activities (Islamic Financial Services Board (IFSB), 2006; Accounting and Auditing Organization for Islamic Financial Institutions (AAOIFI), 2010; Bank Negara Malaysia (BNM), 2010). Hakimi et al. (2018) and Khalil and Chihi (2020a) said that the good organization of a Directors Board could affect the Islamic banks' corporate governance and significantly affect their future.

Therefore, it is important to investigate the Board of Directors' characteristics. This study aims to study the impact of board on the financial stability of Islamic banks. The results indicate that the female director has a positive effect on the financial stability of banks. The other characteristics of the board (the interlocked chairman, the chairman with a shariah degree, the duality practice, and the board's size) do not significantly influence Islamic banks' financial stability. This paper offers new empirical evidence and ideas to enhance our skills in corporate governance-financial stability relationships. Plus, it significantly affects a large audience (academics, regulators, etc.).

The rest of our paper will organize as follows: Section 2 presents the literature review. Section 3 describes the used variables and sample. The empirical results are discussed in Section 4. Finally, section 5 concludes our study.

LITERATURE REVIEW AND HYPOTHESES

Chairman Interlocked

According to the busyness hypothesis, having a high number of board seats limits the director's ability to attend all board meetings and supervise managers, making the director busy (Quttainah, 2012). Iturriaga and Rodríguez (2014) add that the financial market responds positively when interlocked directors leave the financial institution. Consistent with the resource dependency theory, the director, who holds many boards, permits the firm to increase business contacts, receive more resources, and improve its knowledge (Al-Janadi *et al.*, 2013). Furthermore, interlocking facilitates innovation, creates synergies between boards, and increases sustainable development (Mans-Kemp *et al.*, 2018). Proponents of the reputation hypothesis say that the interlocking number show the directors high quality (Fama 1980). Plus, Fama (1980) predicts that the interlocked director improves the institution's return and ameliorates risk control. We hypothesise that:

H_1. The interlocked chairman has negatively influenced the financial stability of banks.

Chairman With a Diploma in Shariah

According to Khalil and Ben Slimene (2021), it seems that it is important for the director to have expertise and knowledge of Islamic laws to make better decisions and facilitate the roles of the Directors Board. Furthermore, a director with good shariah rules skills better understands the decisions of the council and efficiently supervises the shariah members (Tazilah and Abdul Rahman, 2014; Pranata and Laela, 2020). In addition, the president of the Board of Directors has an important role and influences the directors' efficiency and behaviour (Emerton, 2012). Consequently, the chairman has to obtain a shariah degree. This will ameliorate the Director's Board role and the financial stability of Islamic banking.

H_2. The presence of a chairman with a diploma in shariah has positively affected the financial stability of banks.

CEO Duality

The CEO duality allows better cooperation and communication between the directors and the managers, in accordance with the theory of resource dependence (Haniffa and Cooke, 2002; Bukair and Abdul Rahman, 2015; Elhaj *et al.,* 2018). Many researchers argue that the powerful CEO can share more relevant information with other directors. Amine (2018) says that CEO duality increases Islamic banks' performance and stability. Naveed and Abdin (2020) and Khalil and Ben Slimene (2021) add that CEO duality reduces financial risk and improves the sustainable development of firms. Following the stewardship theory, the CEO duality seems to favour shareholders' interests and the financial institution (Anderson and Anthony, 1986). However, proponents of the agency theory predict that CEO duality enhances the strength of the CEO over the board, leading to higher agency costs (Fama and Jensen, 1983).

H_3. The CEO duality has negatively influenced the financial stability of banks.

Women Directors

Following the social role theory, Khalil and Chihi (2020a) predict that Muslim countries have less women on their boards. This can hinder the shareholders of banks from having more women directors. Khan *et al.* (2019), and Yar and Ahmed (2020) indicate the existence of a positive relationship between the board's gender diversity and the bank's financial stability. This follows Adams and Ferriera's (2009) study indicating that having more women directors on supervisory boards can positively influence governed corporations. Khalil and Chihi (2020c) study show that the female director does not affect the financial bank's performance. However, several studies state that male directors are less likely to take risks than female directors. Indeed, women directors convince managers to follow overly conservative policies and certainly makes Islamic banking less competitive (Faccio *et al.*, 2016; Khalil and Chihi, 2020a).

H_4. The presence of women directors has positively influenced the financial stability of banks.

Size

By the resource dependency theory, many directors have various experiences and skills (Amine, 2018). A large board enhances the supervisory quality and meets the stakeholders' needs. According to Ciftci *et al.* (2019) and Rashid *et al.* (2020), many members enable them to manage the risks better, improve sustainable development and enhance Islamic banking's financial performance. In contrast, proponents of the agency theory say that a higher directors number presents difficulties communicating and increases agency costs. According to Jensen (1993) and Prowses (1997), a larger board increases the information asymmetry issues and encourages directors to pursue their interests. Khalil and Chihi (2020a) indicate that the board size does not significantly influence banks' financial soundness. The Islamic banks' corporate governance standards say that the Board of Directors size is defined by the complexity and the size of the IFI's functions (BNM, 2013). We suggest testing our fifth hypothesis:

H_5. The Board of Directors' size has negatively influenced the financial stability of banks.

METHODOLOGY

Sample

Our sample includes 60 banks covering the period of 2015 to 2018. We obtained the annual reports from the official websites of each Islamic bank and the international website for Islamic banks, "IBISONLINE,"[1] to collect the data. Since annual reports are regarded as an important source of information and a mechanism for official disclosure, we primarily used them to collect data (Marston and Shrives, 1991). In addition, the rates of economic growth and inflation for the gross domestic product were extracted from the World Bank website[2].

Variables Measures

According to Khalil and Chihi (2020b,c,d) and Khalil and Taktak (2020), we introduce the bank's financial stability as follows:

$Z\text{-}score = (ROA+K) / \sigma ROA$

Hence, k = total equity/total assets;
ROA = Return on asset;
σ (ROA) = Standard deviation of ROA.

We propose the following model:

$$Z - score_{it} = C + \beta_1 DIP_{it} + \beta_2 INTER_{it} + \beta_3 DUAL_{it} + \beta_4 FEM_{it} + \beta_5 SIZE_{it} + \beta_6 TAI_{it} + \beta_7 AGE_{it} + \beta_8 MO_{it} + \beta_9 SHR_{it} + \beta_{10} NORM_{it} + \beta_{11} CRI_{it} + \beta_{12} GROW_{it} + \beta_{13} IN_{it} + \varepsilon_{it}$$

With C: a constant, β1 ... β13: the coefficients to be estimated, εit: the error term, i: the individual which ranges from 1 to 60, t: the period which ranges from 2015 to 2018.

The following section will use panel data analysis to test our hypotheses and account for unobserved/omitted variable bias. First, we introduce the Panel Corrected Standard Errors (PCSE) approach. The PCSE system removes autocorrelation and heteroscedasticity issues by providing more reliable results (Beck and Katz, 1995).

RESULTS AND DISCUSSION

Descriptive Statistics

The outputs of the descriptive statistics show that the mean of the (INTER) variable is 3.895. The average of the (FEM) variable is 2.560%, which ranges from 0% to 33.333%. The Board of Directors is composed of about 8 directors. The (TAI) variable is estimated at 7.202. The (Z-score) variable has a mean of 14.480.

Table 1. Descriptive statistics

Variables	Mean	SD	Median	Min	Max
INTER	3.895	5.665	2	0	38
FEM	2.560	7.041	0	0	33.333
SIZE	8.432	2.849	9	2	21
TAI	7.202	1.545	7.391	1.571	11.586
AGE	1.455	0.558	1.301	0.568	4.383
CROW	3.061	3.581	3.5	-28	13.4
IN	8.080	13.274	2.8	-26	63.3
z-score	14.480	14.069	10.500	-1.32528	92.414

Table 2 shows that the Director's Board comprises 98.507% of the chairman who does not have a shariah diploma. 7.462% of Islamic banks apply the duality practice. We conclude that duality is not a current practice. 66.417% of Islamic banks have a central council. We note that 35.820% of banks in our sample belong to countries that employ the AAOIFI standards.

Table 2. Frequency of binary variables

Variables	DIP		DUAL	
Frequency %	1	0	1	0
	7.462	98.507	1.608	92.537

Table 3. Frequency of binary control variables

Variables	MO		SHR		NORM	
Frequency %	1	0	1	0	1	0
	66.417	33.582	54.104	45.895	35.820	64.179

Cross-Correlation Matrix

Table 4 highlights that the Cross-Correlation coefficients do not exceed the 0.7 value (Kennedy, 2008).

Table 4. Cross-Correlation Matrix

	INTER	DIP	DUAL	SIZE	FEM	TAI	AGE	MO	SHR	NORM	CROW	IN
INTER	1.0000											
DIP	-0.0195	1.0000										
DUAL	-0.0450	-0.0350	1.0000									
SIZE	0.1388	0.1652	-0.2030	1.0000								
FEM	0.0209	-0.0449	0.0952	0.0210	1.0000							
TAI	0.0300	-0.1197	0.1590	-0.0627	0.0003	1.0000						
AGE	0.1389	-0.0797	0.1407	0.0525	0.0500	0.2489	1.0000					
MO	-0.1431	0.0875	0.2019	0.0415	0.2591	-0.1143	0.0243	1.0000				
SHR	-0.0673	0.1134	0.0336	0.0243	-0.1955	-0.1060	-0.0454	0.5184	1.0000			
NORM	-0.0646	0.1648	-0.2122	0.0642	-0.2074	-0.1411	-0.0762	0.5312	0.6881	1.0000		
CROW	0.0371	-0.0004	0.1599	0.0858	0.1625	0.0424	0.0300	0.2318	-0.1187	-0.1105	1.0000	
IN	-0.1457	-0.0563	-0.0250	-0.0295	-0.0618	0.0661	0.0567	0.2098	0.2982	0.3752	-0.2299	1.0000

Discussion

Table 5 reveals a statistically positive relationship between women directors and financial stability, and the coefficient positively influences (FEM) on the banks' stability. H4, therefore, is supported. This supports the research studies (Pathan and Faff, 2013; Khan *et al.*, 2019) and implies that female directors positively affected financial stability. Furthermore, this result implies that banks with large women's boards foster financial stability. In the same way, the presence of female directors makes Islamic banks more strongly and competitive.

We concluded that the corporate governance standards had proposed any rules on the interlocking number that the chairman can fulfil (INTER), the chairman with a shariah degree (DIP), the duality practice (DUAL), and the board's size (SIZE). These justify the results. Plus, from Table 5, the control variables (TAI, AGE, MO, SHR, NORM, GROW, IN) do not significantly influence the banks' stability.

Table 5. Regression results

Variables	Coef.	Z	P>|z|
INTER	-0.122	-1.10	0.273
DIP	-4.012	-1.34	0.181
DUAL	3.882	0.43	0.670
FEM	0.318	2.18	0.030**
SIZE	0.465	1.43	0.152
TAI	-0.610	-1.55	0.122
AGE	0.536	0.42	0.672
MO	-1.886	-0.60	0.546
SHR	-3.006	-1.03	0.302
NORM	3.781	1.13	0.260
GROW	0.028	0.19	0.852
IN	0.0470	0.68	0.498
Cons	14.665	3.54	0.000***
R^2	30.57%		
N	240		

CONCLUSION

The good organization of a Directors' Board can affect the Islamic banks' corporate governance and significantly affect its future, according to Hakimi *et al.* (2018) and Khalil and Chihi (2020a). This research paper examines the impact of the board on the financial stability of banks. To achieve our hypotheses, we used a sample of 60 banks, where the study period was four years (2015 to 2018).

We found that the female director has a positive influence on the financial stability of Islamic banking. The other characteristics of the board (the interlocked chairman, the chairman with a shariah degree, the duality practice, and the board's size) did not represent any influence on the financial stability of banks.

Thus, this investigation offers theoretical, practical and managerial Contributions. In other words, it highly suggests new empirical evidence and ideas ameliorate our skills in corporate governance-financial stability relationships. The study also offers practical implications. It has significant value to a wide audience. Indeed, this study provides crucial information on how the characteristics of the board can be utilized to increase the stability of banks. It proposes that banks hire female directors in particular. As a result, Islamic bank authorities should consider the research findings while revising the legislation and putting more effort into implementing governance reform measures. Furthermore, supervisory authorities should improve their methods, and ensure that banks are well-governed.

The study has some limitations. There are a few flaws in the study and future studies can yet investigate some possibilities. First, the sample in our study comprises 240 bank years of observations. Even though it is a large sample compared to other Islamic bank research, a future attempt may have a larger sample, increasing the generalizability of the research findings. Second, we need more and better data to explain how to enhance economic growth and foster financial stability. Third, this study does not take into account other important aspects of the board (female ownership, political directors, and so on). As a result, it is suggested that all corporate governance features be included in a future study to better our understanding of the board and the stability of banks relationships.

REFERENCES

AAOIFI. (2010). *Shariah Standards for Islamic Financial Institutions*. Accounting and Auditing Organization for Islamic Financial Institutions.

Abdul Alim, E. (2014). *Global Leaders in Islamic Finance*. Industry Milestones and Reflections, Edition Wiley.

Abdul Latif, R., Kamardin, H., Mohd, K. N. T., & Adam, N. C. (2013). Multiple Directorships, Board Characteristics and Firm Performance in Malaysia. *Management*, *3*(2), 105–111.

Ahn, S., Jiraporn, P., & Kim, Y. S. (2010). Multiple directorships and acquirer returns. *Journal of Banking & Finance*, *34*(9), 2011–2026. doi:10.1016/j.jbankfin.2010.01.009

Al-Janadi, Y., Abdul Rahman, R., & Haj Omar, N. (2013). Corporate Governance Mechanisms and Voluntary Disclosure in Saudi Arabia. *Research Journal of Finance and Accounting*, *4*(4), 25–35.

Al-Musalli, M. A. K., & Ismail, K. N. I. (2012). Corporate Governance, Bank Specific Characteristics, Banking Industry Characteristics, And Intellectual Capital (IC) Performance Of Banks In Arab Gulf Cooperation Council (GCC) Countries. *Asian Academy of Management Journal of Accounting and Finance*, *8*(1), 115–135.

Alanazi, A. S. (2019). Corporate governance and the characteristics of the board of directors: Evidence from an emerging market. *Corporate Board: Role, Duties and Composition*, *15*(1), 17–24. doi:10.22495/cbv15i1art2

Amine, B. (2018). Contribution of Governance to Ensure the Stability of Islamic Banks: A Panel Data Analysis. *International Journal of Accounting and Financial Reporting*, *8*(3), 140–155. doi:10.5296/ijafr.v8i3.13333

Anderson, C. A., & Anthony, R. N. (1986). *The new corporate directors*. John Wiley and Sons.

Bakhouche, A., El Ghak, T., & Alshiab, M. (2022). Does Islamicity matter for the stability of Islamic banks in dual banking systems? *Heliyon*, *8*(4), e09245. Advance online publication. doi:10.1016/j.heliyon.2022.e09245 PMID:35434399

Beck, N., & Katz, J. N. (1995). What to do (and not to do) with time-series cross-section data. *The American Political Science Review*, *89*(3), 634–647. doi:10.2307/2082979

BNM. (2010). *"Shariah Governance Framework for Islamic Financial Institutions", Islamic Banking and Takaful Department, RH/GL/012-23*. Bank Negara Malaysia-Central Bank of Malaysia.

BNM. (2013). *"Guidelines on Corporate Governance for Licensed Islamic Banks (GP1-i)", Islamic Banking and Takaful Department, RH/GL/002-1*. Bank Negara Malaysia-Central Bank of Malaysia.

BNM. (2015). *"Guidelines on Financial Reporting for Licensed Islamic Banks", Islamic Banking and Takaful Department, RH/GL/002-2*. Bank Negara Malaysia-Central Bank of Malaysia.

Boussaada, R. (2012). *L'impact De La Gouvernance Bancaire Et De La Relation Bancaire Sur Le Risque De Crédit: Cas Des Banques Tunisiennes* [Ph.D. thesis]. University Montesquieu-University Tunis.

Buallay, A. (2019). Corporate governance, Sharia'ah governance and performance: A crosscountry comparison in MENA region. *International Journal of Islamic and Middle Eastern Finance and Management*, *12*(2), 216–235. doi:10.1108/IMEFM-07-2017-0172

Bukair, A. A., & Abdul Rahman, A. (2015). Bank performance and board of directors attributes by Islamic banks. *International Journal of Islamic and Middle Eastern Finance and Management*, *8*(3), 291–309. doi:10.1108/IMEFM-10-2013-0111

Chen, C. X., Lu, H., & Sougiannis, T. (2012). The agency problem, corporate governance, and the asymmetrical behavior of selling, general, and administrative costs. *Contemporary Accounting Research*, *29*(1), 252–282. doi:10.1111/j.1911-3846.2011.01094.x

Ciftci, I. E., Tatoglu, G., Demirbag, W. M., & Zaim, S. (2019). Corporate governance and firm performance in emerging markets: Evidence from Turkey. *International Business Review*, *28*(1), 90–103. doi:10.1016/j.ibusrev.2018.08.004

Daly, S., & Frikha, M. (2015). Corporate governance: What about Islamic banks? *International Journal of FinancialServices Management*, *8*(1), 18–41.

Dhouibi, R., & Mamoghli, C. (2013). Determinants of voluntary disclosure in Tunisian Bank's reports. *Research Journal of Finance and Accounting*, *4*(5), 80–94.

Elhaj, M. A., Muhamed, N. A., & Ramli, N. M. (2018). The effects of board attributes on Sukuk rating. *International Journal of Islamic and Middle Eastern Finance and Management*, *11*(2), 312–330. doi:10.1108/IMEFM-03-2017-0057

Elyasiani, E., & Jia, J. (2010). Distribution of institutional ownership and corporate firm performance. *Journal of Banking & Finance*, *34*(3), 606–620. doi:10.1016/j.jbankfin.2009.08.018

Emerton. (2012). *What Makes an Exceptional Independent Non Executive Director?* The Korn/Ferry Institute.

Fama, E. F. (1980). Agency problems and the theory of the firm. *Journal of Political Economy*, *88*(2), 288–307. doi:10.1086/260866

Fama, E. F., & Jensen, M. C. (1983). Separation of ownership and control. *The Journal of Law & Economics*, *26*(2), 301–325. doi:10.1086/467037

Field, L., Lowry, M., & Mkrtchyan, A. (2013). Are busy boards detrimental? *Journal of Financial Economics*, *109*(1), 63–82. doi:10.1016/j.jfineco.2013.02.004

Grassa, R., & Matoussi, H. (2014). Corporate Governance Of Islamic Banks: A Comparative Study Between GCC And Southeast Asia Countries. *International Journal of Islamic and Middle Eastern Finance and Management*, *7*(3), 346–362. doi:10.1108/IMEFM-01-2013-0001

Gujarati, D. (1995). *Basic Econometrics*. McGraw Hill.

Hakimi, A., Rachdi, H., Ben Selma Mokni, R., & Hssini, H. (2018). Do board characteristics affect bank performance? Evidence from the Bahrain Islamic banks. *Journal of Islamic Accounting and Business Research*, *9*(2), 251–272. doi:10.1108/JIABR-06-2015-0029

Haniffa, R. M., & Cooke, T. E. (2002). Culture, Corporate Governance andDisclosure in Malaysian Corporations. *Abacus*, *38*(3), 317–349. doi:10.1111/1467-6281.00112

Hassan, M.K., Sanchez, B., & Safa, M.F. (2013). Impact of financial liberalization and foreign bank entry on Islamic banking performance. *International Journal of Islamic and Middle Eastern Finance and Management*, *6*(1), 7-42.

Hawkamah. (2011). *Policy Brief On Corporate Governance For Islamic Banks And Financial Institutions In The Middle East And North Africa Region*. Hawkamah, The Institute for Corporate Governance.

Ibrahim, S. H. B. M., Wirman, A., Alrazi, B., Nor, M. N. B. M., & Pramono, S. (2012). *Alternative Disclosure & Performance Measures For Islamic Banks*. Working Paper, International Islamic University Malaysia.

IFSB. (2006). Guiding Principles On Corporate Governance For Institutions Offering Only Islamic Financial Services (Excluding Islamic Insurance (Takaful) Institutions And Islamic Mutual Funds). Islamic Financial Services Board.

IMF. (2006). *Financial Stability Indicators*. International Monetary Fund.

Iturriaga, F. J. L., & Rodríguez, I. M. (2014). Boards of directors and firm performance: The effect of multipleDirectorships. *Revista Española de Financiación y Contabilidad*, *43*(2), 177–192. doi:10.1080/02102412.2014.913909

Jensen, M. C. (1993). The modern industrial revolution, exit and the failure of internal control systems. *The Journal of Finance*, *48*(3), 831–880. doi:10.1111/j.1540-6261.1993.tb04022.x

Jensen, M. C., & Meckling, W. H. (1976). Theory of the firm: Managerial behavior, agency cost and ownership structure. *Journal of Financial Economics*, *3*(4), 305–360. doi:10.1016/0304-405X(76)90026-X

Kasim, N., Htay, S. N. N., & Salman, S. A. (2013). Conceptual Framework for Shariah Corporate Governance with Special Focus on Islamic Capital Market in Malaysia. *International Journal of Trade, Economics and Finance*, *4*(5), 336–339. doi:10.7763/IJTEF.2013.V4.312

Kennedy, P. (1998). *A guide to econometrics*. Blackwell.

Kennedy, P. (2008). *A Guide to Econometrics*. Blackwell.

Khalil, A., & Ben Slimene, I. (2021). Financial Soundness of Islamic banks: Does the Structure of the Board of Directors Matter? *Corporate Governance*, *21*(7), 1393–1415. doi:10.1108/CG-06-2020-0237

Khalil, A., & Chihi, S. (2020a). Do board characteristics affect the financial stability of Islamic banks. *African Scientific Journal*, *3*(2), 85–102.

Khalil, A., & Chihi, S. (2020b). Would meetings between the Board of Directors and the Shariah Supervisory Board affect the financial performance of Islamic banks? *Journal of the International Academy for Case Studies*, *26*(6), 1-7.

Khalil, A., & Chihi, S. (2020c). Would foreign directors and women directors affect the financial performance of Islamic banking? *Journal of the International Academy for Case Studies*, *26*(6), 1-5.

Khalil, A., & Chihi, S. (2020d). Does the Shariah Board structure influence the financial performance of Islamic banks? *Journal of the International Academy for Case Studies*, *26*(6), 1-7.

Khalil, A., & Taktak, N. B. (2020). The impact of the Shariah Board's characteristics on the financial soundness of Islamic banks. *Journal of Islamic Accounting and Business Research*, *11*(9), 1807–1825. doi:10.1108/JIABR-08-2018-0127

Khan, M. H., Fraz, A., Hassan, A., & Abedifar, P. (2019). *Board Gender Diversity, Risk taking and Performance: Evidence from Dual Banking Systems.* Working Papers in Responsible Banking and Finance, No.19-003, pp.1-35.

Labaronne, D. (1998). Les lenteurs de la privatisation en Europe de l'Est: Une conséquence de la stratégie d'enracinement des managers. *Revue d'Économie Politique*, *108*(5), 671–689.

Lassoued, M. (2018). Corporate governance and financial stability in Islamic banking. *Managerial Finance*, *44*(5), 524–539. doi:10.1108/MF-12-2016-0370

Mans-Kemp, N., Viviers, S., & Collins, S. (2018). Exploring the causes and consequences of director overboardedness in an emerging market. *International Journal of Disclosure and Governance*, *15*(2), 210–220. doi:10.105741310-018-0048-9

Mans-Kemp, N., Viviers, S., & Weir, J. (2020). Investigating the extent and impact of director overboardedness using a comprehensive measure. *Corporate Governance: The International Journal of Business in Society*, *20*(5), 821–836. doi:10.1108/CG-07-2019-0234

Marston, C. L., & Shrives, P. J. (1991). The use of disclosure indices in accounting research: A review article. *The British Accounting Review*, *23*(3), 195–210. doi:10.1016/0890-8389(91)90080-L

Masulis, R. W., Wang, C., & Xie, F. (2012). Globalizing the boardroom-The effects of foreign directors on corporate governance and firm performance. *Journal of Accounting and Economics*, *53*(3), 527–554. doi:10.1016/j.jacceco.2011.12.003

Nathan, S., & Ribière, V. (2007). From Knowledge To Wisdom: The Case Of Corporate Governance In Islamic Banking. *The Journal of Information and Knowledge Management Systems*, *37*(4), 471-483.

Oud, R. E., & Amedjar, A. (2016). Analyse comparative des normes comptables appliquées à la finance participative – Cas de la Mourabaha. *International Journal of Innovation and Applied Studies*, *15*(4), 812–821.

Pathan, S., & Faff, R. (2013). Does board structure in banks really affect their performance. *Journal of Banking & Finance*, *37*(5), 1573–1589. doi:10.1016/j.jbankfin.2012.12.016

Porter, M. E. (1992). Capital disadvantage: America's Failing Capital Investment System. *Harvard Business Review*, *76*, 65–82. PMID:10121317

Pranata, M. W., & Laela, S. F. (2020). Board characteristics, good corporate governance and maqashid performance in Islamic banking. *Journal of Islamic Monetary Economics and Finance*, *6*(2), 1–24. doi:10.21098/jimf.v6i2.1189

Prowses, S. (1997). The Corporate Governance System In Banking: What Do We Know? *BNL Quarterly Review*, (Special issue), 11–40.

Quttainah, M. A. (2012). *Four Essays on the Impact of Shari'ah (Islamic Law) as an Institutional Governance Mechanism on Organizational Performance and Managerial Behavior* [PhD Thesis]. Institute Rensselaer Polytechnic.

Rafindaa, A., Rafindab, A., Witiastutia, R. S., Surosob, A., & Trinugroho, I. (2018). Board diversity, risk and sustainability of Bank Performance: Evidence from India. *Journal of Security And Sustainability Issues*, *7*(4), 793–806. doi:10.9770/jssi.2018.7.4(15)

Ramly, Z., Datuk, N., & Nordin, M. H. (2018). Shariah Supervision Board, Board Independence, Risk Committee and Risk-taking of Islamic Banks in Malaysia. *International Journal of Economics and Financial Issues*, *8*(4), 290–300.

Shachaf, P. (2008). Cultural diversity and information and communication technology impacts on global virtual teams: An exploratory study. *Information & Management*, *45*(2), 131–142. doi:10.1016/j.im.2007.12.003

Sufian, F. (2006). Size and Returns to Scale of the Islamic Banking Industry in Malaysia: Foreign Versus Domestic Banks. *IIUM Journal of Economics and Management*, *14*(2), 147–175.

Sufian, F. (2010). Does foreign presence foster Islamic banks' performance? Empirical evidence from Malaysia. *Journal of Islamic Accounting and Business Research, 1*(2), 128–147. doi:10.1108/17590811011086723

Sufian, F., & Abdul Majid, M. (2008). Bank Ownership, Characteristics, and Performance: A Comparative Analysis of Domestic and Foreign Islamic Banks in Malaysia. *J.KAU: Islamic Econ., 21*(2), 3–37.

Tazilah, M. D. A. K., & Abdul Rahman, R. (2014). Risk Management and Corporate Governance Characteristics in the Malaysian Islamic Financial Institutions. *Research Journal of Finance and Accounting, 5*(12), 116–128.

Ujunwa, A. (2012). Board characteristics and the financial performance of Nigerian quoted firms. *Corporate Governance, 12*(5), 656–674. doi:10.1108/14720701211275587

Ullah, S., Khokhar, Z.A., Tanveer, N., Khan, M.W., Shabbir, G., & Ahmed, A. (2014). *Shariah Governance Framework For Islamic Banking Institutions*. Islamic Banking Department, State Bank of Pakistan.

Yar, S., & Ahmed, S. Y. (2020). Impact of Board Gender Diversity on The Financial Performance of Conventional and Islamic Banks – An Evidence from Pakistan. *MPRA*, (98798), 1–28.

Zainol, Z., Shaari, R., & Muhamad Ali, H. (2008). A Comparative Analysis of Bankers'Perceptions on Islamic Banking. *International Journal of Business and Management, 3*(4), 157–168.

Zouari, S. Z., & Taktak, N. B. (2014). Ownership structure and financial performance in Islamic banks: Does bank ownership matter? *International Journal of Islamic and Middle Eastern Finance and Management, 7*(2), 146–160. doi:10.1108/IMEFM-01-2013-0002

ENDNOTES

1 www.ibisonline.com

2 www.worldbank.org

Chapter 3
The Influence of Shariah Supervisory Board on the Financial Stability of Islamic Banks:
Do Religious Leaders, Women, and Skilled Shariah Members Matter?

Afef Khalil
ISCAE, University of Manouba, Tunisia

Sabrine Chihi
Cresppa-GTM, UMR 7217, CNRS-University of Paris 8, France & University of Tunis, El Manar, Tunisia

Mohammed El Amine Abdelli
https://orcid.org/0000-0002-5784-4306
University of Western Brittany, France

Imen Ben Slimene
University of Upper Alsace,France

Naima Bentouir
Ain Temouchent University, Algeria

ABSTRACT

The chapter studies the impact of the shariah board's characteristics on the financial stability of Islamic banks. Regression analysis is used to investigate the effect of the shariah board's characteristics on the financial stability of Islamic banks, employing a panel data set of 60 Islamic banking from 2015 to 2018. The findings show that a

DOI: 10.4018/978-1-6684-4834-2.ch003

skilled shariah scholar and a female member have a negative effect on the financial stability of Islamic banks. However, the interlocked shariah scholars and foreigners positively influence the financial stability of banks. Plus, the results indicate that the religious leader (Mufti) and shariah board's size have no significant influence on the financial stability of Islamic banking. This study enhances the literature analysis on corporate governance frameworks and their effect on Islamic banking's financial stability.

INTRODUCTION

The shariah governance is characterized as a collection of organizational and institutional arrangements by which the existence of an efficient and independent shariah control is assured by an Islamic Financial Institution (IFI). Shariah governance may consist of a simple Shariah Board or expand to a Shariah structure (Shariah Board, Department of Shariah control, Department of Shariah risk management, Department of Shariah audit) (Khalil and Taktak, 2020; Khalil, 2021; Alam *et al.*, 2022; Haddad and Bouri, 2022). The Shari'ah Council is a knowledgeable, independent organization of Shari'ah academics, according to Khalil (2020) and Khalil and Taktak (2020). Nomran *et al.* (2018), Buallay (2019), and Khalil and Chihi (2020 b,c) add that members of the Shariah Board issue fatwas and run the sharia risk, which may pose additional dangers (e.g. liquidity risk, credit risk, etc.) and thus menace the sustainable development and the existence of Islamic banking. Besides, the Shariah Board members forbid the bank from such lucrative practices (Hamza, 2013; Khalil and Ben Slimene, 2021). As a result, compliance with shariah laws ensures that investors are attracted, and the reputation of Islamic banking is increased.

We propose investigating the impact of Shariah Council attributes on the stability of Islamic banking in this suggested work. The results show that a skilled shariah member and a female shariah member impact negatively the financial stability of banks. However, the interlocked shariah scholar and the foreign shariah scholar positively influenced the banks' financial stability. Moreover, the findings indicate that the religious leader and Shariah Board's size have no significant influence on the financial stability of bank.

The structure of the study is as follows:The literature review is summarized in Section 2. Then, the third section can find the sample definition and the variables used. Then, the empirical results are discussed in Section 4. Finally, our analysis ends with Section 5.

LITERATURE REVIEW

Skilled Shariah Member

Muhammad *et al.* (2021), Haddad and Bouri (2022), and Kachkar and Yilmaz (2022) say that a professional shariah member meets the needs of shareholders and ensures better supervisory efficiency. Previous research indicates that shariah scholars with accounting or finance experience strengthen coordination between the Shariah Board and the chairman, ensure sustainable development and reduce financial risks. Therefore, Shariah members must obtain skills and experience in accounting, economics and finance. In addition, having a professional shariah member is a better way to ensure Islamic banking sustainability. A positive connection between shariah qualified finance members and the financial stability of Islamic banking was discovered by Quttainah (2012). A trained Shariah scholar is said to have a positive influence on the financial stability of Islamic banks. Lassoued (2018) also confirms this result. Khalil and Taktak (2020) conducted a research paper on 67 Islamic banking from 2005 to 2014. They found that the skilled shariah member does not significantly affect banks' financial soundness. Therefore, we are proposing the following:

H1. A Shariah Board member with financial / accounting expertise positively impacts Islamic banking's financial stability.

Religious Leader Role

The Mufti is a religious leader who has specific attributes (e.g. fair, respectable, trustworthy and tolerant), according to Zepeda (2013). Plus, Zepeda (2013) says the Mufti's job is to issue fatwas and interpret Islam's rules. Hassan and Chachi (2008) expect that the religious leader's involvement increases the shariah conformity of financial products and the position of the board. Therefore, a religious leader (Mufti) should be named a Shariah scholar of Islamic banking. The following is our second hypothesis:

H2. The religious leader's role (Mufti) positively impacts Islamic banking's financial stability.

Female Shariah Member

According to the theory of social position, Islamic countries do not appoint women to the boards of their IFIs (Khalil and Chihi, 2020a,c). This can prevent Islamic banks' shareholders from having more female representatives. In this sense, Kasi and Mahmood (2019) say that the Shariah Board does not observe a woman. Khan *et al.* (2019) note that compared to male scholars, female members are less inclined to take risks. and are negatively linked to Islamic banks' financial performance. The female representatives make the banks less competitive, according to Khalil and Chihi (2020c). Research on a sample of 77 Islamic banks from 2000-2009 has been investigated by Grassa and Matoussi (2014). Their finding indicates that there is no substantial impact on banks' financial performance by the presence of women scholars. Recent Western discourse on the function of women in the islamic world may have concentrated on the veil, but Islam was receptive to women in finance and business from its early years. It will also be essential to discuss how Islamic banking's financial stability is affected by gender disparity in the Shariah Council. This variable's sign is supposed to be cheerful:

H3. The proportion of female Shariah members positively affects Islamic banks' financial stability.

Interlocked Shariah Member

According to the theory of dependence resource, Abdullah *et al.* (2013) argue that interlocking strengthens the expertise of shariah experts and increases their experience. Interlocking reinforces the shariah members' credibility and attracts investors according to the reputation hypothesis (Grassa, 2013). Interlocked expert reduces shariah risk and boosts Islamic banking's financial efficiency. Nomran *et al.* (2018) also confirmed this result for a sample of 82 Islamic banking companies from 1993 to 2014. Proponents of the theory of busyness claim that interlocking makes the shariah member busy (Grassa and Matoussi, 2014; Alabbad *et al.*, 2020; Muhammad *et al.*, 2021). Hamza (2013) and Nomran *et al.* (2018) add that interlocked shariah members contribute to conflicts of interest and confidentiality issues. Interlocked shariah experts drope the legitimacy of the Shariah Board and increase the possibility of fatwa shopping, according to Haridan *et al.* (2018). The next assumption we make is:

H4. The percentage of interlocked Shariah members harms Islamic banking's financial stability.

Foreign Shariah Member

Kachkar and Yilmaz (2022) claim that international shariah representatives strengthen the divergence of shariah understanding and communication issues. This raises the costs and risks of shariah and harms the financial stability of Islamic banking. According to Ben Moussa (2019) and Alabbad *et al.* (2020), international banks promote technology transfer and sustainable development to decrease the availability of services in the financial market. However, a report was conducted by Khalil and Taktak (2020) on a sample of 67 Islamic banking companies from 2005 to 2014. Their findings note that a member of the international shariah has no substantial impact on the bank's financial soundness. Our fourth premise is as follows:

H5. The proportion of foreign shariah members negatively influences Islamic banking's financial stability.

Shariah Board's Size

Agency theory advocates expect that a large board raises the agency's expense and conflicts of interest (Jensen, 1993). A high number of shariah experts have trouble coordinating efforts among shariah members, according to Amine (2018). According to Lassoued (2018), the directors can easily supervise a small Shariah council and strengthen the contact between board members. Rachdi (2014) and Haribowo *et al.* (2021) demonstrate that the Council's size adversely affects the stability of banks and its development. Khalil and Taktak (2020) have also confirmed this finding for a sample of 67 Islamic banking companies from 2005 to 2014. Amine (2018) performed a research report on selecting 30 Islamic banking companies and argues that the large Shariah Board harms bank stability. According to the resource dependence theory, a high number of shariah experts improve awareness that contributes to a good understanding of shariah-compliant practices (Nomran *et al.*, 2018). Farag *et al.* (2014), Haddad and Bouri (2022) suggest that a great Sharia Council minimizes agency expenses and increases control efficiency. Many experts decrease knowledge asymmetry. Saeed and Saeed (2018) and Alam *et al.* (2022) indicate that a large Shariah Council reduces the risk of shariah and benefits banks' financial performance. Besides, Abdul Rahman and Bukair (2013) and Muhammad *et al.* (2021) show that a large Shariah Board reduces the cost of transactions and improves Islamic banking's sustainable development and financial stability. The Bank Negara Malaysia (BNM) Guide (2010) recommends that more than five shariah members should be the Council's size. The AAOIFI (2008) specifies that there be at least three shariah experts on the Shariah Board. We are proposing that:

H6. The Shariah Council's size affects the financial stability of Islamic banking positively.

METHODOLOGY

Sample

The sample consists of 60 Islamic banking operations observed from 2015-2018. Data is gathered manually from the Islamic banking annual reports. From the World Bank website, the inflation and gross domestic product rates are derived. Table 1 describes the sample's composition by country.

Table 1. Sample composition

List of Countries	Number of Islamic Banks
Bahrain	12
Sudan	9
Malaysia	6
Iran	3
Pakistan	4
United Arab Emirates	4
Kuwait	2
Saudi Arabia	3
Turkey	3
Indonesia	2
Qatar	2
United Kingdom	2
Albania	1
Bangladesh	1
Egypt	1
Jordan	1
Palestine	1
South Africa	1
Tunisia	1
Yemen	1
Total	60

Variables Measures

Dependent Variable Measure

Altman developed the Z-score in 1968, and it is a practical method and instrument for assessing financial stability and predicting the possibility of default. Moreover, under the normalcy of bank returns theory, the Z-score ratio representing the number of typical returns required to exhaust the equity (Cihák and Hesse, 2010; Amine, 2018).

According to Bourkhis and Nabi (2013), Khalil and Taktak (2020) and Bakhouche *et al.* (2022), the measurement of the financial stability of banks is defined by Z-score = (ROA+K) / σ (ROA).

Hence, ROA = Return on asset; k = Total equity/Total assets; σ(ROA) = Standard deviation of ROA.

Independent Variables

We are adding six Shariah Board features. The shariah member with accounting/finance expertise (EXP) is the number of Islamic accounting/finance institutions where the shariah member sits; the religious leader (REL) is a binary variable equal to 1 if there is a religious leader and 0 otherwise, the woman (WO) is the percentage of woman shariah members, the interlocked shariah member (INTER) is the percentage of the linked Shariah Board members, the international shariah member (FORE) is the percentage of foreign shariah members. Finally, the Shariah Board's size (SIZE) is the number of shariah members.

Plus, we select seven control variables. TAI is the total asset logarithm of banks, AGE is the age logarithm of Islamic banks, MD is a binary variable equal to 1 if there is a central shariah board, and 0 otherwise, SA is a binary variable equal to 1 if the country of the Islamic bank applies the rules of shariah in its legal framework, and 0 otherwise, NO is a binary variable equal to 1 if the government of the Islamic bank uses the laws of shariah in its legal framework, GRO is the economic growth rate of the gross domestic product, and INFL is the inflation rate.

The following model is suggested:

$$Z\text{-score it} = C + \beta 1\ EXP_{it} + \beta 2\ REL_{it} + \beta 3\ WO_{it} + \beta 4\ INTER_{it} + \beta 5\ FORE_{it} + \beta 6\ SIZE_{it}$$

$$+ \beta 7\ TAI_{it} + \beta 8\ AGE_{it} + \beta 9\ MD_{it} + \beta 10\ SA_{it} + \beta 11\ NO_{it} + \beta 12\ GRO_{it} + \beta 13\ INFL_{it} + \varepsilon it_{it}$$

Therefore, C: is a constant, β1 ... β13: the coefficients to be calculated, εit: the term for the error, I the individual ranging from 1 to 60, and t: is the duration ranging from 2015 to 2018.

The method of Panel Corrected Standard Errors (PCSE) is using to estimate our research paper model. The PCSE approach avoids the problems of auto-correlation and hetero-scedasticity by providing more rugged results. Furthermore, Khalil and Taktak (2020) add that a more stable error mechanism is given by the (PCSE) method than the generalized least squares (GLS) method provides.

RESULTS

Descriptive Statistics

The (WO) variable varies from 0% to 40%, averaging 1.416. The (EXP) variable has a mean of 2.541. 76.772% of scholars are interlocked. Moreover, the (FORE) variable varies from 0% to 100%, which does not support the requirements of AAOIFI (2008). The (SIZE) variable has a mean of 3.701. The board's size is small and confirms the limit set by AAOIFI (2008).

For control variables, Table 2 indicates that the (TAI) variable has an average of 7.190. The mean of the (AGE) variable is 1.455. The (GRO) variable has an average of 3.061. It has a minimum of -28 and a maximum of 13.400. The mean of the (Z-score) variable is 92.414.

Table 2. Descriptive statistics

Variables	Mean	SD	Median	Min	Max
WO %	1.416	5.707	0	0	40
EXP	2.541	2.522	2	0	8
INTER %	76.772	48.250	75	0	100
FORE %	39.179	38.410	33.333	0	100
SIZE	3.701	1.792	3	1	12
TAI	7.190	1.593	7.391	0.001	11.586
AGE	1.455	0.558	1.301	0.568	4.383
GRO	3.061	3.581	3.5	-28	13.4
INFL	8.080	13.274	2.8	-26	63.3
Z-score	14.480	14.069	10.5	-1.325	92.414

18.656% of the banks have a religious leader on their Shariah Boards. A central Shariah Board administers 66.417% of the banks, and 54.104% of the Islamic banking use shariah rules in their legal framework. In addition, 35.820% of Islamic banks employ AAOIFI standards.

Table 3. Frequency of binary variables

Variables	REL		MD		SA		NO	
Fréquence %	1	0	1	0	1	0	1	0
	18.656	80.597	66.417	33.582	54.104	45.895	35.820	64.179

Cross-Correlation Matrix

Table 4 reveals that the variables are less than the Kennedy (2008) limit. The variables are not strongly correlated, it seems.

Discussion

The coefficient on EXP is shown to be harmful in Table 5 (p-values < 0.1). H1, therefore, is not supported. Shariah members with finance/accounting expertise negatively influence the banks' financial stability. This does not support the theory of resource dependence, which says that a trained shariah scholar has the potential to make better decisions and brings experience and skills to the Shariah Board. The qualified shariah member tends to raise disputes and agency costs between directors and shariah scholars. The associated coefficient on the variable (REL) does not have a meaningful impact on bank sustainability, which indicates that the religious leader (Mufti) does not affect the financial stability of banks. This outcome confirms the study of Khalil and Taktak (2020). Besides, Table 5 demonstrates that the (WO) coefficient is negative and essential. H3, therefore, is not authenticated. This suggests that the female Shariah Board's involvement harms Islamic banking's sustainable development and financial stability, which is not confirmed by previous studies (Jimenez *et al.*, 2020; Khalil and Chihi, 2020a). (INTER) variable has a positive effect on banks' financial stability. H4, therefore, is not sponsored. This means that the interlocked shariah representatives strengthen the stabilization bank. Plus, the result means that Interlocking increases the knowledge and expertise of shariah members and attracts investors, which contradicts many studies (Grassa and Matoussi, 2014; Haridan *et al.*, 2018) and supports the resource dependence theory's suggestions. Banks and authorities should promote interlocking practices.

Table 4. Cross-Correlation Matrix

	EXP	REL	INTER	FORE	WO	SIZE	TAI	AGE	MD	SA	NO	GRO	INFL
EXP	1.000												
REL	0.052	1.000											
INTER	0.423	0.108	1.000										
FORE	0.444	-0.004	0.350	1.000									
WO	-0.206	-0.015	-0.063	-0.1645	1.000								
SIZE	-0.064	0.115	-0.074	-0.2872	0.290	1.000							
TAI	-0.164	-0.133	-0.180	-0.1921	0.019	-0.077	1.000						
AGE	-0.122	0.074	0.053	-0.1315	0.115	0.040	0.245	1.000					
MD	-0.151	-0.016	0.066	-0.0520	0.176	0.190	-0.100	0.024	1.000				
SA	0.135	-0.039	0.137	0.0353	-0.270	-0.132	-0.094	-0.045	0.518	1.000			
NO	0.037	-0.210	0.091	-0.0368	-0.185	-0.092	-0.131	-0.076	0.531	0.688	1.000		
GRO	-0.004	0.135	0.066	0.1494	0.130	0.125	0.043	0.030	0.231	-0.118	-0.110	1.000	
INFL	-0.260	-0.139	-0.120	-0.1811	-0.110	-0.080	0.068	0.056	0.209	0.298	0.375	-0.229	1.000

The (FORE) vector coefficient shows a positive impact on the financial stability of Islamic banks. H5 is not authenticated, therefore. Indeed, being a member of the international shariah positively affects financial stability. According to Quttainah (2012), it appears that foreigners reduce the risk of shariah and restrict the issue of the absence of trained experts. However, the research conducted by Khalil and Taktakk (2020) contradicts this result. Thus, banks are invited to recruit more foreigners to improve their financial stability.

Moreover, the (SIZE) variable does not affect the stability of banks. The Shariah Board's number does not influence the stability of banks. Finally, other variables (TAI, AGE, MD, SA, NO, GRO, INFL) do not significantly affect banks' financial stability.

Table 5. Results Regression

Variables	Coef.	Z	P>lzl
EXP	-1.604	-3.33	0.001***
REL	1.918	0.59	0.556
WO	-0.412	-5.30	0.000***
INTER	0.077	2.84	0.005***
FORE	0.090	3.15	0.002***
SIZE	-0.197	-0.46	0.644 .
TAI	-0.205	-0.59	0.553
AGE	0.575	0.39	0.697
MD	1.614	0.42	0.673
SA	-4.133	-1.39	0.165
NO	1.552	0.45	0.656
GRO	-0.056	-0.38	0.707
INFL	0.064	0.99	0.323
Cons	11.450	2.53	0.011
R^2	35.40%		
N	240		

CONCLUSION

Because of the involvement of the Shari'ah Board, the governance structures of Islamic banks are different from those of their traditional peers. Therefore, this work seeks to explore the influence of the characteristics of the Shariah Council on banks' stability. For 2015-2018, we used a sample of 60 banks.

This study shows that a skilled shariah scholar and a female shariah member harm the stability of Islamic banks. The interlocked shariah scholars and the international member of the Shariah Board show a positive influence on banks' stability. The banks must, therefore, promote the interlocking practice and the recruitment of foreigners on their Shariah Council. Moreover, the results indicate that the religious leader (Mufti) and Shariah Board's size have no significant influence on the stability of banks.

This study makes several =new contributions to the literature. First, it draws on resource dependence and agency theories. It uses these theoretical foundations to investigate the Shariah Council's attributes - Islamic banks' stability connection. Second, this paper sheds new light on how corporate governance affects the bank stability. Third, the results point to the role of the Shariah Council and help us to improve our learning. about the relationship between corporate governance and stability.

This paper is useful for researchers, banks, authorities, regulators, etc. Furthermore, Islamic banking authorities should consider the research findings when updating the laws and should implement new governance measures that can ensure the effectiveness of the banks. Furthermore, supervisors need to strengthen their policies, stop inappropriate behaviour, and ensure effective Islamic bank governance. Finally, policymakers need to develop codes and understand the elements that influence the governance practices of banks when establishing their boards.

However, this study has some limitations. More studies need to be conducted on the Islamic banking presence of the religious leader (Mufti). Finally, to realize better governance in banks, it is advisable to include additional corporate governance mechanisms in the next papers.

REFERENCES

AAOIFI. (2005). *Accounting, Auditing and Governance Standards for Islamic Financial Institutions*. Accounting and Auditing Organization for Islamic Financial Institutions.

AAOIFI. (2008). *Governance Standards for Islamic Financial Institutions*. Accounting and Auditing Organization for Islamic Financial Institutions.

AAOIFI. (2010). *Shariah Standards for Islamic Financial Institutions*. Accounting and Auditing Organization for Islamic Financial Institutions.

Abdul Rahman, A., & Bukair, A. A. (2013). The Influence of the *Shariah* Supervision Board on Corporate Social Responsibility Disclosure by Islamic Banks of Gulf Co-operation Council Countries. *Asian Journal of Business and Accounting*, *6*(2), 65–104.

Abdullah, W. A. W., Percy, M., & Stewart, J. (2013). Shari'ah disclosures in Malaysian and Indonesian Islamic banks: The Shari'ah governance system. *Journal of Islamic Accounting and Business Research*, *4*(2), 100–131. doi:10.1108/JIABR-10-2012-0063

Abrar, T., Ahmed, F., & Kashif, M. (2018). Financial Stability of Islamic Versus Conventional Banks in Pakistan. *Journal of Islamic Economics*, *10*(2), 341–366.

Ahmed, M., & Khatun, M. (2013). The Compliance with *Shariah* Governance System of AAOIFI: A Study on Islamic Banks Bangladesh. *Journal of Islamic Economics, Banking and Finance*, *9*(3), 177–191. doi:10.12816/0001617

Alabbad, A., Hassan, K., & Saba, I. (2020). Can Shariah board characteristics influence risk-taking behavior of Islamic banks? *International Journal of Islamic and Middle Eastern Finance and Management*.. doi:10.1108/IMEFM-11-2018-0403

Alam, M. K., Rahman, M. M., Runy, M. K., Adedeji, B. S., & Hassan, M. F. (2022). The influences of Shariah governance mechanisms on Islamic banks performance and Shariah compliance quality. *Asian Journal of Accounting Research*, *7*(1), 2–16. doi:10.1108/AJAR-11-2020-0112

Almutairi, A. R., & Quttainah, M. A. (2017). Corporate governance: Evidence from Islamic banks. *Social Responsibility Journal*, *13*(3), 601–624. doi:10.1108/SRJ-05-2016-0061

Amine, B. (2018). Contribution of Governance to Ensure the Stability of Islamic Banks: A Panel Data Analysis. *International Journal of Accounting and Financial Reporting*, *8*(3), 140–155. doi:10.5296/ijafr.v8i3.13333

Bakhouche, A., El Ghak, T., & Alshiab, M. (2022). Does Islamicity matter for the stability of Islamic banks in dual banking systems? *Heliyon*, *8*(4), e09245. Advance online publication. doi:10.1016/j.heliyon.2022.e09245 PMID:35434399

Beck, N., & Katz, J. N. (1995). What to do (and not to do) with time-series cross-section data. *The American Political Science Review*, *89*(3), 634–647. doi:10.2307/2082979

Ben Moussa, F. (2019). The Influence of Internal Corporate Governance on Bank Credit Risk: An Empirical Analysis for Tunisia. *Global Business Review*, *20*(3), 640–667. doi:10.1177/0972150919837078

BNM. (2010). *"Guidelines on the Governance of Shariah Committee for the Islamic Financial Institutions", Islamic Banking and Takaful Department, RH/GL/012-1*. Bank Negara Malaysia-Central Bank of Malaysia.

Bourkhis, K., & Nabi, M. S. (2013). Islamic and conventional banks' soundness during the 2007–2008 financial crisis. *Review of Financial Economics*, *22*(2), 68–77. doi:10.1016/j.rfe.2013.01.001

Buallay, A. (2019). Corporate governance, Shariah governance and performance: A cross-country comparison in MENA region. *International Journal of Islamic and Middle Eastern Finance and Management*, *12*(2), 216–235. doi:10.1108/IMEFM-07-2017-0172

Čihák, M., & Hesse, H. (2010). Islamic Banks and Financial Stability: An Empirical Analysis. *Journal of Financial Services Research*, *38*(2-3), 95–113. doi:10.100710693-010-0089-0

Daly, S., & Frikha, M. (2015). Corporate governance: What about Islamic banks? *International Journal of Financial Services Management*, *8*(1), 18–41. doi:10.1504/IJFSM.2015.066567

Farag, H., Mallin, C., & Ow-Yong, K. (2014). Corporate social responsibility and financial performance in Islamic banks. *Journal of Economic Behavior & Organization*, *103*, 25–38.

Ghayad, R. (2008). Corporate governance and the global performance of Islamic banks. *Humanomics*, *24*(3), 207–216. doi:10.1108/08288660810899368

Ginena, K., & Hamid, A. (2015). *Foundations of Shariah Governance of Islamic Banks*. Edition Wiley. doi:10.1002/9781119053507

Grassa, R. (2013). Shariah supervisory system in Islamic financial institutions: New issues and challenges: a comparative analysis between Southeast Asia models and GCC models. *Humanomics*, *29*(4), 333–348. doi:10.1108/H-01-2013-0001

Grassa, R., & Matoussi, H. (2014). Corporate Governance Of Islamic Banks: A Comparative Study Between GCC And Southeast Asia Countries. *International Journal of Islamic and Middle Eastern Finance and Management*, *7*(3), 346–362. doi:10.1108/IMEFM-01-2013-0001

Gujarati, D. (1995). *Basic Econometrics*. McGraw Hill.

Haddad, A., & Bouri, A. (2022). *The impact of Shariah Advisory Board characteristics on the financial performance of Islamic banks*. Cogent Economics & Finance. doi:10.1080/23322039.2022.2062911

Hamdi, F. M., & Zarai, M. A. (2014). Corporate Governance Practices and Earnings Management in Islamic Banking Institutions. *Research Journal of Finance and Accounting*, *5*(9), 81–96.

Hamza, H. (2013). Shariah governance in Islamic banks: Effectiveness and supervision model. *International Journal of Islamic and Middle Eastern Finance and Management*, *6*(3), 226–237. doi:10.1108/IMEFM-02-2013-0021

Haribowo, I., Putri, Z. E., & Yulianti, Y. (2021). Corporate Governance and Financial Stability of Islamic Banks in Asia. *Journal of Asian Finance, Economics and Business*, *8*(12), 353–361.

Haridan, N. M., Hassan, A. F. S., & Karbhari, Y. (2018). Governance, religious assurance and Islamic banks: Do Shariah boards effectively serve? *The Journal of Management and Governance*, *22*(4), 1015–1043. doi:10.100710997-018-9418-8

Hassan, A., & Chachi, A. (2008). Corporate Governance of the Islamic Financial Services Industry in Brunei Darussalam. *Journal of Islamic Economics, Banking and Finance*, *4*(1), 1–21.

Hawkamah. (2011). *Policy Brief On Corporate Governance For Islamic Banks And Financial Institutions In The Middle East And North Africa Region*. Hawkamah, The Institute for Corporate Governance.

IFSB. (2006). Guiding Principles On Corporate Governance For Institutions Offering Only Islamic Financial Services (Excluding Islamic Insurance (Takaful) Institutions And Islamic Mutual Funds). Islamic Financial Services Board.

IFSB. (2009). *Guiding Principles On Shariah Governance Systems For Institutions Offering Islamic Financial Services*. Islamic Financial Services Board.

IMF. (2006). *Financial Soundness Indicators*. International Monetary Fund.

Jensen, M. C. (1993). The modern industrial revolution, exit and the failure of internal control systems. *The Journal of Finance*, *48*(3), 831–880. doi:10.1111/j.1540-6261.1993.tb04022.x

Jimenez, R. M., Hernández-Ortiz, M. J., & Cabrera Fernández, A. I. (2020). Gender diversity influence on board effectiveness and business performance. *Corporate Governance*, *20*(2), 307–323. doi:10.1108/CG-07-2019-0206

Kachkar, O., & Yilmaz, M.K. (2022). How diverse are Shariah supervisory boards of Islamic banks? A global empirical survey. *International Journal of Ethics and Systems*. . doi:10.1108/IJOES-10-2021-0195

Kasi, B. R., & Mahmood, N. (2019). Composition and Working of the Sharia Supervisory Boards in Bahrain's Islamic Banks. *Economy*, *6*(2), 76–81. doi:10.20448/journal.502.2019.62.76.81

Kennedy, P. (1998). *A guide to econometrics*. Blackwell.

Kennedy, P. (2008). *A Guide to Econometrics*. Blackwell.

Khalil, A. (2020). Relationship between the Shariah Council and the Board of Directors and its effect on the financial soundness of Islamic banks. *Asian Journal of Accounting and Finance*, *2*(4), 1–10.

Khalil, A. (2021). The impact of the Board of Directors and the Shariah Board on the financial soundness of Islamic banks. *Journal of Islamic Accounting and Business Research*, *12*(5), 646–660. doi:10.1108/JIABR-01-2019-0011

Khalil, A., & Ben Slimene, I. (2021). Financial Soundness of Islamic banks: Does the Structure of the Board of Directors Matter? *Corporate Governance*, *21*(7), 1393–1415. doi:10.1108/CG-06-2020-0237

Khalil, A., & Chihi, S. (2020a). Do board characteristics affect the financial soundness of Islamic banks. *African Scientific Journal*, *3*(2), 85–102.

Khalil, A., & Chihi, S. (2020b). Would meetings between the Board of Directors and the Shariah Supervisory Board affect the financial performance of Islamic banks? *Journal of the International Academy for Case Studies*, *26*(6), 1-7.

Khalil, A., & Chihi, S. (2020c). Does the Shariah Board structure influence the financial performance of Islamic banks? *Journal of the International Academy for Case Studies*, *26*(6), 1-7.

Khalil, A., & Taktak, N. B. (2020). The impact of the Shariah Board's characteristics on the financial soundness of Islamic banks. *Journal of Islamic Accounting and Business Research*, *11*(9), 1807–1825. doi:10.1108/JIABR-08-2018-0127

Khan, M. H., Fraz, A., Hassan, A., & Abedifar, P. (2019). *Board Gender Diversity, Risk taking and Performance: Evidence from Dual Banking Systems*. Working Papers in Responsible Banking and Finance, No.19-003, pp.1-35.

Khorshid, A. (2009). Understanding Derivatives within Islamic Finance. In A. Khorshid (Ed.), *Euromoney Encyclopedia of Islamic Finance. Euromoney Books*.

Lassoued, M. (2018). Corporate governance and financial stability in Islamic banking. *Managerial Finance*, *44*(5), 524–539. doi:10.1108/MF-12-2016-0370

Muhammad, R., Annuar, H. A., Taufik, M., & Nugraheni, P. (2021). *The influence of the SSB's characteristics toward Sharia compliance of Islamic banks*. Cogent Business & Management. doi:10.1080/23311975.2021.1929033

Muneeza, A., & Hassan, R. (2014). Shariah corporate governance: The need for a special governance code. *Corporate Governance*, *14*(1), 120–129. doi:10.1108/CG-02-2011-0015

Nomran, N. M., Haron, R., & Hassan, R. (2018). Shariah supervisory board characteristics effects on Islamic banks' performance: Evidence from Malaysia. *International Journal of Bank Marketing*, *36*(2), 290–304. doi:10.1108/IJBM-12-2016-0197

Oud, R. E., & Amedjar, A. (2016). Analyse comparative des normes comptables appliquées à la finance participative – Cas de la Mourabaha. *International Journal of Innovation and Applied Studies*, *15*(4), 812–821.

Qasim, Y. (2020). Z-Score Application for Jordanian Islamic Banks. *Journal of Public Administration and Governance*, *10*(1), 289–297. doi:10.5296/jpag.v10i1.16335

Quttainah, M. A. (2012). *Four Essays on the Impact of Shari'ah (Islamic Law) as an Institutional Governance Mechanism on Organizational Performance and Managerial Behavior* [Ph.D. Thesis]. Institute Rensselaer Polytechnic.

Rachdi, H. (2014). The role of banking governance in financial and ethical profitability: The case of Malaysian Islamic Banks. *Journal of Islamic Economics, Banking and Finance*, *10*(3), 14–28. doi:10.12816/0025950

Ramly, Z., Datuk, N., & Nordin, M. H. (2018). Shariah Supervision Board, Board Independence, Risk Committee and Risk-taking of Islamic Banks in Malaysia. *International Journal of Economics and Financial Issues*, *8*(4), 290–300.

Rammal, H. G. (2006). The Importance Of Shariah Supervision In Islamic Financial Institutions. *Corporate Ownership and Control*, *3*(3), 204–208. doi:10.22495/cocv3i3c1p5

Saeed, M. B., & Saeed, S. K. (2018). Characteristics of Shariah Supervisory Board, Corporate Governance Mechanisms and Efficiency of Islamic Banks: Evidence from Listed Banks in Asia. *Journal of Islamic Business and Management*, *8*(1), 116–138.

Ullah, S., Khokhar, Z.A., Tanveer, N., Khan, M.W., Shabbir, G., & Ahmed, A. (2014). *Shariah Governance Framework For Islamic Banking Institutions*. Islamic Banking Department, State Bank of Pakistan.

Yar, S., & Ahmed, S. Y. (2020). Impact of Board Gender Diversity on The Financial Performance of Conventional and Islamic Banks – An Evidence from Pakistan. *MPRA*, (98798), 1–28.

Zepeda, R. (2013). Enhancing Islamic Finance through Risk Benchmarking. *The Capco Institute Journal of Financial Transformation*, *38*, 16–36.

Section 2
Case Studies

Chapter 4
How Can Small and Medium Enterprises in the Chinese Market Achieve Sustainable Development Goals Through Blockchain?

Poshan Yu
https://orcid.org/0000-0003-1069-3675
Soochow University, China & Australian Studies Centre, Shanghai University, China

Yao Ge
Independent Researcher, Suzhou, China

Kudzai Mandizvidza
Independent Researcher, Beijing, China

James Mulli
The European University of Luxembourg, Luxembourg

ABSTRACT

Blockchain is one of the most important innovative technologies developed in recent years. It has great potential and capacity to help SMEs prosper due to its decentralized public ledger, which provides a secure infrastructure for transactions between unfamiliar parties without any major influence from a central authority. The use of a decentralized public ledger also makes it possible for SMEs to get credit more easily, thus assisting them in achieving sustainable development. This chapter

DOI: 10.4018/978-1-6684-4834-2.ch004

gives an overview of the functions and applications of blockchain, the situation of SMEs in the Chinese market, and sheds some light on how the Chinese policies on blockchain may affect SMEs. The chapter uses the case of WeBank to show how blockchain technology can accelerate the development of SMEs.

INTRODUCTION

The limited credit access by small and medium-sized enterprises (SMEs) continues to hamper their growth and development in almost every part of the world, and China is no exception. Several reasons have been cited as limiting factors to SMEs' quest to access credit. The most persistent challenge is the severe information disproportionateness between banks and firms. Adverse selection due to information asymmetry leads banks to allocate credit by means of rational choice (Guo et al., 2021). In addition, the lack of adequate collateral by most SMEs is a tenacious stumbling block that hinders deserving SMEs from demonstrating their creditworthiness effectively. This, consequently, sees many SMEs being constrained by the banks' credit rationing (Berger & Udell, 2006).

There has been some transition from traditional information towards a smarter information society due to the increased importance of Cloud Computing, Big Data, Mobile Internet amongst other forthcoming information technologies. One of the significantly growing and crucial technologies which is envisaged to show some great application potential is Blockchain (Peters & Panayi, 2016; Pilkington, 2016). Initially applied in time-stamping transactions (Haber and Stornetta, 1991), blockchain creates a decentralized public ledger that even without a central authority, results in safer transactions between unfamiliar parties (Dai & Vasarhelyi, 2017).

Blockchain has in recent times expanded its technological base to strengthen a number of businesses which include but are not limited to voting systems, banking, insurance, lease contracts, and government services (Reham et al., 2021). Since it arrived in China, blockchain technology has grown significantly in the unique Chinese social environment and is used in various industries.

Blockchain technology has enabled permissionless networks that can be used by independent operators with established incentives, operating without the aid of any individual financial institution or central authority. In particular, the financial services industry is experiencing rapid innovation and change due to blockchain, which has come to be called decentralized finance, or DeFi.

This chapter, that mainly focuses on the Chinese market, will consider the difficulties of SMEs in getting credit, before concentrating on how blockchain can assist them to achieve sustainable development goals.

LITERATURE REVIEW

Role of Blockchain Technology in SMEs Development

Features of Blockchain

Blockchain was introduced by David Chaum (1982)'s work that illustrates the design of a computer system founded, maintained, and relied upon by mutually suspicious groups. The paper is known to be the first to propose the blockchain protocol. The work, together with several other publications such as Satoshi Nakamoto (2008) and Malsa et al. (2021), hold a sustained view that blockchain technology, is broadly a new decentralized computational paradigm. It uses an encrypted chained block structure to authenticate and store data, and a distributed node consensus algorithm to produce and update information. Narrowly speaking, literature refers to blockchain as a book of data shared by each node of a decentralized system (Fanning & Centers, 2016; Yermack, 2017). The process of blockchain data storage entails technical elements like blocks, chain structure, hashing algorithms, Merkle trees, and time stamps (Belchior et al., 2022). Each distributed node can summarize the series of transaction data into time-stamped data blocks that are connected to the current main blockchain by a specific hashing algorithm and Merkle tree data structure. Sun et al. (2021) show that every block is linked to form the longest master chain that records the complete history of the data and provides its traceability and locality.

Blockchain's main features include its strong authentication, decentralization, and tamper-proof. Its decentralization capabilities entails that the entire list of transactions can be accessed by all nodes within the system. Nodes can verify and post new transaction records to the block, which can periodically be added to the end of the leading blockchain with a time stamp (Abuhashim & Tan, 2020). The system can also verify each participating payer's and payee's identity by means of a public key cryptography system (Xie, 2022). In addition, Ghaemi et al. (2021) argued that blockchain technology is highly secure as it employs asymmetric cryptography for data encryption while using proof of workload for each node of the distributed system. It also uses a strong set of rules formed by consensus algorithms that are resistant to external attacks thus ensuring that blockchain data can neither be forged nor be falsified. These features show that financial transaction costs through blockchain can be reduced greatly, processing times shortened, while transaction information security is also improved.

Problems Faced by SMEs

Financing

Wang et al. (2019) shows that financing is difficult and expensive for SMEs. This is because most SMEs are small in scale, have few assets, have low credit scores, and cannot meet banks' lending conditions.

Due to the unevenness in each industry, the degree of digitization of core, upstream, and downstream enterprises in a specific supply chain varies. Although there are plenty of upstream and downstream enterprises, mainly SMEs, even without accounting statements, there is a significant lack of an effective risk assessment basis for banks (Gong, 2021). In practice, banks appear to be biased towards balance sheets, income statements and cash flow statements, to effectively control risks, and also for risk examination of core enterprises and upstream and downstream businesses, making it difficult for many SMEs to obtain financing support (Hu & Fan, 2021). At the same time, cases of fraudulent loans in the form of false trade and self-insured self-financing are common. Therefore, the difficulty of information penetration and risk identification and control has become the top problem restricting financial development amongst SMEs.

In the traditional model, the offline assessment of core enterprises involves multi-dimensional information collection and analysis, especially for projects with a large number of up/downstream enterprises, the identity verification of upstream and downstream businesses and the identification of subject authenticity need to be verified one by one (Yang, 2021). In the operation of trade background audit, Sun et al. (2021) expound that it takes more effort and time to authenticate the transaction documents, register in the registration and inventory of collaterals, etc. Regarding post-credit warnings, high-frequency monitoring is required for accounts receivable reconciliation, market surveillance of goods value, and disposal of movable assets. Many cross-domain businesses, cross-crediting in different places, difficulties in due diligence, and small but high-frequency accounts receivable are all problems that affect efficiency and increase implementation costs (Tang, 2021). Gong (2021) stated that the complex process, cumbersome business procedures, lengthy approval process, detailed information required, and poor timeliness make it especially difficult for asset-light SMEs to raise funds, which greatly increases their operating costs.

Monopoly Tendencies by Internet Giants

Internet giants sometimes monopolize traffic, making it difficult for SMEs to gain users and grow. As a result, the Chinese Internet industry has evolved from free competition to monopolistic competition. Monopoly has become a significant obstacle to the industry development, with massive data and traffic in the hands of the giants on which SMEs depend for survival, with high costs of acquiring users and weak growth (Yang et al., 2020).

The Internet economy is the new engine driving China's economic development. The Internet economy is also typically embodied as a platform economy. Tan (2021) discussed that the Internet platform aggregates many buyers and sellers, facilitating transactions between buyers and sellers by providing massive and accurate information. Due to the existence of the network effect, there is positive feedback and the phenomenon's emergence, which leads to "winner takes all." A particular field often ends up in a minimal number of Internet platforms or the hands of a few Internet giants in the area. With the potential for abuse of power, Internet giants use their long-accumulated users, information, and economic resources to their advantage in capturing new markets, thus squeezing the market share of SMEs.

How Blockchain Can Solve Those Problems

Solving the Financing Difficulties of SMEs

Blockchain technology has the propensity to help financial institutions effectively control risk and optimize credit processes. With the characteristics of blockchain distributed accounting and storage and data non-tameability, information on the operation, assets, and historical financing of SMEs can be recorded on the blockchain platform so that banks can efficiently comprehend the SME financing needs and their repayment ability. Banks can also perform credit management on this basis (Wang et al., 2019). At the same time, Malsa et al. (2021) point out that blockchain can improve the risk control model by providing big data. This will effectively improve the audit efficiency, not to mention reducing the cost of the audit, making accurate decisions, and avoiding the risk of multiple lending.

Innovation in technology and business models to enhance competitiveness

To stand out from the crowd, SMEs must continue to innovate in technology and business models to enhance their competitiveness. Blockchain technology offers unlimited possibilities for SMEs to innovate in technology and business models (Lei et al., 2020); for example, through smart contracts, Abuhashim & Tan (2020) opinions that business processes can be simplified, and smart contracts can complete functions such as invoicing and business contracts at low cost and high efficiency, thus saving costs and improving efficiency for SMEs. In addition, Khan et al. (2022) believe that through blockchain, user privacy and security protection can be improved, reducing the expenditure on protecting user privacy data and making more effective use of data.

Expanding Enterprise Ecology by Uniting Upstream and Downstream Industry Chains

Faced with the monopoly of Internet giants, SMEs can only seek development by grouping together and sharing resources to cut costs, increase efficiency and enhance market competitiveness. Still, it is challenging to solve the trust problem between enterprises that do not know each other (Wong et al., 2020).

Blockchain technology provides a practical solution for SMEs to develop in a group by building a blockchain enterprise alliance with the upstream and downstream industry chains. Within such a blockchain, each enterprise of the enterprise alliance will be on the same business ecological platform based on distributed accounting and data storage, as well as the characteristics of data non-tampering. As a result, the interests of upstream raw material suppliers and downstream customers will be common, and the problems of trust between enterprises and the sharing of users, traffic, and resources will be solved. At the same time, each SMEs can still maintain its own business model and profit model (Long et al., 2019).

Moreover, enterprises from different industries can also join this blockchain business platform for cross-industry cooperation and expand the enterprise ecology (Nandi et al., 2020). For example, sharing medical and health data will not only enable the flow of medical data between hospitals and solve the inefficiency caused by data silos but also enable cooperation between hospitals and insurance companies to simplify the audit and claims process. This improves efficiency and reduces the occurrence of fraudulent insurance cases.

SMEs' Contribution to Economic Growth

SMEs continue to act as capillaries of the national economy and they play an essential role in enhancing labor productivity, creating employment, promoting market competition, and narrowing the income gap (Min, 2021). In the 1980s and 1990s, China established the development idea of "grasping the big and releasing the small." As a result, SMEs benefited from the rapid marketization and globalization dividends development, but the ability to withstand risks was insufficient. For example, in 2008's subprime mortgage crisis, 2011's triangular debt, 2018's trade friction, and 2020's COVID-19 epidemic, the most injured were SMEs. Since 2018, the state has put the development of SMEs in a more critical position, rolling out innovation incentives, financing support for private SMEs as well as offering some tax incentives. In 2018, the National Bureau of Statistics of China presented that the number of SMEs in China were over 30 million. On the other hand, individual entrepreneurs exceeded 70 million, thus contributing about 50% of tax revenue, 60% of GDP, about 70% of technological innovation, 80% of urban labor employment, and 90% of the number of businesses. Figure 1 shows that the total number of market entities is growing, and the small and micro enterprises' share of the market is also increasing.

Figure 1. The share of small and medium enterprises in the market from 2016 to 2025
Data Source: State Administration of Market Supervision and Administration in 2020
Note: LHS=left-hand side; RHS=right-hand side

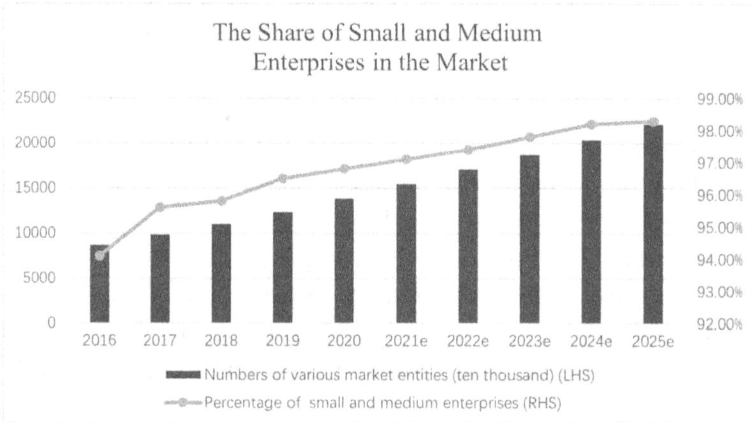

SMEs and Employment Creation in Both Rural and Urban Economies

SMEs are primarily labor-intensive. They are better than large enterprises in both employment capacity and investment elasticity. Most SMEs have a lower technological starting point and require fewer investment costs (Zhang, 2021). They are relatively easy to set up. At the same time, they can absorb many rural employed laborers. This is conducive to promoting the development of rural industrialization and urbanization. The destination of surplus rural labor is always cities, and the occupation is generally non-agricultural industries. Small and medium-sized enterprises are not as demanding as large enterprises in terms of recruitment. There are fewer restrictions on educational qualifications. For example, most construction workers in China were once farmers, and almost all construction companies employed are SMEs.

SMEs Can Revitalize the Regional Economy and Promote Its Harmonious Development

SMEs are the central economic pillar of some prefecture-level cities and counties in China. Only by promoting the service of SMEs well in the local economy can we prosper in development at a local level. In the eastern coastal regions of China, SMEs have become the mainstay of the local economy, as they have formed a distinctive cluster. For many low-income families, self-employment is the only source of income; the poorer the region, the more irreplaceable role SMEs play in poverty reduction. An active SME sector can effectively contribute to local per capita income and reduce the income gap between regions and rural and urban areas in economically underdeveloped western and central regions and rural areas (Zhang, 2021).

SMEs Can Contribute to Technological Innovation

Chinese SMEs have a strong drive for independent innovation, with the number of patents far exceeding the average. Compared with large enterprises, SMEs have higher market sensitivity, more flexible mechanisms, and greater efficiency and often achieve "0 to 1" innovation, with a stronger drive for independent innovation (Zhu, 2019). According to the data by SkyEye in 2021, the number of patents applied by SMEs has increased significantly in the past ten years, reaching 2.28 million in 2020, accounting for 68.4% of the total. According to the State Intellectual Property Office, in 2021, SMEs has accounted for more than 76% of the 5,729 national outstanding model enterprises of IPR (Intellectual Property Rights), and the average number of effective invention patents and IPR pledge financing reached 29.4 and 1.08 respectively, way above the national average of 2.9 and 0.01.

THE DEVELOPMENT OF BLOCKCHAIN

The Development of Blockchain in China

The Rapid Development of China's Blockchain Industry

Figure 2 shows sustained overall growth in the blockchain Chinese market size between 2017 and 2020. The growth rate of the blockchain market also exhibits a sharp increase since 2019. According to International Data Corporation (IDC)'s data, China's blockchain industry moved from 2017's \$0.85 billion level market scale to about \$561 million level industry scale as of 2020.

Figure 2. China's blockchain market size
Data Source: Compiled by IDC Foresight Industry Research Institute

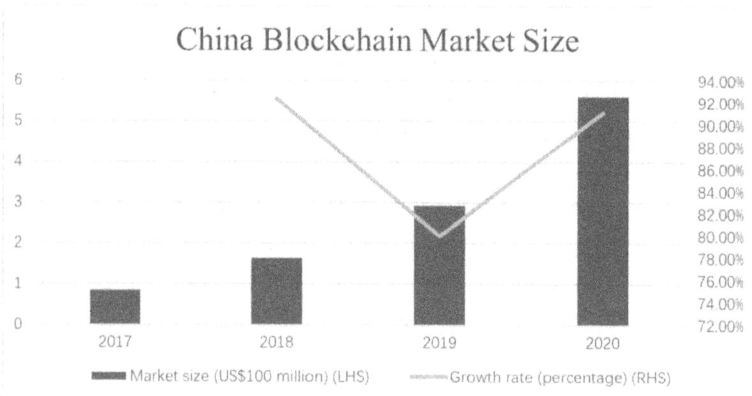

China Has a Large Share of Blockchain Patents in the World, and the Industry-Gathering Effect Is Beginning to Be Evident

China's competitive advantage in the blockchain industry is relatively evident from the global competition patterns perspective. For example, with reference to the number of patents, as shown in Figure 3, according to the data of "Blockchain Invention Patent Ranking of Global Enterprises in the First Half of 2020" released by IPRdaily, a global authoritative intellectual property third-party institution, and incoPat Innovation Index Research Center, the TOP 100 enterprises emanate from 14 countries and regions, with China accounting for 46%, followed by the United States accounting for 25%.

In terms of enterprises population, emerging players providing blockchain professional technical support, solutions and products among other services with inputs or outputs in China reached 303 in the first half of 2020, an increase of 274.07% year-on-year.

China's Blockchain Financial Sector Is the Most Widely Used

From Figure 4, China's blockchain industry applications are popular in sectors like finance, supply chain, traceability, and hardware. These account for nearly 65%. According to the disclosure of "Blockchain Blue Book: China Blockchain Development Report (2019)", there are almost twenty eight thousand blockchain enterprises in China. However, about a thousand blockchain enterprises have investments in the production chain, accounting for only 3.6%, mainly concentrated in areas such as Beijing, Shanghai, Guangdong, and Zhejiang which are more developed regions.

Figure 3. Regional distribution of global blockchain industry-related patents in the first half of 2020
Data Source: Compiled by IPRdaily Foresight Industry Research Institute in 2020

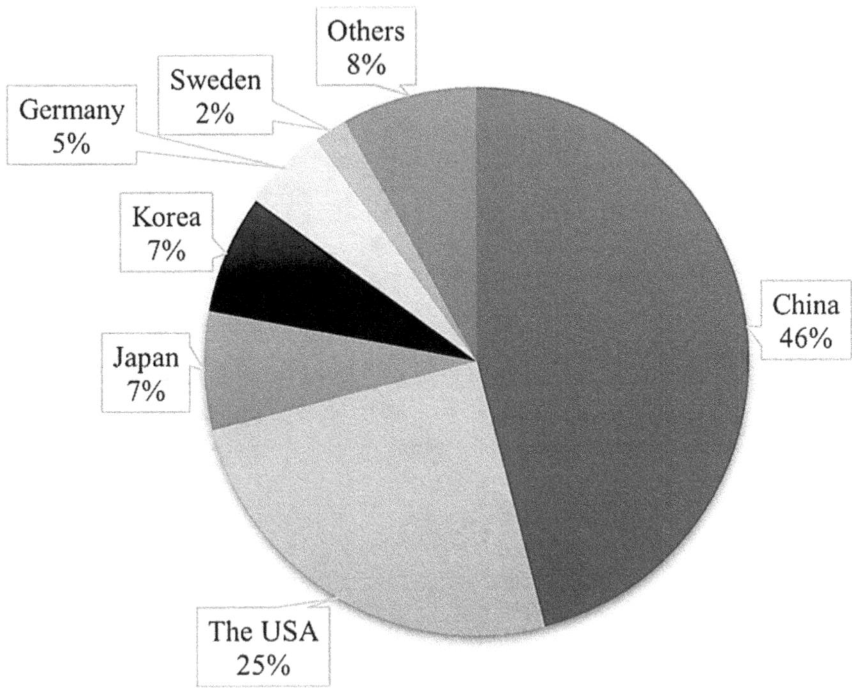

A Comparison of the State of Blockchain Development in China and Abroad (Using CiteSpace)

Brief Introduction of CiteSpace

CiteSpace is a visualization application by Prof. Chaomei Chen, a Chinese scholar in the School of Information Science and Technology at Drexel University, USA, and his team based on Java language, which emerged in the context of scientometrics, data mining technology, and information visualization. Prior, Qiao (2017) had used CiteSpace and Nvivo to study the evolution of blockchain and economic management in the international context and inspired the development of blockchain in China; Wang et al. (2018) used knowledge mapping to analyze the knowledge network and structure of blockchain, and initially analyzed the clusters of disciplines in which it was applied from 2015 to 2017; Wang et al. (2017) used bibliometric methods to study the hot spots in blockchain for the period 2015 to May 2017. CiteSpace provides three visualization options. The default is to use the cluster view to highlight key

Figure 4. Blockchain industry application and distribution in China in 2019
Data Source: Collated by the Foresight Industry Research Institute of the Sadie Blockchain Research Institute in 2019

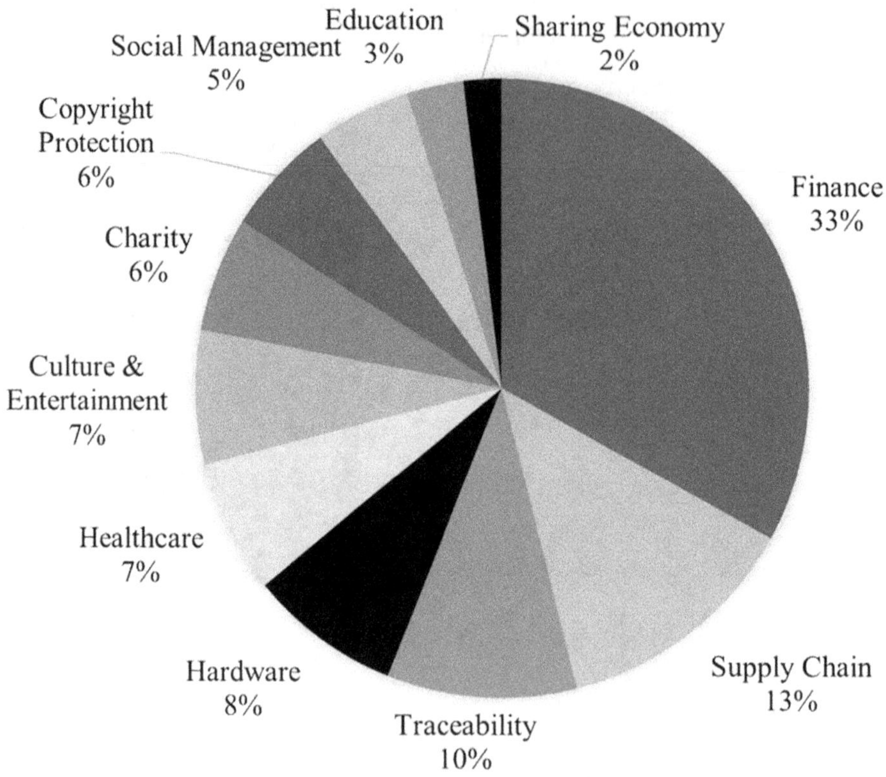

nodes and critical connections. On the other hand, the timeline view concentrates on outlining the connections between clusters and the past span of literature in a cluster. The time zone view focuses on the history of literature in a cluster while representing the knowledge evolution in the time dimension (Chen, 2016). This paper focuses on Log Likelihood Ratio (LLR) network clustering analysis and keyword co-occurrence analysis to study the critical hotspots and development trends in the blockchain field.

Data Sources

To ensure the literature sample's stability and authority, the literature search's scope was limited to the China National Knowledge Internet and Web of Science core collection from 2016 to 2021. In addition, a series of non-research documents, such as conference announcements, news reports, review information, and other non-research documents, were deleted. Reducing the noise of econometric analysis led us to 500 Chinese and 298 English documents.

Keyword Frequency and Research Hotspots Analysis

The term "research hotspot" refers to a topic that has been the focus of many researchers and scholars at a particular time. It is imperative to clarify the high-frequency keywords of blockchain and their distribution for further deepening and developing subsequent blockchain research.

Figure 5. CiteSpace for blockchain development in China
Data Source: China National Knowledge Internet from 2016 to 2021

Table 1. China blockchain keyword frequency statistics

Keyword	Frequency	Centrality
Smart Contracts	50	0.05
Digital Currency	33	0.08
Decentralization	28	0.1
Bitcoin	22	0.01
Consensus Mechanisms	16	0.01
Financial Regulation	14	0.02
Regulatory Sandbox	7	0.01
Trust Mechanisms	6	0.01
Internet of Things	6	0

As we can see in Figure 5 and Table 1, “Smart Contracts” was the most frequent phrase that appeared 50 times between 2016 and 2021. “Digital Currency” appeared 33 times, making it the second most frequent keyword/phrase. Other keywords, such as “Decentralization” and “Bitcoin,” also have a relatively high frequency. This shows that China has been more attentive to the digital currency and virtual currency represented by Bitcoin and has conducted more in-depth research on its core supporting technology, i.e., blockchain technology with decentralization as a distinctive feature. While blockchain technology becomes increasingly mature, the application of blockchain technology is also being gradually promoted as it is used in the finance industry. As the application of blockchain technology spreads, a series of problems also emerge, such as security threats and lack of regulation. Moreover, the emergence of blockchain technology has given birth to some new definitions, such as “Smart Contracts.” In addition, research topics such as “Financial Regulation” and “Trust Mechanisms” are also becoming hot topics in the blockchain field.

As is demonstrated in Figure 6 and Table 2, foreign blockchain research is mainly focused on “Management,” “Challenges,” and “Technology,” which shows that most foreign blockchain research has entered the application stage and is continuing to conquer the challenges. In addition, foreign blockchain researchers attach significant importance to the architecture of the blockchain system, emphasizing the bitcoin use and blockchain technology to develop a decentralized financial system and social system; therefore, keywords like “System,” “Framework,” and “Network” are emerging. In addition, with the heightened research and blockchain application abroad, foreign blockchain research has also paid attention to the use of blockchain technology in the “Internet of Things.”

Figure 6. CiteSpace for blockchain development abroad
Data Source: Web of Science from 2016 to 2021

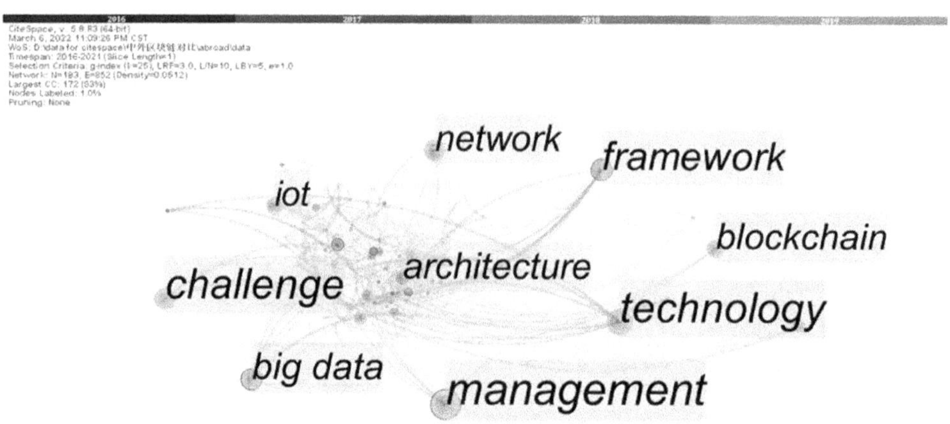

Table 2. Foreign blockchain keyword frequency statistics

Keyword	Frequency	Centrality
Management	45	0.18
Challenge	35	0.08
Technology	34	0.09
Framework	26	0.13
Big data	22	0.11
Blockchain	21	0.05
Network	20	0.07
Architecture	20	0.03
Internet of Things	18	0.09

CHINESE POLICIES OVER BLOCKCHAIN AND SMES

Chinese Policies on SMEs

These policies can be classified into two broad categories. The first classification aims at bettering the business environment, while the second category enhances planning and overall enterprise direction. The government issued the first category of policies to create an environment that is conducive for the development of SMEs. For instance, 2002's approach provides an initial legal framework system that renders legal protection for SMEs and fills a legal gap in this area. Policies from 2012, 2013, and 2018 provide financial and tax support to SMEs and improve their credit guarantee capacity, thus promoting the development of SMEs' economic development. The policies from 2016, 2018, 2020, and 2021 aim to build a better business environment for SMEs, thus helping these enterprises obtain foreign investment and upgrade their industries. These policy reforms show that the Chinese government's support for SMEs unfolds through conducive legal construction and economic support. Such improvement in the overall business environment suggests that the Chinese government has a new vision for creating a new era for SMEs.

The second category of policies focuses on guidance for the direction of SMEs development. The 2011 policy focuses on enhancing innovation and employment absorption capacity, optimizing industrial structure, and improving the level of "specialization and innovation" and industrial cluster development. It further aims to upgrade industrial management and improve SMEs' service systems. Policies of 2016 and 2018 place great emphasis on innovation and specialization, as they set goals of upgrading 200 specialized manufacturing champion model enterprises. They also emphasize discovering and cultivating 600 enterprises with the potential to grow into specialized champions. The policies also targeted nurturing about 600 specialized and innovative "Small Giants" enterprises over three years (2018- 2020). As of 2021, the Chinese government began to focus on improving the stability of the industry chain and promoting digitalization, networking, intelligent transformation, and high-quality enterprises' green development, which shows that the Chinese government is promoting the transformation of SMEs to modern, high-end, and green enterprises (Yu et al. 2022a; 2022d; 2022e; 2022g).

Table 3. Chinese policies affecting SMEs

Time	Regulations	Content
2002	Law on Promotion of Small and Medium-sized Enterprises	The initial formation of the legal framework system for small and medium-sized enterprises.
2011	The 12th Five-Year Plan for the Growth of Small and Medium Enterprises	Enhancing innovation and employment absorption capacity, optimizing industrial structure, improving the level of "specialization and innovation" and industrial cluster development, upgrading industrial management, and improving the service system for SMEs.
2013	Guiding Opinions on Promoting the Development of Small and Medium-sized Enterprises in "Specialization and Innovation"	Increasing financial and fiscal support, establishing, and improving service systems, organizing market development activities, strengthening cultivation and promotion work, and establishing a cooperative working mechanism.
2016	Plan for Promoting the Development of Small and Medium Enterprises (2016-2020)	Using the National SMEs Development Fund to promote the construction of an SME credit guarantee system, implementing the SME Promotion Law. Promoting the establishment of SMEs rights protection mechanism, promoting the establishment and improvement of SME operation monitoring system.
2016	Implementation Plan of Special Action for Cultivating and Enhancing Specialized Manufacturing Champion Enterprises	Summarizing and upgrading 200 specialized manufacturing champion model enterprises by 2025, discovering and cultivating 600 enterprises with the potential to grow into specialized champions.
2018	Implementation Plan on Supporting the Creation of Special Carriers to Promote Innovation and Entrepreneurship Upgrading of Small and Medium Enterprises	Through special funds for SMEs development, 10 billion CNY will be arranged by 2020 to support and guide 200 national and provincial development zones to build different types of special carriers for innovation and entrepreneurship.
2018	Notice on Cultivation of Specialized and Innovative "Small Giant" Enterprises	Using three years (2018- 2020) to cultivate about 600 specialized and innovative "Small Giants" enterprises.
2020	Implementation Opinions on Further Optimizing the Business Environment and Better Serving Market Subjects	Continuously improving the convenience of investment and construction, further simplifying the approval and conditions of production and operation of enterprises, optimizing the business environment of foreign investment enterprises, further reducing the threshold of obtaining employment and entrepreneurship, improving the quality and efficiency of business-related services, and improving the long-term mechanism for optimizing the business environment.

continues on following page

Table 3. Continued

Time	Regulations	Content
2020	Several Opinions on Sound Support Systems for the Development of SMEs	Improving the mechanism of supporting the development of small and medium-sized enterprises, improving the gradient cultivation system for small and medium-sized enterprises, "Small Giants" enterprises, and specialized champion enterprises in the manufacturing industry, standard system and evaluation mechanism, and guiding small and medium-sized enterprises to take the path of "specialization and innovation."
2021	Implementation Opinions on Further Stimulating Private Enterprise Entrepreneurial Enthusiasm. Achieve Entrepreneurial Creativity and Innovation. Promoting High-Quality Development of the Private Economy	Broadening creative channels, strengthening financial support, promoting the development of industrial clusters, enhancing the sense of honor of entrepreneurs, optimizing approval services, and improving the work promotion mechanism.
2021	Notice on Supporting the High-Quality Development of "Specialized and Innovative" Small and Medium-sized Enterprises	Supporting the "small giant" enterprises to increase their investment in innovation, improve their stability in the industry chain, and promote digitalization, networking, and intelligent transformation.
2021	Guiding Opinions on Accelerating the Cultivation and Development of High-Quality Enterprises in the Manufacturing Industry	Building a gradient cultivation pattern of high-quality enterprises, improving the independent innovation capability of high-quality enterprises, promoting the modernization of the industrial and supply chain, guiding the high-end, intelligent and green development of high-quality enterprises, creating an ecology of integrated development of large, medium and small enterprises, promoting high-quality enterprises to strengthen management innovation and cultural construction, and enhancing the level of open cooperation of high-quality enterprises.

Data source: http://www.gov.cn/zhengce/index.htm

Chinese Policies on Blockchain

Policies Oriented on Technology

The Chinese government's promulgation of policy on the technical direction of blockchain technology in 2016, as summarized in Table 4, is evidence of its interest in this kind of technology. Furthermore, the Chinese government has been committed to developing blockchain in conjunction with other high technologies, like, cloud computing, big data, artificial intelligence and the Internet of Things, as policies in 2017 and 2018, which can show that the Chinese government is curious about this new technology and is open to experimenting with the possibilities of using blockchain technology. Furthermore, from the policies of 2020 and 2021, we can learn that the Chinese government is exploring blockchain technology application. They are trying to educate the public about new technologies such as big data, blockchain, cloud computing, artificial intelligence, etc., which, to some extent, prepares SMEs for applying those new technologies (Yu et al., 2022c).

Table 4. Chinese technological policies targeting Blockchain development

Issuing Date	Issuing Departments	Policies	Main Content
2016.10	Ministry of Industry and Information Technology	White Paper on Blockchain Technology and Application Development (2016)	It summarizes the current status of blockchain development and its application scenarios at home and abroad. The policy also introduces the roadmap of blockchain technology development in China and the future direction and process of blockchain technology standardization.
2016.12	State Council	Circular on the National Informatization Plan for the 13th Five-Year Plan	For the first time, "blockchain" is included in the plan as a strategic frontier technology.
2017.1	Ministry of Commerce	Guidance on Further Promoting the Construction of National E-Commerce Demonstration Bases	Promoting the incubation of entrepreneurship in demonstration bases and the innovative application of technologies such as big data, cloud computing, the Internet of Things, artificial intelligence, and blockchain.
2017.7	State Council	Circular on the Development Plan of New Generation Artificial Intelligence	Promoting the integration of blockchain technology and artificial intelligence to establish a new social trust system.
2017.8	State Council	Guiding Opinions on Further Expanding and Upgrading Information Consumption to Unleash the Potential of Domestic Demand Sustainably	Proposal to carry out pilot applications based on blockchain, artificial intelligence, and other technologies.
2018.6	Ministry of Industry and Information Technology	Action Plan for the Development of Industrial Internet (2018- 2020)	Encouraging research on the application of edge computing, deep learning, blockchain, and other emerging frontier technologies in the industrial Internet.
2020.11	Culture and Tourism Department	Opinions on Promoting the High-Quality Development of the Digital Culture Industry	Supporting the integrated application and innovation of 5G, big data, cloud computing, artificial intelligence, the Internet of Things, and blockchain in the cultural industry and building several digital application scenarios for the cultural sector.
2021.6	State Council	Notice of the State Council on the Issuance of the Outline of the Action Plan for the Quality of Science for All People (2021- 2035)	Promoting the deep integration of science popularization with technologies such as big data, cloud computing, artificial intelligence, and blockchain. Strengthening the concepts of demand perception, user stratification, and situational application. Promoting innovation and upgrading of communication methods, organization and mobilization, and operation services, strengthening the construction of "Science Popularization China," and making full use of existing platforms to build a national science communication network platform and a science popularization platform.

Data source: http://www.gov.cn/zhengce/index.htm

Policies Oriented Toward Blockchain Application

In October 2017, the Chinese government released its first policy related to the direction of the blockchain technology application, as summarized in Table 5. The policies use several tools, including artificial intelligence together with emerging technologies, aimed at establishing a credit evaluation mechanism. After that, the Chinese government committed to combining blockchain with other high-techs like cloud computing, big data, artificial intelligence, virtual reality, and augmented reality, among others. In 2017, 2018, 2019, and 2021, the Chinese government promoted the application of blockchain and other high-techs in industrial Internet, postal, logistics, education, finance, livelihood, agriculture, human resources, and other sectors. The Chinese government has further established several demonstration zones, and relevant laws and regulations have been introduced to regulate blockchain technology's legal and reasonable application (Yu et al., 2022b; 2022f).

Table 5. Chinese policies on Blockchain Applications

Issuing Time	Issuing Department	Policies	Main Content
2017.10	State Council	The Guidance on Actively Promoting Supply Chain Innovation and Application	Study of the use of blockchain, artificial intelligence, and other emerging technologies to establish a credit evaluation mechanism based on the supply chain.
2017.11	State Council	Guiding Opinions on Deepening "Internet + Advanced Manufacturing" and Developing Industrial Internet	Promoting the research and exploration of edge computing, artificial intelligence, augmented reality, virtual reality, blockchain, and other emerging frontier technologies in the industrial Internet.
2017.12	National Post Office	Guiding Opinions on Promoting Postal Services for the Construction of "One Belt, One Road"	Exchanging experiences with countries along the postal route on integrating and developing the postal industry and the Internet, big data, cloud computing, artificial intelligence, and blockchain, jointly carrying out demonstrations of technological applications.
2018.2	Ministry of Industry and Information Technology	Notice on Organizing the Declaration of Pilot Demonstration Projects on Information Consumption	Actively exploring the use of blockchain technology to carry out the process of information logistics testing and promoting the reduction of costs and increasing efficiency of information consumption in the logistics industry.
2018.4	Ministry of Education	The Education Informatization 2.0 Action Technology	Proposes to actively explore effective ways of recording, transferring, exchanging, and certifying intelligent learning effects based on blockchain, big data, and other new technologies, forming a ubiquitous and intelligent learning system, promoting the deep integration of information technology and intelligent technology into the education teaching process, and developing new growth poles for international competition.

continues on following page

Table 5. Continued

Issuing Time	Issuing Department	Policies	Main Content
2019.8	State Council	Opinions on Supporting Shenzhen in Building an Advanced Demonstration Zone of Socialism with Chinese Characteristics	Improving the capacity of financial services for the real economy, studying and improving the system of issuance and listing, refinancing, mergers and acquisitions and restructuring the Growth Enterprise Market, and creating conditions to promote the reformation of the registration systems and supporting the development of innovative applications such as digital currency in Shenzhen. Promotion of the interconnection and interoperability of financial markets and mutual recognition of financial (fund) products with Hong Kong and Macao. Promoting RMB internationalization at an early stage and on a pilot basis and exploring innovations in cross-border financial supervision.
2021.10	State Council	Opinions of the State Council on Pilot Work on Innovation in the Business Environment	Promoting the exploration and application of blockchain technology in government services, livelihood services, logistics, accounting, and other fields.
2021.11	State Council	Several Measures to Enhance the Competitiveness of Small and Medium Enterprises	Supporting financial institutions to deepen the use of big data, artificial intelligence, blockchain, and other technical means. Improving credit approval and risk management models and continuously increasing the scale and intensity of investment in small and medium-sized enterprises.
2021.11	Ministry of Rural Affairs	The Guidance on Expanding Multiple Functions of Agriculture to Promote Quality Development of Rural Industries	Promoting the role of rural e-commerce in dovetailing science, industry, and trade. Implementing the "Internet + agricultural products" out of villages and into cities project, using 5G, cloud computing, Internet of Things, blockchain, and other technologies. Accelerating the construction of network systems, front-end warehouses, and logistics facilities. Introducing modern information technology into all agricultural production, processing, and marketing aspects. Establishing big data on agricultural products in counties and cities and cultivating rural e-commerce entities and businesses such as webcasting.
2021.11	Ministry of Human Resources and Social Security	Opinions on Promoting Quality Development of Human Resources Services in the New Era	Implementing the "Internet + Human Resources Services" initiative, innovating and applying new information technologies such as big data, artificial intelligence, and blockchain to promote the efficiency of recruitment, training, outsourcing of human resources services, and labor dispatch.
2021.10	People's Bank of China, Central Internet Information Office	Opinions on Regulating the Application and Development of Open-Source Technology in the Financial Sector	Exploring independent open-source ecology, focusing on accelerating ecological construction in the fields of essential software such as operating systems, databases, and middleware and emerging technologies such as cloud computing, big data, artificial intelligence, and blockchain. Using the open-source model to accelerate the development of information technology innovation.

Data source: http://www.gov.cn/zhengce/index.htm

Policies Oriented Towards Regulation and Standards

Since January 2017 (and prior), the Chinese government has been issuing numerous policies, as shown in Table 6. This indicates that The Government of China has always been supportive and optimistic about blockchain from its onset. However, as some domestic and foreign institutions used various types of deceptive propaganda to participate in some financing activities in the name of ICO, the Chinese government began to clean up and rectify token issuance activities until January 2018, when it rigorously provided services for transactions involving virtual currency. The government, also instituted some financial measures, that prevented virtual currency transactions through certain payment channels. Since then, the Chinese government has also paid great attention to the security of blockchain technology applications. In addition, the 'Blockchain Information Service Management Regulations' introduction has standardized the basis for filing within China's blockchain industry. The "Management Regulations" introduction also means that the "regulatory era" for blockchain information services in China has officially arrived.

Table 6. Chinese policies on Blockchain regulation and standards

Issuing Time	Issuing Department	Policies	Main Content
2017.1	Ministry of Industry and Information Technology	Information Technology Services Development Plan (2015- 2020)	Putting forward the blockchain and other areas of innovation to reach the advanced international level and other requirements.
2017.8	China Internet Finance Association	Tips on Preventing Risks Related to Various Types of Investment Absorption in the Name of Initial Coin Offering (ICO)	Guidelines on preventing some domestic and foreign institutions that use various types of misleading propaganda to engage in financing activities in the name of ICO.
2017.9	Internet finance special rectification work leading group office	Notice the clean-up and rectification work on token issuance and financing	Comprehensively stop new issuance of token and financing activities, establishing a mechanism for detecting activities of token issuance and financing to prevent resurgence; conducting a case-by-case study of completed ICO projects, clearing out those issued for the general public, and cracking down on illegal and irregular behavior.
2018.3	Ministry of Industry and Information Technology	Highlights of Standardization Work in the Information Technology and Software Service Industry in 2018	Proposes to promote the formation of the National Technical Committee for the Management of Information and Industrialization Integration Standards, the National Technical Committee for Blockchain and Distributed Bookkeeping.
2018.1	China Internet Finance Association	Alert on Preventing the Risks of Overseas ICO and "Virtual Currency" Transactions	Investors are warned to guard against overseas coin issuers. It is pointed out that the act of providing payment and other services for "virtual currency" transactions will face policy risks, and investors should take the initiative to strengthen risk awareness and remain rational.

continues on following page

Table 6. Continued

Issuing Time	Issuing Department	Policies	Main Content
2018.1	Payment and Settlement Department of the Central Bank of China	Notice on Self-Inspection and Rectification Work on Providing Payment Services for Illegal Virtual Currency Transactions	The notice requires all units and branches to carry out self-investigation and rectification work, strictly prohibiting services for virtual currency transactions and preventing payment channels from being used for virtual currency transactions through financial measures.
2019.1	State Internet Information Office	Regulations on the Administration of Blockchain Information Services	Blockchain information service providers and users shall not use blockchain information services to engage in activities prohibited by laws and administrative regulations, such as endangering national security, disturbing social order, and infringing on the legitimate rights and interests of others.
2019.2	State Internet Information Office	Blockchain Information Service Management Regulations	The "Blockchain Information Service Management Regulations" regulate the record basis for developing the blockchain industry in China. The "Management Regulations" introduction also means that the "regulatory era" for blockchain information services in China has officially arrived.
2019.3	State Internet Information Office	Announcement on the First Batch of Domestic Blockchain Information Service Filing Numbers	The first batch of a total of 197 blockchain information service names and filing numbers were publicly released. The main types of companies in the list are Internet companies, financial institutions, listed companies, etc. The key directions are blockchain technology platforms, traceability, confirmation, anti-counterfeiting, and supply chain finance.
2019.10	Standing Committee of the National People's Congress	The Cryptography Act	The Cryptography Law came into force on January 1, 2020. Designed to regulate the application and management of passwords. Promoting the development of the cryptographic industry, protecting the network and information security, and enhancing the scientific, standardized, and legal level of cryptographic management is a comprehensive and fundamental law in the field of cryptography in China.
2019.10	State Internet Information Office	Announcement of Blockchain Information Service Management Regulations	The regulations clarify the target and scope of blockchain regulation and the principle of lenient rule for schools. Blockchain information service providers must file with the State Internet Information Office and carry out class real identity information authentication for blockchain information service users, etc.
2019.10	Political Bureau of the CPC Central Committee	The 18th collective study of the Political Bureau of the CPC Central Committee on the current status and trends of blockchain technology development	The integrated application of blockchain technology plays a vital role in new technological innovation and industrial change. Therefore, we should take blockchain as a significant breakthrough in independent innovation of core technology, as it clarifies the main direction of research and increases investment.

continues on following page

Table 6. Continued

Issuing Time	Issuing Department	Policies	Main Content
2019.11	The central bank and the regulatory authorities of Shanghai, Beijing, Shenzhen, Dongguan, Inner Mongolia, and many other places	The central bank and relevant regulatory authorities around the world have issued a series of blockchain regulatory policies intensively	Risk alerts have been issued for digital currency trading-related activities, followed by mapping and checking of trading platforms and shutting down and rectifying them one after another.
2019.11	Development and Reform Commission	Guidance Catalogue for Industrial Restructuring (2019)	The entry of virtual currency 'mining,' which had been included in the category of eliminated industries in the "Catalogue for the Guidance of Industrial Structure Adjustment (2019, Draft for Comments)", was deleted.
2020.3	China Central Bank	Financial Distributed Ledger Technology Security Specification	Specifies the security system of financial distributed ledger technology, including basic hardware, basic software, cryptographic algorithm, node communication, ledger data, and consensus protocol. The Specification defines management, privacy protection, regulatory support, operation and maintenance requirements, and governance mechanisms.
2020.6	Standing Committee of the National People's Congress	The 2020 Legislative Work Plan of the Standing Committee of the National People's Congress	The NPC Standing Committee's 2020 Legislative Plan emphasizes the study of legal issues related to new technologies and fields such as artificial intelligence, blockchain, and gene editing.
2020.12	The China Banking and Insurance Regulatory Commission	Measures for the Regulation of Internet Insurance Business	The Regulation of the Internet Insurance Business is formulated following the Insurance Law of the People's Republic of China and other laws and administrative regulations to regulate the Internet insurance business, effectively prevent risks, protect the legitimate rights and interests of consumers, and enhance the level of the insurance industry in serving the real economy and the livelihood of the society.

Data source: http://www.gov.cn/zhengce/index.htm

The timeline in Table 7 will help us better understand the Chinese government's policy on blockchain technology as a whole.

CASE STUDIES

Qianhai WeBank's Development Status

Qianhai WeBank is a private pilot enterprise in Shenzhen that applied to the China Banking Regulatory Commission for the right to set up a bank in 2014 and has been growing rapidly since then. The company was incorporated as 'Shenzhen Qianhai WeBank Co.' in less than half a year. The company then officially launched its

Table 7. The development process of China's blockchain industry policy

2013—2014 Severe regulation	– At the end of 2013, the People's Bank of China, the Ministry of Industry and Information Technology, and the China Banking Regulatory Commission. In addition, China Securities Regulatory Commission (CSRC) and China Insurance Regulatory Commission (CIRC) jointly issued the Notice on Preventing the Risk of Bitcoin.
2015—2017 Active response	– The Central Bank started studying the feasibility of legal digital currency and the development of the trading platform. – The Ministry of Industry and Information Technology (MIIT) released a white paper on the development of blockchain technology and applications in China (2016). – The Central Bank added blockchain to the 13th Five-Year Plan.
2018—2019 Strengthening of research and regulation	– In 2018, the Central Bank issued Tips on Preventing Illegal Fund Raising in the Name of 'Virtual Currency' and 'Blockchain.' – The central government pointed out that blockchain should be taken as an essential breakthrough in independent innovation of core technology.
2020—2021 Active promotion	– Actively promote the joint application of blockchain in various industries.

Data source: Collated by Foresight Industry Research Institute

official website and raised the slogan of 'technology, inclusive, link,' with the help of the network as a platform to develop inclusive financial products and encourage 'personal loan and a small deposit.' It has provided highly efficient, quality Internet banking services for their customers which helped the bank achieve a good brand image. Premier Li Keqiang witnessed how the bank conducted credit transactions through the Internet during his inspection of WeBank in 2015. Although the loan amount was only RMB 35,000, it was the first time in China's history that financial activity was conducted through the Internet. With this move, WeBank entered into an official trial phase, which may have been just the beginning for the bank but meant a milestone reality for online banking in China as a whole, which marked the stage of modern network development for banks in China since then (Hu, 2020). Shortly after that, the bank established a partnership with the then-famous Huaxia Bank, where the time between the authorization of the China Banking Regulatory Commission (CBRC) and the establishment of WeBank was only a few months, but its development potential was clear to all, and its future was unlimited.

As one of the first private banks in China, Qianhai WeBank has received much media attention since its development. Throughout its development history, Wan (2018) held the view that WeBank is a young and innovative bank compared to traditional banks and a new type of bank with no counters and purely online operations compared to other private banks. WeBank became prominent for their purely online business model and were active among individuals and SMEs for their special personal savings and small loans business. WeBank's operations are supported by financial technology, such as big data, blockchain technology, artificial intelligence, and cloud computing, reflecting its reliance on Tencent's technological development. At the same time, WeBank has tapped many technology personnel in its staff system to support financial technology.

Qianhai WeBank's Development Features

5'Purely Online' Operation of 'Personal Loan and Small Deposit' Business

Unlike the operation of ordinary banks that require the establishment of counters, all business of WeBank can be conducted through the Internet, so geographical constraints will not bind its transaction business, and all clients are able to transact with the bank via the Internet, just by downloading an APP, which can be successfully linked with QQ and WeChat ports, so the model has significant advantages:

Cost saving. While brick-and-mortar banks require to install counters, hire sales staff, and meet some high overhead costs, WeBank operations only need a computer and Internet technology, which maximizes its cost savings.

Increased efficiency. Due to the popularity of the Internet, users around the world can conduct business anytime and anywhere, which not only gets rid of geographical restrictions but also greatly improves business efficiency. In addition, WeBank collects and credits customer information through the Internet, so its business model is objective and fair, truly creating a sound business platform for customers.

In line with its business philosophy of providing universal access to the world, WeBank has always been committed to providing financial services to ordinary people as well as small and medium-sized enterprises. As a result, its scope of business is mainly related to micro loans or bill payment agencies. Moreover, WeBank faces lower- and middle-class customers and therefore undertakes financial services of a personal nature. This distinguishes them from many large commercial banks, which provide high-end and high-value financial products,

The first product launched by WeBank is the "Microloan," which, as the name suggests, is a small-scale, petty loan business with the advantage of being "instant." This type of business does not require the necessary collateral and guarantees from the customer, as the online system identifies the customer through facial recognition technology and establishes a credit profile through the credit system. Customers can make online applications via their mobile social media platforms such as QQ or WeChat client, and the status of their loan application is often concluded within a week without having to fill out detailed information. In some instances, clients have been able to receive the money in just half an hour, which demonstrates how fast and efficient the model is. Furthermore, there is no specific limit to the loan amount, as long as it does not exceed 300,000; many of these credits are between 20,000 CNY to 200,000 CNY, so the amount can fully meet customers' needs.

According to the official data from WeBank, shown in Table 8, as of 15 May 2017, the total amount of loans granted by Microloan, which has been online for two years, was 360 billion yuan, representing a wide range of customers and a large amount of loans granted. As for repayment, it is also very convenient, with a daily interest rate of 0.05%, and customers can repay up to the amount they can afford. Therefore, it is so popular, with around 83% of the country's cities currently using it, and WeBank's lending performance is increasing.

Table 8. Development performance of "Microloan" as of May 2017

Total loan amount	360 billion CNY
Total number of loans	44 million
Proactive Credit Customers	98 million
City coverage	567
Open and activate users	22 million

Data source: http://finance.ce.cn/bank/

Application of Patented Blockchain Technology

In 2016, WeBank began a major rollout of blockchain technology, which is in use in more than 20 institutions. Shortly afterward, a kick-off meeting on the systematic study of blockchain technology was officially held in Beijing, with the Ministry of Industry and Information Technology's Electronic Standards Researchers taking the lead and proposing to proceed with the preparation of the "White Paper on Blockchain Technology and Applications in China," including WeBank (Wan, 2018). Subsequently, the "Blockchain Lab" was established, and WeBank and Wanxiang Holdings worked together to establish an alliance to do research and development work on blockchain technology in the financial industry.

In terms of scenario application, to improve the efficiency of bank loan clearing, in 2016, WeBank launched the operation of a joint inter-bank loan clearing platform, the main application of which is "microloan," which is still supported by the in-depth use of blockchain technology. Through blockchain technology, the platform can obtain a more systematic set of standard operational schematics to complete the necessary reconciliation operations if some of the information is successfully entered into the corresponding blockchain by the partner banks. Based on the standardized data provided by the schematic, staff can simply cross-reference it to comprehensively and systematically understand the credit situation. This allows for risk prevention in the transaction process. Due to the reliability and practicality of the technology, many other banks, including Luoyang Bank, have joined the platform in succession.

WeBank has also developed a blockchain BaaS cloud service system regarding underlying technology. The use and operation of BaaS cloud service technology are the first of their kind in the domestic financial industry, which not only greatly reduces costs, but also allows transactions to take place even between different institutions, making operations more convenient and services more thorough.

This makes it easier to operate and provides a better service. However, the underlying support for this technology still comes from Tencent Cloud, with which WeBank has developed a new financial system platform that makes banking procedures more formal, data processing more secure, and operations more professional. Since then, many other institutions in the industry have been competing to adopt the technology, with WeBank taking care of the specific services.

Figure 7 shows changes in loans that were given to small and medium enterprises by banking institutions between 2018 and 2021.

Figure 7. Changes in loans received by small and medium enterprises from banking institutions (2018 Q1-2021 Q2)
Data Source: Wind Economic Database in 2021

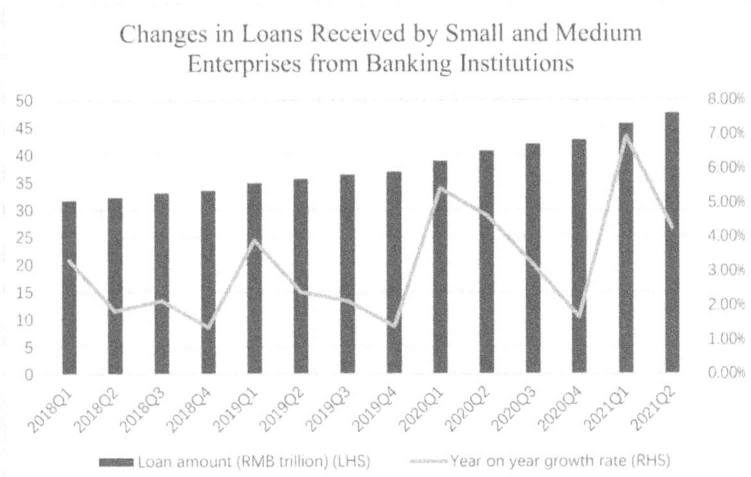

According to Figure 7, loans received by small and medium enterprises from banking institutions have generally increased between 2018 and 2021. Credit is due to the development and effective application of financial technology, banking institutions can access SMEs' credit qualifications more easily and accurately, thus enabling them to delegate more and process loans faster. In recent years, SMEs have received more loan amounts from the banking sector to cush them from the adverse impacts of the COVID-19 epidemic. A sustained application of blockchain technology and its associated measures has the odds of helping businesses as they embark on a sustainable development path.

CONCLUSION

We must use blockchain technology correctly and efficiently to achieve sustainable growth for SMEs. For example, the development of blockchain technology enables SMEs to access loans more quickly and efficiently, thus ensuring a stable and sustainable funding chain. In addition, blockchain development can also reduce SMEs' administrative costs and facilitate industrial clusters' development, which can increase output efficiency and reduce overall costs.

In the Chinese market, government plays a notable role, and enabling policy engineering greatly influences any industry's development. As is propounded in this study, the Chinese government is not only committed to creating a suitable economic environment for SMEs to grow but also provides them with appropriate legal support. Moreover, these days, the Chinese government is also offering some incentive policies to encourage SMEs to innovate and specialize.

Blockchain technology, there are, however, mixed attitudes. The Chinese government holds a positive view of blockchain technology research and willingly promotes its application in many industries. Just like in the case of the development and flourishment of Webank, credit is due to the approval and promotion efforts by the government. However, the Chinese government discourages using bitcoin or non-fungible tokens (NFT). Transactions in Bitcoin and NFT in the domestic market are heavily monitored due to their high price volatility. In turn, the regulation of blockchain technology is intensified to guard the stable development of China's economy.

This chapter focused on the role played by blockchain technology in the development of Chinese SMEs. It delved on providing valuable insights into the future part of its application. Since blockchain technology is somewhat intelligible, its practicality and positive influence go beyond the Chinese SMEs market. The authors also acknowledge the uncapped potential and need for close monitoring and regulation of the application of this technology so that benefits may continue to outweigh the threats. Ways of expanding blockchain technology globally and ensuring its application are over a wider geographic spectrum remain a grey area, particularly in developing economies. This, moving forward, may present the subject as the research hotspot over the unforeseeable future.

ACKNOWLEDGMENT

The authors would like to acknowledge:

- Our colleagues from various institutions including but not limited to, Soochow University, The European Business University Of Luxembourg, The Australian Studies Centre of Shanghai University, and Krirk University, as well as the independent research associates who provided insight and expertise that greatly assisted the research, although they may not agree with all of the interpretations/conclusions of this chapter.
- China Knowledge for valuable support to our research.
- The Editor and the International Editorial Advisory Board (IEAB) of this book, who desk reviewed, rigorously put this work through double/triple-blind review processes. We appreciate their thorough, minute, and final critical reviews leading to the acceptance of this chapter for publication.
- All anonymous reviewers for their valuable and constructive feedback that powered intense revision, enhancement, and fine-tuning of this chapter.

REFERENCES

Abuhashim, A. A., & Tan, C. C. (2020). Smart Contract Designs on Blockchain Applications. *2020 IEEE Symposium on Computers and Communications (ISCC)*, 1-4.

Belchior, R., Vasconcelos, A., Guerreiro, S., & Correia, M. P. (2022). A Survey on Blockchain Interoperability: Past, Present, and Future Trends. *ACM Computing Surveys*, *54*(8), 1–41. doi:10.1145/3471140

Berger, A. N., & Udell, G. F. (2006). A more complete conceptual framework for SME finance. *Journal of Banking & Finance*, *30*(11), 2945–2966. doi:10.1016/j.jbankfin.2006.05.008

Chaum, D. L. (1982). *Computer systems established, maintained and trusted by mutually suspicious groups* [Unpublished doctoral dissertation]. Department of Computer Sciences, The University of California, Berkeley, CA.

Chen, C. (2004). Searching for intellectual turning points: Progressive Knowledge Domain Visualization. *Proceedings of the National Academy of Sciences of the United States of America*, *101*(Suppl.), 5303–5310. doi:10.1073/pnas.0307513100 PMID:14724295

Chen, C. (2006). CiteSpace II: Detecting and visualizing emerging trends and transient patterns in scientific literature. *Journal of the American Society for Information Science and Technology*, *57*(3), 359–377. doi:10.1002/asi.20317

Chen, C. (2010). *System and method for automatically generating systematic reviews of a scientific field.* US Patent US20110295903A1.

Chen, C. (2016). *CiteSpace: A Practical Guide for Mapping Scientific Literature*. Nova Science Publishers.

Chen, C. (2017). Science mapping: A systematic review of the literature. *Journal of Data and Information Science*, *2*(2), 1–40. doi:10.1515/jdis-2017-0006

Chen, C. (2020). A Glimpse of the First Eight Months of the COVID-19 Literature on Microsoft Academic Graph. *Frontiers in Research Metrics and Analytics*, *5*, 607286. doi:10.3389/frma.2020.607286 PMID:33870064

Chen, C., Ibekwe-SanJuan, F., & Hou, J. (2010). The structure and dynamics of co-citation clusters: A multiple-perspective co-citation analysis. *Journal of the American Society for Information Science and Technology*, *61*(7), 1386–1409. doi:10.1002/asi.21309

Chen, C., & Song, M. (2019). Visualizing a field of research: A methodology of systematic scientometric reviews. *Public Library of Science ONE*, *14*(10), e0223994. doi:10.1371/journal.pone.0223994 PMID:31671124

Dai, J., & Vasarhelyi, M. A. (2017). Toward blockchain-based accounting and assurance. *Journal of Information Processing Systems*, *31*(3), 5–21.

Fanning, K., & Centers, D. P. (2016). Blockchain and its coming impact on financial services. *Journal of Corporate Accounting & Finance*, *27*(5), 53–57. doi:10.1002/jcaf.22179

Ghaemi, S., Rouhani, S., Belchior, R., Cruz, R., Khazaei, H., & Musílek, P. (2021). *A Pub-Sub Architecture to Promote Blockchain Interoperability.* ArXiv, abs/2101.12331.

Gong, L. (2021). Microbank's supply chain financial service model for small and micro enterprises. *Banker*, *6*, 123–124.

Guo, L., Liu, Q., Shi, K., Gao, Y., Luo, J., & Chen, J. (2021). A blockchain-driven electronic contract management system for commodity procurement in electronic power industry. *IEEE Access: Practical Innovations, Open Solutions*, *9*, 9473–9480. doi:10.1109/ACCESS.2021.3049562

Haber, S., & Stornetta, W. S. (1991). How to time-stamp a digital document. *Journal of Cryptology*, *3*(2), 99–111. doi:10.1007/BF00196791

Hu, B., & Fan, Y. (2021). Internet joint lending: Theoretical logic, potential problems and regulatory directions. *Journal of Wuhan University*, (03), 131–142. doi:10.14086/j.cnki.wujss.2021.03.013

Hu, F. (2020). The role and potential of blockchain to advance sustainable development. *Journal of Sustainable Development Economics*, *5*, 59–61.

Hu, L. (2020). *Analysis of micro-credit business of WeBank* [Master's thesis]. Hebei University.

Khan, S.A., Piprani, A.Z., & Yu, Z. (2022). Digital technology and circular economy practices: future of supply chains. *Operations Management Research*, 1-13.

Long, Y., Zhang, J., & Ai, R. (2019). Blockchain technology-based supply s chain financial system optimization research. *Southwest Finance*, *1*, 72–79.

Luo, Y., & Hou, Y. (2016). Development strategies and policy regulation of China's Internet banks - A case study based on Wezuo Bank and Online Business Bank. *Modern Economic Exploration*, (07), 42–46. doi:10.13891/j.cnki.mer.2016.07.009

Malsa, N., Vyas, V., Gautam, J., Shaw, R. N., & Ghosh, A. (2021). *Framework and Smart Contract for Blockchain Enabled Certificate Verification System Using Robotics*. Machine Learning for Robotics Applications. doi:10.1007/978-981-16-0598-7_10

Min, Z., Sawang, S., & Kivits, R. (2021). Proposing Circular Economy Ecosystem for Chinese SMEs: A Systematic Review. *International Journal of Environmental Research and Public Health*, *18*(5), 18. doi:10.3390/ijerph18052395 PMID:33804522

Nakamoto, S. (2008). *Bitcoin: a peer-to-peer electronic cash system.* https://bitcoin.org/bitcoin.pdf

Nandi, M. L., Nandi, S., Moya, H., & Kaynak, H. (2020). Blockchain technology-enabled supply chain systems and supply chain performance: A resource-based view. *Supply Chain Management*, *25*(6), 841–862. doi:10.1108/SCM-12-2019-0444

Peters, G. W., & Panayi, E. (2015). Understanding modern banking ledgers through blockchain technologies: future of transaction processing and smart contracts on the Internet of money. Springer International Publishing.

Pilkington, M. (2016). Blockchain technology: principles and applications. In F. Xavier Olleros & M. Zhegu (Eds.), *Research Handbook on Digital Transformations* (p. 225). doi:10.4337/9781784717766.00019

Rehman Khan, S. A., Yu, Z., Sarwat, S., Godil, D. I., Amin, S., & Shujaat, S. S. (2021). The role of block chain technology in circular economy practices to improve organisational performance. *International Journal of Logistics Research and Applications*, *25*(4-5), 605–622. doi:10.1080/13675567.2021.1872512

Sun, W., Dedahanov, A. T., Shin, H. Y., & Li, W. P. (2021). Using extended complexity theory to test SMEs' adoption of Blockchain-based loan system. *PLoS One*, *16*(2), 16. doi:10.1371/journal.pone.0245964 PMID:33544745

Sun, Y., Chen, Y., Li, D., Lu, H., Li, B., Liu, C., & Lu, W. (2021). The research of source-load transaction mechanism based on blockchain. *IOP Conference Series. Earth and Environmental Science*, *675*(1), 675. doi:10.1088/1755-1315/675/1/012142

Tan, Y. (2021). The dilemma and the way out of the regulation of the abuse of market dominance by Internet platforms. *Research on the Rule of Law*, *4*, 110–123. doi:10.16224/j.cnki.cn33-1343/d.20210701.004

Tang, Y. J. (2021). An overview of commercial banks' credit risk management and the difficulty of financing for small and medium-sized enterprises. *Business News*, *12*, 73–74.

Wan, J. (2018). *Countermeasures for the characteristic development of Qianhai WeBank in Shenzhen* [Master's thesis]. Hebei University.

Wang, R., Lin, Z., & Luo, H. (2019). Blockchain, bank credit and SME financing. *Quality & Quantity*, *53*(3), 1127–1140. doi:10.100711135-018-0806-6

Wong, P. F., Chia, F. C., Kiu, M. S., & Lou, E. C. (2020). *Potential integration of blockchain technology into smart sustainable city (SSC) developments: A systematic review*. Smart and Sustainable Built Environment.

Xie, W. S. (2022). Study on Enterprise Financial Risk Prevention and Early Warning System Based on Blockchain Technology. *Mobile Information Systems*, *2022*(1), 5–10. doi:10.1155/2022/4435296

Yang, H., Zhang, W., Xi, X., Liu, Y., & Zhai, T. (2020). Block Research on the game of supply chain finance based on accounts receivable model in a chain environment. *Mathematical Practice and Understanding*, *13*, 313–320.

Yang, J. (2021). China's small and medium-sized enterprise financing dilemma and countermeasures research. *Economist*, *11*, 288–290.

Yermack, D. (2017). Corporate governance and blockchains. *Review of Finance*, *21*(1), 7–31.

Yu, P., Chen, D., & Ahuja, A. (2022a). Smart and Sustainable Economy: How COVID-19 Has Acted as a Catalyst for China's Digital Transformation. In S. Kautish & G. Kaur (Eds.), *AI-Enabled Agile Internet of Things for Sustainable FinTech Ecosystems* (pp. 106–146). IGI Global. doi:10.4018/978-1-6684-4176-3.ch006

Yu, P., Gong, R., & Sampat, M. (2022b). Blockchain Technology in China's Digital Economy: Balancing Regulation and Innovation. In P. Tehrani (Ed.), *Regulatory Aspects of Artificial Intelligence on Blockchain* (pp. 132–157). IGI Global. doi:10.4018/978-1-7998-7927-5.ch007

Yu, P., Gu, H., Zhao, Y., & Ahuja, A. (2022c). Digital Transformation Driven by Internet Data Center: Case Studies on China. In D. Piaggesi, H. Landazuri, & B. Jia (Eds.), *Cases on Applying Knowledge Economy Principles for Economic Growth in Developing Nations* (pp. 203–230). IGI Global. doi:10.4018/978-1-7998-8417-0.ch011

Yu, P., Jiao, A., & Sampat, M. (2022d). The Effect of Chinese Green Transformation on Competitiveness and the Environment. In P. Ordóñez de Pablos, X. Zhang, & M. Almunawar (Eds.), *Handbook of Research on Green, Circular, and Digital Economies as Tools for Recovery and Sustainability* (pp. 257–279). IGI Global. doi:10.4018/978-1-7998-9664-7.ch014

Yu, P., Liu, Z., Hanes, E., & Mumtaz, J. (2022e). Integration of IoT and Blockchain for Smart and Secured Supply Chain Management: Case Studies of China. In S. Goyal, N. Pradeep, P. Shukla, M. Ghonge, & R. Ravi (Eds.), *Utilizing Blockchain Technologies in Manufacturing and Logistics Management* (pp. 179–207). IGI Global. doi:10.4018/978-1-7998-8697-6.ch010

Yu, P., Lu, S., Hanes, E., & Chen, Y. (2022f). The Role of Blockchain Technology in Harnessing the Sustainability of Chinese Digital Finance. In P. Swarnalatha & S. Prabu (Eds.), *Blockchain Technologies for Sustainable Development in Smart Cities* (pp. 155–186). IGI Global. doi:10.4018/978-1-7998-9274-8.ch009

Yu, P., Yu, M., & Sampat, M. (2022g). Smart Management for Digital Transformation in China. In B. Barbosa, S. Filipe, & C. Santos (Eds.), Handbook of Research on Smart Management for Digital Transformation (pp. 411-438). IGI Global. doi:10.4018/978-1-7998-9008-9.ch019

Zhang, L. (2021). The role of SME business administration in promoting economic development. *China Small and Medium Enterprises*, *5*, 142–143.

Zhou, L., Qiu, X., Liu, J., & Chen, W. (2020). Research on FinTech innovation to serve small and micro enterprises' financing - a survey based on 840 small and micro enterprises in FinTech pilot areas. *Southwest Finance*, *10*, 24–35.

Zhu, Y. (2019). *R&D input, innovation output and firm performance* [Master's thesis]. Zhongnan University of Economics and Law. https://kns.cnki.net/KCMS/detail/detail.aspx?dbname=CMFD202002&filename=1019862670.nh

KEY TERMS AND DEFINITIONS

Adverse Selection: In financial markets, adverse selection refers to a situation wherein one party in a potential transaction uses some extra information the other part does not have such that the transaction likely favors the former.

Credit Rationing: At a micro level, there are two aspects to this: (1) some of the loan applicants are accepted, while others are denied a loan even if they are willing to pay a high interest rate, and (2) loan applications are only partially met (e.g., a $1 million loan application can only be granted up to $500,000).

Cryptocurrency: A medium of exchange that uses cryptographic principles to secure transactions and control the creation of units of exchange. A cryptocurrency is a type of digital currency (or virtual currency) such as Bitcoin.

Data Silos: A data silo is a group of raw data that is only accessible to one department, and not to the rest of the other divisions within that same organization. This results in a severe lack of transparency, efficiency, and trust within that organization.

Decentralized Public Ledger: A way for untrusted parties to reach a consensus on a common digital history.

Hashing Algorithms: Hashing is a method of processing information in computer science. It is commonly used as a practical method of information security. Hashing algorithms are also used to encrypt password strings in databases, as the hash value calculated by the hashing algorithm cannot be reversed back to its original value, thus providing effective password protection.

ICO: Initial Coin Offering, derived from the stock market concept of Initial Public Offerings (IPO), are the first issuance of tokens by blockchain projects to raise general purpose digital currencies such as bitcoin and ethereum.

Idea of "Grasping the Big and Releasing the Small": The emphasis is on the government supporting the development of large enterprises to make them more competitive in the international market. The idea sees the central government relinquishing control over SMEs.

Merkle Trees: Merkel tree is a binary tree that can be used to quickly check and summarise large amounts of data which can be used to verify the integrity of transaction records in a block.

Timestamps: A timestamp is data generated by digitally signing an object containing information such as the signature parameters of the original document, the time of signing and others using digital signature technology. Timestamps are used to prove that the original document existed before the time of signing.

Chapter 5
Sustainability Within Italian SMEs and Its Effect on Their Financial Stability

Daniele Giordino
https://orcid.org/0000-0001-5507-6270
University of Turin, Italy

Cinzia Revello
https://orcid.org/0000-0002-1370-3130
University of Turin, Italy

ABSTRACT

This study attempts to investigate the relationship between sustainability innovation, firm performance, financial stability, and competitive advantage. In order to do so, the authors explore the effects that the implementation of a new business process which targets sustainability has on three small and medium sized businesses (SMEs) operating in Italy. Within the methodology section the authors have discussed the various criteria utilized to select an appropriate and adequate sample of SMEs. Semi-structured interviews were utilized to gather qualitative data so as to reflect the lived experiences of various members of SMEs' personnel. Data, charts, and various reports were utilized. The findings suggest the presence of a positive relationship between sustainability innovation and firm performance. Furthermore, the authors have gathered and analyzed evidence which supports the hypothesis that sustainability innovation has a positive correlation when it comes to financial stability.

DOI: 10.4018/978-1-6684-4834-2.ch005

INTRODUCTION

The growth of the global population and the continuous development of the economy is causing increased consumption of resources. Therefore, the materials utilized to support the production of assets increase the emissions produced while also causing a burden to the environment. Due to the aspects above, entities, institutions, and, more broadly, stakeholders are pressuring firms to respond to these challenges and deal with environmental degradation (El-Kassar et al., 2019). Businesses are increasingly under pressure from different stakeholders to be more sustainable while maintaining a high degree of competitiveness due to the new challenges highlighted by globalization and technological advancements (Ikram et al., 2021). However, external pressure motivates organizations and firms globally to innovate their business to reduce their environmental impact (Le and Ikram, 2022). Part of the literature supporting the revisionist approach to sustainability innovation believes that it can aid and support businesses in improving their competitive advantages (Zefeng et al., 2018). However, previous studies that have examined the effects of sustainability innovation on firm performance and competitiveness usually target and focus on a single relationship and rarely investigate multiple effects within a single search model (Le and Ikram, 2022; Gurlek and Tuna, 2018).

Moreover, most studies concerning the impact of sustainability innovation examine and focus on data produced by the companies within a short and set period (Ikram et al., 2019; Maletič et al., 2021). Therefore, studies which utilize more qualitative data and investigate the lived experiences of key personnel within firms are necessary (Thanh et al., 2021). Qualitative data obtained from individuals directly correlated to a firm's development and innovation permit the gathering of longitudinal data to critically observe the real effects of sustainability innovation on firms' performance (Doluca et al., 2018; Ikram et al., 2021). Therefore, the lived experiences of employees and entrepreneurs who have worked within the same context enable the collection and analysis of data which grants the assessment of the real impact of sustainable innovation (Kusi-Sarpong et al., 2019). The elements mentioned above highlight the existence of a gap in the literature that can be further researched and developed. This study analyzes small and medium-sized enterprises (SMEs) that have introduced a new business process that focuses on improving the firm's environmental performance. The selected SMEs operate in Italy.

Moreover, the sample under study operates within the farming and agricultural sector. Three SMEs agreed to participate in the study. Thus, the gathered data reflect the experiences of said three firms. To gather the necessary data, the authors have adopted a qualitative approach. Semi-structured interviews were conducted with the key personnel of the various firms to gather the necessary data.

Moreover, the firms allowed the researchers to analyze reports, charts, and various other forms of documents produced over numerous periods. The authors also utilized their personal observations on the effects and effectiveness of sustainability innovation. By doing so, the researchers could triangulate data to strengthen the validity of the proposed findings (Yin, 2018). A set of research questions are developed using multiple theoretical approaches that combine stakeholder theory, sustainability vision theory, resourced-based innovation theory, and integrated innovation theory.

Thus, this study addresses the previously reported gap by answering the following research questions:

RQ1: Do sustainability innovation boost firm competitiveness and firm performance of SMEs?

RQ2: Does sustainability innovation improve the financial stability of SMEs?

This study contributes to the current literature in a multitude of ways. Firstly, it extends the existing literature on sustainability innovation and firm performance by assessing how it impacts three different SMEs operating within the same sector. The selected SMEs have implemented a new business process that targets the improvement of their environmental performances. Secondly, it empirically investigates the effects of sustainability innovation on firms' accounting profitability performance measures for Italian firms. Finally, the article provides a detailed description of the business process, which enabled the achievement of the presented findings so that other firms operating within the same sector can benefit from the open innovation nature of the information shared.

Nonetheless, it is important to consider the various limitations of the study. First, the obtained data reflect the experience of three SMEs operating within the Italian context. Therefore, the presented results should not be generalized. Moreover, future studies should adopt a quantitative approach to investigate better the correlation between sustainability innovation and firm competitiveness and performance.

LITERATURE REVIEW

Theoretical Framework

To conduct this study, the authors have utilized the stakeholder theory as the underpinning theory. Stakeholders are defined as those that can be impacted and affected by business outcomes (Freeman, 2010; Sachs & Kujala, 2021). Moreover, stakeholders can condition the obtained results of business operations (Freeman et al., 2021; Valentinov & Chia, 2022). The current literature identifies different categories, such as customers, governments, employees, shareholders, and communities, as well as many others, as examples of stakeholders (Freeman 2020).

Companies pursue sustainability innovation to stimulate the interest of stakeholders through the development of social, environmental, and economic elements to hopefully trigger a positive response from the stakeholders of a particular business (Tang, 2022; Verma et al., 2022). Authors have suggested that the practice mentioned above would enhance the firms' competitiveness and environmental and financial performance (Le and Ikram, 2022; Ma et al., 2022).

This study considers the grounded theories, including sustainability vision, resource-based, and integrated innovation theories (Le and Ikram, 2022, Kantabutra, 2020). By doing so, the research assumes that sustainability innovation needs to be implemented if firms want to remain competitive and improve their performance. On the other hand, when it comes to the analyzed context, resourced-based innovation theory explicates the condition in which innovation should be considered to utilize SMEs' resources to develop a competitive advantage (Zefeng et al., 2018; Hojnik and Ruzzier, 2016).

Sustainability Innovation and Firm Performance and Competitiveness

The current state of the art does not present a consensus regarding the relationship between sustainability innovation and firm competitiveness (Hussain et al., 2018).

Previous literature defines sustainability innovation as the process which incorporates environmental, societal, and economic values into the company system from the stage of development, R&D, and commercialization (Kibler et al., 2018). The process of sustainability innovation applies to products, services, and business processes (Kibler et al., 2018). Companies engage with sustainability innovation since they perceive it to be important for the evolution and enhancement of corporate sustainability performances (Arcese et al., 2015).

The current state of the art presents two main approaches to sustainability innovation. The first approach proposed by the existing literature is the revisionist view. The revisionist view supports the idea that sustainability innovation leads companies to refine their competitiveness by improving firm performance (Gurlek et al., 2018). On the contrary, the second approach, which is defined as a traditionalist view, advocates how sustainable innovation requires a large investment from companies which results in increased prices which reduce the firm's ability to compete on a costs basis hindering the enterprises' competitive advantage (Blowfield et al., 2008; Kuzma et al., 2020; Shin et al., 2018). Furthermore, the traditionalist view supports that companies should engage in sustainability innovation only if they want to generate environmental benefits (Le and Ikram, 2022). The second approach does not support the hypothesis that sustainability innovation can lead to improved financial performance (Rauter et al., 2019). However, other publications have found a positive correlation between sustainability innovation and firm competitiveness (Kusi-Sarpong et al., 2019).

Furthermore, published research in 2018 highlights how sustainability is linked with improved business efficiency and competitiveness (Cherrafi et al., 2018). Again, Cherrafi et al. (2018) link sustainability practices to a higher degree of profitability. However, sustainability innovation is extremely complex and cannot be reduced to a simple technical specificity. Therefore, it integrates innovation within multiple different aspects of the business, such as products, management, and technology, towards sustainability. The literature refers to this approach as the integrated innovation theory (Le and Ikram, 2022; Wang et al., 2016). The paper's authors have approached the research questions mainly utilizing the revisionist view, which positively correlates firm competitiveness and profitability with sustainability innovation (Albort-Morant et al., 2017; Diaz-Garcia et al., 2015; Xavier et al., 2017).

Sustainability Within SMEs

Small and medium-sized businesses compose most organizations operating within the European and Italian economic structure (Muller et al., 2015). Therefore, it is important to research said entities to understand how structured changes and policies can affect the economic system of the areas mentioned above. When implementing practices safeguarding the environment, larger companies tend to benefit from cultural and managerial aspects. In contrast, SMEs must rely on the chief executive officer/entrepreneur's values to implement CSR practices (El Batz et al., 2016). It has been studied and discussed that SMEs often engage in CSR out of ethical motives (Jamali et al., 2009). However, it has been reported that larger corporations and firms mainly engage with CSR to promote their brand and image and pursue better economic performance (Cantele and Zardini, 2018). Small and medium-sized businesses perceive their environmental impact as something that can be negligible due to their operational size (Battisti and Perry, 2011).

Moreover, due to low visibility, small and medium-sized firms are not incentivized to communicate their adopted practices to external stakeholders (Giordino and Crocco, 2022; Stekelorum, 2020). The current state of the art highlights how environmental management tools can positively impact SMEs' performance (Agan et al., 2013). Researchers have shown evidence that small and medium businesses can achieve increased competitiveness and cost reduction by adopting environmental practices that tackle CSR issues (Bagur-Femenias et al., 2013). However, small and medium-sized businesses encounter various challenges when implementing sustainability practices (Giordino and Crocco, 2022; Ukko et al., 2021). The limited size of SMEs often equates to limited financial resources that can be allocated to the innovation and development of business processes that target CSR objectives (Halila, 2007). However, public entities and institutions are allocating part of their budget to financially support the sustainable development of SMEs to create a more sustainable and socially responsible economy (European Commission, 2020). For example, the European Commission (2021) allocated 30% of the EU funds to fight climate change, protect biodiversity, and gender equality and discuss many other objectives of social nature. By doing so, larger entities aim to foster and promote the widespread adoption of CSR practices within SMEs and large corporations. Small and medium-sized businesses have limited numbers of employees. As a result, their personnel often lack the necessary skills and training to innovate the business processes in favour of a more socially responsible approach to their business model (Christmann, 2000; Hart, 1995). The chief executive officer/entrepreneur also suffers from this deficiency of know-how (Biondi, Frey, and Iraldo, 2000). The lack of time and resources further affects SMEs' abilities to adopt sustainable practices. Employees within such organizations are often responsible for multiple different activities and business functions. Therefore, it becomes tedious to include new tasks targeted at the CSR development of new processes and activities (Johnson & Schaltegger, 2015).

Additionally, the low priority given to CSR activities by SMEs results in a low degree of priority (Journeault, Perron, and Vallières, 2021). An additional barrier to SMEs' implementation of sustainable practices is caused by the misinformation of small and medium-sized organizations' CEO/entrepreneurs (Vo, 2011). The professionals mentioned above often lack the necessary tools and knowledge to understand the present costs and benefits associated with sustainable practices (Friedman and Miles, 2002; Revel et al., 2010). Researchers have previously collected data that indicate how managers of small and medium-sized companies tend to overestimate the costs and underestimate the benefits of CSR practices (Revel and Rutherford, 2003).

METHODOLOGY

The authors conducted a qualitative study using a multiple case study methodology since it allows one to investigate a contemporary phenomenon within a real context without relying on a single evidence source (Yin, 2018). Benbasat et al. (1987) indicate how a case study methodology examines a phenomenon in its natural environment and permits researchers to collect data and information from one or few entities to comprehend the studied circumstance better. Moreover, the multiple case study approach is extremely beneficial for exploratory investigations where the variables are not clearly understood (Eisenhardt and Graebner, 2007). The following steps have been adopted to conduct this research's data collection and analysis. Firstly, the authors defined the selection criteria for the research population from which the final sample was drawn (Sardi et al., 2020). The final sample was selected based on the following criteria, which have been established by the researchers conducting this study:

1. Only small and medium-sized businesses operating within Italy can be selected. The adopted definition of SMEs is the one utilized by the European Union (EU). The EU indicates SMEs as businesses that have 50 up to 249 employees, as well as an annual turnover not exceeding 50 million euros (Ulrich, 2000).
2. Firms must operate in traditional agriculture, farming, and manufacturing sectors.
3. The firms must have implemented a new business process focusing on sustainability.

By doing so, the researchers believe that it would allow them to understand better how implementing business processes that focus on sustainability might affect the firm's ability to improve its financial performance.

Within these criteria, only four firms were selected. However, only three of the four companies have agreed to participate in the study. The selected firms were named A, B, and C to ensure anonymity, as reported in *Table 1.*

Table 1. Authors' own elaboration

Company Name	Sector	Interviewed Personnel
Company A	*Agricultural/Farming*	*Chief Executive Officer, Accountant*
Company B	*Agricultural/Farming*	*Chief Executive Officer, Accountant*
Company C	*Agricultural/Farming*	*Chief Executive Officer, Line Manager, Accountant*

A qualitative approach was chosen since it permits the authors to capture a detailed description of a particular instance (Eisenhardt & Graebner, 2007). The researchers have used semi-structured interviews with a cross-section of employees from different departments of the analyzed SMEs to gather data. Several interviews were conducted with the various accounting departments, business development, and human resources. Moreover, due to the nature of the selected sample, the chief executive officer has also been interviewed multiple times.

Furthermore, companies' documents, charts, and reports have been gathered and analyzed. Finally, direct observations of the effects and effectiveness of the implemented business process made by the authors were taken into account, allowing the researchers to triangulate the data to strengthen the validity of the proposed findings (Yin, 2018). The open-ended nature of the research questions was chosen to explicitly understand how applying a new business process that focuses on improving a company's sustainability can affect the financial performance of the said firm. Moreover, semi-structured interviews have been carried out with multiple different departments to fully investigate and understand how a new sustainable business process might affect different elements and aspects of an organization. A total of 60 hours of interviews were recorded. Data collected through interviews were then recorded and transcribed (Sergeeva et al., 2017). Firstly, the transcripts were coded using NVivo version 12 to highlight keywords, quotes, and thematic patterns. Both authors have individually coded the transcripts twice. However, no material differences between the two authors' codes have been found.

Moreover, one month after the first coding session, both researchers manually analyzed the transcribed data; however, no material differences were found. The secondary data obtained from reports, charts, and other SME documents were also transcribed, added to the analysis tool, and coded with the interview transcripts. The qualitative data collected through in-depth semi-structured interviews were analyzed following the guidance of the Gioia method to ensure rigour and trustworthiness (Gioia et al., 2013). The approach, as mentioned earlier, forces researchers to utilize an interview protocol and informant quotes to make sense of the data being collected based on similarities and differences between the various categories. The first round of coding, also known as the open coding phase, forces the authors to group codes deemed similar. Secondly, the researchers must conduct axial coding to conceptualize the codes found in the first phase and group them into several themes. Moreover, the authors utilized the literature to make sense of and group the codes into distinct categories while cross-referencing the results with previous works mentioning sustainability innovation and its effects on companies' performance. Finally, the authors approached the final round of coding in which they developed the identified aggregate themes.

FINDINGS

In the following section, the authors present the aggregate themes identified and developed through the use of the Gioia method to ensure rigour and trustworthiness to the qualitative data gathered through the semi-structured interviews (Gioia et al., 2013). As previously reported within section 3, the use of the literature aided the authors in structuring the following four paragraphs, which focus on how the newly implemented sustainability process works, how it affects the environmental performance of those companies implementing it, as well as how it enhances the business side of performance. The following paragraphs present the ecological benefits obtained through the anaerobic digestion of animal manure, how the digester operates, and which benefits are generated by the various companies adopting it. Moreover, the first section highlights the environmental damage caused by livestock production to emphasize the effects of sustainability innovation on some key production processes of businesses operating within the farming and agricultural sector.

The Environmental Impact of Livestock Production Systems

The selected SMEs operate within the farming and agricultural sector. Therefore, the following elements describe the challenges SMEs must overcome to reduce their environmental impact. Livestock production systems affect the environment and must be reduced by applying more efficient on-farm management systems (Maranon et al., 2011). In fact, many pollutants deriving from livestock farming deplete the quality of air, water, and soil. Cattle farming is a major source of livestock waste production and a major cause of pollution. Atmospheric pollutants from these systems include odors, methane (CH_4), nitrous oxide (N_2O), and ammonia (NH_3); these molecules are mainly responsible for the contribution to the greenhouse effect of livestock farms (Maranon et al., 2011). Methane emissions from dairy farms are directly related to enteric fermentation and manure handling.

Moreover, pollution from nitrogen (N) leads to an immediate release of ammonia (NH_3) and nitrous oxide (N_2O) into the atmosphere and an indirect emission in the soil following the leaching of nitrates (NO_3^-). In addition, a further contribution to soil pollution can derive from contamination following traces of pathogens, antibiotics, and heavy metals potentially contained in animal waste. In terms of annual tons of CO_2 equivalent, agricultural activities are responsible for 405 $MtCO_{2eq}$ per year (10% of the total Europe GHG emissions), of which approximately 210 $MtCO_{2eq}$ are related to nitrous oxide emissions. In comparison, methane emissions account for about 195 $MtCO_{2eq}$ (Bacenetti et al., 2013).

To prevent greenhouse gas (GHG) emissions, the leaching of nutrients and organic matter into the environment, and respect the objectives of the Kyoto agreement, increasingly sustainable solutions are required for managing and recycling animal manure and organic waste. Failure to use or underuse production waste materials leads to losses of potential revenues and increases costs incurred with their disposal practice. Indeed, if managed correctly, these products are a valuable resource that can produce renewable energy as an alternative to the fossil fuel economy and as a source of nutrition for agriculture. Furthermore, recycling the products, as mentioned earlier, reduces emissions and pollutants emitted into the environment. In this regard, anaerobic digestion plays an increasingly important role.

The New Business Process: The Anaerobic Digestion of Animal Manure

The SMEs examined have all adopted an anaerobic digestion process to reduce their environmental impact. Anaerobic digestion is a complex biochemical process of conversion of animal manure into biogas that involves different and specific microorganisms. The degradation of organic material without oxygen is a naturally occurring process. This treatment consists of the decomposition of organic matter in the absence of free oxygen since it is a process that happens in anaerobiosis and at variable temperatures based on the type of microorganism involved (psychrophilic, mesophilic, or thermophilic). However, it typically takes place at around 35 °C. The optimal pH range for anaerobic digestion is around values between 6,7, and 7,5 units of the input mixture. The process inside the reactor takes place in four stages: hydrolysis, fermentation, acetogenesis, and methanogenesis. The anaerobic process produces a gas mixture called biogas, consisting mainly of methane with a high percentage of carbon dioxide, ammonia, and traces of other gasses. In addition to the oxidation of organic substances to methane, there is the production of thermal energy and the formation of the undigested residue, called digestate. This waste is typically used as an agricultural fertilizer. At the same time, the biogas produced is sold or used as fuel to produce electricity fed into the Italian national grid system. Anaerobic digestion is estimated to reduce the carbon content in manure and dry matter by approximately 50% (Amon et al., 2006).

The Anaerobic Digestion Process

The process involves the collection of animal waste through systems that convey such waste inside tanks equipped with a cover that isolates them from the environment, with significant volumetric capacities depending on the size of the farm. Animal waste (both solid and liquid) is introduced into these tanks; moreover, other types of waste can be added, such as those of food origin or coming from crop residues, to increase the quantity (and quality) of biogas produced and reduce the costs associated with the disposal of such waste. Inside the biodigester reactor, some mixers are used to mix the contents. The anaerobic digestion process takes a few days for the reaction to be complete (between 12 and 25 days). However, the digester is fed waste daily to have stable biomethane production over time. Inside the reactor

The fermented fraction is removed from the digester through the use of pumps and placed in a storage tank, which often requires the presence of a cover. Subsequently, the fermented fraction can be used and spread on fields as fertilizer. Otherwise, it can undergo further physical separation through the utilization of a mechanical separator. The obtained solid fraction is used as bedding for animals or as organic fertilizer within various crops utilized to produce multiple types of fruits. On the other hand, the liquid part can be used as fertilizer in crops that target the production of vegetables and fruits. The transformation of livestock waste into digestate reduces the costs incurred by the company for alternative disposal of this product and allows the transformation of waste into a resource. In fact, the digestate obtained can be used directly as a fertilizer on the companies' land. Otherwise, it can be sold to improve further the companies' ability to generate revenue. When directly utilized by the company, it results in a reduction of costs. Moreover, it enhances the firm's profit margin since they can reduce their costs with materials that would have been previously classified as liabilities due to their disposal costs.

The overlying gas phase, called biogas, is removed from the reactor through pipes and pumps. Biogas can be used directly for heating or combined thermal and electrical generation. Moreover, biogas can also be transformed into biomethane, which has similar characteristics to natural gas and can therefore be used as a fuel for vehicles' engines to replace fossil fuels. For biogas to be used as fuel, it is necessary to remove carbon dioxide (CO_2), hydrogen sulphide (H_2S), and other molecules before introducing it into the natural gas network. Instead of being used as fuel for electricity generation, At the end of the moisture removal process, the biogas is converted into electricity by means of a cogeneration unit (CHP) with an alternating internal combustion engine and fed into the Italian national electricity grid (Battini et al., 2014). The production of biogas (and its possible treatments) determines an economic gain for the organization. Furthermore, it promotes the reduction of pollutants compared to traditional disposal methodologies.

The heat developed by the anaerobic degradation reaction can be used in situ. For example, the heat developed can heat the milking parlour or be distributed to consumers through a heating pumping system. Therefore, the firm obtains an economic and environmental gain, improving the entity's financial stability.

The Observed Benefits of the Anaerobic Digestion

The main advantage deriving from the use of manure in anaerobic digestion is the use of waste instead of an energy crop as a renewable energy source to avoid competition with food production. Moreover, it reduces the emission of dangerous emission gasses. Secondly, adopting anaerobic digestion to treat manure reduces emissions normally produced when utilizing fossil fuels. Additionally, electricity and heat are obtained from the production of biogas, which can be used directly in the production plant itself or as a source of thermal energy. Consequently, using said resources reduces the costs associated with the various production plants, resulting in a more advantageous business cost structure. For example, Company A and Company C have both shown white papers that report a large sum of energy savings, consequently leading to a higher profit margin. Moreover, Company B has demonstrated evidence that they have created a new profit centre thanks to the utilization of the anaerobic digestor since they would get paid by other local farmers to deal with their production waste in exchange for the natural biogas produced by the new implant. Therefore, sustainability innovation can reduce the costs associated with production lines, create new revenue streams, and diversify the company's portfolio, which improves the company's performance and competitiveness (Hermundsdottir & Aspelund, 2021; Momaya, 2019).

The reduction of greenhouse gas emissions following this method's adoption for electricity production is approximately 1,2 kg CO_{2eq}/kWh (Bacenetti et al., 2013). Another advantage deriving from the treatment of livestock manure for the generation of biogas is that the biogas can be produced when needed and can be easily stored. Furthermore, exploiting the existing natural gas infrastructure for distribution and use is possible. Consequently, the biogas produced sustains the system that generated it in the first place, creating a truthfully self-sustaining system that reduces energy consumption costs and improves profit margins (Ghisetti & Rennings, 2014). Usually, the digesters are fed daily and continuously with different raw materials to obtain stable biogas production. This ensures continuous electricity production increasing the system's efficiency while lowering the incidence of load losses on the entire system. Finally, it is important to consider how part of the energy produced (both electrical and thermal) is consumed by the system (pumps, mixers, and separators). Typically, electricity self-consumption is less than 10% of the total amount of energy produced by the digester (Bacenetti et al., 2013).

Biogas is a more versatile renewable energy source than wind, solar, or any other energy source since it is not limited by geographical area or season. The development of biogas production in European countries has been influenced strongly by environmental regulations and the EU Renewable Energy Directives (Hou et al., 2018). One of the EU's policy goals is to achieve a 40% reduction in greenhouse gasses and improve renewable energy production capability by 32% by 2030 (Li et al., 2021). The main EU countries where agricultural biogas plants are most present are Germany, Denmark, Austria, and Sweden. However, other countries are slowly adopting such a system to a lesser extent. Those countries are the Netherlands, France, Spain, Italy, the United Kingdom, and Belgium. Germany is the leading European country in developing anaerobic digestion, with over 8000 functioning plants and total electricity production from biogas of more than 3530 MW (Shih et al., 2015). Sweden is the main proponent of using biogas as a fuel for vehicles. As a result, the market based on this fuel is constantly growing, with over 15000 cars in circulation running on biomethane (Holm-Nielsen, 2009). When it comes to Italy, the production of biogas from animal manures and other agricultural biomass has undergone extraordinary growth, which is largely due to the biogas support programs implemented in Italy (the introduction of Tradable Green Certificate and feed-in-tariff and increased investment subsidies) (Hou et al., 2018).

DISCUSSION AND RESEARCH IMPLICATIONS

Discussion

The previously presented findings support the positive correlation between sustainability innovation and the improvement of firms' competitiveness (Kiveu et al., 2019). Therefore, the researchers can respond to the RQ1 indicating that sustainability innovation does improve the firms' competitiveness and performance. Moreover, the reported findings highlight how the implementation of new business processes which target sustainability can also affect the incurred costs of a company. Within the selected sample, it has been observed how the various firms can transform something previously seen as production waste into an asset that can be utilized to generate energy, heat, and animal bedding. For example, the chief executive officer of firm A says in one of the recorded files:

"We have been able to significantly reduce the costs directly correlated to the production of our animal-based products. Consequently, we have improved our profit margin. Moreover, we have access to more contracts with big retailers because we can sustain their continuous requests to improve our pricing systems to attract more customers to their stores." Chief Executive Officer, Firm A

Furthermore, the production line manager of firm C discusses how important it is for their business to transform livestock waste into something that can be utilized and monetized:

"The disposal of the produced animal waste has lifted great pressure from our business. Before implementing our new anaerobic digester, we would receive complaints from local governments since a great deal of odor would disturb the newly built houses near our main implant. The entire business took a hit since it affected our reputation. Locals would not support our products. However, we looked into potential solutions that would not force us to relocate our plants....the anaerobic digester reduced a great deal of odor emission. We have never received complaints since then. The local population has appreciated the investment that we have made

to better their lives. Moreover, we have been able to hire new employees because the digester requires new personnel.....our reputation has improved, and now we cannot satisfy the demand for our in-house dairy products." Line Manager, Firm C

When considering RQ2, the researchers have been able to gather evidence indicating how SMEs can improve their financial stability. For example, the accountant operating within firm A says:

"The digester generates a profit for us. We generate revenues from it. The biogas produced is enough to support our gas consumption. Moreover, we sell the surplus to Snam Rete Gas. It brings into the business a pretty good amount of cash that we can use to finance the acquisition of new assets. Actually, we now generate more revenues from the digester rather than from our main operations of meat and various vegetables and fruits production." Accountant, Firm A

Moreover, the accountant of firm B reports:

"We have reduced our costs and increased our revenue streams. We have not taken out a loan since the implementation of the digester." Accountant, Firm B

Additionally, the article's authors have gathered evidence and data that might suggest an improved business resilience of firms that adopt sustainability innovation. Two of the three selected SMEs discuss how important it has been to them to have a new revenue stream that is not directly correlated to crop production. During the summer of 2020, Italy faced a heat wave that damaged the production of various fruits and vegetables. However, two SMEs have been able to support their businesses thanks to the digester. Various participants report:

"It is difficult to predict the output we might get from our crops. However, it is quite easy to predict the amount of animal waste that we produce over a specific period of time. Therefore, we can now accurately estimate the quantity of biogas generated over a specific period." Chief Executive Officer, Firm A

"Summer 2020 ruined our entire production. We lost our sales from more than half of our fields. As a result, our net profit took a massive hit. However, the production of biogas saved us." Chief Executive Officer, Firm C

However, further investigations are necessary to understand the reported finding better since it might be something limited to the specific sector under analysis. Moreover, the nature of our research does not allow the generalization of our findings since most of the data gathered refers to lived experiences of a small group of individuals that operate within three different SMEs. Nonetheless, the authors believe that the data mentioned above might support the positive correlation between sustainability innovation and the ability of an entity operating within the analyzed sector to endure the effects of climate change better. Moreover, when it comes to RQ1 and RQ2, the authors believe that the gathered evidence, company reports, and observations can lead to thinking that sustainability innovation does have a positive effect on the company's financial performance and competitiveness.

Theoretical Implications

This study contributes to the current state of the art in the domain of firm innovation and firm performance in some ways. Firstly, the research adopts the stakeholder theory (Freeman, 2010) by asserting that enterprises pursue sustainability innovation to satisfy and fulfil stakeholders based on balancing economic, social, and environmental benefits. As a result, this should generate a positive response from various stakeholders enhancing the firms' competitiveness and ecological and financial performance. In fact, the gathered evidence and data suggest that sustainability innovation enhances the firm's competitiveness and financial performance. Consequently, the authors have responded to the research questions in this study, RQ1, and RQ2. Secondly, the application of sustainability innovation within the context of SMEs reinforces its theoretical contributions towards the role of innovation in enhancing SMEs' competitive advantage from both a financial and environmental perspective. Finally, this study provides a detailed description of the implemented process to share the necessary knowledge to further promote sustainable innovation within SMEs operating within the agricultural and farming sector, promoting the idea of open innovation.

Practical Implications

This research has the following practical implications. Firstly, this study provides additional evidence of the positive effects of sustainability innovation on firms' performance and competitiveness. As shown by the selected sample, introducing a new business process that directly targets sustainability allowed them to utilize waste to generate something that could either be commercialized or sold to outside entities to generate more revenues. Therefore, this study encourages business leaders to consider sustainability innovation as a long-term plan that positively affects the company's sustainability and improves its financial stability and competitiveness. Secondly, this study provides insights into the important role of sustainability in ensuring the basis for a balanced long-term strategy that tackles economic and environmental values.

Moreover, the reported findings support the revisionist view. Consequently, the view mentioned above supports the idea that sustainability innovation can be regarded as a tool that benefits organizations thanks to the reduced consumption of input materials, energy, waste, and water. Finally, this research highlights the barriers that SMEs face when it comes to the implementation of sustainability practices and processes. Therefore, small and medium-sized firms must carefully evaluate their approach to sustainability innovation and decision-making strategies. Due to their limited financial resources, SMEs need to assess the potential impact of sustainability innovation. The misallocation of resources could potentially lead to a reduced competitive advantage. Therefore, SMEs should break down their innovation goals and optimize the utilization of internal and external resources.

CONCLUSION

The results of this research directly correlate with the proposed research questions. Accordingly, the first research question was responded with the affirmation that sustainability innovation positively correlates with firm competitiveness and performance. The cost structure of the various SMEs has been improved since the implementation of the newly developed process. Moreover, the analyzed companies have been able to generate a new revenue stream which increases their profit margin. Additionally, sustainability innovation positively affects various elements influencing a firm's competitiveness. The image and reputation of a brand also have been positively affected by the implementation of the digester since it improves the company's relationships with local communities. Hence, the findings mentioned above can be interpreted as follows: sustainability innovation might have a positive connection with the multidimensional performance of the selected SMEs (Le and Ikram, 2022).

Likewise, the gathered evidence responded to the second research question, affirming that sustainability innovation improves the firms' financial stability. This is especially true when sustainability innovation is implemented through adopting a new business process that targets waste reuse, cost reduction, and profit margin increase.

The findings also suggest how sustainability innovation could potentially be responsible for improved resilience for SMEs operating within the selected sector. The gathered data suggest how part of the analyzed SMEs have been able to reduce the negative effects correlated with climate change. The findings have also reported anecdotal experiences since they offer new elements that could be utilized to investigate different aspects of sustainability innovation further.

As previously discussed, the selected sector greatly impacts resource consumption and the emission of pollutants in various elements of our environment. Moreover, SMEs are the majority of organizations present within the Italian economy. Therefore, the presented findings support the necessity of sustainability innovation within SMEs. Moreover, the discussed process utilized by the selected SMEs should support the process of open innovation. Consequently, the authors of this body of work hope to promote adopting this business process by various SMEs globally.

LIMITATIONS AND FUTURE RESEARCH

The conducted research has some limitations. Firstly, the analyzed sample operates within the agricultural and farming sector and has some peculiarities that cannot be applied to other industries. Moreover, the selected firms are SMEs. Therefore, the obtained data cannot and should not be generalized to large companies. Secondly, the investments necessary to implement the reported process are financially significant, time-consuming, and require the essential know-how to plan and implement it correctly. Finally, the implementation of a chemical process of this size cannot be generalized and used as a universal benchmark. On the contrary, this business process needs to be planned and evaluated case by case, depending on the company's specific needs.

This research lends itself to multiple scientific paths which need to be explored in future research. Notably, the agricultural sector features unique peculiarities not present in other products or services of different industries. Consequently, it would be interesting to investigate the financial implications of implementing new business processes that target sustainability in different contexts and initiatives and highlight how sustainability and financial capabilities reinforce one another. Moreover, it would be interesting to investigate further the relationship between sustainability innovation and the ability of a firm to endure the negative effects caused by climate change.

REFERENCES

Agan, Y., Acar, M. F., & Borodin, A. (2013). Drivers of environmental processes and their impact on performance: A study of Turkish SMEs. *Journal of Cleaner Production*, *51*, 23–33. doi:10.1016/j.jclepro.2012.12.043

Albort-Morant, G., Henseler, J., Leal-Millán, A., & Cepeda-Carrión, G. (2017). Mapping the field: A bibliometric analysis of green innovation. *Sustainability*, *9*(6), 1011. doi:10.3390u9061011

Amon, B., Kryvoruchko, V., Amon, T., & Zechmeister-Boltenstern, S. (2006). Methane, nitrous oxide and ammonia emissions during storage and after application of dairy cattle slurry and influence of slurry treatment. *Agriculture, Ecosystems & Environment*, *112*(2-3), 153–162. doi:10.1016/j.agee.2005.08.030

Arcese, G., Flammini, S., Lucchetti, M. C., & Martucci, O. (2015). Evidence and experience of open sustainability innovation practices in the food sector. *Sustainability*, *7*(7), 8067–8090. doi:10.3390u7078067

Bacenetti, J., Negri, M., Fiala, M., & González-García, S. (2013). Anaerobic digestion of different feedstocks: Impact on energetic and environmental balances of biogas process. *The Science of the Total Environment*, *463*, 541–551. doi:10.1016/j.scitotenv.2013.06.058 PMID:23831800

Bagur-Femenias, L., Llach, J., & del Mar Alonso-Almeida, M. (2013). Is the adoption of environmental practices a strategical decision for small service companies? An empirical approach. *Management Decision*, *51*(1), 41–62. doi:10.1108/00251741311291300

Battini, F., Agostini, A., Boulamanti, A. K., Giuntoli, J., & Amaducci, S. (2014). Mitigating the environmental impacts of milk production via anaerobic digestion of manure: Case study of a dairy farm in the Po Valley. *The Science of the Total Environment*, *481*, 196–208. doi:10.1016/j.scitotenv.2014.02.038 PMID:24598150

Battisti, M., & Perry, M. (2011). Walking the talk? Environmental responsibility from the perspective of small-business owners. *Corporate Social Responsibility and Environmental Management*, *18*(3), 172–185. doi:10.1002/csr.266

Benbasat, I., Goldstein, D. K., & Mead, M. (1987). The case research strategy in studies of information systems. *Management Information Systems Quarterly*, *11*(3), 369–386. doi:10.2307/248684

Biondi, V., Frey, M., & Iraldo, F. (2000). Environmental management systems and SMEs. *Greener Management International*, *2000*(29), 55–69. doi:10.9774/GLEAF.3062.2000.sp.00007

Blowfield, M., Visser, W., & Livesey, F. (2008, September). Sustainability innovation: mapping the territory. In *Corporate Responsibility Research Conference*, Cambridge University Press.

Cantele, S., & Zardini, A. (2018). Is sustainability a competitive advantage for small businesses? An empirical analysis of possible mediators in the sustainability–financial performance relationship. *Journal of Cleaner Production*, *182*, 166–176. doi:10.1016/j.jclepro.2018.02.016

Cherrafi, A., Garza-Reyes, J. A., Kumar, V., Mishra, N., Ghobadian, A., & Elfezazi, S. (2018). Lean, green practices and process innovation: A model for green supply chain performance. *International Journal of Production Economics, 206*, 79–92. doi:10.1016/j.ijpe.2018.09.031

Christmann, P. (2000). Effects of "Best practices" Of environmental management on cost advantage: The role of complementary assets. *Academy of Management Journal, 43*(4), 663–680. doi:10.2307/1556360

Díaz-García, C., González-Moreno, Á., & Sáez-Martínez, F. J. (2015). Eco-innovation: Insights from a literature review. *Innovation, 17*(1), 6–23. doi:10.1080/14479338.2015.1011060

Doluca, H., Wagner, M., & Block, J. (2018). Sustainability and environmental behaviour in family firms: A longitudinal analysis of environment-related activities, innovation and performance. *Business Strategy and the Environment, 27*(1), 152–172. doi:10.1002/bse.1998

Eisenhardt, K. M., & Graebner, M. E. (2007). Theory building from cases: Opportunities and challenges. *Academy of Management Journal, 50*(1), 25–32. doi:10.5465/amj.2007.24160888

El Baz, J., Laguir, I., Marais, M., & Staglianò, R. (2016). Influence of national institutions on the corporate social responsibility practices of small-and medium-sized enterprises in the food-processing industry: Differences between France and Morocco. *Journal of Business Ethics, 134*(1), 117–133. doi:10.100710551-014-2417-z

El-Kassar, A. N., & Singh, S. K. (2019). Green innovation and organizational performance: The influence of big data and the moderating role of management commitment and HR practices. *Technological Forecasting and Social Change, 144*, 483–498. doi:10.1016/j.techfore.2017.12.016

European Commission. (2020). EU budget: European Commission welcomes agreement on €1.8 trillion package to help build greener, more digital and more resilient. *Europe*.

European Commission (2021) *EU's Next Long-Term Budget & NextGenerationEU: Key Facts and Figures.* EC. https://ec.europa.eu/info/publications/eus-next-long-term-budget-nextgenerationeu-key-facts-and-figures_en

Freeman, R. E. (2010). *Strategic management: A stakeholder approach.* Cambridge university press. doi:10.1017/CBO9781139192675

Freeman, R. E., Dmytriyev, S. D., & Phillips, R. A. (2021). Stakeholder theory and the resource-based view of the firm. *Journal of Management*, *47*(7), 1757–1770. doi:10.1177/0149206321993576

Freeman, R. E., Phillips, R., & Sisodia, R. (2020). Tensions in stakeholder theory. *Business & Society*, *59*(2), 213–231. doi:10.1177/0007650318773750

Friedman, A. L., & Miles, S. (2002). SMEs and the environment: Evaluating dissemination routes and handholding levels. *Business Strategy and the Environment*, *11*(5), 324–341. doi:10.1002/bse.335

Ghisetti, C., & Rennings, K. (2014). Environmental innovations and profitability: How does it pay to be green? An empirical analysis on the German innovation survey. *Journal of Cleaner Production*, *75*, 106–117. doi:10.1016/j.jclepro.2014.03.097

Gioia, D. A., Corley, K. G., & Hamilton, A. L. (2013). Seeking qualitative rigor in inductive research: Notes on the Gioia methodology. *Organizational Research Methods*, *16*(1), 15–31. doi:10.1177/1094428112452151

Giordino, D., & Crocco, E. (2022). Sustainable Development: A New Frontier for SMEs. In *Management Strategies for Sustainability, New Knowledge Innovation, and Personalized Products and Services* (pp. 68–93). IGI Global. doi:10.4018/978-1-7998-7793-6.ch003

Gürlek, M., & Tuna, M. (2018). Reinforcing competitive advantage through green organizational culture and green innovation. *Service Industries Journal*, *38*(7-8), 467–491. doi:10.1080/02642069.2017.1402889

Halila, F. (2007). Networks as a means of supporting the adoption of organizational innovations in SMEs: The case of environmental management systems (EMSs) based on ISO 14001. *Corporate Social Responsibility and Environmental Management*, *14*(3), 167–181. doi:10.1002/csr.127

Hermundsdottir, F., & Aspelund, A. (2021). Sustainability innovations and firm competitiveness: A review. *Journal of Cleaner Production*, *280*, 124715. doi:10.1016/j.jclepro.2020.124715

Hojnik, J., & Ruzzier, M. (2016). The driving forces of process eco-innovation and its impact on performance: Insights from Slovenia. *Journal of Cleaner Production*, *133*, 812–825. doi:10.1016/j.jclepro.2016.06.002

Holm-Nielsen, J. B. (2009). Seadi tA, Oleskowicz-Popiel P. *Bioresource Technology*, *100*, 5478–5484. doi:10.1016/j.biortech.2008.12.046 PMID:19217772

Hou, Y., Velthof, G. L., Case, S. D. C., Oelofse, M., Grignani, C., Balsari, P., Zavattaro, L., Gioelli, F., Bernal, M. P., Fangueiro, D., Trindade, H., Jensen, L. S., & Oenema, O. (2018). Stakeholder perceptions of manure treatment technologies in Denmark, Italy, the Netherlands and Spain. *Journal of Cleaner Production, 172*, 1620–1630. doi:10.1016/j.jclepro.2016.10.162

Hussain, N., Rigoni, U., & Cavezzali, E. (2018). Does it pay to be sustainable? Looking inside the black box of the relationship between sustainability performance and financial performance. *Corporate Social Responsibility and Environmental Management, 25*(6), 1198–1211. doi:10.1002/csr.1631

Ikram, M., Zhang, Q., Sroufe, R., & Ferasso, M. (2021). Contribution of certification bodies and sustainability standards to sustainable development goals: An integrated grey systems approach. *Sustainable Production and Consumption, 28*, 326–345. doi:10.1016/j.spc.2021.05.019

Jamali, D., Zanhour, M., & Keshishian, T. (2009). Peculiar strengths and relational attributes of SMEs in the context of CSR. *Journal of Business Ethics, 87*(3), 355–377. doi:10.100710551-008-9925-7

Journeault, M., Perron, A., & Vallières, L. (2021). The collaborative roles of stakeholders in supporting the adoption of sustainability in SMEs. *Journal of Environmental Management, 287*, 112349. doi:10.1016/j.jenvman.2021.112349 PMID:33735683

Kibler, K. M., Reinhart, D., Hawkins, C., Motlagh, A. M., & Wright, J. (2018). Food waste and the food-energy-water nexus: A review of food waste management alternatives. *Waste Management (New York, N.Y.), 74*, 52–62. doi:10.1016/j.wasman.2018.01.014 PMID:29366796

Kiveu, M. N., Namusonge, M., & Muathe, S. (2019). Effect of innovation on firm competitiveness: The case of manufacturing SMEs in Nairobi County, Kenya. International. *Journal of Business Innovation and Research, 18*(3), 307–327. doi:10.1504/IJBIR.2019.098251

Kusi-Sarpong, S., Gupta, H., & Sarkis, J. (2019). A supply chain sustainability innovation framework and evaluation methodology. *International Journal of Production Research, 57*(7), 1990–2008. doi:10.1080/00207543.2018.1518607

Kuzma, E., Padilha, L. S., Sehnem, S., Julkovski, D. J., & Roman, D. J. (2020). The relationship between innovation and sustainability: A meta-analytic study. *Journal of Cleaner Production, 259*, 120745. doi:10.1016/j.jclepro.2020.120745

Le, T. T., & Ikram, M. (2022). Do sustainability innovation and firm competitiveness help improve firm performance? Evidence from the SME sector in vietnam. *Sustainable Production and Consumption*, *29*, 588–599. doi:10.1016/j.spc.2021.11.008

Li, Y., Zhao, J., Krooneman, J., & Euverink, G. J. W. (2021). Strategies to boost anaerobic digestion performance of cow manure: Laboratory achievements and their full-scale application potential. *The Science of the Total Environment*, *755*, 142940. doi:10.1016/j.scitotenv.2020.142940 PMID:33348487

Ma, L., Chen, X., Zhou, J., & Aldieri, L. (2022). Strategic Management Accounting in Small and Medium-Sized Enterprises in Emerging Countries and Markets: A Case Study from China. *Economies*, *10*(4), 74. doi:10.3390/economies10040074

Maletič, M., Gomišček, B., & Maletič, D. (2021). The missing link: Sustainability innovation practices, non-financial performance outcomes and economic performance. *Management Research Review*, *44*(11), 1457–1477. doi:10.1108/MRR-09-2020-0562

Maranon, E., Salter, A. M., Castrillon, L., Heaven, S., & Fernández-Nava, Y. (2011). Reducing the environmental impact of methane emissions from dairy farms by anaerobic digestion of cattle waste. *Waste Management (New York, N.Y.)*, *31*(8), 1745–1751. doi:10.1016/j.wasman.2011.03.015 PMID:21504844

Momaya, K. S. (2019). The past and the future of competitiveness research: A review in an emerging context of innovation and EMNEs. *International Journal of Global Business and Competitiveness*, *14*(1), 1–10. doi:10.100742943-019-00002-3

Muller, P., Caliandro, C., Peycheva, V., Gagliardi, D., Marzocchi, C., Ramlogan, R., & Cox, D. (2015). *Annual report on European SMEs 2014/2015: SMEs start hiring again.* European Commission.

Rauter, R., Globocnik, D., Perl-Vorbach, E., & Baumgartner, R. J. (2019). Open innovation and its effects on economic and sustainability innovation performance. *Journal of Innovation & Knowledge*, *4*(4), 226–233. doi:10.1016/j.jik.2018.03.004

Revell, A., & Rutherfoord, R. (2003). UK environmental policy and the small firm: Broadening the focus. *Business Strategy and the Environment*, *12*(1), 26–35. doi:10.1002/bse.347

Revell, A., Stokes, D., & Chen, H. (2010). Small businesses and the environment: Turning over a new leaf? *Business Strategy and the Environment*, *19*(5), 273–288.

Sachs, S., & Kujala, J. (2021). *Stakeholder engagement in management studies: Current and future debates.* Oxford Research Encyclopedia of Business and Management.

Sardi, A., Sorano, E., Garengo, P., & Ferraris, A. (2020). The role of HRM in the innovation of performance measurement and management systems: A multiple case study in SMEs. *Employee Relations: The International Journal*, *43*(2), 589–606. doi:10.1108/ER-03-2020-0101

Sergeeva, A., Huysman, M., Soekijad, M., & van den Hooff, B. (2017). Through the eyes of others: How onlookers shape the use of technology at work. *Management Information Systems Quarterly*, *41*(4), 1153–1178. doi:10.25300/MISQ/2017/41.4.07

Shih, J. C. (2015). Development of Anaerobic Digestion of Animal Waste: From Laboratory, Research and Commercial Farms to a Value-Added New Product. In Anaerobic Biotechnology: Environmental Protection and Resource Recovery (pp. 339-352).

Shin, J., Kim, C., & Yang, H. (2018). The effect of sustainability as innovation objectives on innovation efficiency. *Sustainability*, *10*(6), 1966. doi:10.3390u10061966

Stekelorum, R. (2020). The roles of SMEs in implementing CSR in supply chains: A systematic literature review. *International Journal of Logistics Research and Applications*, *23*(3), 228–253. doi:10.1080/13675567.2019.1679101

Tang, X. (2022). New Schemes for Investment in of Small and Medium-Sized Enterprises of China: Role of Access to Finance, Innovation, and Sustainability. *Frontiers in Psychology*, *13*, 13. doi:10.3389/fpsyg.2022.857193 PMID:35558710

Thanh, T. L., Huan, N. Q., & Hong, T. T. T. (2021). Effects of corporate social responsibility on SMEs' performance in emerging market. *Cogent Business & Management*, *8*(1), 1878978. doi:10.1080/23311975.2021.1878978

Ukko, J., Nasiri, M., Saunila, M., & Rantala, T. (2019). Sustainability strategy as a moderator in the relationship between digital business strategy and financial performance. *Journal of Cleaner Production*, *236*, 117626. doi:10.1016/j.jclepro.2019.117626

Ulrich, L. (2000). Small and medium-sized enterprises – delimitation and the European definition in the area of industrial business. *European Business Review*, *12*(5), 261–264. doi:10.1108/09555340010373537

Valentinov, V., & Chia, R. (2022). Stakeholder theory: A process-ontological perspective. *Business Ethics, the Environment & Responsibility*, *31*(3), 762-776.

Verma, V., Bisht, P., & Joshi, S. (2022). Sustainable Supply chain Systems of Food and Beverages SMEs in developing countries: Theoretical perspective. *Journal of Decision Analytics and Intelligent Computing*, *2*(1), 36–52. doi:10.31181/jdaic10011062022v

Vo, L. C. (2011). Corporate social responsibility and SMEs: A literature review and agenda for future research. *Problems and Perspectives in Management*, 9(4), 89–97.

Wang, W., & Wang, Y. (2016). Integrated Innovation Theory: Theory Exploration of a Complex System. *Management & Engineering*, (23), 228.

Xavier, A. F., Naveiro, R. M., Aoussat, A., & Reyes, T. (2017). Systematic literature review of eco-innovation models: Opportunities and recommendations for future research. *Journal of Cleaner Production*, *149*, 1278–1302. doi:10.1016/j.jclepro.2017.02.145

Yin, R. (2018). *Case Study Research: Design and Methods* (6th ed.). Sage.

Zefeng, M., Gang, Z., Xiaorui, X., Yongmin, S., & Junjiao, H. (2018). The extension of the Porter hypothesis: Can the role of environmental regulation on economic development be affected by other dimensional regulations? *Journal of Cleaner Production*, *203*, 933–942. doi:10.1016/j.jclepro.2018.08.332

KEY TERMS AND DEFINITIONS

Cost Centre: Part of an organization whose costs are charged for accounting purposes.

Environmental Impact: Any change caused to the environment due to human activities

Environmental Performance: Are indicators whose aim is to report the natural resource utilization, waste and emission of businesses and firms' processes.

Profit Centre: Part of an organization that directly adds to the entire organization's bottom line by generating revenues and earnings.

Small and Medium Enterprises: Companies with fewer than 250 employees and an annual turnover not exceeding 50 million euro.

Sustainable Management: Business processes whose aim is to avoid the deterioration of natural resources and environment in which the company operates.

Sustainability: Meeting the needs of businesses and society without compromising the ability of future generations to meet their own needs.

Sustainability Innovation: Is the making of intentional changes to a company's processes, products, or services to generate long term environmental and social benefits while also generating revenues for the firm.

Chapter 6
The Corporate Social Responsibility of the Family SMEs:
A Descriptive Analysis in the Context of Tunisia

Zouhayer Mighri
ISIGK, Tunisia & LARTIGE, Tunisia

Sana Ben Ghodbane
IHEC Carthage, Tunisia & LARIMRAF, La Manouba, Tunisia

Mohamed Soufeljil
IHEC Sousse, Tunisia

Adel Redouane
Faculty of Economics, Commercial, and Management Sciences, Eloued University, Algeria

ABSTRACT

The social responsibility of business is a topical theme, which is of interest to both the researchers and the leaders of the companies. This paper aims to respond to the following problem: if the family companies adopt CSR then what about the social dimensions to their counterparts among non-family members? The study that the authors conducted with 141 enterprises shows that the adoption of the social responsibility of the small business family is progressive and slow. The authors find that the family SME is characterized by societal choices that differ from those of the non-family business. Our results have a considerable professional contribution. In this

DOI: 10.4018/978-1-6684-4834-2.ch006

paper the authors provide to the manager an analysis of the behavior of leaders in a family SME around their CSR commitments. This paper is organized as follows: first, there is presented an introduction and review of literature and research hypotheses. The third section describes the study's sample and methodology choice where the authors briefly describe the main methods or treatments applied. The fourth section presents the discussion of results, and the last section concludes the study.

INTRODUCTION

The concept of corporate social responsibility (CSR) is a real controversy in society that queries researchers and business leaders. This topic has been booming this third millennium, given the structural change that has known the business environment and the challenges that pose these changes on its sustainability. The concept of CSR was addressed initially by Bowen in 1953, this economist who is regarded as the founding father of CSR has analyzed this subject following the request of the Protestant Church, which leads us to say that this concept is based on a religious basis of solidarity: "*those who have received must give*." CSR was intended to participate in the moralization of the functioning of the enterprise and to greater social justice. Unfortunately, it doesn't seem easy to give an exact date to the genesis of CSR in the literature. The Fugitive borders that exist between this concept and concepts often neighbours such as the moral, ethics, or ethics further complicate any attempt to opt for a specific duration of its genesis and even of its definition. The concept of CSR has not had an echo extended among researchers and professionals. The existing literature nourishes the idea that the family business reacts slowly to changes in its environment and that it is less prone to the appropriation of CSR, in particular (Dick and al. (2021), Morsing and al. (2019)). Therefore, it explains the existence of companies that are highly citizen's family but simultaneously. And what are the determinants of the CSR of the family business? This paper will attempt to bring elements of response to these questions. We aim to investigate the determinants of the Corporate Social Responsibility of the family business in Tunisia.

Furthermore, we aim to study the effect of small family business characteristics on adopting CSR. The family SME is characterized by societal choices that differ from those of the non-family business. Indeed, the behaviour of small family businesses is due to the slow process of developing an understanding of CSR, explained by certain factors identified in this paper. Our results have a considerable professional contribution. In our paper, we provide the manager with an analysis of the behaviour of leaders in a family SME around their CSR commitments.

The chapter is structured in the following way. The second section presents a review of the literature and the research hypothesis. The third section deals with methodological choice. The fourth section presents the results and their discussions. Finally, the last section presents the conclusion.

A SUMMARY OF THEORETICAL LITERATURE

The literature review on the social responsibility of family businesses provides several dimensions that stimulate the appropriation of CSR strategy. Our research proposes studying the effect of small family business characteristics on adopting CSR. Several studies have examined the association that can relate family business characteristics to teheir social responsibility in the context of developed countries without detecting any unanimity on the effect of these characteristics on CSR.

The CSR in the SME Family

The literature review shows that the research on CSR has paid particular attention to CSR in the SMES concerning CSR in large companies. Previous studies reported that CSR in SMES differs from that in large enterprises in various aspects such as the models, practices, strategies, tools, influential factors, problems, and barriers (Russo & Tencati, 2009; Besser1999; Spence and Lozano, 2000; Spence, 2015). Research in the past has suggested that CSR in SMES tends to be informal rather than CSR in large firms (Fassin, 2008; Spence & Lozano, 2000). CSR depends mainly on the founders' or managers' attitudes and values (Murillo and Lozano, 2006). In addition, the cultural context, beliefs, religion, families, and friends of the business owners affect CSR. SMEs prefer to use informal tools such as personal links to treat ethical issues (Graafland et al., 2003). Smes prefer to learn through networks and peers (Jenkins, 2006). Compared to large enterprises, SMES often encounter more obstacles in CSR, particularly the lack of financial resources, knowledge, and skills.

The idea of the social responsibility of the company was broadcast in the society and the business community at the end of the xixth century, in the context of the mutation of American Capitalism. In this spirit, other research had shown that the speech at the time was very marked by the concepts of a strong religious connotation of " *stewardship* " and " *trusteeship,* "which stipulate the idea of an implied contract specifying the relationship between the company and the society. These two concepts showed that the exercise of any power or property of a Well had to be justified before God and the community. The question of CSR has become less critical in the middle of the business, and he has had to wait until the end of the 1960s and the beginning of the 1970s to see the polemics resurface. Several research studies have been carried out during this period to axiomatize a body of doctrine for CSR. In this framework, Davis thinks that each company should participate in the policy for the community's well-being, education, employees' satisfaction, etc. This shows, among other things, that there was an awareness of the company's role in its environment. A doctrinal body begins to formulate as early as the 1960s, with the work of several researchers. Still, we cannot mention the work on CSR during this period without recalling Carroll's research, which led to editing an article founder in 1979 entitled " *A Three-Dimensional Conceptual Model of Corporate Social Performance.* " Carroll (1979) shows that the concept of CSR covers four dimensions: economic, legal, ethical, and discretionary, and added that the company must be listening to society by realizing its dimensions. The book of Carroll (1979) remains a reference for most studies that have dealt with the theme of CSR. The current research aims to transform the first reflections on CSR. It is, therefore, a part of a philosophical design to a pragmatic design and managerial one in which CSR is mainly interested in managing problems and tensions social issues faced by businesses.

These two decades have been largely marked by the proliferation of research on the theme of CSR. In effect, this notion has experienced considerable enlargement, giving birth to several other new concepts and creators: Societal performance, societal sensitivity (*responsiveness*), business ethics, and to a lesser degree, the theory of stakeholders (Carroll, 1999). There is, first of all, the passage of a narrow design centered on the principles of CSR to a design based on the processes that promote the actions of response to societal pressures or " *corporate social responsiveness*, "then, to the emergence of a new conceptualization enlarged more societal performance of enterprises (PSE) or " *Corporate Social Performance* " which incorporates, in addition to the principles and the process, the results of the societal behaviors. This step has been marked by the concentration of the research on the concept of PES and the purpose of operationalizing the concept. There was a bottom-up approach toward integrating the various previous visions within the PSE.

After viewing CSR in its historical context, we will subsequently advance the factors influencing this concept in the literature.

The Factors Influencing the Social Responsibility of the Family Business

Few studies have tried to identify the factors influencing, in particular, the process of appropriation of the CSR of the family business. However, the contributions of some authors try to answer these questions.

The Knowledge of the Officer

Several researchers are interested in identifying the factors involved in the leader's decision-making. Among these factors figure the knowledge of the leader. It is not here to speak of knowledge as truths in the sense of scientific knowledge but of representations of reality that will guide the choice of the Leader (Spence & Rutherfoord (2001)). The underlying idea is that the more a manager knows about CSR, the more it will tend to engage in concrete actions and changes of attitude (Saulquin & Schier (2007). The question which arises at this level is to know what types of knowledge the family business leader has- the need to engage in CSR? The answer is twofold. The knowledge that encourages the company's change concerning its own practices is not the same as those that stimulate the business to support actions from other companies (Gadenne et al. (2009). In the first case, the leader must know about the social and environmental impact of its business, concerning practices and existing initiatives, but also regarding the cost/benefit ratio of the CSR, which Gadenne et al. (2009) appoint the degree of conscience.

Leaders who lack knowledge about their environmental influence and who consider that the improvement of the ecological footprint is not in their interest do not see the relevance of engaging in CSR. In the second case, it is the degree of attitude which is important, that is, the general beliefs that will shape the positive representation of the Leader vis-a-vis CSR (Vives (2006)). This knowledge will lead the leader in support of external stakeholders through financial donations but are not wide enough to stimulate a reflexive attitude of the leader as to their own actions and influences Gadenne et al. (2009). In this context, CSR is seen as a means to achieve precise objectives and does not constitute an end.

As well, CSR does not fall directly within the personal values of the leader and does not respond on a priority basis to a moral duty. It is here in the presence of an instrumental transposition of the CSR. However, note that the objectives sought by the leaders are multiple and do not concern only the search for immediate profit. Families businesses are approaching CSR rather as a means of ensuring their "*license to operate* " in their own community, to invest in the relations with stakeholders, in particular with the social partners, suppliers, customers, and investors, or to improve the different processes, such as the production, the quality of the products. Finally, CSR is perceived as a moral duty, an obligation to respect and fulfill stakeholders' needs to give back to the community.

The Influence of the Environment: Likely Trigger of the Principles of CSR

Typically, the company adopts a societal behavior in response to stimuli received by the officer. Internal stimuli or external causes of motivations, proactive or reactive. The stimuli are appointed factors attracting the officer's attention since they lead the leader to recognize an opportunity in *CSR*. They reflect the response of the company to a constantly changing environment. CSR allows the company to reconcile economic, social, and environmental dimensions. It is particularly the external motivations that relate in the first place, the fear of the company losing a share of the market for the benefit of the local and international competitors and the fight against the competitive threats to respond to these threats. It should be listening to its stakeholders by adopting a strategy that embodies the company's citizenship concerning its competitors. Thanks to our descriptive questionnaire, the findings identified somewhat the idea of the impact of the competition on the decision of appropriation of the CSR. A proposal based on the idea of the weakness of the competition as an explanation of the absence of societal commitment has been advanced, «A low competition characterizes our market. We record that 78,57% of respondents seem to disagree with this idea. Thus, we cannot say that the perception of strong competition can constitute an incentive concerning the search for an approach to social responsibility.

CSR can also be explained by the desire to benefit from government aid to adopt social actions and the support provided by public bodies. In particular, government programs are specific benefit businesses of benefits and tax and non-tax incentives to encourage the adoption of measures that promote the protection of the environment and the development of local communities. The company is also confronted with other motivations which relate, among other things, to the influence of stakeholders; elsewhere, it is clear from the literature that CSR is stimulated above all by pressure from stakeholders (Worthington et al. 2008). For Lepoutre and Heene (2006), the engine of the CSR in SMES is situated more concerning internal stakeholders (staff, customers, and suppliers) and much less concerning external stakeholders and the natural environment, as it is more widely the case with larger companies. In this context, Gadenne et al. (2009) believe that the suppliers, the legislator, the clients, and the community are the parties the more influential for the SMES. This is evident from the responses to the proposals of our investigation; 78,57% of the respondents stated that they were favorable, well with an intensity divergent, with the proposition " *We have stable relations with our stakeholders.* " Similarly, most companies in our study seem to agree with the proposal: «*We live in a favorable environment to our activity*. Nevertheless, if it is found that the influence of the Environment on the making of the decision by the CSR must be taken into account, it should not exaggerate the deterministic nature of the latter.

The analysis must, in addition, be focused on the business. Indeed, the external stimuli previously mentioned could not explain to them only the company's commitment to CSR. The combination of stimuli and explanatory variables can trigger the process of decision. Far from being only forced by the barriers of external nature, the CSR of the small family business is conditioned by other factors relating to the company's internal organization and the behaviors of senior leaders. So that a decision of societal commitment is taken, a set of prerequisites must be met. A favorable internal context must also allow the family business to adopt CSR. To do this, the family business must overcome several internal obstacles. The struggles for power within the family business, a phenomenon quite frequent, as well as the particular conflicts relating to the decision of appropriation of the CSR, are, first, antagonistic to this strategy. In addition, it may be common to observe a strong opposition to CSR on the part of the principal owners.

The possible lack of support for CSR on the part of the Board of Directors would also have a negative impact. Once the internal conditions are met, the family business can initiate its CSR policy if a set of explanatory variables is present. In effect, the willingness of the family to ensure the company's survival to transmit to future generations is a factor encouraging the establishment of CSR. Generally, the family business manifests a strategic conservatism, especially when the previously adopted strategy has shown its efficiency. The sense of stability and profitability appear to constitute an obstacle to the willingness to invest in CSR. Obviously, it is a strategy that works or has worked well in the past all the chances to see erected in a "paradigm" strategic company. The managers are, in this sense, prudent to seek other routes to performance and prefer to stick to the policy that has proven its worth in the past. Such a company devotes long-term sustainability and non-financial performance as objectives to pursue. The societal behavior of the family culture certainly allows us to commit to CSR. The company cement of Enfidha (EC), known under the «Group Uniland, "provides a good illustration of this societal orientation.

Created in 1896, the company remains faithful to the spirit of its origins, that of a family business. She has been able to reconcile the different dimensions of CSR. After its installation on the Tunisian market in the framework of the privatization of national companies, it has been obligated to meet its stakeholders' expectations. In this spirit, Director General says, *"at Uniland, we are convinced that our success depends on the unswerving respect we committed to our customers, suppliers, employees, and our community in general. Seeing a guarantee of future success, we pay special attention to developing our employees, and we are a company firmly committed to sustainable development. Our active participation in various solidarity actions carried out in the countries and regions where we are present is the best evidence, as well as the links we have with global organizations and local governments dedicated to this task."*

However, 64,28% of respondents agree with our proposal: " *We do not need a CSR policy*." Furthermore, our investigation shows that half of the interviewees think that CSR remains a matter of public authority; w*e believe that social responsibility is a matter of public authority*. Similarly, most of the companies in our survey agree with the proposal: that the adoption of CSR seems very expensive. Moreover, 92,86% of them believe that: This CSR approach is not currently included among the strategic concerns of our company. This said that the weakness of managerial skills, coupled with the pursuit of objectives, is more urgent than CSR, which implies a lack of interest in this strategy. In effect, 78,57% of the surveyed respondents disagree with the proposal the exploration of information on CSR.

The Illustrative Variables of the CSR: Organizational Characteristics and Role of Resources

Given the previously made conditions, the company should consider CSR to respond to some objectives. The first of these goals is the search for competitive advantage: the management of the Company may collect the commitment to the environmental approach and the improvement of personal working conditions as sources of competitive advantages to acquiring new projects and, in particular, reduce the barriers to entering the international market. The pioneering studies of the eighties advocated that the link between CSR and the company's performance is linear. Such studies state that CSR can only be beneficial. More recent research recognizes this strategy's benefits, costs, and constraints. The first question to analyze is the influence of organizational characteristics such as size on CSR. In a second point, we will develop the influence of resources on the adoption decision of CSR. Social commitment appears necessary for businesses of all sizes to adapt to stakeholders' expectations, and it becomes a reform from the typology of stakeholders to manage stakeholder expectations. The real challenge lies at the level of the SME family. In this spirit, many researchers argued that size was a predictive factor in structuring organizations. However, few studies are interested in the influence of the size of the organizations on their CSR practices. To this title, the study of Lepoutre and Heene (2006) is rich with lessons. Noting the existence of contradictory research findings on the issue, these authors have distinguished the specificities related to the leader, organizational specificities, and specificities of context to explain more finely dissimilarities in CSR practices observed in the field.

Concerning the environmental pillar of CSR, ecological awareness increases remarkably with the size of the firms (Glachant and al (2004)). These authors add that this effect size can be explained by the existence of fixed costs linked to the implementation of practices respectful of the environment more easily absorbable by companies of larger sizes. The investigation of Glachant and al (2004) showed a strong positive relationship between the establishment of an Environmental Management System (EMS) and the size of the studied firms. Also, enterprises with less than 100 employees are only 42.9% to adopt an EMS against 84.4% of those with a workforce between 100 and 500 employees.

The descriptive research that we have conducted allows us to establish a correlation between the resources of businesses and their absence of CSR. Both quantitatively (lack of human resources, financial resources, or time) and qualitatively (absence of experience and competence), the resources constitute a major obstacle to CSR. Regarding the answers of the majority of the companies in our survey to the proposal: our human and financial means do not always allow us to respond immediately to the expectations of our stakeholders, 71.43% of the respondents to our questionnaire seem to agree with this proposal.

Our survey also shows that 92,86% of respondents agree with our proposal: Currently, we do not have the necessary skills to adopt CSR. We can affirm that the human and financial resources loaded to lead CSR policy seem to have adverse effects. Our test of explanation of the absence of societal commitment of 14 Tunisian SMES was nevertheless able to join this attitude to the fear of loss of autonomy. Most of its companies agree with this proposal of recourse to financial institutions for borrowing money. In response to this proposal, keep the profits of the last three fiscal years accountants, "100% of respondents were not in agreement. The study shows that 71.43% of the interviewed disagree with the proposal: the recruitment of managers outside of the family," this said that companies want to retain the decision-making at the family level. Today, family businesses can compensate for their delay in size, for example, thanks to the use of information technologies, such as the Internet, to adopt an approach of CSR.

We do not succeed in explaining these companies' low social commitment to the low use of technologies of information. On the contrary, most of the companies in our study declare favour of the use of the Internet," the use of the new technologies of information transmissions. Throughout this section, we have tried to analyze the family business and its social responsibility theoretically. Observing the founding particularities of this entity has helped generate arguments concerning the specificity of this process. As well we can formulate the hypothesis related to the adoption of the principles of CSR in the small family business in the following manner:

Hypothesis 1: *Family businesses do not adopt the same social dimensions as their non- family counterparts.*

RESEARCH METHODOLOGY

This part plays a fundamental role in the presentation of this research. It focuses on the collection of data, the construction of the questionnaire of the research, and the choice of the sample.

Data Collection and Processing

To familiarize ourselves with the field of research, we first explored the theme, which has enabled us to have a general vision of the process of CSR and the establishment of a Maintenance Guide. This exploratory phase has been conducted within some familial SMEs that have adopted a CSR approach. We have orchestrated the interviews for exploratory reasons and for confirmation of items that would constitute the main questionnaire of our research. The ideal was that the respondent would be, for example, the founder or manager who has triggered the CSR. During this exploratory phase on the ground, we conducted three interviews with three family businesses in the region of Sousse. Indeed, the choice of the governorate of Sousse has been dictated by hardware order and practice circumstances.

Nevertheless, this exploratory phase also allowed us to conduct interviews with the inhabitants of the local community of Ain Mdhaker affected by the extraction activities of EC. Furthermore, the main questionnaire of the research has been carried out as a result of a review of the literature, and semi-structured interviews were carried out with three leaders of family businesses. Nevertheless, we noticed that problems relating to the ambiguity of a few statements and the representation of some of the concepts are explained without doubt by the length of our draft questionnaire. Following its observations, some changes have been made: the questionnaire has been widely abstract to embed only the most congruent variables to the study. In addition, the statements of the scales have been reformulated to represent their concepts better. In the final analysis, our research approach is synthesized by the attached figure 1.

Our method is to fix appointments with the firms chosen by our database. We have taken care of these appointments through telephone communications and e-mails sent to companies with Internet access. Once our respondents fixed the appointments, we tried to obtain a reasonable timetable so that the meetings with our respondents would be well-organized. That is to say, and we have chosen to perform five visits per day, each service can last between one hour less quarter and one hour. We have tried in these discussions to present our research objective and the causes of choosing the company in question. However, other questionnaires were sent by postal way or by intermediaries (employees) who work within its businesses. These questionnaires have been accompanied by letters of presentation of our research objective and the reasons for the choice of the company in question.

We have received no response for some questionnaires due to false postal addresses. These questionnaires were conducted between June and September 2012. The main questionnaire of the study is directed indiscriminately at business families and non-family ones. Therefore, the respondent has the opportunity to respond to the proposals that it considers interesting. Similarly, we tried to ensure that the family businesses that meet our measurement scales are not necessarily socially responsible. But, before embarking on the collection of data necessary for measuring variables of our research model, we wanted to detect the process of appropriation of CSR within companies other than family (public, managerial, etc.).

Figure 1. Phase of data collection

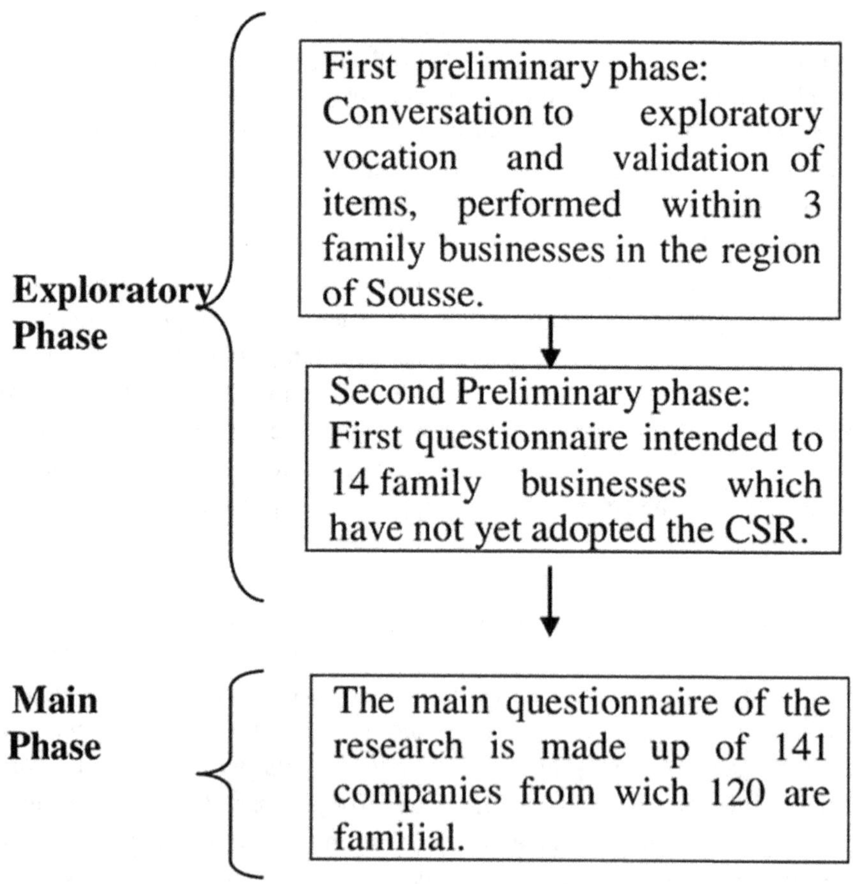

Choice of the Research Sample

The great difficulty in choosing family SMES has consisted of the fact that in Tunisia, there is no recognized legal status of the family business. For this reason, we have had recourse to the API (Agency for the Promotion of industry) to help us select this type of business. The research companies have also been chosen from the electronic database of the Investment Promotion Agency (API) and the Websites of the coveted companies. Our formed database consists of 200 family and non-family businesses according to the criteria of the possession of the capital and the exercise of the power of government. We have retained the threshold of 33% of capital as a quantitative criterion to incorporate a company into our database. Therefore, if a shareholder owns less than 33%, it is considered a minority. As soon as he holds more than 33% of the capital, the company he controls could have the qualifier of family. However, it is clear that these choices induce some risks to the study and its results. Even if we are looking to examine and describe the process of appropriation of CSR principles of family businesses of small and medium size, this objective does not exclude collecting the responses of large firms, assuming that they have evolved from SMES to large enterprises. The second dimension is a little sensitive because it focuses on the companies that have adopted the approach of CSR. This phase has been carried out based on the criteria of the following choices:

- Companies that have achieved economic performance during the fiscal years 2009-2010.
- The certified companies (ISO9001, ISO 26000, etc.) or have a certification program in the next years.
- The companies that have not committed breaches of regulations in force have not been the subject of a tax adjustment during the last three years.
- Companies are constantly seeking the sustainability of the company and its transmission to future generations.
- The companies are concerned about the ethical, ecological, and social (values Dialogue, transparency, listening, and anticipation of stakeholders' expectations). This strategy seems to us to be relevant to be able to create a consistent set of socially responsible companies. Finally, our database comprises 141 companies, of which 120 are familial.

RESULTS AND DISCUSSION

The empirical validation study will focus on presenting the research results while testing the advanced hypothesis on the collected data and relying on descriptive and

Table 1. The distribution of the different social dimensions adopted by companies

Dimension	Order
Economic responsibility (profit, profitability, productivity, etc.)	
Ethical Responsibility (confidence business-to-customer, etc.).	
Legal responsibility (compliance with the regulations in force, etc.).	
Discretionary responsibility (protection of the environment, etc.).	

comparative analysis to enter the societal dimensions of two groups of family and non-family businesses. It is to draw lessons about these processes' nature and conduct comparisons. The theory advocates dissimilarity in the adoption of the dimensions of CSR. In fact, Aupperle and al (1985) show that the economic responsibility of CSR remains dominant, followed by the responsibilities: legal, ethical, and philanthropic for several countries, namely the USA, England, France, Germany, Switzerland, Sweden, and Japan. The final stages of the analysis will be the subject of theorizing the conclusions and interpretation of the final results.

The Seizure of the Social Dimension of the Company: A Descriptive Analysis

Far from wanting to analyze all the identified sizes, our study of the process of CSR will focus only on the adoption of the societal dimension of the company. This analysis is based on a question from our research questionnaire where the respondents were asked to classify by chronological order the dimensions that their companies have adopted in the course of their ownership of CSR. Such a study would require, among other things, temporal boundaries. For example, the researcher must know when the studied phenomenon begins and ends. Although the present research is not on a single firm, such delimitation is hardly feasible since the studied process is temporally separate for each. Furthermore, the selected companies are composed of a large diversity of companies where age, social maturity, and the degree of CSR differ. Therefore, we do not define any observation period during which the event of change must occur.

We have asked the respondents to rank the different dimensions the company has adopted during its appropriation process of CSR following a chronological order of their achievement. Accordingly, the following table was submitted to them.

In this framework, it was necessary to introduce contextual help in our questionnaire to explain some of the terms that respondents may misunderstand. Here, the terms which could be misunderstood were illustrated by examples that explain the four dimensions.

Table 2. Distribution of Social Dimensions adopted by EF and ENF

Mode	EF, n=120		ENF, n=21		TOTAL, n=141	
	Staff	%	Staff	%	Staff	%
ECO RES	37	86,05%	6	13,95%	43	100.00%
ETH RES	52	91,23%	5	8.77%	57	100.00%
LEG RES	25	73,53%	9	26,47%	34	100.00%
DIS RES	6	85.71%	1	14,29%	7	100.00%

Source: Prepared by authors

Summary of the Results of the Research

We propose in what follows to expose the descriptive results of our study on the confiscation of the societal dimension. The following analysis will provide additional information to help us understand the company's behavior. The four dimensions of the social responsibility of the company advanced by Carroll (1979) are:

- **ECO RES**: Economic responsibility
- **ETH RES**: Ethical responsibility
- **LEG RES**: Legal responsibility
- **DIS RES**: Discretionary responsibility

Our study consists of 151 undertakings (128 families and 23 non-families). Ten firms are eliminated because they do not have the intention of adopting the principles of CSR. Thus, the companies used to consist of 120 families businesses and 21 non-families businesses.

Figure 2. Number of Social Dimensions adopted

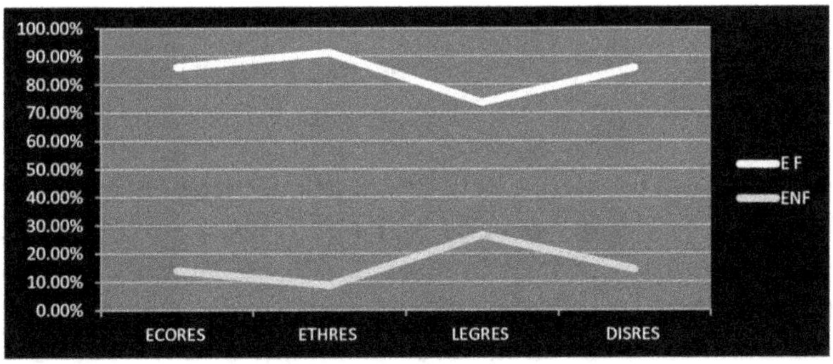

Ethical and economic responsibilities are the dimensions most adopted by the family businesses[1] of our study. Legal responsibility comes in a second position. However, legal and Economic responsibility is the most used dimensions by non-family companies. Ethical responsibility comes in a second position. Given this figure, we can see that the family business presents an attraction for ethical responsibility. Nevertheless, his counterpart, non-families, reflects a desire for legal responsibility. The following table will provide more information.

Table 3. Distribution of the social responsibilities between the EF and the ENF

Mode	EF, n=120		ENF, n=21		TOTAL, n=141	
	Staff	%	Staff	%	Staff	%
ECO RES	37	30,83%	6	28.57%	43	30.50%
ETH RES	52	43,33%	5	23.81%	57	40,43%
LEG RES	25	20,84%	9	42.86%	34	24,11%
DIS RES	6	5.00%	1	4.76%	7	4.96%
TOTAL	120	100.00%	21	100.00%	141	100.00%

Source: Prepared by authors

According to this table, we note that the passage of its companies toward discretionary responsibility is very long. In fact, only six among 120 surveyed families' businesses have adopted the dimension discretionary (DIS RES).

The passage of the family businesses toward responsibility is discretionary and very slow.

In addition, we can conclude that for surveyed family businesses, priority is given to the ethical responsibility followed respectively by the economic dimension, legal and discretionary. In fact, the contribution of the societal responsibility of firms to the financial performance of Tunisian-rated businesses confirms the predominance of the legal dimension, followed successively by the ethical, economic, and discretionary responsibilities. Aupperle and al (1985), also, postulate that the economic dimension is a priority followed by legal, ethical and discretionary responsibilities.

In addition, the research conducted by Pinkston and Carroll (1996), aimed at identifying the directions of CSR in seven developed countries (USA, England, France, Germany, Switzerland, Sweden, and Japan, confirms the finding issued by Aupperle and al (1985). The economic responsibility of CSR remains dominant, followed by the legal, ethical, and philanthropic responsibilities.

Figure 3. The distribution of social responsibilities between the EF and the ENF

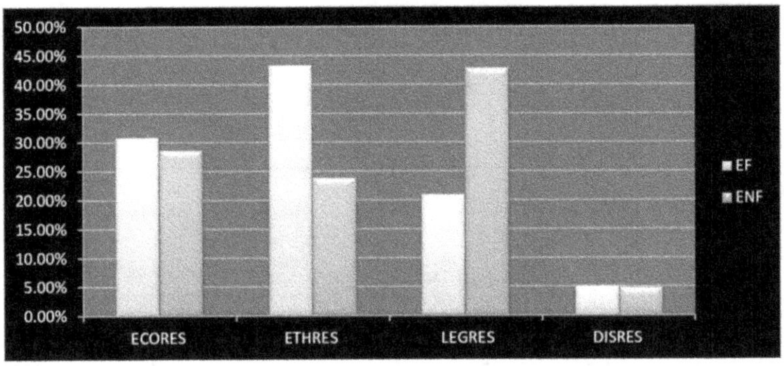

The overall trend of the societal responsibility of business is strongly oriented toward the ethics component. This can be explained by the importance that surveyed families' businesses attach to " *corporate governance.* " In fact, the Ethics takes the form of a strategic asset to seduce more investors and arrive to mobilize the funds in their favour, since; the family businesses must demonstrate a certain responsibility, especially in the area of transparency of information with the stakeholders to establish a climate of shared confidence.

The prominent place of the economic dimension, which occupies the second position, can be explained by the importance of economic interest and profit maximisation for the surveyed family businesses. The legal dimension occupies the third place; this can be translated into a commitment of families' enterprises to respect the laws and regulations in force and, in particular, the provisions laid down by the Labor Code. Finally, the discretionary or philanthropy responsibility (Carroll, (1979, 1999)) is returned to the last position. Its low intake in forming CSR returns to a low investment in charitable shares.

Nevertheless, we observe among non-families businesses the predominance of the legal dimension followed by the economic, ethical and discretionary dimensions.

A principal component analysis (ACP) has been carried out to purify the items of our measurement scale. This phase was followed by a confirmatory factor analysis (AFC). Finally, a scoring study was carried out in our sample to check the research's advanced hypothesis.

Table 4. Selected items after (AFC)

	Latent Variable	Selected Items
Corporate Social Responsibility	CSR	LEGRES2 ECORES1 ETHRES3 DISRES1

Source: Prepared by authors

Table 5. Score of items of CSR of families businesses

Items	EF
LEGRES2	453
ECORES1	503
ETHRES3	548
DISRES1	407

Table 6. Score of the items of CSR of the non-families businesses

Items	ENF
Legres2	92
Ecores1	84
Ethres3	74
Disres1	31

Source: Prepared by authors

The following figure will bring a complement of information.

Figure 4. Distribution of the dimensions of CSR of EF

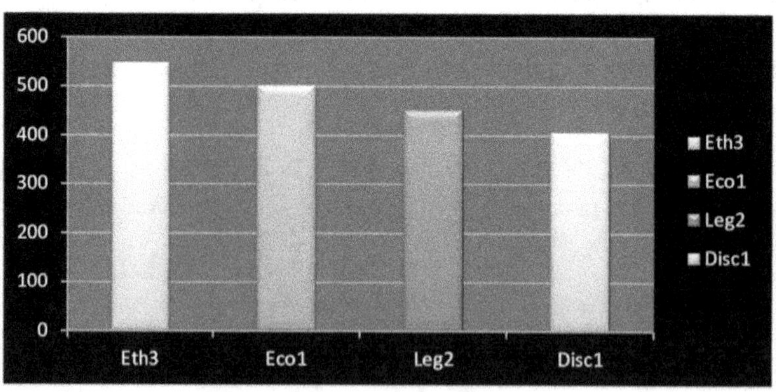

Figure 5. Distribution of the dimensions of CSR and ENF

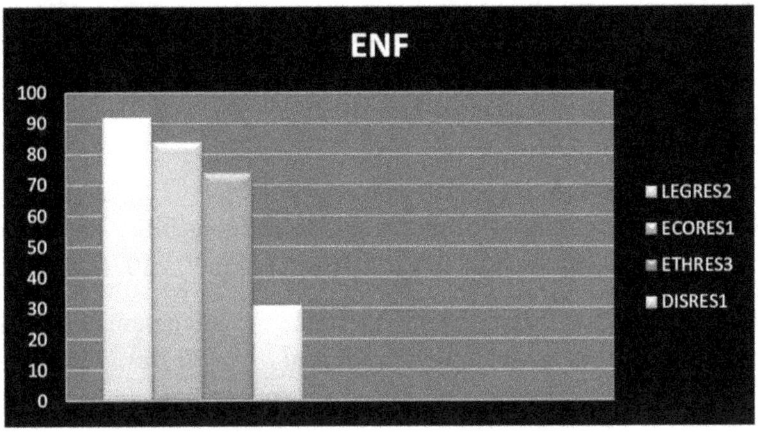

In light of these two figures, several observations can be highlighted. First, the family businesses adopt the ethical dimension in the first place with a score of (548). Family businesses adopt the economic dimensions in the second place. The discretionary dimension is the least used for companies in our study. However, it is observed that non-families businesses adopt the legal dimension first (92). The figure shows the decrease in the share of family businesses from the ethical dimension as soon as we approach the legal dimension.

On the contrary, there is a growth of non-families businesses from the same dimension. The descriptive analysis conducted here, which highlights the adoption of societal dimensions by two groups of families and non-families businesses, leads to the following result: the family businesses do not adopt the same societal dimensions as their non-families counterparts. In sum, we can say that our hypothesis is validated.

CONCLUSION

The analyzes carried out throughout this empirical investigation permit us, in some way, to respond to our research's objective, which is to compare the process of adoption of the societal dimensions between two groups of families and non-family businesses. The study recognizes the deficiencies of the theoretical framework of CSR but uses it to analyze the process of appropriation of CSR between these two entities. The family SMES adopts a pyramid of societal dimensions, which differs from the non-family business and is progressing slowly; this finding is established through this descriptive phase. Accordingly, the behaviour of small family businesses is due to the slow process of developing knowledge of CSR, explained by the negative impact of some of its characteristics. Finally, it is important to report that the empirical results consolidate our findings.

REFERENCES

Aupperle, K. E., Carroll, A. B., & Hatfield, J. D. (1985). An Empirical Examination of the Relationship between Corporate Social Responsibility and Profitability. *Academy of Management Journal*, *28*(2), 446–463. doi:10.2307/256210

Besser, T. L. (1999). Community involvement and the perception of success among small business operators in small towns. *Journal of Small Business Management*, *37*(4), 16–30.

Carroll, A. B. (1979). A three dimensional conceptual model of corporate social performance. *Academy of Management Review*, *4*(4), 97–505. doi:10.2307/257850

Carroll, A. B. (1999). Corporate Social Responsibility. Evolution of a definitional construct. *Business & Society*, *38*(3), 268–295. doi:10.1177/000765039903800303

Dick, M., Wagner, E., & Pernsteiner, H. (2021). Founder-Controlled Family Firms, Overconfidence, and Corporate Social Responsibility Engagement: Evidence From Survey Data. *Family Business Review*, *34*(1), 71–92. doi:10.1177/0894486520918724

Fassin, Y. (2008). SMEs and the fallacy of formalising CSR. *Business Ethics: a European Review*, *17*(4), 364–378. doi:10.1111/j.1467-8608.2008.00540.x

Gadenne, D. L., Kennedy, J., & McKeiver, C.Gadenne and al. (2009). An Empirical Study of Environmental Awareness and Practices in SMEs. *Journal of Business Ethics*, *84*(1), 45–63. doi:10.100710551-008-9672-9

Glachant M., Vicarelli M. et Vincent F., (2004), Management environnemental: Une enquête auprès de 270 Etablissements Industriels Français. Rapport pour *l'ADEME et l'OCDE.*

Jenkins, H. (2006). Small Business Champions for Corporate Social Responsibility. *Journal of Business Ethics*, *67*(3), 241–256. doi:10.100710551-006-9182-6

Lepoutre, J., & Heene, A. (2006). Investigating the Impact of Firm Size on Small Business Social Responsibility: A Critical Review. *Journal of Business Ethics*, *67*(3), 257–273. doi:10.100710551-006-9183-5

Maignan, I. (2001). Consumers' perceptions of Corporate Social Responsibilities: A Cross-Cultural Comparison. *Journal of Business Ethics*, *30*(1), 57–72. doi:10.1023/A:1006433928640

Morsing, M., & Spence, L. J. (2019). Corporate social responsibility (CSR) communication and small and medium sized enterprises: The governmentality dilemma of explicit and implicit CSR communication. *Human Relations*, *72*(12), 1920–1947. doi:10.1177/0018726718804306

Murillo, D., & Lozano, J. (2006). SMEs and CSR: An Approach to CSR in their own words. *Journal of Business Ethics*, *67*(3), 227–240. doi:10.100710551-006-9181-7

Pinkston, T. S., & Carroll, A. B. (1996). A retrospective examination of CSR orientations: Have they changed? *Journal of Business Ethics*, *15*(2), 199–206. doi:10.1007/BF00705587

Poza, F. and T. Messer (2001). Spousal leadership and continuity in the family firm, *Family Business Review*, *14*(1), pp. 25-36.

Russo, A., & Tencati, A. (2009). Formal vs. Informal CSR strategies: Evidence from Italian Micro, Small, Medium-sized, and Large Firms. *Journal of Business Ethics*, *85*(S2), 339–353. doi:10.100710551-008-9736-x

Spence, L., & Rutherfoord, R. (2001). Social Responsibility, profit maximization and the small firm owner-manager. *Journal of Small Business and Enterprise Development*, *8*(2), 126–139. doi:10.1108/EUM0000000006818

Spence, L. J. (2015). (in press). Small business social responsibility: Expanding core CSR theory'. *Business & Society*. doi:10.1177/0007650314523256

Spence, L. J., & Lozano, J. (2000). Communicating About ethics with small firms: Experiences from the U.K. and Spain. *Journal of Business Ethics*, *27*(1/2), 43–53. doi:10.1023/A:1006417425446

Vives, A. (2006). Social and Environmental Responsibility in Small and Medium Enterprises in Latin America. *Journal of Corporate Citizenship*, *21*(21), 39–50. doi:10.9774/GLEAF.4700.2006.sp.00006

Worthington, I., Ram, M., Boyal, H., & Shah, M. (2008). Researching the Drivers of Socially Responsible Purchasing: A Cross-National Study of Supplier Diversity Initiatives. *Journal of Business Ethics*, *79*(3), 319–331. doi:10.100710551-007-9400-x

ENDNOTE

1 We have taken into consideration the staffing to arrive at this conclusion.

Chapter 7
Innovative Performance Management Practices for the Sustainable Development of Moroccan Construction SMEs

Abdelali Ezziadi
https://orcid.org/0000-0001-5857-9156
Polydisciplinary Faculty of Sidi Bennour, Chouaïb Doukkali University, Morocco

Mohamed Wadie Lahouirich
Polydisciplinary Faculty of Sidi Bennour, Chouaïb Doukkali University, Morocco

Aziza Chachdi
Polydisciplinary Faculty of Sidi Bennour, Chouaïb Doukkali University, Morocco

ABSTRACT

The construction industry plays a crucial role in the economic and social development of every country However, the construction sector uses 36% of total energy, 30% of raw materials, 39% of energy-related CO2 emissions, and 35% of solid waste production. In fact, the emergence of sustainable development has been accompanied by a profusion of research dealing with the impact of the integration of sustainability on managerial practices. In Morocco, the orientation to sustainable construction implies an evolution of construction project management practices to not only ensure that projects meet time, cost, and technical quality requirements, but also to guarantee that the construction project is sustainable. This paper aims to study the sustainable project management practices developed within Moroccan companies. For this purpose, the authors have used secondary data and activity reports from seven Moroccan companies in the construction sector. The results of this study show that the seven companies adopt very heterogeneous practices, ranging from continuous actions to specific actions

DOI: 10.4018/978-1-6684-4834-2.ch007

INTRODUCTION

The construction industry is crucial to every country's economic and social development. According to market survey data, the scale of the world construction market has grown from USD 9.5 trillion in 2014 to USD 11.4 trillion in 2019, with a compound annual growth rate of 3.71% from 2014 to 2019 (United Nations Environment Programme, 2021). In Morocco, the construction industry is a levered sector of the Moroccan economy; It contributes 6% to the GDP, generated a turnover of 5.44 million euros in 2018, and employs more than 900,000 jobs (Ministry of Housing and Urban Policy, 2020).

The success and failure of the construction organizations significantly affect the construction industry, other industries linked to it, and thus the entire nation (Tripathi and Jha, 2018). Construction organizations are primarily small and medium-sized enterprises whose activities are organized in projects dispersed in time and/or space. The success of these projects depends on several factors and constraints, including cost, quality, and time.

The future of the global construction industry looks good, with opportunities in residential, non-residential, and infrastructure. However, the consumption of natural resources in the coming years will be explored, especially with a linear economy model (Ezziadi and Chachdi, 2021). According to Global Alliance for building and construction, the construction sector uses 36% of total energy, 30% of raw materials, 39% of energy-related CO2 emissions, and 35% of solid waste generation (United Nations Environment Programme, 2021). For that, construction organizations need innovative performance management practices to plan, implement, monitor, and improve the efficiency and effectiveness of their projects, not only focused on traditional indicators but also integrating those related to sustainable performance.

An analytical-descriptive approach was adopted to study and identify how Moroccan Small and Medium Enterprises (SMEs) in the construction sector develop or develop their performance management practices to realize sustainable performance projects. We have collected and exploited informative data from seven major Moroccan companies operating in the construction sector through the transposition of the concept of sustainable development in business by evaluating its three fundamental pillars: economic, environmental, social, and economical.

On the other hand, difficulties were encountered when carrying out this study, such as the restricted access to empirical data relating to our field of research and the limited number of our sample (seven case studies relating to SMEs in construction). Nevertheless, despite the small number of Moroccan SMEs surveyed, we have highlighted original adaptation strategies.

The results show that construction project management practices must evolve to monitor whether projects meet deadlines, costs, and technical quality requirements and ensure that construction projects are sustainable. Suggestions and recommendations were finally developed to carry out a possible integration of new construction project management practices.

RETHINKING MANAGEMENT CONTROL IN THE CONTEXT OF SMEs: TOWARDS A PERFORMANCE MANAGEMENT SYSTEM

The metamorphosis from a management control system to a performance management system takes its essence from the will of managers "to capture a holistic approach to the management and control of organizational performance" (Ferreira and Otley, 2009). Indeed, the context in which companies operate, and more particularly SMEs (more dependent on contextual factors), no longer allows them to survive and perpetuate without having a more global vision based on relevant and reliable information. Moreover, available statistics show that one of the causes of SME failure is the absence of a long-term vision (D'Amboise & Bakanibona, 1990) and the lack of analytical knowledge of the company's current situation. The evolution of the missions of management control and the new issues that it must take into account (cash management, the social and societal dimension, risk management, the evolution of information systems, etc.) lead researchers to no more extended focus on the instrumental approach of management control, but to seek to understand the functioning of SMEs by developing a path to the management system in the broad sense (Meyssonnier, 2015).

In addition, the state of SMEs (accounting and financial information system failing or even absent, non-formalized objectives, poorly computerized information systems, scarcity of human, financial and technical resources, etc.), especially in Morocco (Sadeq, 2013), means that today the engineering approach to the engineering approach to management control no longer solves the managerial problems of SMES. Therefore, recent developments in work on management control do not cease to encourage the rethinking of the management control system. to rethink the performance management system in its entirety.

Lorino defined performance management in his book "Methods and practices of performance management as the definition and implementation of methods that allow "learning to act together efficiently and to act together in an increasingly efficient way" (Lorino, 2003). Further on in the same reference, he defined it as being the accomplishment of "two complementary functions in a continuous manner: deploying the strategy in rules of operational actions (deployment) and capitalizing on the results and lessons learned from the action to enrich the reflection on the objectives (feedback). Thus, he presents management as a loop between strategy and operations (figure1).

Figure 1. The steering loop
Source: Lorino (2003)

The literature review on performance management reveals the existence of more than 20 definitions for this concept (Ates et al., 2013). The scope of the concept can explain these different meanings of performance management. For example, is it a human dimension (Aguinis, 2009), an operational dimension (Parthiban & Goh, 2011) or a strategic dimension (Otley, 1999). To give just a few definitions, Meyssonnier (2015), drawing on the work of Ferreira and Otley, specifies that the overall performance management system includes, in particular: the formulation of strategic objectives, the identification of causal chains that allow them to be achieved, the determination of the required levels of performance in each responsibility center and incentive system of managers" (Ferreira & Otley, 2009).

More recently, Barbelivien defined the performance management system as "a complete and coherent system of tools for forecasting, measuring and controlling financial and non-financial performance" (Barbelivien, 2014).

PROBLEM STATEMENT AND METHODOLOGICAL APPROACH

The Construction industry is one of the significant sector generators of waste worldwide. Construction waste comes mainly from demolition and rehabilitation works (90%), of which 73% is internal waste. In Morocco, the statistics published by the Secretariat of State in charge of sustainable development indicate a total quantity of waste in the sector of 41.9 million tons and 40.48 million tons of inert waste (97.3%).

The World population Growth and increase in housing and infrastructure needs would grow these statistics and lead to an explosion of waste quantities, explained in particular by the extensive exploitation of natural resources associated with an inefficient use of end-of-life materials (Fořt & Černý, 2020). Consequently, Project management practices and success criteria theoretically validated in the linear economic model (Take-Maste-Waste) are no longer supported in the sustainability and circular model approach (Ezziadi & Chachdi, 2021). Moroccan construction enterprises, especially Small and medium enterprises, would also rethink their practices of project management control to comply with their projects' economic, environmental and social requirements.

For that, this paper aims to answer the following question: *How do Moroccan construction companies integrate the dimensions that constitute the "triple Bottom Line" business concept, namely environmental, social and economic practices for managing their projects?*

To answer it, the design of this study is based on a literature review and an analytical-descriptive approach through the collection and exploitation of informative data from a sample of seven main Moroccan companies operating in the construction sector, through the transposition of the concept of sustainable development in business, by the evaluation of its three fundamental pillars, namely environmental, social and economic practices.

CONCEPTUALIZATION OF THE PERFORMANCE OF SMEs IN THE CONSTRUCTION INDUSTRY

"Although all economic actors consider performance part of their short-or medium- or long-term objectives, we quickly realize that it leaves room for many interpretations" (St-Pierre & Cadieux, 2011). Indeed, the definition of the notion of performance is a subject that has aroused the interest of several researchers and practitioners and has been widely used, in all fields and at all levels (Ehrenberg, 1991; Bessire, 1999), without them agreeing on a clear and universal definition of "this ambiguous notion" (Gauzente, 2000; Montes et al., 2003). Moreover, Khlif considers that the search for a clear, standard, and fair definition of performance is not an easy task (Khlif, 1998). Performance is a concept that refers to several meanings depending on the field of use (physical, sport, art, etc.), and its definition keeps evolving over time. Thus, the contingency of performance (Marmuse, 1997) means that it has attributes and evaluation criteria specific to the construction sector, particularly by focusing on project performance, which is the management unit for this sector.

As is the case for any organization, the quest for performance in a fiercely competitive and riskier environment (Ezeldin & Sharara, 2006) is the primary concern of SMEs operating in the construction sector. Nevertheless, being a complex notion and a social construct, performance is apprehended based on complementary and sometimes contradictory attributes (Lebas, 1995). Thus, before beginning to reflect on management practices and the factors that determine them, defining the notion of performance in the context of SMEs in the construction industry is essential.

Furthermore, the heterogeneity of perceptions of performance (Bourguignon, 2000; Salgado, 2013; Ezziadi & Ouhadi, 2016) implies a diversity of steering practices (St-Pierre & Cadieux, 2011). Therefore, identifying the main attributes of the performance of SMEs in the construction sector constitutes the first line of thought in studying the performance management systems of these companies. In reviewing the literature on the performance of SMEs in the construction sector, we identified two groups of works. The first group focuses on project performance, in which most researchers are interested. The second, which remains less explored, focuses on the firm's performance.

Bassioni et al. conceptualize the performance of construction companies in terms of two dimensions of performance: financial performance and non-financial performance (Bassioni et al, 2005). Each of these two facets covers a range of indicators and measures. Therefore, the difficulty lies in choosing an appropriate measure to understand each dimension (Nivyintizo, 1995). This choice is crucial, as the use of inappropriate measures explains, in part, the failure of SMEs (Maduekwe & Kamala, 2016). As for project performance, the available literature identifies a multiplicity of performance criteria with a common core of cost, quality, and time.

Given that there is no general consensus on the key indicators of project performance (Chan et al., 2004; Toor & Ogunlana, 2010) and the diversity of perceptions of this performance among stakeholders (Wang & Huang, 2006; Toor & Ogunlana, 2008), the identification of a set of common attributes is a crucial phase in the process of steering the performance of SMEs at the project level (Cox et al., 2003). There is indeed no consensus on the criteria for evaluating and measuring project performance, but the majority of the works mentioned above, and many others, cite the three criteria of cost, quality, and time. These form the Iron Triangle theorized by Atkinson (1999).

The study of all the criteria raised in the literature (Table 1) looks at both the macro-performance of the project - which concerns the users and beneficiaries of the project - and its micro-performance - which concerns the contractors and consultants (Lim and Mohamed, 1999), reveals that the assessment of project performance is no longer based solely on the cost-quality-delay triptych.

In the context of this work, to evaluate the performance of a project, we use the matrix of Toor and Ogunlana (2010) insofar as it includes the three classic criteria of the Iron Triangle, which are enriched and completed by six other criteria, the most cited by all the works. This provides both an objective and subjective assessment of project performance.

Table 1. Key attributes of construction project performance

Authors	Performance Attributes
Maloney (1990)	Time, cost, quality, productivity, and efficiency
Norris (1990)	On-budget, financial performance, and profitability
Ashley et al. (1987)	Cost, schedule, quality, safety, and participant satisfaction
Shenhar et al. (1997)	Project efðciency, impact on the customer, direct and business success, and preparing for the future
Lipovetsky et al. (1997)	Meeting design goals; beneðts to the customer; beneðts to the developing organization; and beneðts to the defense and national infrastructure
Cheung et al. (2004)	Time, cost, quality, customer satisfaction, customer-initiated changes, health and safety
Luu et al. (2008)	Cost, schedule, customer satisfaction, quality management, team performance, change management, material management, safety
Toor and ogunalan (2010)	On-time delivery, minimum budget, conformance to specifications, efficient use of resources, effectiveness, safety, defects, stakeholder satisfaction, and the reduction of conflicts and disputes
Ali and Rahmat (2010)	Functionality, customer satisfaction, health and safety, number of complaints, time, and cost
Construction industry institute (2011)	Cost, delay, accidents, defects, and productivity
Tunji-Olayeni and al (2016)	Cost, schedule, quality, customer satisfaction, project profitability, productivity, safety, and teamwork
Demirkesen and Ozorhon (2017)	Lead time, cost, quality, safety, and customer satisfaction
Adeleke et al. (2019)	Resolve cost, schedule, and quality

SUSTAINABILITY AND PERFORMANCE MANAGEMENT SYSTEM IN CONSTRUCTION SME

As we have explained, the traditional criteria for managing construction projects are essentially based on the three dimensions of the golden triangle (cost, quality, and time). Nevertheless, they have revealed their limits with the emergence of new actors and other project objectives emphasizing the sustainability of construction projects and adapting to the concept of sustainable development. We recall that sustainable development is defined as “a mode of development that meets the needs of present generations without compromising the ability of future generations to meet their own needs” (WCED, 1987).

Figure 2. Project performance attributes
Source: Toor and Ogunlana (2010)

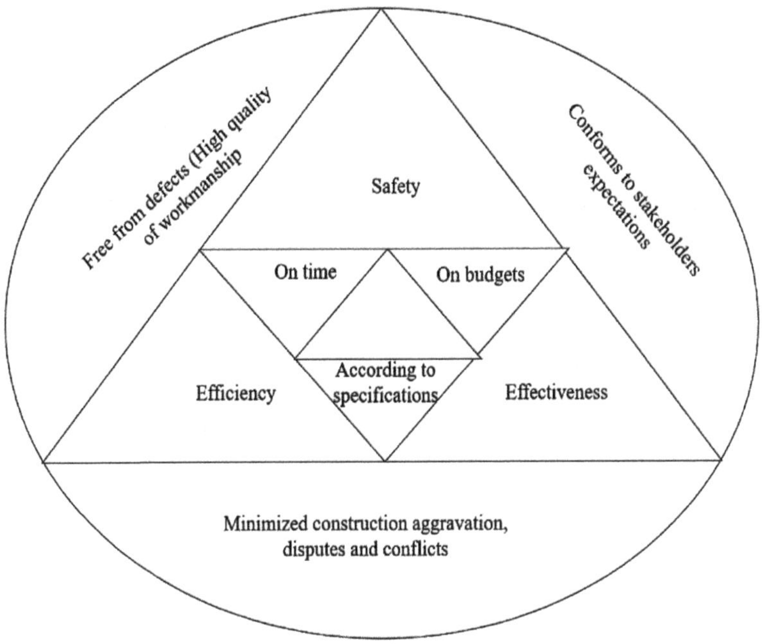

In the construction sector, sustainable building began to develop around the world almost two decades ago. The concept of the sustainable building refers to considering their impact on the environment and their sustainability. It is about a balance between the environmental, economic, and social dimensions, with the objectives of improving the living environment of citizens, strengthening the sustainable management of natural resources, and promoting environmentally friendly economic activities. As Araújo et al. (2013) note, "it is about establishing construction practices that minimize the impacts of buildings, constructing and managing buildings with an appropriate balance between the environment, society, and the economy."

Furthermore, IMANOR (2020) points out that throughout their life cycle, buildings are responsible for 40% of CO2 emissions, 40% of natural resource consumption, and 40% of waste generated worldwide. The sector also has important social (health, safety, quality of life) and economic (employment, productivity, link between development and infrastructure needs, corruption) impacts. Also, Šelih (2007) notes that construction activities have raised serious concerns about their significant environmental impacts, which stem from their consumption of materials, many of which are non-renewable.

Four main findings can be drawn from the analysis of the construction sector:

- Site construction produces numerous air pollutants
- Large volumes of waste result from production, transportation, and construction materials and products.
- Large amounts of energy are consumed in the manufacture of construction products
- The production processes occur in a less controlled and more vulnerable environment than in other industrial environments.

Overcoming this critical situation and promoting sustainable buildings requires a revision of the performance criteria for construction projects. This evolution of the construction project's success criteria is linked to the success factors that are the inputs that lead to the project's success. Green technical and managerial innovation in the construction industry significantly influences these success factors and the company's financial performance (Junaid et al., 2022). Thus, the environmental issues could be "lean manufacturing and energy saving," "recycling of materials," "waste control," "noise reduction," and "air and water pollution reduction."

Small and Medium enterprises contribute to most of the world's pollution, and their negative impact on a global scale is great. For this reason, Kamali and Hewage noted that assessing the life cycle sustainability of different construction methods is imperative (Kamali & Hewage, 2017). The evaluation criteria cover the Triple Bottom Line sustainability categories (TBL), a phrase coined by Elkington in 1995 (El Kington, 1997): environmental, economic, and social. According to Hammer and Pivo, these three dimensions of sustainability are called Profit, People, and the Planet (3Ps) (Hammer and Pivo, 2016),. Each category includes numerous sustainability performance indicators associated with the different phases of a building's life cycle.

According to Marsden, "The TBL objective is a holistic business policy that integrates corporate citizenship into the values and practices of the entire company in such a way that its environmental, social and financial performance is managed as one" (Marsden, 2000).

The three dimensions of the TBL, economic, social, and environmental, are closely related and mutually influential. It is challenging to separate them since they share common elements called "sweet spot," shown in the Figure 3 (Elkington, 1997).

Nevertheless, no universal standard method exists for assessing aspects of the triple bottom line, and no universally accepted standard exists for determining the subcategories of each balance sheet. As a result, companies adapt the general framework and design it according to the structure of their projects and the requirements of their stakeholders.

Figure 3. Sweet Spot (SS)
Source: Elkington (1997)

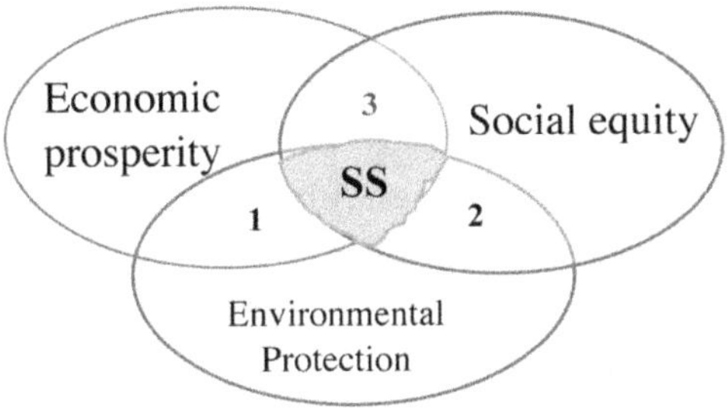

This flexibility allows two entities to assess a sustainability project similarly but record it differently. Thus, the lack of a standard measurement methodology can be a strength. However, ultimately, the TBL calculations will be determined by data availability. Currently, the TBL exists, as Savitz noted, as "*a kind of balanced scorecard that captures in numbers and words the degree to which any company is or is not creating value for its shareholders and society*." (Savitz, 2013).

According to an analysis of 30 articles with 45 case studies, most of which were published from 2014 to 2020, Magdalina (2021) shows that the companies surveyed are characterized by a moderate implementation of sustainable activities and an economic dimension critical.

Table 2. The Triple Bottom Line criteria

	Economic	Environmental	Social
Typical measures	Sales, profit, and ROI	Pollutants emitted	Health and safety record
	Taxes Paid	Carbon footprint	Community impacts
	Monetary flows	Recycling and reuse	Human rights and privacy
	Jobs created	Water and energy use	Product responsibility
	Supplier relations	Product impacts	Employee relations
	Total	**Total**	**Total**

Source: Savitz (2013)

MOROCCAN CONSTRUCTION COMPANIES AND SUSTAINABILITY

Regarding Habitat, the government is working on developing national strategies and technical supervision of the sector to improve the housing production process regarding safety, quality, and sustainability. However, the construction sector faces several shortcomings, including (MDCE 2016):

- The dispersion of standards in different texts (law relating to urbanism, communal road regulations development regulations, development regulations, ministerial orders, circulars, etc.) and reference to the RGC through existing laws and texts: Energy efficiency n° 47-09, accessibility n° 10-03, building code, General Architecture Specification...
- Except for some provisions, most of the legal and regulatory arsenal in force regulatory arsenal in force seems to be outdated to the reality and the requirements of the evolution of the socio-economic context and the technical and technological progress.
- The considerable delay was recorded at the level of the application of the texts governing urbanism, notably law 12/90, which stipulates the elaboration of the general regulation of construction and communal rules.
- To the future challenge in government policy (urban renewal, urban upgrading ...), advanced regionalization, and governance of cities (investment drainage, quality in the city investment, quality in the city ...).

In Morocco, the orientation toward sustainable construction was manifested well before COP 22 and reaffirmed during this event. And one of the sectors concerned is the building industry to reduce the carbon footprint. But, in fact, ecologic construction in Morocco is based, technically and essentially, on implementing thermal and acoustic insulation, and some actions are scattered.

To frame the reflection on sustainable management practices in small and medium enterprises, we referred to the study of sustainable practices reported by large Moroccan companies in the construction sector. According to the analysis of activity reports of the seven-construction company selected, the integration of sustainability in Moroccan construction companies can be summarized as shown in Table 3.

The construction sector plays an essential role in the Moroccan economy. It is characterized, among other things, by the predominance of micro-enterprises and SMEs, which represent considerable potential and a major source of solutions and innovations.

Even if some authors and professionals consider that regulations in the construction sector could hamper innovation and act as a constraint for certain companies, they are also a gas pedal for sustainable construction, particularly in the energy field (PWC, 2018).

Table 3. Sustainable management practices in Moroccan construction companies

Company	Environnemental Practices	Social Practices
Afric industries	• Use of propane instead of fuel oil • Installation of an underground tank (instead of an overhead tank) • Existence of a waste compactor • Equipping all workshops with LED fittings and tubes (70% to 90% energy savings) • Water heater powered by solar energy	• Participation in the management fund for COVID-19 • Granting of donations to public utility associations • Distribution of Ramadan baskets for the benefit of the staff • Organization of an annual draw for a pilgrimage to Mecca • A supplementary pension and health insurance scheme • Safety equipment provided to the staff • Establishment of an infirmary for first aid • Quarterly meeting of the health and safety committee
Aluminum du Maroc	• Planting of 100 trees in the company's garden • The signing of a partnership for the recycling of obsolete computer equipment with the association Green Ship Al jisr	• Partnership agreements with educational and training institutions • Financial support from the Moroccan Association for Sustainable Development and other associations of public utility • Participation in fairs, events, and demonstrations led by professionals, students, and other stakeholders (Sustainable Development Days, Pollutec international fair)
Ciment du Maroc	• Organization of educational outings in the quarries to raise awareness of the biodiversity of different species and the protection of birds for schoolchildren • Sponsoring the Solar Decathlon to design and build high-energy performance solar houses • All our cement production sites are ISO 14001 certified. • Implementation of an energy recovery policy with the objective of reducing its carbon footprint • It equips all kiln stacks with real-time analyzers that continuously measure gas and dust emissions from the firing process. • carrying out a backfilling campaign for excavations generated by the operation	• Strengthening and extending to all our staff the digital training programs offered by the Group: more than 2,000 hours of training have been provided • The signing of agreements with medical organizations to improve and diversify medical and social security coverage • Organization of mornings for employees' young children (children aged between 4 and 12), collective meals by site, convention for executives and thematic managers • Granting of training, advanced training, and professional integration internships at all the company's sites (more than 560 internships) • Participation in student forums at engineering and business schools and in research projects • Support for the construction project of the Koranic and cultural complex • Rehabilitation of several schools near our production sites • Various donations of cement and materials for the construction of roads, the rehabilitation of mosques, the renovation of schools, and the reconstruction of dike walls or fences of some "douars."
Colorado	• Renewal of the certification according to the iso 14001 v2015 standard for the environment • Renewal of the certification • "Eco-Label" certification for the entire product range	• Supporting and sponsoring sports clubs and associations • Ensuring gender equality and promoting access to positions of responsibility based on merit • Adjustment of working conditions for a good balance between private and professional life • Organization of celebrations for the benefit of employees and their children (baccalaureate celebration, "Achoura" celebration, "Ftour Ramadan," women's day...)

continues on following page

Table 3. Continued

Company	Environnemental Practices	Social Practices
Jet Contractors	• Management of hazardous products through the identification and design of appropriate storage areas and the integration of good chemical storage conditions into operational monitoring • Implementation of an internal procedure detailing the different phases of waste management • Development of solutions that reduce the carbon footprint of buildings (high environmental quality certification) • Introduction of environmental and social requirements in the consultation of external service providers • Use of renewable energy as an energy source in the industrial park (696 KWp photovoltaic roof and 140 KWp concentrated photovoltaic modules) • Provision of public transportation and carpooling for a large number of employees • Recovery and reuse of rainwater for watering plants in the administrative offices • Systematically turning off lighting and air conditioning equipment outside of working hours.	• Annual salary increase to encourage the employee for his efforts, motivate him, and encourage him to give more next year. • Social security coverage, emergency management, solidarity, team building, signing agreements with banks for preferential rates • Increasing gender diversity in the company's businesses and reaching 35% of women managers by 2025 (currently 26%).
Holcim Maroc	• Implementation of the ISO 14001 environmental management system • Equipping its main plant with its own wind farm, with a total capacity of 32MW, which allows for an 80% electricity substitution • Implementing continuous monitoring and online monitoring of the stacks at the various sites (dust emission rates below 50 mg/nm3) • Promoting innovation and sustainable construction (50% of R&D resources) • Favoring alternative fuels and creating a platform dedicated to waste treatment (218 KT of alternative fuels) • Replacement of part of the basic materials with by-products from other industries (330 KT of alternative materials) • Establishment of an advanced metering system and equipping factories with water treatment plants • Rehabilitation of quarries after their exploitation (414 Ha rehabilitated and 300 000 trees planted)	• Support for 145 projects with 110,000 beneficiaries • Fight against school dropouts through the distribution of scholarships and school bags: 14,000 bags and 31,000 beneficiaries • Preparation and monitoring of skills development plans, both for its own needs and those of territorial actors (2300 beneficiaries) • Contribute to the opening up of certain villages by developing several roads and access routes. • Ensuring the development of employees' skills: 81% of employees have received training
SONASID	• All suppliers and subcontractors are subject to our convention compliance requirements • 90% of the company's electricity consumption is of renewable origin • reduction of greenhouse gas emissions by more than 200,000 t of CO_2/year • Obtained ISO 50001 certification for energy efficiency • Consumption of nearly one cubic meter of water per ton of steel produced • Implementation of semi-closed circuit water treatment plants • The activity is a manufacturing process based on recycling; nearly 50% of the needs are met locally. • Recycling and recovery of industrial waste: replacing up to 50% of fuel oil with used lubricating oils. • Valorization of 90% of the waste produced by the company	• Setting up weekly Safety Committees (SC) at the unit level and monthly at the site level • Monthly field audits and specific audits of the application and knowledge of the rules • Daily "OHS Minutes" with employees. • Development of team skills through training programs in collaboration with leading Moroccan engineering schools and management experts • Construction of school classes for disabled students • Renewal each year of the "Ramadan baskets" operation • Creation of a sewing and hairdressing room for illiterate women • Support for the development of the local entrepreneurial fabric

As seen from the table above, large companies integrate sustainability differently while accepting that financial indicators (triple bottom line economic dimension) occupy a predominant place.

Some of them privilege continuous actions of sustainability aiming at the reduction of the harmful and undesirable effects of their activity on the environment and society, such as the certification ISO 140001, the installation of ecological equipment and installations, the commissioning of waste management equipment's, the favoring of alternative materials, the establishment of rules of supplies and subcontracting linked to sustainability. Others are more oriented toward specific and temporary actions, signing partnership agreements with associations and non-governmental organizations, tree planting actions, support for local residents, and social actions to benefit staff.

Few companies have been able to provide quantified and objective indicators of their sustainable actions:

- Recovery, Recycling, and Valorisation of the waste produced
- % reduction of greenhouse gas emissions
- % of renewable origin of electricity consumption

CONCLUSION

The emergence of sustainable development and its declination at all strategic and operational levels has been accompanied by a profusion of research work dealing with the impact of the integration of sustainability on managerial practices. Thus, concepts of environmental accounting, green finance, environmental management control, responsible investment, etc., have emerged.

Effectively, the construction sector plays a vital role in Morocco. It contributed 6.2% to the total value added at current total value added at current prices and 21.3% to that of secondary activities between activities between 2008 and 2017. In addition, it employed more than one million people in 2017, or 9.8% of the employed population, of which 11.2% were in urban areas. in urban areas (MEF; 2020). But, it is also one of the most pollutant sectors and consumers of natural and energy resources, so sustainability is essential. Moreover, several countries have revised their construction regulations to consider the sector's negative effects on society and the environment.

As a result, construction project management practices should evolve to monitor that projects meet the time, cost, and technical quality requirements and ensure that the construction project is sustainable.

To do this, SMEs, like large companies, have an interest in integrating new construction project management practices and highlighting new performance indicators such as:

- Improving materials and waste management practices by introducing just-in-time production and privileging alternative inputs;
- Integrate alternative sustainable construction methods which are more efficient than traditional methods. For example, prefab and modular construction;
- Reducing rework and construction waste by implementing construction management software.

REFERENCES

Adeleke, A. Q., & … . (2019). Project Management Performance and Its Influence on Malaysian Building Projects, KnE. *Social Sciences*, 313–329.

Aguinis, H. (2009). *Performance Management* (2nd ed.). Prentice Hall/Pearson Education.

Araújo, C., Bragança, L., & Almeida, M. (2013). Sustainable construction key indicators. *IOP Conference Series. Materials Science and Engineering*, *660*(1), 505–512.

Ates, A., Garengo, P., Cocca, P., & Bititci, U. (2013). The development of SME managerial practice for effective performance management. *Journal of Small Business and Enterprise Development*, *20*(1), 28–54. doi:10.1108/14626001311298402

Atkinson, R. (1999). Project Management: Cost, Time and Quality, Two Best Guesses and a Phenomenon, It's Time to Accept Other Success Criteria. *International Journal of Project Management*, *17*(6), 337–342. doi:10.1016/S0263-7863(98)00069-6

Barbelivien D. (2014). *La structuration du système de pilotage de la performance au sein d'une ETI la différencie-t-elle de la PME? Le cas d'une ETI familiale du Grand Ouest*, [Working Papers]. hal-00934226, HAL

Bassioni, H. A., Price, A. D. F., & Hassan, T. M. (2005). Building a conceptual framework for measuring business performance in construction: An empirical evaluation. *Construction Management and Economics*, *23*(5), 495–507. doi:10.1080/0144619042000301401

Bessire, D. (1999). Définir la performance. *Comptabilité Contrôle Audit*, *5*(2), 127–150. doi:10.3917/cca.052.0127

Bourguignon, A. (2000). *Performance et contrôle de gestion. Encyclopédie de Comptabilité, Contrôle de gestion et Audit*. Ed. Economica.

Chan, A. P. C., Scott, D., & Chan, A. P. L. (2004). Factors affecting the success of a construction project. *Journal of Construction Engineering and Management*, *130*(1), 153–155. doi:10.1061/(ASCE)0733-9364(2004)130:1(153)

Cox, R. F., Issa, R. R. A., & Ahrens, D. (2003). Management's perception of key performance indicators for construction. *Journal of Construction Engineering and Management*, *129*(2), 142–151. doi:10.1061/(ASCE)0733-9364(2003)129:2(142)

D'Amboise, G., & Bakanibona, A. (1990). La planification dans les PME: une synthèse de résultats empiriques: conclusions et recommandations. *Revue internationale P.M. E (Norwalk, Conn.)*, *3*(2), 147–166.

Ehrenberg, A. (1991). *Le Culte de la performance*. Calmann-Lévy.

El Kington, J. (1997). *The triple Bottom Line: sustainability's accountants in Russo M. V. (2008), Environmental Management: Reading and cases* (2nd ed.). Sage.

Ezeldin, A. S., & Sharara, L. M. (2006). Neural Networks for Estimating the Productivity of Concreting Activities. *Journal of Construction Engineering and Management*, *132*(6), 650–656. doi:10.1061/(ASCE)0733-9364(2006)132:6(650)

Ezziadi, A., & Chachdi, A. (2021). Using of the Circularity Indicators in the Financial Communication of Listed Companies in the Construction Industry, *Journal of Economics. Finance and Management Studies*, *4*(6), 766–771.

Ezziadi, A., & Ouhadi, S. (2016). Les perceptions de la performance des PME marocaines. *Economie et société*, 16.

Ferreira, A., & Otley, D. (2009). The design and use of performance management systems: An extended framework for analysis. *Management Accounting Research*, *20*(4), 263–282. doi:10.1016/j.mar.2009.07.003

Fořt, J., & Černý, R. (2020). Transition to circular economy in the construction industry: Environmental aspects of waste brick recycling scenarios. *Waste Management (New York, N.Y.)*, *118*, 510–520. doi:10.1016/j.wasman.2020.09.004 PMID:32980730

Gauzente, C. (2000). Mesurer la performance des entreprises en l'absence d'indicateurs objectifs: Quelle validité? Analyse de la pertinence de certains indicateurs. *Revue Finance Contrôle Stratégie*, *3*(2), 145–165.

Hammer, J., & Pivo, G. (2016). The Triple Bottom Line and Sustainable Economic Development Theory and Practice. *Economic Development Quarterly*, *31*(1), 25–36.

Institut, IMANOR (2020). Guide développement durable dans la construction: Rôles des normes pour une meilleure assimilation des principes et pratiques de développement durable dans la construction. IMANOR.

Junaid, M. (2022). Effects of sustainable supply chain integration on green innovation and firm performance. *Sustainable Production and Consumption*, *30*, 145–157.

Kamali, M., & Hewage, K. (2017). Development of performance criteria for sustainability evaluation of modular versus conventional construction methods. *Journal of Cleaner Production*, *142*(4).

Khlif, W. (1998). *La Conception et la Mesure de Performance dans l'Industrie Hôtelière: Cas de Trois Entreprises Tunisienne, In la Gestion des Entreprises: Contextes et Performances, Actes du Colloques Organisé le 28, 29 et 30 Novembre 1996 par la Faculté des Sciences Economiques et de Gestion de Sfax*. Centre de Publication Universitaire.

Lebas, M. J. (1995). Performance Measurement and Performance Management. *International Journal of Production Economics*, *41*(1-3), 23–35. doi:10.1016/0925-5273(95)00081-X

Lim, C. S., & Mohamed, M. Z. (1999). Criteria of project success: An exploratory re-examination. *International Journal of Project Management*, *17*(4), 243–248. doi:10.1016/S0263-7863(98)00040-4

Lorino, P. (2003). *Méthodes et pratiques de la performance*. Collection Références.

Chidinma Maduekwe, C., & Kamala, P. (2016). Performance measurement by small and medium enterprises in Cape Metropolis, South Africa. *Problems and Perspectives in Management*, *14*(2), 46–55. doi:10.21511/ppm.14(2).2016.05

Magdalina, Z. (2021). *Adapting and Mitigating Environmental, Social, and Governance Risk in Business*. IGI Global.

Marmuse C. (1997). In Ed. Economica (Ed.), Performance in SIMON Y. & JOFFRE P. (sous la direction de): Encyclopédie de Gestion, 2, (pp. 2194–2207).

Marsden, C. (2000). The New Corporate Citizenship of Big Business: Part of the Solution to Sustainability? *Business and Society Review*, *105*(1), 9–25.

Meyssonnier, F. (2015). Quel contrôle de gestion pour les start-ups? *Comptabilité Contrôle Audit*, *21*, 33–61.

Ministère de l'économie et des finances. (2020). *Tableau de bord Sectoriel de l'année 2019*. Ministère de l'économie et des finances.

Ministère délégué chargé de l'environnement. (2016), *Plan sectoriel « Eco-Construction et bâtiment durable* . MDCE.

Ministry of Housing and Urban policy. (2020). *Immobilier 2020: Eléments de prospective*. Ministry of Housing and Urban policy. http://www.mhpv.gov.ma/?page_id=1168

Lloréns Montes, F. J., Verdú Jover, A., & Miguel Molina Fernández, L. (2003). Factors affecting the relationship between total quality management and organizational performance. *International Journal of Quality & Reliability Management*, *20*(2), 189–209. doi:10.1108/02656710310456617

Nivyintizo S. (1995), *Déterminants de performance dans le secteur du bâtiment et travaux publics: le cas des entreprises de construction du Burundi*. Mémoire de maîtrise, Université du Québec à Chicoutimi.

Otley, D. (1999). Performance management: A framework for management control systems research. *Management Accounting Research*, *10*(4), 363–382. doi:10.1006/mare.1999.0115

Parthiban, P., & Goh, M. (2011). An integrated model for performance management of manufacturing units. *Benchmarking*, *18*(2), 261–281. doi:10.1108/14635771111121702

PWC. (2018). *Innovation et BTP: la transformation du secteur est en marche*. PWC. www.pwc.fr

Sadeq H. (2013), Les programmes d'appui à la PME. Publications de l'IRES, p. 32

Salgado M. (2013). *La performance: une dimension fondamentale pour l'évaluation des entreprises et des organisations*. hal-00842219

Savitz, A. (2013). *Talent, Transformation, and the Triple Bottom Line: How Companies Can Leverage Human Resources to Achieve Sustainable Growth*. John Wiley & Sons.

Savitz, A. W. (2013). *The Triple Bottom Line: How Today's Best-Run Companies Are Achieving Economic, Social and Environmental Success - and How You Can Too*. John Wiley & Sons.

Šelih, J. (2007). Environmental management systems and construction SMES: A case study for Slovenia. *Journal of Civil Engineering and Management, 13*(3), 217–226. doi:10.3846/13923730.2007.9636440

St-Pierre, J., & Cadieux, L. (2011). La conception de la performance: Quels liens avec le profil entrepreneurial des propriétaires dirigeants de PME? *Revue de l'Entrepreneuriat, 10*, 33–52.

Toor, S.-R., & Ogunlana, S. O. (2010). Beyond the 'iron triangle': Stakeholder perception of key performance indicators (KPIs) for large-scale public sector development projects. *International Journal of Project Management, 28*(3), 228–236. doi:10.1016/j.ijproman.2009.05.005

Toor, S.-R., & Ogunlana, S. O. (2008). Critical COMs of success in large-scale construction projects: Evidence from Thailand construction industry. *International Journal of Project Management, 26*(4), 420–430. doi:10.1016/j.ijproman.2007.08.003

Tripathi, K. K., & Jha, K. N. (2018). An empirical study on performance measurement factors for construction organizations. *KSCE Journal of Civil Engineering, 22*(4), 1052–1066. doi:10.100712205-017-1892-z

Tripathi, K.K., & Jha, K.N. (2018). Determining success factors for a construction organization: A structural equation modeling approach. *Journal of Management Engineering, 34*(1), 1–15.

United Nations Environment Programme. (2021). *Global Status report for building and construction*.

Wang, X., & Huang, J. (2006). The relationships between key stakeholders ' project performance and project success: Perceptions of Chinese construction supervising engineers. *International Journal of Project Management, 24*(3), 253–260. doi:10.1016/j.ijproman.2005.11.006

World Commission on Environment and Development. (1987). Our Common Future, United Nations. WCED.

Chapter 8
Assessing the Impact of Financial Performance on the Entrepreneurship Dynamic for Social and Economic Development in Businesses:
A Case Study of the Marrakech-Safi Region

Mohamed Wadie Lahouirich
Polydisciplinary Faculty of Sidi Bennour, Chouaïb Doukkali University, Morocco

Abdelali Ezziadi
Polydisciplinary Faculty of Sidi Bennour, Chouaïb Doukkali University, Morocco

ABSTRACT

Considering the weight of SMEs on an international scale, mainly in times of crisis, entrepreneurship becomes an important factor for achieving economic and social development that meets the demands of society. However, entrepreneurship requires motivations and implies objectives, and especially a financial performance, which will play the role of vector for entrepreneurship, and by extension for socio-economic development. In other words, it is about connecting 3 concepts: Financial performance, entrepreneurship, and socio-economic development. For that, this paper will first focus on the motivations and objectives of entrepreneurs, before developing in detail the concept of financial performance, its evolution to the sustainable development, as well as its importance in the entrepreneurial environment, as vector and objective.

DOI: 10.4018/978-1-6684-4834-2.ch008

INTRODUCTION

Since the signing of Agenda 21 by 173 countries at the Earth Summit of Rio in 1992, sustainable development has become a priority and an opportunity to reconcile business and strategic issues, whether individual or collective. In addition, the adoption of resolution 73/225 by the General Assembly of the United Nations in December 2018 about entrepreneurship for sustainable development gave rise to many reports and studies linking entrepreneurship as a vector for the creation of jobs, promoting economic growth, improving the social conditions and resolving social and environmental problems in society. However, the advent of the COVID-19 pandemic has led to a decline in the global economy. The International Labor Organization (ILO) estimates job losses between 5 and 25 million jobs, with labor income falling between 860 billion and 3.4 trillion dollars. In addition, some alarming forecasts point to 70 million people who will fall back into extreme poverty with the pandemic (Mahler and al., 2020). Because VSEs and SMEs are the sources of 2/3 jobs worldwide, and the fact that job losses recorded with the pandemic of COVID-19 would be oriented towards entrepreneurship, thus absorbing the challenges of society and contributing to the achievement of the objectives of sustainable development, we note that entrepreneurship and VSE/SME play an essential and preponderant role in the social and economic development of nations. But this role should be put into an upstream perspective concerning the sustainability of companies, which is strongly impacted by performance.

Indeed, performance is at the center of SME strategy, whatever the phase of its life cycle and size, since it represents a triggering factor for the act of entrepreneurship, the sustainability of companies, and territorial development. However, the concept of performance is still debated because it is polysemous and sometimes even subjective. Indeed, performance can range from simple economic growth to achieving Sustainable Development Goals, including job creation and profit. Whatever meaning we give to performance, it is clear that the financial dimension is omnipresent in the entrepreneurial process and all its phases. Indeed, any entrepreneurial approach involves the mobilization of financial resources and automatically includes a financial dimension. Barneto and Verstraete (2008) mention that the financial question is part of the daily life of entrepreneurship and goes beyond project financing to cover a broader spectrum in the entrepreneur's everyday life. Faced with this omnipresence of both performance and the financial question in the daily life of entrepreneurs and considering the objectives of sustainable development, several questions deserve to be asked. First, what are the objectives and motivations of entrepreneurs? Second, what triggers the entrepreneurial process? Third, how can we determine financial performance? Fourth, what is the relationship between financial performance and entrepreneurship? Finally, how can entrepreneurship, in its quest for financial performance, contribute to achieving more global objectives, namely the Sustainable Development Goals?

MOTIVATIONS AND OBJECTIVES OF ENTREPRENEURS

Entrepreneurship designates the action of the undertaking, carrying out a project; it is a process of discovery, evaluation, and exploitation, so we can say that entrepreneurship is the fact of carrying out an activity.

Entrepreneurial Motivations

The study of entrepreneurial motivations amounts to determining the factors influencing the entrepreneurial approach of individuals. It is, therefore, a question of understanding the entrepreneurial activity upstream and determining the elements triggering the entrepreneurial process. Several authors have looked at the facts that trigger entrepreneurship. For example, Gabarret and Vedel (2012) propose two visions called "pull" and "push." First, it is a positive fact that triggers the entrepreneurial process (business opportunity, improved income, or the desire to evolve socially, etc.). The second, that is to say, push, is a negative fact that triggers the entrepreneurial process (loss of employment, loss of income, salary frustrations, etc.). Based on the contribution of Gabarret and Vedel (2012), it is possible to deduce that the financial performance of the economic actors in place can motivate and encourage an entrepreneur to start a business.

On the other hand, Julien and Marchesnay (1996) are interested in the motivations of individuals and evoke the theory of triggers, which is based on individual, family, social or organizational factors. According to the authors (Julien and Marchesnay), the action of entrepreneurship can emanate from the individual's own skills or the will to follow in the footsteps of someone whom he considers an example and who has succeeded in his entrepreneurial experience. In other words, the trigger for the action to be taken could be observing a third-party entrepreneur's good financial or non-financial performance. For their part, Wiklund and al. (2005) and LeCornu and al. (1996) mention the specific case of SMEs and conclude in their respective studies that financial and non-financial motivations are on the top list of factors that triggered their entrepreneurial action. Moreover, economic rationality, resulting from observation or not, dictated their choice to start businesses.

Objectives of the Managing Entrepreneur

Without going into the general debate relating to values, training, and experience, we will focus instead on the conception of the performance of the entrepreneur-manager. We will admit the limits of this approach which will not consider certain contingents factors. In doing so, and based on the results of several empirical studies such as those of Cliff (1998), Baum and Locke (2004), Morris and al. (2006), or Reijonen and Komppula (2007), we can say that the managing entrepreneur pays particular attention to the growth of his business while seeking several types of performance:

- Personal performance: Aiming for social recognition, financial independence, and building personal wealth.

Table 1. Listing of the main personal objectives of managing entrepreneurs

Personal Objectives	Authors
Financial security	St-Pierre and Cadieux (2011), Raymond and al. (2013)
Quality of life	Reijonen and Komppula (2007), Raymond and al. (2013)
Independence	Morris and al. (2006), Cassar (2007), Raymond and al. (2013)
Personal assets and wealth	St-Pierre and Cadieux (2011), Raymond and al. (2013)

- The economic performance integrates the company's growth, profit, performance, and financial autonomy.

Table 2: Listing of the main economic objectives of managing entrepreneurs

Economic Objectives	Authors
Growth and turnover	St-Pierre and Cadieux (2011), Raymond and al. (2013)
Financial performance	LeCornu and al. (1996), St-Pierre and Cadieux (2011), Raymond and al. (2013)
Dividend and profitability	LeCornu and al. (1996),

- Sustainable performance: This takes into account the creation of jobs, the reputation of the company, and other societal and environmental considerations.

Table 3. Listing of the main sustainable objectives of managing entrepreneurs

Sustainable Objectives	Authors
Creation of jobs	Westhead and Wright (1999), Gets and Petersen (2005), St-Pierre and Cadieux (2011).
Ethics and reputation	Cohen and al. (2006), St-Pierre and Cadieux (2011).
Respect the environment	Cohen and al. (2006), Choi and Gray (2008), St-Pierre and Cadieux (2011).

The various studies relating to the motivations and objectives of managing entrepreneurs provided ample information on either upstream or downstream performance, i.e., the performance of economic actors already in place as a triggering factor for the entrepreneurial process, but also the performance as a goal and expected objective. To fully understand the link between financial performance, entrepreneurship, and sustainable development, it is, therefore, necessary to first focus on the outlines of the concept of performance.

CONCEPTUAL FRAMEWORK OF PERFORMANCE

Generally, any entrepreneur or owner-manager pursues a quest for performance. The empirical work of Smith and al. (2000) or Ondoua et al. (2008) highlights the relationship between performance and entrepreneurial behavior and demonstrates a strong positive correlation between the two variables.

Origins of Performance

Dealing with a notion as complex as performance refers to its historical origins. Pesqueux (2004) dwells on the epistemology of the word performance, recalling that it derives from the word performer, which, in the 13th century, meant "to accomplish and execute." This word appears in the 15th century in English with to perform, which means the accomplishment of a process or a task with the resulting results and the success that can be attributed to it.Guenoun (2009) offers another semantic approach to the word performance, combining two possible meanings. The first, based on the French origin of performance, defines it as the process of forming perfection (Aubert, 2006), a word with which it shares its prefix "per," "formance" in turn refers to the idea of a "process in the process of formation." The second acceptance comes from the English origin and refers to the conduct of action and achieving objectives (Lorino, 2003). From these two acceptances arise two semantic definitions, the first is that performance is the search for something that cannot be improved, and the second is that performance is the carrying out of action. Performance is not a concept exclusive to organizations. As such, Pesqueux (2004) highlights the difficulty of understanding the concept of performance due to its polysemous nature and proposes some applications of the word performance in specific fields. Through the application of the word performance in several areas, Pesqueux (2004) concludes that the latter is a "catch-all" since this concept refers to two essential elements, namely the action and the result.

Performance as Seen by Entrepreneurs

The question of absolute performance is widely raised in the literature, through its multiple dimensions and facets, with all this concept implies in terms of confusion and lack of unanimity. But when it comes to performance as perceived by entrepreneurs or start-ups, there isn't much work and research. First, performance is a wide-ranging concept that captures the interest of both researchers and professionals. Defining it means consulting many research works, each offering a distinct definition. For Bourguignon (1997), performance is a sum of 3 primary senses. Success represents the result of the action, which means the evaluation of the results obtained without value judgment, and the action which represents the process and not only a result obtained at a given moment. Marchesnay (1991) considers performance as the degree of achievement of an objective and believes that it depends on the triptych effectiveness, efficiency, and effectiveness, representing the ability to achieve results and optimize resources. The satisfaction was ultimately obtained thanks to the results. The literature offers wide coverage of the concept of performance, with definitions that sometimes resemble each other but differ at other times. And if the definition of performance is consistent, so is its measurement.

Performance Measurement

When we discuss measuring performance, this supposes establishing indicators for evaluating it to assess the results of action according to a certain methodology. Concretely, this involves collecting information relating to the action, its objectives, and its results, then compiling and cross-referencing them to analyze them, interpret them, and give them meaning and value. According to Bouckaert and Halligan (2008), any element related to performance reflects a distinct level of reality but mainly reflects a non-neutrality that makes understanding the concept and its derivatives complex.Briefly, Pesqueux (2004) defines performance indicators according to their relevance and contributions. In other words, he does not propose to limit it to the simple objective evaluation of a phenomenon. Still, he adds that it is imperative to consider the context and the nature of the phenomenon object of the assessment. For this, the author proposes three relevance criteria that each measurement indicator must have. First is operational relevance, which considers the indicator's process and difficulty level; then strategic relevance, which compares the objectives and results; and finally, cognitive relevance, which allows the understanding and interpretation of the indicator. Unfortunately, the literature does not show a consensus on performance measurement indicators. Still, Stiglitz et al. (2009) consider performance evaluation a good and very useful exercise, which can federate opinions and avoid situations of blockage in the apprehension of performance.

Financial Performance

Historically, performance has been apprehended according to quantitative and financial logic (Walker and Brown, 2004) for several decades. However, it is essential to point out that the predominance of financial performance is not monopolistic but rather stems from the overlap between several quantitative performance measurement indicators, which are mainly linked or attached to financial performance. For example, Ittner and Larcker (1999) and Banker et al. (2000) use economic performance as an example, which is only an anticipated financial performance. The predominance of financial indicators for measuring performance encourages tracing their evolution over time. One of the first financial indicators for measuring performance is the Return On Investment (ROI), which has been so successful that it has been generalized in several companies. This success has given rise to a significant development of indicators for measuring financial performance, as evidenced by the emergence of Return On Equity (ROE) or Return On Net Asset (RONA). Lorino believes that if performance is essentially economic, then it is assimilated to the net creation of wealth, making it a quantitative performance. This quantitative aspect refers to the work of Ampuero and al. (1998), who were interested in measuring performance, highlighting some of the quantitative literature that is based not only on accounting and financial data but also on other information from the market. The literature work of Ampuero and al. traces a good number of indicators and performance evaluation models from the 1920s to the 1990s.

The work of Ampuero and al. represent the basis of the representation of indicators for measuring financial performance since, in addition to tracing the evolution of indicators, they consider that the measurement of performance is similar to the ex-post evaluation of the results obtained, which refers to monitoring and measuring results. For this reason, these authors emphasize a panoply of indicators such as ROI, ROE, and ROIC and defend the thesis that they represent an excellent way to measure financial performance.

Figure 1. Time evolution of performance measurement.
Source: Ampuero and al., 1998.

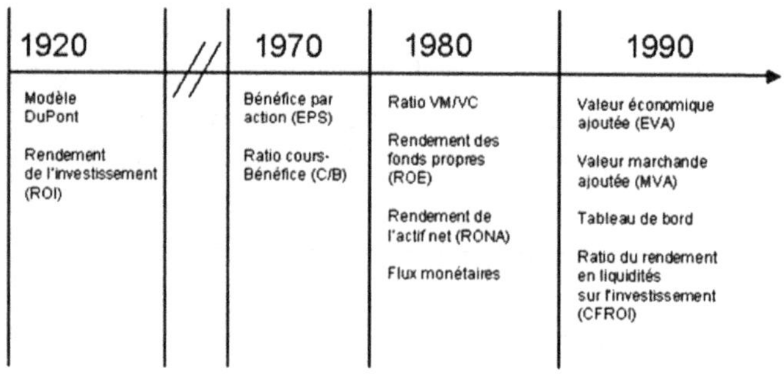

Critics of Financial Performance Measurement Indicators

Since the 1980s, several authors have criticized performance measurement indicators based on accounting and financial data. These authors argue that this type of indicator is susceptible to accounting manipulation by company managers and therefore risks biasing the real performance of companies. For example, Lahouirich and al. (2022), Lahouirich (2021) or Kennerly and Neely (2003) believe that the financial statements of companies reflect the historical situation of the company and not its future prospects, while the evaluation of the performance of the company does not depend only of its past achievements but also of its future prospects and its projected cash flows. Thus, Lahouirich and Ouhadi (2017) mention that market-oriented and investor perception indicators are more relevant for evaluating the financial performance of companies, in particular Economic Value Added (EVA), Market to Book (M/B) or the Market Value Added (MVA).

Financial Performance in Entrepreneurship

The keen interest in financial performance is not new, and its importance in the entrepreneurial sphere is well established. Indeed, all levels of the entrepreneurial process evoke the financial question, either directly or indirectly. Thus, Rédis and Paré (2008) propose a diagram of the different stages of the entrepreneurial process and their main prerequisites, which are as follows:

According to the authors (Rédis and Paré), the financial question arises in all stages of the entrepreneurial process. In the pre-creation phase, an entrepreneur must have a minimum of knowledge and skills in finance, both for the launch of his business and for the financial support and planning of his project. In the creation phase, the entrepreneur attaches importance to the financial evaluation and to the various financing methods of his company, which implies the integration of the financial evaluation and the follow-up in his entrepreneurial approach. Finally, in the post-creation phase, the entrepreneur performs financial management of his business and monitors performance to ensure the sustainability and development of his business. Thus, we notice that the financial question is omnipresent in the entrepreneurial sphere, giving rise to a new concept: entrepreneurial finance. Indeed, the development of entrepreneurship imperatively requires the implementation of new financial specificities adapted to entrepreneurs.

Figure 2. Stages of entrepreneurial process.
Source: Adapted from Rédis and Paré (2008)

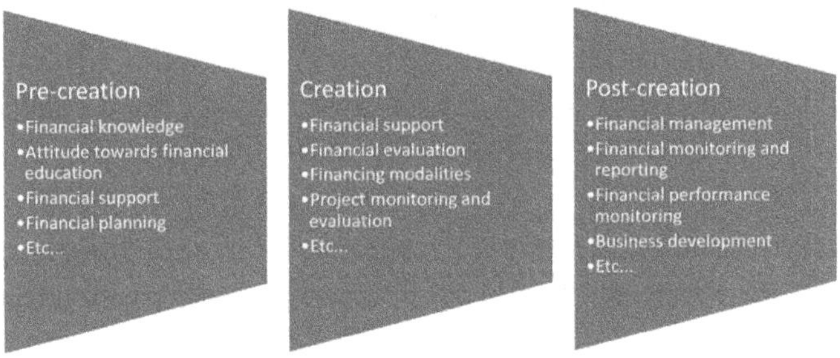

Entrepreneurial Finance and SMEs

Rédis (2009) defines entrepreneurial finance as the set of relationships between the entrepreneur and the financial sphere, with all that this implies in terms of specificity. Paré and Demerens (2011) consider that finance intended for SMEs and business leaders is quite distinct from that of large groups and their shareholders. They argue that it is necessary to distinguish between entrepreneurial finance and traditional finance. This observation is rooted in the financial objectives and the separation between ownership and management of companies. Indeed, in SMEs, the company is an extension of the person of the entrepreneur, which implies confusion between ownership and management as the same person carries out the two functions. Similarly, the objectives of a managing entrepreneur are not oriented exclusively towards the maximization of projects but extend towards sustainability and the minimization of risks.

THE GENESIS OF CSR AND SUSTAINABLE DEVELOPMENT ORIENTATION

The Emergence of CSR in Business

According to Spence and al. (2007), the concept of CSR is the managerial translation of sustainable development. This concept is closely linked to certain concepts such as ethics, commitment, deontology, or even morality. The connection of these concepts makes it difficult to determine the exact date of its genesis. Indeed, several writings exist, inspired in particular by religions, and implicitly deal with the exercise of any power with ethics and deontology to serve the community and ensure its well-being. However, among the first scientific works, Abrams (1951) and Bowen (1953) highlighted the notion of CSR. Bowen (1953), in his book "Social Responsibilities of Businessman," was the first to have built a theoretical model of CSR. This author, who deals with the American context, points the finger at large companies through the influences they exert on the lives of the population through the conduct of their activities.

Bowen believes that corporations have not only an economic responsibility to themselves and their shareholders but also a responsibility to the community. He defines CSR as follows: "*CSR refers to the obligation of businessmen to implement policies, make decisions and follow courses of action that meet the objectives and values considered desirable by our society.* "The vision and contribution of Bowen (1953) represent a notable evolution in the field of management since it allowed the introduction of several dimensions that were historically disconnected and absent from the business world. Since then, work has contributed to developing the concept of CSR. Therefore, as we deal with financial and non-financial performance, we propose to go around the idea of CSR without pretending to trace the exhaustiveness of the works that contributed to its development. For Davis (1966), companies must make decisions that promote the community's well-being. The author believes that companies are like any other citizen and must act fairly and responsibly. The author says that "*CSR refers to the obligation of leaders to consider the effects of their actions on the social or societal system as a whole. These managers apply CSR when considering that the firm's actions are likely to affect other people's interests. Thus, they must look beyond their firm's economic and technical interests*".For Johnson (1971), CSR reflects the ability of the company to find the right balance between its own interests and those of the various actors. The author is based on the work of Davis (1966) and defines CSR as "*the pursuit of socio-economic objectives through the development of particular social norms enabling the business world to respond to particular situations.*" Johnson's major contribution lies in the integration of the notion of long-term profit into the concept of CSR. Indeed, the author believes that companies that adopt societal programs expect a return on investment that materializes in long-term profit. Abrams, Bowen, Davis, and Johnson have contributed to the CSR concept's emergence and development. Still, the most popular work remains that of Carroll (1979) since he was the first to have linked the CSR concept with corporate social performance. According to the author, "*CSR covers the economic, legal, ethical and discretionary expectations of society at a given moment*." The definition provided by Carroll reflects the ethical and moral behavior of the company, expected by society, even if the latter is not the subject of any regulation or law. In other words, this ethical behavior results from a voluntary approach by company managers to meet society's expectations. The contribution of Carroll (1979) was followed by several works dealing with the notion of CSR, giving rise to several related concepts such as societal performance, societal sensitivity, business ethics, etc.

Conceptual Approaches to CSR

The concept of CSR has greatly evolved over time and continues to evolve until today. Historically, we identify three conceptions of this notion. First, a design reflects a voluntary approach and a philanthropic dimension emanating from business managers to promote certain values and ethics in business. In this conception, companies are players with rights and obligations toward third parties, but CSR actions are considered outside the company's scope. That is to say that they are not part of the company's normal activity. Still, as they come from a voluntary approach, the main objective is to repair any damage caused by normal activity by creating and financing foundations and other charitable actions. According to Capron (2008), the voluntary and philanthropic conception of CSR is a means of justifying, legitimizing, and correcting the impacts of the economic activity of companies.

Then, we find the strategic-utilitarian conception, which stipulates that CSR actions promote companies' economic and financial performance. According to this conception, socially responsible companies do not struggle to achieve their economic and financial performance insofar as they manage to align the interests of their stakeholders with their own interests. For Capron and Quairel (2004), this conception was born in Europe and is the result of the dialogue maintained between companies and their stakeholders, particularly the unions, which makes it possible to regulate and federate the interests of the various stakeholders.

Finally, the managerial conception is oriented toward sustainable development. Although this is the most recent conception, the proponents stipulate that the company's prosperity depends on its environment. If the latter is healthy, then she can maximize her long-term interests. For Capron and Quairel (2004), companies that subscribe to this concept take social and environmental concerns into account in their management, focusing on prevention and anticipating the expectations of their stakeholders.

Even if these three conceptions result from an evolution of the CSR concept, we find them all in the field. Indeed, the first approach is ubiquitous in developing countries, the second greatly affects Anglo-Saxon companies, and the third is mainly distributed in Europe and Asia. What we can learn from these three approaches is the voluntary aspect and the mandatory aspect. The first aspect reflects a logic of corporate commitment, while the second reflects a binding aspect for them.

Dimensions of CSR

CSR, whether approached through a voluntary or mandatory approach, involves a certain number of responsibilities on the part of companies. Carroll (1979) identifies four categories of responsibilities that the company must observe for it to qualify as socially responsible:

- **Economic responsibility**: The primary vocation of a company is to make profits and meet the profitability requirements of its shareholders. Therefore, this requires the production of goods and services in compliance with quality and safety standards to guarantee the satisfaction of all stakeholders.
- **Legal responsibility**: In addition to the repressive aspect, companies must respect the law and regulations.
- **Ethical responsibility**: The author defines the ethical responsibility of companies as being a voluntary approach on their part, even in the absence of a regulatory and legal framework, aimed at promoting ethics in the conduct of normal business activities.
- **Discretionary or philanthropic responsibility**: These are charitable actions carried out by the company.

The categorization operated by Carroll (1979) greatly contributed to the development of the CSR concept. Moreover, it represented the basis for several other works, including that of Wood (1991), which proposes three categories of social responsibilities:

- **Institutional legitimacy**: The Company, as an economic actor and legal entity, have certain rights and prerogatives granted by society. The author believes that the company must use its prerogatives in such a way as to respond favorably to the expectations of society. Otherwise, the company risks losing its legitimacy and thereby jeopardizing its existence.

- **Organizational public responsibility**: Every action leads to a reaction. Based on this observation, companies have a public responsibility because their actions have consequences for their stakeholders, whether primary/ direct or secondary/indirect.
- **Individual managerial discretion**: As a company representative responsible for operationalizing and implementing the company's strategy, the company's manager must use his discretionary power and act ethically to promote the interests of all stakeholders.

It is clear that Wood's contribution is at no time contradictory to that of Carroll, but we note a certain complementarity between the two works. A complementarity, which was also underlined and treated in detail by Attarça and Jacquot (2005), who set up a reading grid grouping together the two works cited above, and which they present as follows:

Table 4. Levels and dimensions of CSR

	Institutional Level	Organizational Level	Individual Level
Economic responsibilities	Produce goods and services, provide jobs, create wealth for shareholders	The prices of goods and services reflect the true costs of production and include all externalities	Produce ecologically, using non-polluting technologies, reduce costs by promoting recycling
Legal Responsibilities	Comply with laws and regulations. Do not lobby or wait for privileged positions in public policy	Work for public policy by defending enlightened interests	Take advantage of regulatory instructions to innovate in products or technologies
Ethical responsibilities	Follow fundamental ethical principles	Provide accurate and complete information to increase the safety of use beyond legal requirements	Develop use information for specific users and promote it as a product benefit
Discretionary Responsibilities	Act as a model citizen in all areas: Beyond regulations and ethical rules. Return part of the turnover to the community	Invest company resources in charitable actions related to the first and second circles of the company's social environment	Choose charitable investments that are profitable in terms of social problem solving

Source: Attarça and Jacquot (2005)

CSR as a Tool to Achieve Sustainability

According to Bouquin (2004), the classic approach to performance is based mainly on a short-term economic system that measures the profitability of the funds invested in the company. Introducing new concepts drawn from CSR enriches the debate around performance through several questions on the dimensions to be integrated to evaluate and measure performance. The response provided by Gomez (2001) evokes sustainable development and the link between generations. According to the author, sustainable development "*is not only respect for the environment...it is also the assurance given to today's generations of shareholders that companies will be sufficiently sustainable to benefit from the fruits of their savings. It is, therefore, the assurance that the strategies are not blows and that the company is managed seriously over the long term.* ". As a result, the concept of global performance is closely linked to the notion of sustainable development. Castelnau and Nöel (2004) insist on the long-term vision of performance and the integration of the notion of sustainable development. The authors believe that it cannot be achieved without considering the dimensions drawn from CSR. Thus, the evolution of the concept of performance, which was initially based on the financial dimension, to which the literature has added other CSR dimensions, gradually led to the idea of global performance.

According to Douhou and Berland (2007), global performance is, first and foremost, a social convention involving three actors: the company, its managers, and its stakeholders. The authors justify this postulate through three elements:

- Global performance only makes sense if the three players mentioned above adhere to CSR and sustainable development principles. In other words, the overall performance, which results from the company's actions and decisions, can only be achieved if the various stakeholders (shareholders, employees, customers, suppliers, State, etc.) consider them normal.
- Global performance acts as a means of raising awareness and federating stakeholders' interests with the company's interests, the latter already integrating concerns oriented toward sustainable development.
- Global performance implies the participation of all actors in compliance with Lewis' five conditions, namely:
    - Each actor complies with the convention
    - Each actor expects everyone to comply
    - Each actor prefers general compliance
    - The existence of an alternative regularity
    - The first four conditions are commonly known and accepted by the actors

For Germain and Trébucq (2004), the performance combines financial, social, and societal performance. Several authors support this definition, such as Capron and Quairel (2006), who believe that global performance is a tool for evaluating, measuring, and implementing strategies oriented toward sustainable development.

Nevertheless, global performance comes up with the same difficulties linked to the concept of performance and PSE, namely the polysemous nature and the integration and operationalization of several dimensions. As such, some authors have attempted to simplify the concept of global performance on the operational level to facilitate its understanding. For example, Reynaud (2003) suggests breaking global performance down into economic, socio-environmental, or societal performance.

Measuring Sustainable Development

The Global Reporting Initiative (GRI), in its guideline for sustainable development reporting, proposes to measure global performance based on the axes of sustainable development by suggesting certain indicators:

Table 5. Examples of sustainable development indicators 1

Categories of Indicators	Examples of Core Indicators
Economic performance indicators	- Turnover - Net profit - Total wages and benefits paid - Payments to capital providers - Taxes paid
Environmental performance indicators	- Consumption of raw materials - Water consumption - Energy consumption - Waste generated by production - Greenhouse gas emissions
Social performance indicators	- Distribution of the workforce by region, gender, by type of contract - Net job creation per financial year - Workplace accidents, absenteeism rate - Number of hours of training per person and per exercise

Source: Global Reporting Initiative (2001)

For their part, Callens and Tyteca (1999) introduce the time dimension to sustainable development indicators. They believe that the quest for global performance is primarily a question of efficiency rather than effectiveness while keeping the company's social responsibility in mind. They, therefore, propose the following indicators:

Faced with the great diversity that characterizes the notion of performance, researchers, like professionals, apprehend this concept out of opportunism to meet their objectives. However, the fact remains that this diversity represents an asset in the field of research since it places performance in an evolving and timeless framework.

Table 6. Examples of sustainable development indicators 2

Component	Short Term	Long Term
Economic	- Turnover - Added value - Quantities produced - Raw materials - Energy consumed	- Profitability - Competitiveness - Market shares - Product durability
Social	- Employment, wages - Work intensity - Productivity - Risk of accident - Noises smells	- Well-being, level of education - Availability of resources - Size of the company - Staff turnover rate
Environmental	- Natural Resources - Waste, pollution, emissions - Modes and distances of transport	- Global impacts - Landscape impact - Closure of the industrial system - Dematerialization

Source: Callens and Tyteca (1999)

THEORETICAL MODEL: ENTREPRENEURSHIP, SMES, AND SUSTAINABLE DEVELOPMENT

This research work seeks to establish links between financial performance, entrepreneurial dynamics, and sustainable development. To do this, we made two hypotheses. For our first hypothesis, we assume that the historical financial performance achieved by established companies can influence new entrepreneurs and positively impact entrepreneurial dynamics. For our second hypothesis, we estimate that the entrepreneurial dynamic recorded in a region will positively impact macro magnitudes concerning sustainable development, in this case, measured by average employment and job creation.

Figure 3.
Source: established by the authors

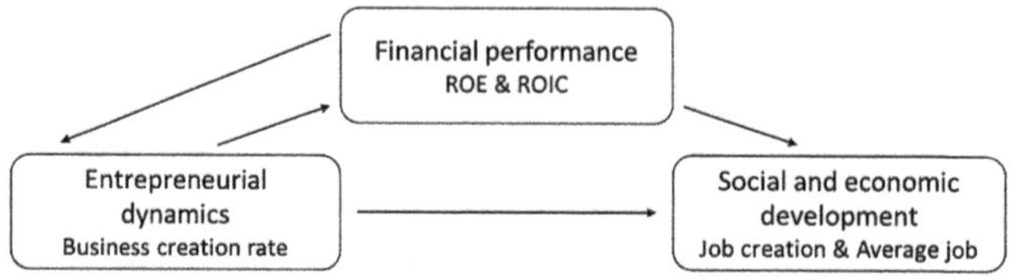

METHODOLOGY

This paper aims firstly to study the cause-and-effect relationships between the financial performance of companies and the entrepreneurial dynamics at the level of the Marrakech – Safi region. In other words, the objective is to determine whether companies' historical financial performance can directly or indirectly impact entrepreneurial dynamics. The ROE and the ROIC measure the historical financial performance from 2017 to 2019 of all the companies listed in the Marrakech – Safi region. The evolution of entrepreneurial dynamics is determined by the rate of business creation from 2020 to 2021. Secondly, this paper aims to study the contribution of entrepreneurship in the socio-economic development of the Marrakech – Safi region through the linking of the entrepreneurial dynamics of the region as well as the evolution of its macro magnitudes reflecting the progress made in terms of socio-economic development. To do this, we were interested in comparing the evolution of business creation with the evolution of job creation at the level of the Marrakech – Safi region, based on data communicated by the Social Security Fund (CNSS), but also through the employment of investment projects approved by the Unified Regional Investment Commission.

Figure 4. Distribution by Turnover.
Source: established by the authors from OMPIC's Database

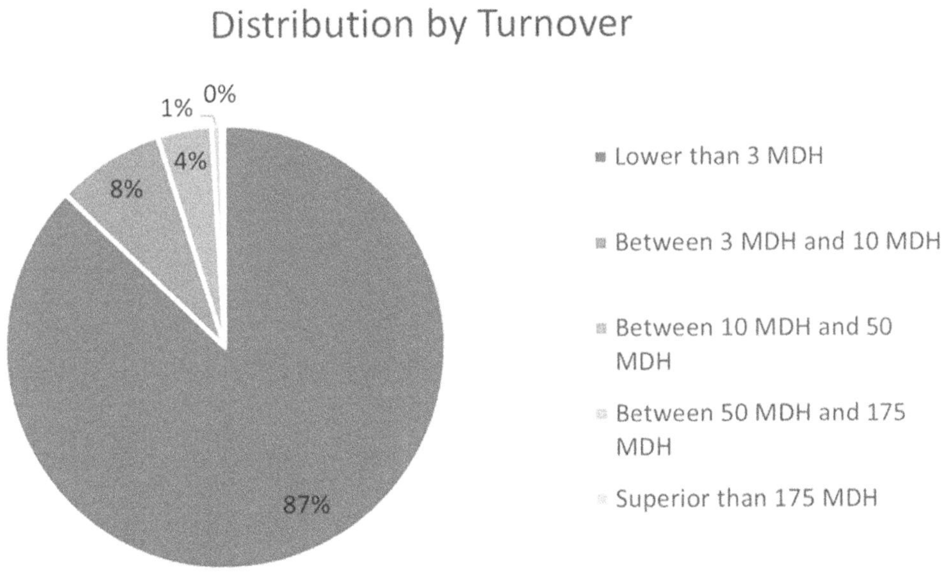

RESULTS

Profile of Companies in the Marrakech – Safi Region

Company Size by Turnover

The Marrakech – Safi region is dominated by the presence of SMEs, with 87% of companies having a turnover of fewer than 3 million dirhams. Companies with a turnover of more than 175 million dirhams represent barely 0.2%.

Figure 5. Distribution by Age.
Source: established by the authors from OMPIC's Database

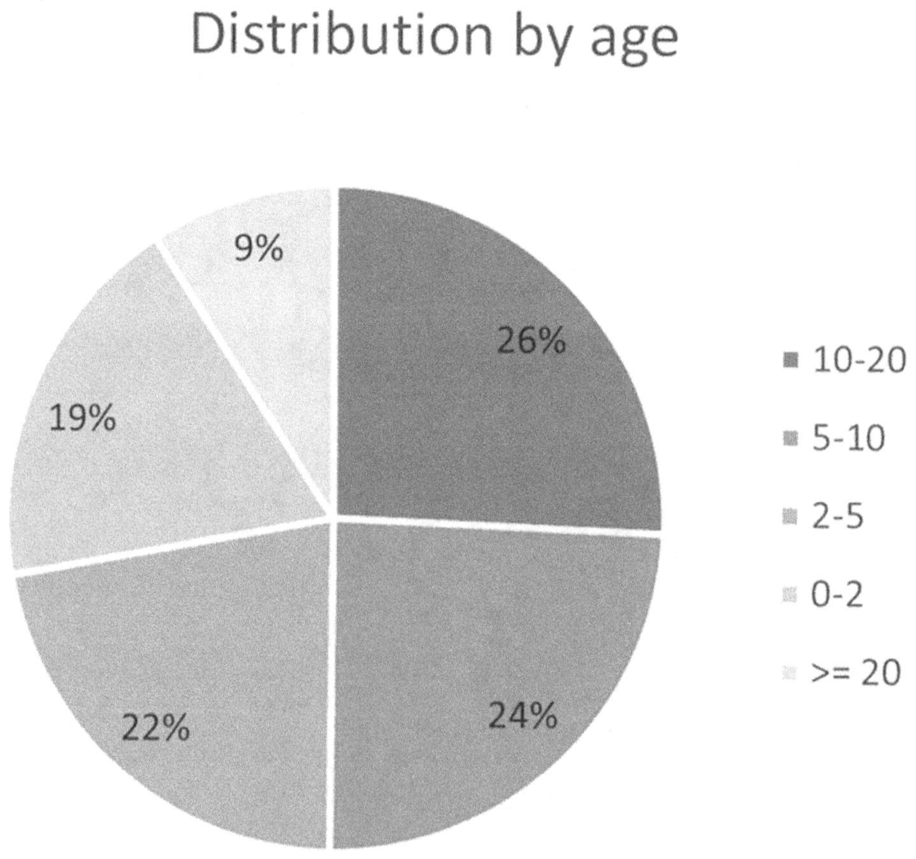

Age of Companies

9% of companies in the Marrakech – Safi region are more than 20 years old, compared to 19%, which are less than two years old. Between these two extremes, companies display a more or less similar distribution.

Legal Form

More than 95% of regional companies have opted for the limited liability form. The other legal forms remain marginal in the distribution of companies.

Figure 6. Legal from Distribution of companies in the Marrakech – Safi Region.
Source: established by the authors from OMPIC's Database

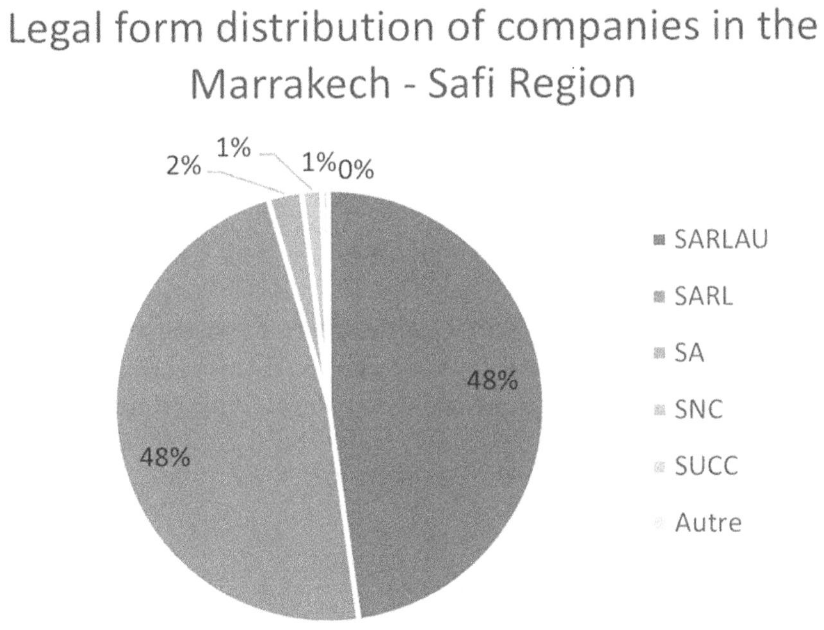

Sectorial Distribution

The economy of the Marrakech – Safi is dominated by commercial activity since it represents more than 40%. Followed by the construction and real estate sector, then services. The industrial sector represents barely 8% of the region's economy.

Figure 7. Sectorial Distribution of companies in the Marrakech – Safi Region.
Source: established by the authors from OMPIC's Database

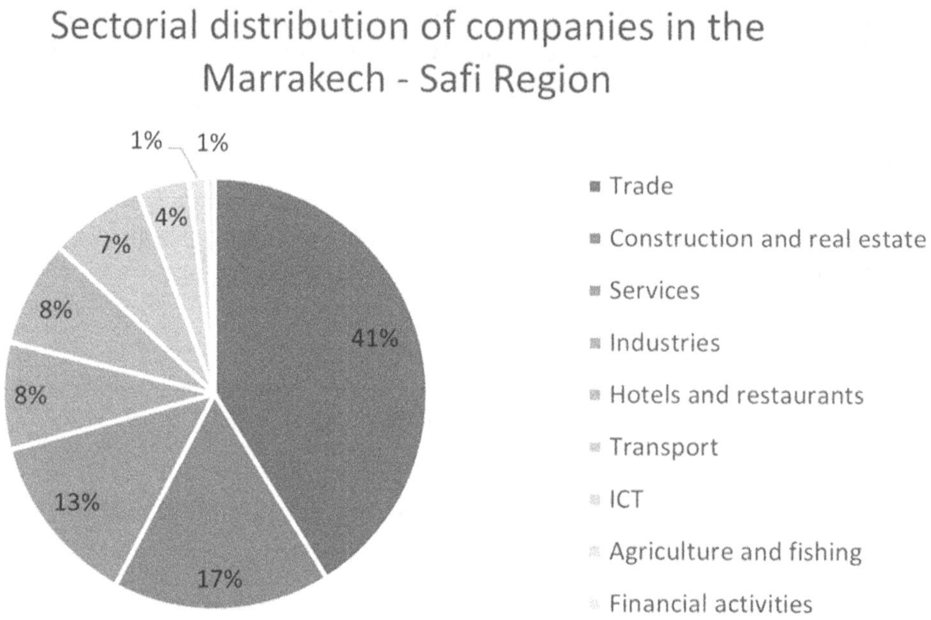

Typical Profile Dominating the Marrakech – Safi Region

From the data presented above, we find that the most represented company profile in the region is a young SME oriented towards commercial activity, achieving a turnover of fewer than 3 million dirhams and opting for a legal form that limits its liability.

The Performance Profile of Companies in the Region 2017 – 2019

ROE in the Marrakech – Safi Region

Financial performance, measured by ROE and observed at the level of companies in the Marrakech – Safi region, has improved over the three years studied, namely 2017, 2018, and 2019. The average ROE has gone from -15% in 2017 to +21% in 2019, thus testifying to an improvement in the financial performance of companies in the Marrakech – Safi region.

Table 7. Descriptive statistics of ROE

	N	Minimum	Maximum	Mean
ROE 2019	13051	-340,36%	873,71%	21,9794%
ROE 2018	12059	-905,09%	809,56%	5,2362%
ROE 2017	14294	-969,23%	1017,38%	-15,4106%
Valid N (listwise)	12059			

Source: established by the authors by SPSS, from OMPIC's database

ROIC in the Marrakech – Safi Region

Since most companies in the Marrakech – Safi region operate are oriented toward Trade and Services, this significantly impacts their invested capital, leading to a significant increase in the ROIC indicator. Concerning this indicator at the Marrakech – Safi region level, we note that it has recorded strong growth over the three years studied and a marked improvement in average. Thus, based on the observation of the two financial performance indicators that we have retained for this study, we note that historically (2017-2019), companies in the Marrakech – Safi region have recorded an improvement in their financial performance. This is an encouraging factor for entrepreneurship and business creation, both for pre-established operators and new ones.

Table 8. Descriptive statistics of ROIC

	N	Minimum	Maximum	Mean
ROIC 2019	13051	-4800,00%	9400,00%	7063,6113%
ROIC 2018	12059	-3550,00%	8900,00%	6225,5424%
ROIC 2017	14294	-2200,00%	6500,00%	4546,1357%
Valid N (listwise)	12059			

Source: established by the authors by SPSS, from OMPIC's database

Entrepreneurial Dynamics in the Marrakech – Safi Region

The total number of business creations in the Marrakech – Safi region was almost stable between 2019 and 2020, despite the advent of the Covid-19 health crisis, which testifies to a good entrepreneurial dynamic at the regional level. Moreover, a dynamic was confirmed in 2021 since the rate of business creation has increased by 27%.In other words, we are witnessing an improvement in the historical financial performance of companies in the Marrakech – Safi region, which is accompanied by an increase in the rate of business creation.

Figure 8. Evolution of Business Creations.
Source: established by the authors from CRI Marrakech – Safi database (crianalytics)

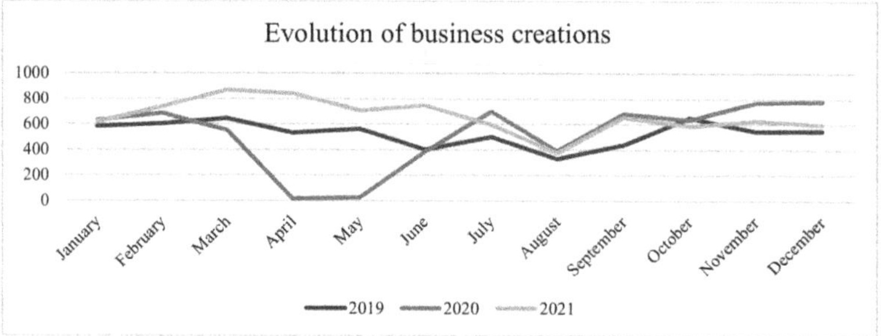

Evolution of Variables Relating to Sustainable Development in the Region

Average Job

The average employment per company in the Marrakech – Safi region recorded a slight increase between 2020 and 2021, despite the increase in business creation. Although some sectors recorded a decline, most sectors either rose or stagnated, meaning that every business, existing or new, employs more people than before.

Job Creation

Based on the data from the Regional Center of Investment of Marrakech – Safi and the work of the Unified Regional Investment Commission, we note that the total number of jobs created has increased significantly between 2020 and 2021, despite the impact of the Covid-19 crisis.

Figure 9. Average Job.
Source: established by the authors from CNSS

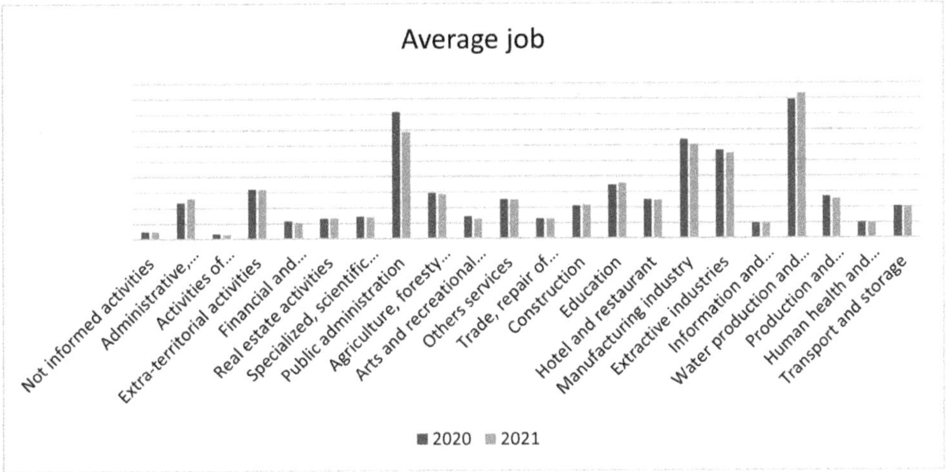

Figure 10. Job creation.
Source: established by the authors from CRI Marrakech – Safi database (crianalytics)

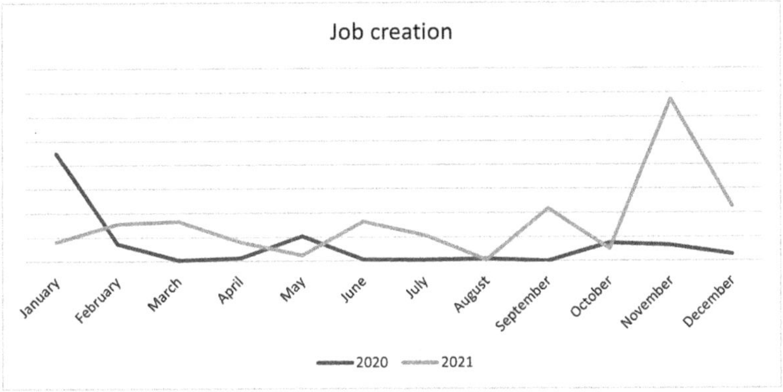

CONCLUSION

From the results presented above, some conclusions can be drawn:

- Financial performance as a vector of entrepreneurial dynamics: Companies established in the Marrakech – Safi region show an improvement in financial performance between 2017 and 2019, representing a positive, encouraging fact for entrepreneurship. Indeed, according to the "pull" vision proposed by Gabarret and Vedel (2012), a positive fact observed or experienced by an individual can become a factor encouraging the entrepreneurial process. Similarly, Julien and Marchesnay (1996) who had mentioned the weight of individual, family, social or organizational factors in the entrepreneurial process and the possibility of inspiration in the successful entrepreneurial path; we can say that the historical financial performance of companies of the region has contributed, directly or indirectly, to the development of entrepreneurial dynamics at the regional level.

- Entrepreneurial dynamics as a locomotive of the socio-economic development of the territories: With the number of business creations increasing between 2019 and 2021, and taking into account the effects of the health crisis due to Covid-19, we note two important facts. The first one is the increase in average employment per company in the Marrakech – Safi region for both old and new companies. The second concerns the net increase in job creation, which recorded significant growth between 2020 and 2021. Therefore, if we consider job creation as an indicator of socio-economic development and, therefore, of sustainable development, such as stipulated by Callens and Tyteca (1999), we can say that the entrepreneurial dynamics of the Marrakech – Safi region could have contributed, directly or indirectly, to the socio-economic development of the region.

REFERENCES

Abrams, F. (1951). Management Responsibilities in a Complex World. *Harvard Business Review*, *9*(3).

Ampuero, M. (1998), Solving the measurement dilemma: How EVE and the balanced scorecard fit toether. *Strategic performance management series, (Vol. 2).*

Attarça, M., & Jacquot, T. (2005). *La représentation de la responsabilité sociale des entreprises: Une confrontation entre les approches théoriques et les visions managériales, Journée de Développement Durable, AIMS*. IAE Aix-en-Provence.

Aubert, N. (2006). *Pourquoi les salariés achètent des actions de leur entreprise? Le cas d'une augmentation de capital réservée aux salariés, Congrès International de l'Association Française de Finance*. IAE de Poitiers.

Aubert, N., Garnotel, G., Lapied, A., & Rousseau, P. (2014). Employee ownership: A theoretical investigation of management entrenchement vs reward management. *Economic Modelling*, *40*, 40. doi:10.1016/j.econmod.2013.12.011

Banker, R. D., Potter, G., & Srinivasan, D. (2000). An empirical investigation of an incentive plan that includes nonfinancial performance measures. *The Accounting Review*, *75*(1), 75. doi:10.2308/accr.2000.75.1.65

Barneto, P., & Verstraete, Th. (2008), Finance et entrepreneuriat. Revue du financier, 170, 3-8.

Baum, J. R., & Locke, E. A. (2004). The Relationship of Entrepreneurial Traits, Skill, and Motivation to Subsequent Venture Growth. *The Journal of Applied Psychology*, *89*(4), 587–598. doi:10.1037/0021-9010.89.4.587 PMID:15327346

Bouckaert, G., & Halligan, J. (2008). *Managing performance, International comparison*. Routledge.

Bouquin, H. (2004). Le contrôle de gestion. Presses Universitaires de France, Collection Gestion, 6ème édition, Paris.

Bourguignon, A. (1997). *Sous les pavés, la plage... ou les multiples fonctions du vocabulaire comptable: Exemple la performance*. Comptabilité Contrôle Audit.

Bowen, H. (1953). *Social Responsibilities of the Businessman*. Harper & Brothers.

Callens, I., & Tyteca, D. (1999). Towards indicators of sustainable development for firms - A productive efficiency perspective. *Ecological Economics*, *28*(1), 41–53. doi:10.1016/S0921-8009(98)00035-4

Capron, M. and Quairel-Lanoizelee, F. (2004). *Mythes et réalités de l'entreprise responsable.* La Découverte.

Carroll, A. (1979). A Three-Dimensional Conceptual Model of Corporate. *Academy of Management Review*, *4*(4), 497–505. doi:10.2307/257850

Cassar, G. (2007). *Money, money, money? A longitudinal investigation of entrepreneur career reasons, growth preferences and achieved growth* (Vol. 19). Entrepreneurship & Regional Development, Taylor & Francis Journals.

Castelnau, P., & Noël, C. (2004). *Engagement pour un développement durable et performance des entreprises: Le cas français, Actes des journées La performance: de la mesure à l'action*. CERMAT.

Choi, D., & Gray, E. (2008). The venture development processes of sustainable entrepreneurs. *Management Research News*, *31*(8), 558–569. doi:10.1108/01409170810892127

Cliff, J. (1998). Does one size fit all? Exploring the relationship between attitudes towards growth, gender and business size. *Journal of Business Venturing, 13*(5), 523–542. doi:10.1016/S0883-9026(97)00071-2

Cohan, B. and al. (2006). Toward a sustainable conceptualization of dependent variables in entrepreneurship research. *Business Strategy and the Environment*, 17.

ILO Monitor. (2021). Covid-19 and the world of work, (7th ed.): Updated estimates and analysis. International Labor Organization.

Davis, L. (1966). The design of jobs. *Industrial Relations, 6*(1), 21–45. doi:10.1111/j.1468-232X.1966.tb00833.x

Demerens, F., & Paré, J. L. (2011). *Quel enseignement de la finance entrepreneuriale? Une proposition pragmatique* (Vol. 24). Revue Internationale PME.

Douhou, A., & Berland, N. (2007). *Mesure de la performance globale des entreprises.* Congrès de l'Association Francophone de Comptabilité.

Gabarret, I. & Vedel, B. (2012). Pour une nouvelle approche de la motivation entrepreneurial. *Congrès international francophone en Entrepreneuriat.* PME.

Germain, C. and Trébucq, S. (2004). *La performance globale de l'entreprise et son pilotage: quelques réflexions.* Semaine sociale Lamy.

Gets, D., & Petersen, T. (2005). Growth and profit-oriented entrepreneurship among family business owners in the tourism and hospitality industry. *Hospital Management, 24*(2), 219–242. doi:10.1016/j.ijhm.2004.06.007

Gomez, F. (2001). Financing investment. *The American Economic Review*, 91.

Guenoun, M. (2009), *Le Management de la performance publique locale: Etude de l'utilisation des outils de gestion dans deux organisations intercommunales* [Thèse de doctorat en Sciences de Gestion, Université de Paul Cézanne, Marseille, France].

Ittner, C. D., & Larcker, D. F. (1998). Are nonfinancial measures leading indicators of financial performance? An analysis of customer satisfaction. *Journal of Accounting Research, 36*, 1. doi:10.2307/2491304

Johnson, H. (1971). *Business in contemporary society: Framework and issues.* Wadsworth.

Julien, P. A., & Marchensay, M. (1996). *L'entrepreneuriat.* Economica.

Kennerley, M., & Neely, A. (2003). Measuring performance in a changing Business Environment. *International Journal of Operations & Production Management, 23*(2), 23. doi:10.1108/01443570310458465

Lahouirich, M. W and al. (2017). Autour de la performance, de l'évaluation au pilotage: Une revue de littérature, *3ème Colloque International de Recherche en Economie & Gestion.*

Lahouirich, M. W. (2021). De la performance financière et la performance globale: Un panorama multidimensionnel et des approches complémentaires, (2nd ed.). *Colloque International Gouvernance. Entrepreneuriat et Performance.*

Lahouirich, M.W. (2022), Impact of family shareholding on firm's performance: Cas of listed companies in Casablanca stock exchange. *International Review of Management and Computer, 1.*

Lahouirich, M.W. (2022). From financial performance to sustainable development: A great evolution and an endless debate. *Financial Markets, Institutions and Risks (FMIR), 6.*

LeCornu, M. and al. (1996). The small entreprise financial objective function. *Journal of Small Business Management*, 34.

Lorino, P. (2001). *Le balanced scorecard revisité: Dynamique stratégique et pilotage de performance, exemple d'une entreprise énergétique.* Actes du 22ème congrès de l'A.F.C., Metz.

Mahler. (2020). *Lives and Livelihoods: Estimates of the Global Mortality and Poverty Effects of the COVID-19 Pandemic. Policy [Research Working Paper; No. 9277].* World Bank.

Marchesnay, M. (1991). *Économie d'entreprise*. Eyrolles.

Morris, M., Miyasaki, N. N., Watters, C. E., & Coombes, S. M. (2006). The dilemma of growth: Uinderstanding venture size choice of women entrepreneurs. *Journal of Small Business Management, 44*(2), 221–244. doi:10.1111/j.1540-627X.2006.00165.x

Ondua, B.V. (2008). *Stratégies de développement durable dans les PME: Une étude exploratoire auprès des PME camerounaises.* Communication présentée au CIFEPME 9, Belgique.

Paré, J. L., & Rédis, J. (2011). Réorienter la recherche en finance entrepreneuriale. Gestion 2000, 28.

Pesqueux, Y. (2004). *La notion de performance globale, 5ème forum internationale sur La Performance Globale de l'Entreprise*. Université Tunis Carthage.

Raymond, L., Marchand, M., St-Pierre, J., Cadieux, L., & Labelle, F. (2013). Dimensions of small business performance from the owner-manager's perspective: A reconceptualization and empirical validation. *Entrepreneurship and Regional Development*, *25*(5-6), 468–499. doi:10.1080/08985626.2013.782344

Rédis, J. (2009). *Finance entrepreneuriale, L'Harmattan.* Collection De Boeck.

Rédis, J., & Paré, J. (2007). *Qu'est-ce que la finance entrepreneuriale? Séminaire de finance entrepreneuriale Advancia – Institut pour la recherche CDC – CDC Entreprises, 25 septembre 2007*. Advancia-Négocia.

Reijonen, H. & Komppula, R. (2007). Perception of success and its effect on small firm performance. *Journal of Small Business Entreprise Development, 14*.

Reynaud, E. (2003). *Développement durable et entreprise: vers une relation symbiotique, Journée AIMS, Atelier développement durable*. ESSCA Angers.

Smith, A. (2000), Small firms and the environment: Factors that influence small and medium sized entreprises environmental behaviour. *Small and medium-sized entreprises and the environment*.

Spence, M. (2007). *Développement durable et PME: Une étude exploratoire des déterminants de leur engagement* (Vol. 20). Revue Internationale PME.

St-Perre, J. & Cadieux, L. (2011), La conception de la performance: Quels liens avec le profil entrepreneurial des propriétaires dirigeants de PME?, *Revue de l'entrepreneuriat, 10*.

St-Pierre, J. (2012), *Configuration de capacités stratégiques et performance des PME: Une étude exploratoire de l'influence de l'environnement national*. CIFEPME, Brest, France.

Stiglitz, J. (2009). The measurement of economic performance and social progress revisited: Reflections and overview. *Sciences Po Publications, 33*.

The Global Reporting Initiative (GRI) (2001). *Guidelines for sustainability reporting*. GRI.

Walker, E., & Brown, A. (2004). What success factors are important to small business owners? *International Small Business Journal*, *22*(6), 577–594. doi:10.1177/0266242604047411

Westhead, P., & Wright, M. (1999). Portfolio and serial founders located in rural and urban area. *Regional Studies*, *33*(2).

Wiklund, J., & Shepherd, D. (2005). Entrepreneurial orientation and small business performance: A configurational approach. *Journal of Business Venturing*, *20*(1), 71–91. doi:10.1016/j.jbusvent.2004.01.001

Wood, D. J. (1991). Corporate social performance revisited. *Academy of Management Review*, *16*(4), 691. doi:10.2307/258977

APPENDIX: ABREVIATIONS

CNSS: Caisse Nationale de Sécurité Sociale
CRI: Centre Régional d'Investissement
CSR: Corporate Social Responsibility
EVA: Economic Value Added
GRI: Global Reporting Initiative
ILO: International Labor Organization
M/B: Market to Book
MVA: Market Value Added
OMPIC: Office Marocain de Propriété Industrielle et Commerciale
ROE: Return On Equity
ROI: Return On Investment
ROIC: Return On Invested Capital
RONA: Return On Net Asset
SME: Small and Medium Entreprises
VSE: Very Small Entreprises

Chapter 9
Can Industry 4.0 Technologies Offer a Solution for the Sustainability of SMEs?
Case Studies From Turkey

Güzide Karakuş
Necmettin Erbakan University, Turkey

ABSTRACT

Digital transformation tools within the scope of the fourth industrial revolution continue to improve with changing needs and are an issue that maintains its importance. The fact that these technologies have an important place in the sustainability of businesses is a primary motivation of this study. Similarly, it is critical for SMEs, which have an important place in the national and global economy, to protect their assets in this process. In this study, semi-structured interviews were conducted with five SME managers in Turkey to understand whether SMEs, which are important actors of economic development, see Industry 4.0 technologies as an opportunity for their sustainability. In line with the findings obtained, it has been concluded that SMEs see Industry 4.0 technologies as an opportunity in terms of their sustainability, ability to perform digital transformations in line with their own needs in business functions, and ability to prepare a roadmap for the future.

DOI: 10.4018/978-1-6684-4834-2.ch009

INTRODUCTION

Industrial revolutions are events that enable the production of goods and services to be produced faster, cheaper, and in larger quantities, creating effects to improve the quality of life of people (Carvalho, 2017: 9). Industry 4.0, the fourth industrial revolution, is a continuous change and transformation process fed by a transformation approach (Dengiz, 2017: 39). The most important feature that distinguishes Industry 4.0 from other industrial revolutions is that information and communication technologies play a more prominent role than ever before in production and the substitution of labour with machines is in question (Günaydın, 2018: 76). Industry 4.0 is a term used to describe the new industrial revolution that emphasizes automation, innovation, big data, cyber-physical systems, processes and people (Javaid, Haleem, Singh, Rab, & Suman, 2021: 3).

However, the fourth industrial revolution is not limited to smart and connected machines and systems but has a broader scope. In this period, the interactions of technologies that develop simultaneously in areas ranging from gene sequencing to nanotechnology, from renewable resources to quantum computing (Schwab, 2016: 12), affect all sectors and life, from producing goods and services to public services. Industry 4.0, which affects the competitiveness of businesses, is also of great importance in terms of the position of countries in the global economy. For this reason, programs are implemented in developed and developing countries to disseminate Industry 4.0 concepts and technologies in local companies. However, it is an important requirement to develop different approaches to analyzing and structuring digital technologies in developing countries compared to developed countries (Dalenogare, Benitez, Ayala, & Frank, 2018: 383-384).

The fourth industrial revolution has four main effects on business: 1. Customer expectations are shifting, 2. products are being enhanced, 3. Companies forge new partnerships as they learn the importance of new forms of collaboration, 4. Operating models are evolving into new digital models (Schwab, 2016: 54). These effects should be understood by all stakeholders of the business world and translated into action plans. The digital transformation that takes place with Industry 4.0 enables companies to establish closer coordination with all stakeholders throughout the value creation process and allows them to respond faster to customers by identifying the change in customer needs faster (Schulte, 2016: 11). The digital transformation is based on the uninterrupted flow of products and information throughout the supply chain, and to ensure this, companies need to be digitized in all relevant areas of the value chain (Bogner, Voelklein, Schroedel, & Franke, 2016: 16).

While globalization provides great opportunities for companies to expand the market in all sectors, it also creates pressure on cost and speed due to competitive conditions. Although this pressure leads some companies to reduce costs by sacrificing quality, this action causes a loss of customers in the long run. These business-based losses create a disadvantageous position for countries, and low-cost, poor-quality products cause job losses in global supply chains. For this reason, it should be accepted that the main factor that increases the competitiveness of countries in the face of the challenges brought by globalization is to develop technologies that can produce low-cost and high-quality products (Metin, 2019: 1). In this direction, country-based programs should be designed for the effective use of Industry 4.0 tools.

Digital transformation tools within the scope of the fourth industrial revolution continue to improve with changing needs and is an issue that maintains its importance. The fact that these technologies have an important place in the sustainability of businesses is a primary motivation for this study. Similarly, it is critical for SMEs, which have an important place in the national and global economy, to protect their assets in this process. In the 2021 report of the World Trade Organization, referring to the data of 2016, it is stated that SMEs represent more than 90% of the business volume, more than 60% of the employment, and 55% of the GDP in developed economies and make significant contributions to international trade (WTO, 2021: 138). In line with the importance of Industry 4.0 and the sustainability of SMEs, this study seeks answers to the following questions.

- *Do SMEs see Industry 4.0 as an opportunity for their sustainability?*
- *Which Industry 4.0 technologies are implemented in SMEs?*
- *Does the use of Industry 4.0 technologies contribute to the economic sustainability of SMEs?*

Firstly, the effects of Industry 4.0 on production were examined within the scope of the study. Then, sustainability in SMEs, the relationship between Industry 4.0 and sustainability, and the use of Industry 4.0 technologies in SMEs were conceptually examined. In the application part, semi-structured interviews were conducted with five SME companies operating in different sectors in Turkey using multiple exploratory case studies, one of the qualitative research methods, and answers to the research questions were sought. Lastly, in the conclusion part, suggestions are presented in line with the information obtained in the study.

BACKGROUND

Manufacturing From Industry 4.0 Perspective

Today, Industry 4.0 is a popular term used to describe recent changes, especially in the manufacturing industry (Brettel, Friederichsen, Keller, & Rosenberg, 2017: 56).

Trying to find a definition that would accurately describe Industry 4.0 is not an easy task, as many features of this new Industrial Revolution depend on the technologies and process components being implemented (Carvalho, 2017: 17). Industry 3.0 focuses on the automation of a single machine or process, while industry 4.0 focuses on the end-to-end digitization of all physical assets and their integration into digital ecosystems with value chain partners. Industry 4.0 applications aim to combine all the possibilities of technology on a common platform and transform the future industrial environment into a fully knowledge-based form, managed with analytical solutions using real and reliable data. Intelligent robotics and automation systems are used intensively (Dengiz, 2017: 39). Industry 4.0 describes the transition from centralized production to a very flexible and self-controlled production phase (Leyh, Bley, Schäffer & Forstenhäusler, 2016: 1297).

Industry 4.0 exists and opens new horizons in the manufacturing industry with many innovative technologies such as cyber-physical systems, cloud computing, artificial intelligence (AI), Internet of Things (IoT), autonomous vehicles, additive manufacturing, robotic applications, new materials, blockchain, 5G, and virtual/augmented reality (Schwab, 2016: 19; Carvalho, 2017: 17; Javaid vd., 2021: 3). While these technologies provide more powerful networking between business processes, creation of efficient interfaces, integrated data exchange, and management (Bogner et al., 2016: 15), they also enable production with tactical intelligence (Trappey, Trappey, Govindarajan, Chuang, & Sun, 2017: 209). Furthermore, digital transformation in line with Industry 4.0 offers various opportunities to create new products and services in all sectors, to find more efficient ways of doing business (Schwertner, 2017: 388), and to optimize business models by removing the barriers between people, companies, and objects. While there are many expected benefits of this transformation, the most important ones can be listed as maximum efficiency, high quality, speed, and ease in decision making, increased profitability, and decreased labour costs (Karabacak & Aras 2019: 43). Similarly, thanks to these technologies, improvements in stock and shipping costs can be achieved by increasing traceability in the entire supply chain (Sert, 2020: 16). Preventive maintenance, benchmarking, real-time monitoring of data, operational intelligence, big data analysis, energy efficiency and providing a safer work environment are stated as other advantages of Industry 4.0 applications (Javaid vd., 2021: 3).

Companies have entered a digital transformation process with the perspective of changing how they work to increase business agility and optimize the performance of employees to meet customer demands better and against the volatility of the markets (Henriette, Feki, & Boughzala, 2015: 432). There are six dimensions on the way to the digitalization of businesses: Strategy and organizational structure, smart factory, smart operations, smart products, data-driven services, and personnel competencies (Sert, 2020: 56). All of these dimensions are interconnected and should be carried out by businesses with equal importance. Among these elements, smart factories, which are in the centre of manufacturing, have an important place in terms of technological and organizational structure. Lee, Jun, Chang & Park (2017) created a conceptual framework to define the main elements of smart factories, which require a comprehensive transformation from traditional methods to advanced technologies and aim for flexible production (Oztemel & Gursev, 2020: 23):

- **Objective**: Optimum management of the production process, zero waste, maximum efficiency, product customization, increasing production competitiveness, efficient use of assets, innovation in supply chain and logistics.
- **Direction to pursue:** Intellectualization and optimization, response to changes in the external environment, integration of processes into computing technologies, organic linking of functions, and improvement in control systems.
- **Necessary technologies:** Automation technology, IoT, big data, cyber-physical systems (CPS), etc.
- **Applicable object:** Facilities, devices, workers, material/part/product.
- **Applied processes:** Throughout the product life cycle, product design, production planning, process control, stock control, logistics, sales, and quality control.

Although the advantages of Industry 4.0 have begun to be accepted by practitioners, some uncertainties also cause various negative approaches in the workforce. The most controversial aspect of Industry 4.0 is the expected change in the structure and size of employment and the predicted unemployment rate. The common point of the studies on this subject in the literature is that there will be a change in the structure of employment and the qualifications of the workforce (Günaydın, 2018: 84). In this direction, governments, companies, and individuals should undertake different tasks. First, public works should be carried out, and education policies should be formed following the expectations of the future workforce. Individuals should train themselves in line with the technologies of the future and work to increase their technical abilities and competencies. Finally, to overcome the prejudices against the transformation experienced in line with Industry 4.0, companies should harmonize their business strategies and operations (Schumacher, Erol & Sihn, 2016: 162) and ensure the active participation of employees in the change in the entire organization.

MAIN FOCUS OF THE CHAPTER

Sustainability in SMEs

Small and medium-sized enterprises (SMEs) are the heart of the economy worldwide and have been the subject of many studies in different fields. The sustainability of SMEs is also very important in terms of economic, social, and environmental sustainability. Understanding and achieving all dimensions of sustainability by SMEs will significantly contribute to the effective use of existing resources and social and economic development. It should not be forgotten that SMEs must sustain their economic existence for a sustainable world. For the continuity of SMEs, the priority is to ensure sustainable operation management, and at this point, insufficient resources and stakeholder pressure are important constraints and require effective strategic management. The key to organizing the company for sustainable operations is that leadership establishes a proactive culture in formulating environmental and social goals, pursues a continuous strategy of environmental and social improvement, and adopts a learning culture that recognizes and reinforces the benefits and value of training and developing its employees (Kerr, 2006: 32). While effective use of resources and technological developments that reduce environmental impacts contribute to the ecological dimension of sustainability, other dimensions should not be ignored. For example, companies' growth and development, employment creation, and financial sustainability development contribute to sustainability's economic dimension. Similarly, the development of employment opportunities, improving the quality of business life as a result of the improvement of working conditions, and the development of social state opportunities through the taxes they pay are the contributions of SMEs to the development of social sustainability.

SMEs, the backbone of the economy, are more vulnerable to internal and external factors and have a fragile structure because they have few resources (Eggers, 2020: 199). Zapata, Berrah, & Tabourot (2020) defined the general characteristics of SMEs operating in the field of production as follows:

- Limited resources (financial, technical, human),
- Less complex organizational structure with informal strategy and decision-making mechanisms,
- Culture with low flexibility for change and experimentation,
- Employees working in more than one field,
- Poor adherence to business processes and standards,
- Product development with a high level of customization,
- Industry knowledge focused on a specific area,
- Strong customer/supplier relationships,

- Low investment in R&D and lack of alliances with universities,
- Low adoption of new technologies.

While some of the features mentioned above offer various advantages, such as cost advantages, rapid decision-making, and agile production practices, some create disadvantages in operating on a global scale. As a result, SMEs do not have sufficient opportunities for growth compared to globally competitive large companies. Therefore, to strengthen the overall competitiveness of production and narrow the productivity gap between SMEs and large companies, it is necessary to significantly accelerate the development of the productivity of SMEs (Lee vd., 2017: 2), and Industry 4.0 applications are important tools in this direction.

RELATIONSHIP WITH INDUSTRY 4.0 AND SUSTAINABILITY

Companies are faced with the reality of limited resources. They are looking for ways to integrate sustainability concepts into their product designs, operations, and supply chains (Sloan, Klingenberg & Rider, 2013: 19). The Fourth Industrial Revolution, Industry 4.0, is capable of making significant contributions to sustainability along with the various advantages created by developing technologies. Digital business transformation is the integration of new digital technologies into all business areas, leading to fundamental changes in how the organization works (Schwertner, 2017: 389). The limited resources of the world will be used much more efficiently in various fields of production and industry with Industry 4.0 (Dengiz, 2017: 44). Industry 4.0 applications, whose starting point is to increase the efficiency of enterprises and improve their competitiveness (Vrchota, Volek, Novotná, 2019: 2), also contribute to their sustainability.

Large companies use Industry 4.0 technologies to maintain their existence and contribute to environmental, economic, and social sustainability. However, it is impossible to say the same for SMEs trying to survive with limited opportunities in global economic conditions. SMEs, which carry out their activities, especially in developing countries, have difficulties implementing sustainability and Industry 4.0 approaches. Especially SMEs in developing countries have challenges implementing sustainability and Industry 4.0 processes. Jayashree, Hassan Reza, Malarvizhi, Maheswari, Hosseini & Kasim (2021) investigated the relationship between the application of Industry 4.0 technologies and sustainability goals within the context of SMEs and have concluded that technological innovations have a significant impact on SMEs to develop effective Industry 4.0 practices and achieve their sustainability goals. However, reaching these technological innovations and Industry 4.0 tools is difficult for SMEs struggling to maintain their current operations.

While the lack of resources for digitalization in SMEs is a major problem, it is not as important as the type of leadership in the organization that defines the organizational culture. Frequently, in a family-owned SME, the leader's poor vision for the future and the leader's unwillingness to risk their current comfortable position are major barriers to digital transformation. Similarly, the structure of SMEs that focuses on managing daily operations (Zapata et al., 2020: 7) prevents them from allocating the necessary time and resources to digital transformation and slows down the transformation. However, it should not be forgotten that in terms of the sustainability of their assets, SMEs should become smarter and develop their production and management structures with technologies that detect and improve production problems (Lee et al., 2017: 2). Because the advantages such as profitable growth, cost reduction and increase in productivity to be achieved with new products, new services and innovative business models to be obtained with digital transformation are important opportunities for the sustainability of SMEs. SMEs that realize these opportunities start their digitalization journey and try to reshape their business models towards digitalization (Bley, Leyh, & Schäffer, 2016: 2). Because the Industry 4.0 concept offers a great potential for the future, especially for medium-sized businesses (Vrchota et al., 2019: 8).

OBSTACLES TO THE USE OF INDUSTRY 4.0 TECHNOLOGIES IN SMEs

While the fourth industrial revolution has led to various differentiations in growth models, labour markets and working life, it has also greatly impacted the management and organization. For example, efficient use of resources with Industry 4.0 technologies that have been developed and implemented (Schwab, 2016: 52). Industry 4.0 applications initially only affected large companies, as SMEs considered such issues too complex and expensive and remained uninterested. However, it has been understood that digitalization can no longer be limited to large companies and separate functional areas such as the information technology departments (Leyh vd., 2016: 1297). Businesses of every size and structure, operating in every sector, are affected by this change and transformation and must continue to exist by using digital transformation tools suitable for their own structure.

Digital transformation is undoubtedly an institutional change and requires an infrastructure beyond certain innovations and organizations. Institutional infrastructure connects different actors and, most importantly, creates action plans with governance and regulation (Hinings, Gegenhuber, & Greenwood, 2018: 55). Digital business transformation is an objective process that responds to changing business environments. Implementation of the process requires a clear strategy and prioritization supported by financial resources, leadership, and active participation of all employees in the organization. The flow rate depends on the characteristics of the industry. (Schwertner, 2017: 393).

The use of Industry 4.0 technologies is an important change and transformation process, and various obstacles may occur in this transformation. Prause (2019) stated that market uncertainty, external factors, and senior management support are the most important factors in the transition to digital technologies due to his study to understand the difficulties of Japanese SMEs in adopting Industry 4.0 technologies. According to different sources, the barriers to digital transformation are listed below (Ebert & Duarte, 2018: 16; Sarvari, Ustundag, Cevikcan, Kaya, & Cebi, 2018: 97, Aygün & Satı, 2022: 242).

- Lack of knowledge about the social benefits of this transformation,
- Lack of skilled workforce,
- Incomplete or insufficient infrastructure,
- Incomplete or inadequate regulations,
- Uncertainties regarding consumer protection,
- Lack of knowledge about new technologies and opportunities,
- Uncertainty regarding the benefits of technology investments in products and processes,
- Lack of information about customer demand for new products and business models within the scope of Industry 4.0 vision,
- Limited financial resources,
- Difficulties in identifying the starting point and milestones of the planning horizon,
- The need for efficient portfolio management for technology investments,
- Requirements for prioritizing and scheduling new product and process projects,
- Inability to allocate limited resources to projects and cooperate with reliable partners,
- Lack of communication in the organization about the benefits of Industry 4.0 transformation projects,
- Organizational resistance,
- Information technology security issues.

While the aforementioned barriers remain valid for SMEs, insufficient access to finance (Ebert & Duarte, 2018: 16) is one of the most important barriers. Other risks for SMEs are the lack of a qualified workforce that can use and run Industry 4.0 applications for a radical transformation, lack of information security policy, and unprotected network connections (Karabacak & Aras 2019: 41). Due to these obstacles, SMEs cannot use the advantages that some of their qualifications will provide them in the digitalization journey. For example, while SMEs have the advantage of interacting more with customers and suppliers compared to large-scale companies, they cannot use this advantage in research and development activities due to their lack of information technology integration (Mittal, Khan, Romero & Wuest, 2018: 195).

Another issue that should not be ignored is the **human factor**. The human factor, which is a more important obstacle to digital transformation than technology or finance, may appear as cultural traditions, employees' resistance to change, lack of relevant knowledge and good practices, lack of resources, lack of motivation and inability to take risks (Schwertner, 2017: 392). For this reason, it is important for the leader of SMEs to be aware of digital transformation, to determine the necessary training and consultancy services and a digitalization roadmap for the enterprise, and to define the opportunities and risks in this transformation and direct the entire organization in this direction.

METHOD

In the research, by using literature research, observation, interview and document review techniques, it has been investigated whether SMEs see Industry 4.0 as an opportunity for their sustainability, which Industry 4.0 technologies they apply, and whether the use of Industry 4.0 technologies contribute to their economic sustainability. In the application part, multiple exploratory case studies, one of the qualitative research methods, were preferred. An exploratory case study provides an opportunity to understand a situation in its entirety (Yin 2018). Since SMEs have an important position in the economy in Turkey and the whole world, the research has been determined as enterprises with SME status operating in Turkey. As of 2020, there are 3.2 million SMEs registered in Turkey. SMEs provide 99.8% of the enterprises in Turkey, 73.8% of the total employment, make 64.5% of the total turnover of the enterprises and constitute 56.3% of the total exports in Turkey (TOBB, 2020). Within the scope of the research, purposive and convenience sampling methods were used. While determining the participating companies, attention was paid to the fact that they were operating in different sectors and sizes and had implemented at least one application within the scope of Industry 4.0 to increase the validity of the findings. In line with the determined conditions, businesses were contacted, and interviews were held with businesses that agreed to participate. At the end of the interviews with five companies, it was decided that theoretical saturation was achieved due to the repetition of the answers. The interviews were held between January 10 and February 20, 2022, and each interview lasted 50-90 minutes. While interviews were conducted with company A using the online meeting program, face-to-face meetings were held with companies B, C, D and E. All interviewees are people who work as General Managers in companies, and 4 of them (Companies A, B, C, D) are also business partners. Therefore, interviewing the General Managers, who can best describe the situation, contributed to the reliability of the data obtained.

During the interviews, a short briefing was provided on Industry 4.0 technologies. Afterwards, semi-structured questions created in line with the information obtained from similar studies in the literature were directed to the participants. The questions are listed below.

- Do you see Industry 4.0 tools (robotic technologies, automation systems, RFID, software, different digital applications, cloud computing, etc.) as an opportunity for the economic sustainability of your business?
- Which Industry 4.0 technologies are applied in business functions to improve your sustainability?
- Since what year have you been using these technologies?
- Did Industry 4.0 technologies contribute to your economic sustainability?
    - The effect of these technologies on your productivity,
    - The impact of these technologies on your costs,
    - The effect of these technologies on your product quality,
    - The impact of these technologies on the business reputation,
    - The result of these technologies on your sales volume, market share, entry into new markets, and your competitiveness,
    - How did these technologies affect your profitability?

In the interviews, the disadvantages of Industry 4.0 technologies and ideas about future plans were also expressed and included in the interview findings.

Although there are different applications in the analysis of qualitative data, the method consisting of description, analysis and interpretation categories developed by Walcott (1994) was preferred to understand the Industry 4.0 approaches of SMEs. In the method proposed by Walcott (1994), the researcher is suggested to tell the events in a certain order, and the direct transfer of the analyzed event to the reader is emphasized (Walcott, 1994: 23-29; Özdemir, 2010: 331).

RESULTS

It is important that Industry 4.0 technologies, which are one of the important concepts of our age, are understood and applied by SMEs, which have an important place for economies. In this study, which was implemented with this motivation, the findings obtained through semi-structured interviews with five SME general managers are presented in this section. First of all, information about the participating companies is given in Table 1.

Table 1. Information on participating companies

Company	Industry	Year of Establishment	Number of Employees	Job Titles	Industry 4.0 Tools Are Used	How Many Years Has the Business Been Using Industry 4.0 Tools?
A	Casting	1968	151	General Manager (Business Partner)	Yes	2
B	Hydraulic Equipment Manufacturing	2001	31	General Manager (Business Partner)	Yes	4
C	Shelf Manufacturing	1977	130	General Manager (Business Partner)	Yes	5-6
D	Pump manufacturing	1988	65	General Manager (Business Partner)	Yes	5-6
E	Hydraulic and electronic automation system	1998	42	General Manager	Yes	4-5

As seen in Table 1, all participating companies are small and medium-sized businesses operating in different sectors. Company A operates in the province of Kocaeli in Turkey, while companies B, C, D and E operate in the province of Konya (known as an SME city). All the participants work as General Managers in the companies, and all of the companies use at least one of the Industry 4.0 technologies. A 1-hour online interview was held with the participant, one of the business partners, who works as the General Manager in Enterprise-A, which operates in the casting industry. The participant's responses to the semi-structured interview questions and their views on the subject are presented in Table 2.

Table 2. Company A (Casting facility) interview findings

COMPANY: A **Industry: Casting** **Size: Medium sized business**	
Are the Industry 4.0 tools used?	Yes. Since 2020, the orientation towards Industry 4.0 tools have started in order to meet customer expectations.
In which units are they used?	- *ERP (Enterprise Resource Planning) system* has been established and is being used to monitor all purchasing, production planning and control, quality control, stock tracking, delivery and maintenance activities. - *3D Printing* started to be used for production and R&D. - *CMM (Coordinate Measurement Machine)* measurement system has been established and used in order to reduce measurement errors within the scope of quality control.
Advantages	- 15% reduction in heat treatment waste, - Improvement in production planning and stock tracking, - 5% improvement in compliance with deadlines, - Increase in traceability in all processes, - Improvement in product quality, - 15-18% increase in sales to USA,
Disadvantages	- 3% increase in costs - There was resistance among senior employees at the beginning in the transition to digital technologies. However, with the understanding of its benefits, this resistance turned into support.
Is it planned for the future?	- Increasing the use of digital technologies in production, - Carrying out studies on digital marketing, - To transition to digital technologies within the scope of energy efficiency, - To follow the developments in 3D printing technology and to ensure the use of these printers in production.

Some remarkable comments in the interviews with the participant of Company A are as follows:

Industry 4.0 tools are inevitable for the future of the casting industry and offer great opportunities. ERP system is a very important tool for traceability, efficiency, profitability, reduction of waste and effective use of energy. With the data transferred directly from the machines to the ERP system, tracking our production system became easier and independent of the human factor.

With the digital measuring device (CMM), integration between the furnaces, the laboratory, and the foundry furnaces has been achieved. This way, we can produce products with correct hardness, strength, yield, and tensile values. As a result, significant improvement was achieved in our product quality.

With the 3D printer, the part to be processed can be printed out, all necessary measurements can be made, and errors can be detected. Therefore, this application offers a very important advantage for investment casting. After the necessary improvements are made, the casting process is started, and possible errors are minimized.

One of the industry's main problems is the energy use intensity. So we think that thanks to Industry 4.0 tools, it will be beneficial in terms of efficient use of energy, reduction of costs and reduction of negative environmental effects.

Table 3. Company B (Hydraulic Equipment Manufacturer) interview findings

COMPANY: B **Industry: Hydraulic Equipment Manufacturing** **Size: Small business**	
Are the Industry 4.0 tools used?	Yes. Since 2018, efforts on digital sales have been carried out, and it has been actively used for a year.
In which units are they used?	Digital transformation was initiated within the scope of *sales* activities in the company. Within the scope of increasing sales, a B2B (buyer to buyer) *digital sales system* was established. The system, in which purchasing, sales, accounting and warehouse follow-up are carried out in an integrated manner, was implemented by our company for the first time in the hydraulic equipment sector in Turkey. The customer creates his own request on the sales site, makes the payment and can follow the delivery.
Advantages	- Saving on human resources, - Fulfilling customer demands, - Reduction in errors, - Increase in delivery speed, - Reduction in data loss, - 30% increase in sales, - Increase in the number of customers, - Improvement in product traceability, - More accurate stock control, - 20% increase in productivity, - Reduction in costs due to savings in labour, - Increase in service quality (due to reduction of wrong products, wrong invoices, etc.) - The fact that the business leads the sector has contributed to the business reputation by standing out from its competitors.
Disadvantages	- High investment cost, - The need for qualified labour in the installation is high.
Is it planned for the future?	- Increasing the use of digital technologies in production, - To ensure the use of 3D printing for use in R&D and production activities. - Automation in production.

A 1.5-hour face-to-face meeting was held with the General Manager, one of the partners of Enterprise B, which manufactures and sells hydraulic equipment. The obtained results are presented in Table 3.

Some remarkable comments in the interviews with the participant of Company B are as follows:

Targets for the use of Industry 4.0 tools have been determined in our enterprise. Investments in digital technologies will increase our efficiency and profitability in the market.

Due to the fact that SMEs have a constantly dynamic work pace, they consider digitalization as non-urgent work and act slowly in this regard.

Although financing is an important constraint for digital transformation in SMEs, the most important thing is the knowledge and approach of the top management.

A one-hour face-to-face interview was held with the participant, who is the owner and General Manager of Company C, which manufactures warehouse shelves. The obtained results are presented in Table 4.

Some remarkable comments in the interviews with the Company C participant are as follows.

The use of Industry 4.0 tools in manufacturing provides a significant advantage for the sustainability of businesses, as well as the high investment costs and a significant disadvantage. However, the obstacle that is more important than the financing requirement is the need for a qualified workforce to adapt to digital systems.

Another important obstacle is the economic stability of the country. Even businesses that are able to make these investments avoid making investments in order not to take risks in an economic system where there is no stability.

A one-hour face-to-face meeting was held with the participant, who is the General Manager and one of the partners of Company D, which manufactures pumps. The obtained results are presented in Table 5.

Table 4. Company C (Shelf Manufacturer) interview findings

COMPANY: C **Industry: Shelf Manufacturing** **Size: Medium sized business**	
Are the Industry 4.0 tools used?	Yes. Since 2016, the change and transformation in the market have been followed, and digital transformation steps have been taken in line with the needs.
In which units are they used?	- MRP (Manufacturing Resource Planning) system has been used in the enterprise's production, purchasing, quality control, assembly and storage departments. - A transition to digitalization has been ensured in the *sales* process, and our customers have been able to visit our factory site online. A tracking system is used in sales, delivery and assembly, - Digitalization has been achieved in *human resources* with face recognition and personnel tracking systems, - Quality and traceability improvements are carried out in *production* processes with robots, painting facilities, welding robots and sheet metal cutting robots.
Advantages	- Savings on human resources (80% savings on labour in the cutting and dyeing shop), - Improvement in quality control processes, - Decrease in dependency on personnel, - Fulfilling customer demands, - Reduction of errors in purchasing, sales and production processes, - Increase in delivery speed, - Increase in domestic and international sales, - Increase in the number of customers, - Improvement in product traceability, - More accurate stock control, - Increase in productivity, - 40% reduction in costs due to labour savings, - Increase in product and service quality, - Increase in profitability, - Increase in employee satisfaction by reducing the workload of the personnel, - Improvement in the quality of the working environment, - Reduction in occupational safety risks.
Disadvantages	- High investment cost, - The convenience of the ecosystem is important, - It requires qualified human resources.
Is it planned for the future?	- Smart shelf systems can be produced, - Full automation in production (sustainable mechanization can be achieved by switching to mass production).

Some remarkable comments in the interviews with the participant of the Company D are as follows:

Although most companies are willing to accept the investment costs that will arise in digital transformation, the most important constraint is the resistance of the existing staff in the transition to new systems and the difficulties in finding qualified personnel.

Table 5. Company D (Hydraulic Pump Manufacturer) interview findings

COMPANY: D **Industry: Hydraulic Pump Manufacturing** **Size: Medium sized business**	
Are the Industry 4.0 tools used?	Yes. Investments in digitalization started in 2016 and 2017.
In which units are they used?	- By establishing the MRP (Manufacturing Resource Planning) system, *purchasing, accounting, quality control, sales, and warehouse* records were transferred to digital media, and the processes' traceability was ensured. In the production process, the transition to the ERP system continues. - Work has begun on *digital sales*, - Works on the transition to automation in *production* and *assembly lines* were started, and renovation works were carried out on the benches. - Research studies on the use of robots in *production* and sub-investment for automation in the paint facility were made. - Digital measurement systems were introduced in the *quality control* unit.
Advantages	- Increase in traceability, - Labour saving, - 20% reduction in costs due to labour savings, - Increase in product quality, - Increase in profitability, - Improvement in productivity, - Improvement in quality control processes, reduction in the number of errors, - Reduction of errors in purchasing, sales and production processes, - More accurate stock control, - Increase in employee satisfaction by reducing the workload of the personnel, - Reduction in occupational safety risks, - Saving time loss, - Improvement in business reputation.
Disadvantages	- Employee resistance is high in the transition to digital technologies, - High investment cost, - It requires qualified human resources.
Is it planned for the future?	- Transition to full automation in assembly lines will be realized - Work will be carried out on digital marketing.

On behalf of both the company and the country, we should not miss this train (Industry 4.0). We should be in it. This is the only way to produce products with high added value.

An 80-minute face-to-face interview was held with the participant, who is the General Manager of Company E, which manufactures hydraulic and electronic automation systems. The obtained results are presented in Table 6.

Table 6. Company E (Hydraulic and electronic automation system manufacturer) interview findings

COMPANY: E **Industry: Hydraulic and electronic automation systems** **Büyüklük: Small business**	
Are the Industry 4.0 tools used?	Yes. Investments in digitalization started in 2017 and 2018.
In which units are they used?	- By establishing an ERP (Enterprise Resource Planning) system, records of *purchasing, production planning, accounting, quality management, quality control, maintenance, sales and warehouses* were transferred to digital media and traceability of processes was ensured. - The production module is customized and effectively used in line with business needs. Data entries have been mobilized with hand terminals and kiosks, and more effective production monitoring has become possible. - Work on *digital marketing* is carried out. - Digital measurement systems were introduced in the *quality control* unit. - Adaptation of new technologies was started in line with the needs of customers. The hydraulic and electronic systems have been developed in line with the particle counter, sensors for vibration, distance and pressure measurement, and machine learning and predictive maintenance.
Advantages	- Increase in traceability and controllability, - Improved detection of bottlenecks, - Increase in product/system quality, - Increase in competitiveness, - Improvement in staff productivity, - Reduction in the number of errors, - Effective stock management, - Saving time loss, - Improvement in business reputation.
Disadvantages	- Employee resistance in the transition to digital technologies, - Increase in errors in the transition process, - Increase in costs, - Increase in need for skilled labour, - Intensive labour requirement in the transition period.
Is it planned for the future?	- Studies are planned to support the production process with simulation to minimise system production errors.

Some remarkable comments in the interviews with the participant of the Company D are as follows:

We were at the 2011 Hannover Fair, where the term Industry 4.0 was first used. We have always followed the subject and investigated what kind of work can be done in our business.

While we are working on digitalization in our business processes, we use Industry 4.0 tools intensively in the systems we offer to our customers. In addition, since the manufacturers of the components we use in our systems are the implementers of Industry 4.0, we play an intermediary role in transferring these technologies to our customers.

In the Industry 4.0 transition process, our costs increased, the employees have resisted, there was an increase in errors, we have not seen a positive reflection on our sales yet, and our profitability has decreased due to increased costs. However, we believe that we will begin to experience the advantages of transitioning to digital technologies with our increasing competitive power and product quality in 4-5 years.

CONCLUSION

All of the industrial revolutions have caused great changes and transformations in production structures all over the world. With the transformation of Industry 4.0, thanks to the technological tools to be used in all functions in the value chain and the big data to be obtained, personalized products/services can be offered, production costs are reduced, quality, flexibility, timeliness, transparency, efficiency, reliability, and traceability are improved. Therefore, at this moment, it contributes to the sustainability of the business. This study investigated whether SMEs, which are important actors in economic development, see Industry 4.0 technologies as an opportunity for their sustainability, and semi-structured interviews were conducted with five SME managers. All of the companies participating in the interviews are SMEs (Small and Medium Sized Enterprises) and operate in different sectors. All the companies have taken initiatives on Industry 4.0 technologies and determined a roadmap for the future. In the interviews, business managers were first asked whether they see Industry 4.0 tools as an opportunity for their sustainability. All the participants answered the question "YES" and explained what kind of work they had done. Four of the participating companies stated that they use MRP and ERP systems. For example, Mathrani, Mathrani & Viehland (2013) stated that one of the most used digital transformation tools in SMEs is enterprise systems, also known as ERP systems. They also added that these systems, which were originally developed to meet the functional needs of the business, become part of the business in the modern digital economy and support tactical movements and strategic direction. Similarly, Cardoni, Zanin, Corazza & Paradisi (2020), as a result of their study investigating the effect of knowledge management and performance measurement systems on the sustainability of SMEs, stated that the implementation of knowledge management and performance management strengthened the sustainability and suggested entrepreneurs design a coherent knowledge management approach to support economic sustainability. The findings obtained from the interviews are in this direction; all four business participants stated that these systems provide significant benefits and create an important infrastructure for their digital transformation and sustainability.

When the interviewees were asked which business functions they used Industry 4.0 technologies, A, C, D and E companies stated that they used them in purchasing, production planning, quality control, warehouse management, accounting, maintenance, and sales functions. In addition, Company A stated that they used it in the R&D function and company C in the human resources function. Enterprise B indicated that they started their digital transformation by establishing a digital sales system for the first time in their sector. Javaid et al. (2021) similarly state that Industry 4.0 applications provide advantages in the control and traceability of all operations. Companies should change their daily working styles to improve their productivity and performance. Dutta, Kumar, Sindhwani & Singh (2021) emphasized that manufacturing SMEs need to digitize their quality practices to develop successfully in the global market and ensure synergy in the value chain. The findings align with the literature and show that SMEs operating in Turkey use different Industry 4.0 tools in various functions and gain benefits.

To understand whether the use of Industry 4.0 technologies contributes to the economic sustainability of SMEs, the interviewees were asked what kind of benefits Industry 4.0 tools provide them, and the answers of the participants are presented below:

- Saving on human resources (B, C, D),
- Improvement in production planning and stock tracking (A),
- Improvement in quality control processes (B, C, D),
- Reduce dependence on employees (C),
- Fully meeting customer demands (B, C),
- Reduction in errors/wastes (A, B, C, D, E),
- Increase in delivery speed (A, B, C),
- Increase in domestic and international sales (A, B, C),
- Improvement in product traceability (A, B, C, D, E),
- Effective stock management (A, C, B, D, E),
- Increase in productivity (B, C, D, E),
- Cost reduction due to labour savings (C, B, D)
- Increase in product and service quality (A, B, C, D, E),
- Increase in profitability (C, D),
- Increase in employee satisfaction by reducing the workload of the employee (C, D),
- Improvement in the quality of the working environment (C),
- Reduction in occupational safety risks (C, D),
- Improvement in business reputation (B, C, D, E),

- Improved detection of bottlenecks (E),
- Increase in competitiveness (E),
- Reduction in time loss (D, E),
- Reduction in data loss (B).

As can be seen, the perceived benefits of Industry 4.0 by business managers differ and are compatible with similar studies in the literature (see Dengiz, 2017; Karabacak & Aras, 2019; Vrchota vd., 2019; Sert, 2020; Javaid vd., 2021; Henriette, Feki & Boughzala, 2015). However, all interviewees stated that reduction in errors and wastage, improvement in product traceability, effective stock management, and increase in product and service quality were benefits and came to the fore as the most important items. In addition, the interviewees defined items such as reduction in staff dependency, improvement in the quality of the working environment, improvement in the detection of bottlenecks, and reduction in data loss as the benefits obtained based on the enterprise. Still, these were not included in the literature.

All the stated benefits of Industry 4.0 are also critical for the sustainability of SMEs. Yusoff, Wahab, Latiff, Osman, Zawawi & Fazal (2018), in their study examining the factors related to sustainable growth in SMEs through literature research, stated that by providing employee satisfaction and motivation, it can contribute to sustainability with effective energy and raw material consumption and waste reduction programs. Mohiuddin, Al Azad, Ahmed, Ed-Dafali & Reza (2022) stated that, together with Industry 4.0 technologies, businesses could achieve positive results such as increasing product quality, efficiency and flexibility, saving costs, increasing customer satisfaction with personalized products and reducing environmental impacts and improving the value and competitiveness of the business. However, they also stated that there might be various difficulties regarding skills, technological problems and ethics.

During the interviews, the interviewees expressed the difficulties and disadvantages of the transition to Industry 4.0 and added research findings. A consolidated version of the challenges voiced by the participants is as follows:

- High investment cost (A, B, C, D, E),
- Employee resistance occurs during the transition process (B, D, E),
- High skilled labour requirement (B, C, D, E),
- Availability of the ecosystem is important (C),
- An increase in errors in the transition process (E),
- Requires intensive labour in the transition process (B, E).

When the findings are examined, it is seen that all interviewees agree that the investment cost of digital transformation is high. While the high costs are seen as an important disadvantage for all businesses, it is a remarkable issue expressed by the interviewees that the vision and leadership of the business manager is a more important factors. The high need for qualified labour and the difficulty recruiting employees stand out as another important issue. The importance of the appropriate ecosystem and the tendency of errors to increase in the transformation process is striking responses expressed by each participant. Günaydın (2018) and Schwertner (2017) similarly pointed out that the need for a qualified workforce will increase in digital transformation and the importance of the human factor. The importance of the ecosystem in which the business operates, which the general manager of enterprise C expressed, should not be overlooked. It is critical for businesses that the country of operation should have a stable economic structure for digital transformation investments that require large costs.

Finally, the participants were asked whether they had plans for using Industry 4.0 tools in the future, and all of the participants stated that they had determined a roadmap in this context and talked about their plans.

As seen in the research findings, SMEs see Industry 4.0 tools as an opportunity for their sustainability, perform digital transformations in line with their own needs in business functions and make plans for the future. This situation has similarities with the literature, and Lee et al. (2017), Jayashree et al. (2021) and Vrchota et al. (2019) state that Industry 4.0 technologies offer significant advantages for SMEs to achieve their sustainability goals. Therefore, the current situation is promising for SMEs, which can be considered the heart of the economy in Turkey, and shows that the state administration has duties within the scope of ensuring economic stability and developing initiatives to train qualified personnel.

The most important limitation of the study is that it was carried out with qualitative research within five companies. Therefore, it is impossible to generalize the findings to all SMEs in Türkiye. Thus, in future studies, it is recommended to expand the scope of the results by conducting quantitative studies with a larger sample size.

ACKNOWLEDGMENT

I want to thank Akgül Kalıp A.Ş., Alp Raf A.Ş., Hiposan A.Ş., Simya Ltd. Şti. and Anadolu Döküm for their participation and contributions to this study.

REFERENCES

Aygün, D. & Satı, Z. E.(2022). Evaluation of Industry 4.0 transformation barriers for SMEs in Turkey. *Eskişehir Osmangazi Üniversitesi İktisadi ve İdari Bilimler Dergisi/Eskişehir Osmangazi University Journal of Economics and Administrative Sciences, 17*(1), 239-255.

Bley, K., Leyh, C., & Schäffer, T. (2016). Digitization of German enterprises in the production sector-Do they know how "digitized" they are? *Twenty-second Americas Conference on Information Systems.*

Bogner, E., Voelklein, T., Schroedel, O., & Franke, J. (2016). Study based analysis on the current digitalization degree in the manufacturing industry in Germany. *Procedia CIRP, 57*, 14–19. doi:10.1016/j.procir.2016.11.004

Brettel, M., Friederichsen, N., Keller, M., & Rosenberg, M. (2017). How virtualization, decentralization and network building change the manufacturing landscape: An industry 4.0 perspective. *FormaMente, 12*.

Cardoni, A., Zanin, F., Corazza, G., & Paradisi, A. (2020). Knowledge management and performance measurement systems for SMEs' economic sustainability. *Sustainability, 12*(7), 2594. doi:10.3390u12072594

Carvalho, R. M. D. C. (2017). *Industry 4.0–Is Portugal prepared for the future?* [Doctoral dissertation]. The School of Technology and Management of the Polytechnic Institute of Leiria, Portugal.

Dalenogare, L. S., Benitez, G. B., Ayala, N. F., & Frank, A. G. (2018). The expected contribution of Industry 4.0 technologies for industrial performance. *International Journal of Production Economics, 204*, 383–394. doi:10.1016/j.ijpe.2018.08.019

Dengiz, O. (2017). Endüstri 4.0: Üretimde kavram ve algı devrimi [Industry 4.0: A revolution of concepts and perceptions]. *Makina Tasarım ve İmalat Dergisi/Journal of Machine Design and Manufacturing, 15*(1), 38-45.

Dutta, G., Kumar, R., Sindhwani, R., & Singh, R. K. (2021). Digitalization priorities of quality control processes for SMEs: A conceptual study in perspective of Industry 4.0 adoption. *Journal of Intelligent Manufacturing, 32*(6), 1–20. doi:10.100710845-021-01783-2

Ebert, C., & Duarte, C. H. C. (2018). Digital Transformation. *IEEE Software, 35*(4), 16–21. doi:10.1109/MS.2018.2801537

Eggers, F. (2020). Masters of disasters? Challenges and opportunities for SMEs in times of crisis. *Journal of Business Research, 116*, 199–208. doi:10.1016/j.jbusres.2020.05.025 PMID:32501306

Günaydın, D. (2018). Türkiye'de dördüncü sanayi devrimini beklerken: Çerkezköy Organize Sanayi Bölgesi'nde bir araştırma [While waiting for fourth industrial revolution in Turkey: A case study in Çerkezköy Organized Industrial Zone]. *Istanbul Management Journal, 29*(85), 73–106.

Henriette, E., Feki, M., & Boughzala, I. (2015). The shape of digital transformation: A systematic literature review. *MCIS 2015 Proceedings, 10*, 431-443.

Hinings, B., Gegenhuber, T., & Greenwood, R. (2018). Digital innovation and transformation: An institutional perspective. *Information and Organization, 28*(1), 52–61. doi:10.1016/j.infoandorg.2018.02.004

Javaid, M., Haleem, A., Singh, R. P., Rab, S., & Suman, R. (2021). Upgrading the manufacturing sector via applications of Industrial Internet of Things (IIoT). *Sensors International, 2*, 100129. doi:10.1016/j.sintl.2021.100129

Jayashree, S., Hassan Reza, M. N., Malarvizhi, C. A. N., Maheswari, H., Hosseini, Z., & Kasim, A. (2021). The Impact of Technological Innovation on Industry 4.0 Implementation and Sustainability: An Empirical Study on Malaysian Small and Medium Sized Enterprises. *Sustainability, 13*(18), 10115. doi:10.3390u131810115

Karabacak, N., & Aras, N. (2017). Kobi'lerin malzeme aktarma ve depolama sistemlerine yönelik Endüstri 4.0 uygulamalarında karşılaşılan güçlükler ve çözüm önerileri [Challenges in Industry 4.0 applications and solutions to material handling and storage systems of SMEs]. *Makina Tasarım ve İmalat Dergisi/Journal of Machine Design and Manufacturing, 17*(2), 39-45.

Karakuş, G., & Güneş, K. (2021). An Action Research to Identify Problems Experienced in the ERP System Installation Process in SMEs: Sample of an SMEs Operating in Turkey. In Handbook of Research on Recent Perspectives on Management, International Trade, and Logistics (pp. 352-372). IGI Global. doi:10.4018/978-1-7998-5886-7.ch019

Kerr, I. R. (2006). Leadership strategies for sustainable SME operation. *Business Strategy and the Environment, 15*(1), 30–39. doi:10.1002/bse.451

Lee, J., Jun, S., Chang, T. W., & Park, J. (2017). A smartness assessment framework for smart factories using analytic network process. *Sustainability, 9*(5), 794. doi:10.3390u9050794

Leyh, C., Bley, K., Schäffer, T., & Forstenhäusler, S. (2016, September). SIMMI 4.0-a maturity model for classifying the enterprise-wide it and software landscape focusing on Industry 4.0. In 2016 federated conference on computer science and information systems (fedcsis) (pp. 1297-1302). IEEE.

Mathrani, S., Mathrani, A., & Viehland, D. (2013). Using enterprise systems to realize digital business strategies. *Journal of Enterprise Information Management, 26*(4), 363–386. doi:10.1108/JEIM-01-2012-0003

Metin, S. (2019). *İşletmelerin Dijital Dönüşüm (Endüstri 4.0) Farkındalık ve Algı Düzeyinin Değerlendirilmesi: Elazığ OSB Örneği* [Assessment of Businesses Awareness and Perception Level of Digital Transformation (Industry 4.0): The Case of Elazığ OIZ] [PhD Thesis]. Firat University Social Sciences Institute Technology and Information Management, Elazığ, Türkiye.

Mittal, S., Khan, M. A., Romero, D., & Wuest, T. (2018). A critical review of smart manufacturing & Industry 4.0 maturity models: Implications for small and medium-sized enterprises (SMEs). *Journal of Manufacturing Systems, 49*, 194–214. doi:10.1016/j.jmsy.2018.10.005

Mohiuddin, M., Al Azad, M. S., Ahmed, S., Ed-Dafali, S., & Reza, M. N. H. (2022). *Evolution of Industry 4.0 and Its Implications for International Business.* . doi:10.5772/intechopen.101764

Özdemir, M. (2010). Nitel veri analizi: Sosyal bilimlerde yöntembilim sorunsalı üzerine bir çalışma [Qualitative data analysis: A study on methodology problem in social sciences]. *Eskişehir Osmangazi Üniversitesi Sosyal Bilimler Dergisi/Eskişehir Osmangazi University Journal of Social Sciences, 11*(1), 323–343.

Oztemel, E., & Gursev, S. (2020). Literature review of Industry 4.0 and related technologies. *Journal of Intelligent Manufacturing, 31*(1), 127–182. doi:10.100710845-018-1433-8

Prause, M. (2019). Challenges of industry 4.0 technology adoption for SMEs: The case of Japan. *Sustainability, 11*(20), 5807. doi:10.3390u11205807

PwC. (2016). *Global Industry 4.0 Survey. Industry 4.0: Building the Digital Enterprise 2016*. Available online: https://www.pwc.com/gx/en/industries/industries-4.0/landing-page/industry-4.0-building-yourdigitalenterprise-april-2016.pdf

Sarvari, P. A., Ustundag, A., Cevikcan, E., Kaya, I., & Cebi, S. (2018). Technology roadmap for Industry 4.0. In *Industry 4.0: Managing the digital transformation* (pp. 95–103). Springer. doi:10.1007/978-3-319-57870-5_5

Schulte, M. A. (2016). *Digital transformation in the manufacturing industry, Industry 4.0: From Vision to Reality*. IDC White Paper.

Schumacher, A., Erol, S., & Sihn, W. (2016). A maturity model for assessing Industry 4.0 readiness and maturity of manufacturing enterprises. *Procedia CIRP*, *52*, 161–166. doi:10.1016/j.procir.2016.07.040

Schwab, K. (2016), *The fourth industrial revolution*. World Economic Forum, Geneva, Switzerland.

Schwertner, K. (2017). Digital transformation of business. *Trakia Journal of Sciences*, *15*(1, Suppl.1), 388–393. doi:10.15547/tjs.2017.s.01.065

Sert, E. (2020), *Dijital Dönüşümde Endüstri 4.0 Değer Zinciri Temel Faaliyetler Analizi: Otomotiv Sektörü için Model Önerisi* [Industrial 4.0 value chain primary activities model analysis in digital transformation: Proposal fort he automotive sector] [PhD Thesis]. İstanbul Üniversitesi, Sosyal Bilimler Enstitüsü, İşletme Anabilim Dalı, İstanbul/Istanbul University, Institute of Social Sciences, Department of Business Administration, Türkiye.

Sloan, K., Klingenberg, B., & Rider, C. (2013). Towards sustainability: Examining the drivers and change process within SMEs. *Journal of Management and Sustainability*, *3*(2), 19. doi:10.5539/jms.v3n2p19

TOBB. (2020), *Türkiye'nin KOBİ'leri / Turkey's SMEs*. https://www.tobb.org.tr/KobiArastirma/Documents/TOBB_T%C3%BCrkiyenin%20KOBIleri%20B%C3%BClteni.pdf

Trappey, A. J., Trappey, C. V., Govindarajan, U. H., Chuang, A. C., & Sun, J. J. (2017). A review of essential standards and patent landscapes for the Internet of Things: A key enabler for Industry 4.0. *Advanced Engineering Informatics*, *33*, 208–229. doi:10.1016/j.aei.2016.11.007

Vrchota, J., Volek, T., & Novotná, M. (2019). Factors Introducing Industry 4.0 to SMES. *Soc. Sci.*, *8*(5), 130. doi:10.3390ocsci8050130

Walcott, H. F. (1994). *Transforming qualitative data: Description, analysis and interpretation*. SAGE Publications.

WTO (World Trade Organization). (2021). *World Trade Report 2016: Economic resilience and trade.* https://www.wto.org/english/res_e/booksp_e/wtr21_e/00_wtr21_e.pdf

Yin, R. K. (2018). *Case Study Research and Applications: Design and Methods* (6th ed.). SAGE.

Yusoff, T., Wahab, S. A., Latiff, A. S., Osman, S. I., Zawawi, N. F., & Fazal, S. A. (2018). Sustainable growth in SMEs: A review from the Malaysian perspective. *Journal of Management and Sustainability*, *8*(3), 43. doi:10.5539/jms.v8n3p43

Zapata, M. L., Berrah, L., & Tabourot, L. (2020, August). Towards the Definition of an Impact Level Factor of SME Features Over Digital Transformation. In *IFIP International Conference on Advances in Production Management Systems* (pp. 123-130). Springer.

ADDITIONAL READING

de Sousa Jabbour, A. B. L., Ndubisi, N. O., & Seles, B. M. R. P. (2020). Sustainable development in Asian manufacturing SMEs: Progress and directions. *International Journal of Production Economics, 225*, 107567.

Lawrence, S. R., Collins, E., Pavlovich, K., & Arunachalam, M. (2006). Sustainability practices of SMEs: The case of NZ. *Business Strategy and the Environment*, *15*(4), 242–257. doi:10.1002/bse.533

Prabawani, B. (2013). Measuring SMEs' sustainability: A literature review and agenda for research. *International Journal of Management and Sustainability*, *2*(12), 193–207. doi:10.18488/journal.11/2013.2.12/11.12.193.207

Shields, J., & Shelleman, J. M. (2015). Integrating sustainability into SME strategy. *Journal of Small Business Strategy*, *25*(2), 59–78.

KEY TERMS AND DEFINITIONS

Digitization/Digital Transformation: It is the structural changes that occur with the inclusion of digital technologies in all organizational structures and business processes.

Enterprise Resource Management (ERP): It is an information system designed to support strategy development, operational management, data analysis and decision making functions in businesses. The system provides controlling routine operations such as sales, purchasing, inventory management, production planning and control, service and financial management under one roof (Karakuş & Güneş, 2021: 372).

Industry 4.0: It is the 4th Industrial Revolution, which includes many new automation systems, data management and new production technologies.

SME: Although it differs in different regions of the world, SMEs in Turkey are economic units that employ less than 250 people and whose annual net sales revenue or financial balance sheet does not exceed 125 million TRY and are classified as micro-enterprises, small enterprises, and medium-sized enterprises in the regulation.

Sustainability: It is to act by considering environmental, economic, and social parameters in all processes of businesses in order to be permanent.

Compilation of References

AAOIFI. (2005). *Accounting, Auditing and Governance Standards for Islamic Financial Institutions*. Accounting and Auditing Organization for Islamic Financial Institutions.

AAOIFI. (2008). *Governance Standards for Islamic Financial Institutions*. Accounting and Auditing Organization for Islamic Financial Institutions.

AAOIFI. (2010). *Shariah Standards for Islamic Financial Institutions*. Accounting and Auditing Organization for Islamic Financial Institutions.

Abbas, Z., & Salman, D. (2020). *Egyptian small and medium sized enterprises' battle against COVID-19 pandemic: March–July 2020*. https://www.emerald.com/insight/content/doi/10.1108/JHASS-09-2020-0161/full/pdf

Abdul Alim, E. (2014). *Global Leaders in Islamic Finance*. Industry Milestones and Reflections, Edition Wiley.

Abdul Latif, R., Kamardin, H., Mohd, K. N. T., & Adam, N. C. (2013). Multiple Directorships, Board Characteristics and Firm Performance in Malaysia. *Management*, *3*(2), 105–111.

Abdul Rahman, A., & Bukair, A. A. (2013). The Influence of the *Shariah* Supervision Board on Corporate Social Responsibility Disclosure by Islamic Banks of Gulf Co-operation Council Countries. *Asian Journal of Business and Accounting*, *6*(2), 65–104.

Abdullah, W. A. W., Percy, M., & Stewart, J. (2013). Shari'ah disclosures in Malaysian and Indonesian Islamic banks: The Shari'ah governance system. *Journal of Islamic Accounting and Business Research*, *4*(2), 100–131. doi:10.1108/JIABR-10-2012-0063

Abrams, F. (1951). Management Responsibilities in a Complex World. *Harvard Business Review*, *9*(3).

Abrar, T., Ahmed, F., & Kashif, M. (2018). Financial Stability of Islamic Versus Conventional Banks in Pakistan. *Journal of Islamic Economics*, *10*(2), 341–366.

Abuhashim, A. A., & Tan, C. C. (2020). Smart Contract Designs on Blockchain Applications. *2020 IEEE Symposium on Computers and Communications (ISCC)*, 1-4.

Adeleke, A. Q., & … . (2019). Project Management Performance and Its Influence on Malaysian Building Projects, KnE. *Social Sciences*, 313–329.

African. (2021). *The role of Small and Medium Enterprises (SMEs) in making Egypt self-sufficient.* African Association of Entrepreneurs. https://aaeafrica.org/home

Agan, Y., Acar, M. F., & Borodin, A. (2013). Drivers of environmental processes and their impact on performance: A study of Turkish SMEs. *Journal of Cleaner Production, 51*, 23–33. doi:10.1016/j.jclepro.2012.12.043

Aguinis, H. (2009). *Performance Management* (2nd ed.). Prentice Hall/Pearson Education.

Ahmed, M., & Khatun, M. (2013). The Compliance with *Shariah* Governance System of AAOIFI: A Study on Islamic Banks Bangladesh. *Journal of Islamic Economics, Banking and Finance, 9*(3), 177–191. doi:10.12816/0001617

Ahn, S., Jiraporn, P., & Kim, Y. S. (2010). Multiple directorships and acquirer returns. *Journal of Banking & Finance, 34*(9), 2011–2026. doi:10.1016/j.jbankfin.2010.01.009

Alabbad, A., Hassan, K., & Saba, I. (2020). Can Shariah board characteristics influence risk-taking behavior of Islamic banks? *International Journal of Islamic and Middle Eastern Finance and Management*. . doi:10.1108/IMEFM-11-2018-0403

Alam, M. K., Rahman, M. M., Runy, M. K., Adedeji, B. S., & Hassan, M. F. (2022). The influences of Shariah governance mechanisms on Islamic banks performance and Shariah compliance quality. *Asian Journal of Accounting Research, 7*(1), 2–16. doi:10.1108/AJAR-11-2020-0112

Alanazi, A. S. (2019). Corporate governance and the characteristics of the board of directors: Evidence from an emerging market. *Corporate Board: Role, Duties and Composition, 15*(1), 17–24. doi:10.22495/cbv15i1art2

Albort-Morant, G., Henseler, J., Leal-Millán, A., & Cepeda-Carrión, G. (2017). Mapping the field: A bibliometric analysis of green innovation. *Sustainability, 9*(6), 1011. doi:10.3390u9061011

Al-Janadi, Y., Abdul Rahman, R., & Haj Omar, N. (2013). Corporate Governance Mechanisms and Voluntary Disclosure in Saudi Arabia. *Research Journal of Finance and Accounting, 4*(4), 25–35.

Al-Musalli, M. A. K., & Ismail, K. N. I. (2012). Corporate Governance, Bank Specific Characteristics, Banking Industry Characteristics, And Intellectual Capital (IC) Performance Of Banks In Arab Gulf Cooperation Council (GCC) Countries. *Asian Academy of Management Journal of Accounting and Finance, 8*(1), 115–135.

Almutairi, A. R., & Quttainah, M. A. (2017). Corporate governance: Evidence from Islamic banks. *Social Responsibility Journal, 13*(3), 601–624. doi:10.1108/SRJ-05-2016-0061

Amine, B. (2018). Contribution of Governance to Ensure the Stability of Islamic Banks: A Panel Data Analysis. *International Journal of Accounting and Financial Reporting, 8*(3), 140–155. doi:10.5296/ijafr.v8i3.13333

Amon, B., Kryvoruchko, V., Amon, T., & Zechmeister-Boltenstern, S. (2006). Methane, nitrous oxide and ammonia emissions during storage and after application of dairy cattle slurry and influence of slurry treatment. *Agriculture, Ecosystems & Environment, 112*(2-3), 153–162. doi:10.1016/j.agee.2005.08.030

Ampuero, M. (1998), Solving the measurement dilemma: How EVE and the balanced scorecard fit toether. *Strategic performance management series, (Vol. 2).*

Anderson, C. A., & Anthony, R. N. (1986). *The new corporate directors.* John Wiley and Sons.

Araújo, C., Bragança, L., & Almeida, M. (2013). Sustainable construction key indicators. *IOP Conference Series. Materials Science and Engineering, 660*(1), 505–512.

Arcese, G., Flammini, S., Lucchetti, M. C., & Martucci, O. (2015). Evidence and experience of open sustainability innovation practices in the food sector. *Sustainability, 7*(7), 8067–8090. doi:10.3390u7078067

Ates, A., Garengo, P., Cocca, P., & Bititci, U. (2013). The development of SME managerial practice for effective performance management. *Journal of Small Business and Enterprise Development, 20*(1), 28–54. doi:10.1108/14626001311298402

Atkinson, R. (1999). Project Management: Cost, Time and Quality, Two Best Guesses and a Phenomenon, It's Time to Accept Other Success Criteria. *International Journal of Project Management, 17*(6), 337–342. doi:10.1016/S0263-7863(98)00069-6

Attarça, M., & Jacquot, T. (2005). *La représentation de la responsabilité sociale des entreprises: Une confrontation entre les approches théoriques et les visions managériales, Journée de Développement Durable, AIMS.* IAE Aix-en-Provence.

Aubert, N. (2006). *Pourquoi les salariés achètent des actions de leur entreprise? Le cas d'une augmentation de capital réservée aux salariés, Congrès International de l'Association Française de Finance.* IAE de Poitiers.

Aubert, N., Garnotel, G., Lapied, A., & Rousseau, P. (2014). Employee ownership: A theoretical investigation of management entrenchement vs reward management. *Economic Modelling, 40,* 40. doi:10.1016/j.econmod.2013.12.011

Aupperle, K. E., Carroll, A. B., & Hatfield, J. D. (1985). An Empirical Examination of the Relationship between Corporate Social Responsibility and Profitability. *Academy of Management Journal, 28*(2), 446–463. doi:10.2307/256210

Aygün, D. & Satı, Z. E.(2022). Evaluation of Industry 4.0 transformation barriers for SMEs in Turkey. *Eskişehir Osmangazi Üniversitesi İktisadi ve İdari Bilimler Dergisi/Eskişehir Osmangazi University Journal of Economics and Administrative Sciences, 17*(1), 239-255.

Bacenetti, J., Negri, M., Fiala, M., & González-García, S. (2013). Anaerobic digestion of different feedstocks: Impact on energetic and environmental balances of biogas process. *The Science of the Total Environment, 463*, 541–551. doi:10.1016/j.scitotenv.2013.06.058 PMID:23831800

Bagur-Femenias, L., Llach, J., & del Mar Alonso-Almeida, M. (2013). Is the adoption of environmental practices a strategical decision for small service companies? An empirical approach. *Management Decision*, *51*(1), 41–62. doi:10.1108/00251741311291300

Bakhouche, A., El Ghak, T., & Alshiab, M. (2022). Does Islamicity matter for the stability of Islamic banks in dual banking systems? *Heliyon*, *8*(4), e09245. Advance online publication. doi:10.1016/j.heliyon.2022.e09245 PMID:35434399

Banker, R. D., Potter, G., & Srinivasan, D. (2000). An empirical investigation of an incentive plan that includes nonfinancial performance measures. *The Accounting Review*, *75*(1), 75. doi:10.2308/accr.2000.75.1.65

Barbelivien D. (2014). *La structuration du système de pilotage de la performance au sein d'une ETI la différencie-t-elle de la PME? Le cas d'une ETI familiale du Grand Ouest*, [Working Papers]. hal-00934226, HAL

Barneto, P., & Verstraete, Th. (2008), Finance et entrepreneuriat. Revue du financier, 170, 3-8.

BaryA. (2019). SMEs Sector: A Key Driver to The Egyptian Economic Development. https://www.researchgate.net/publication/331037085

Bassioni, H. A., Price, A. D. F., & Hassan, T. M. (2005). Building a conceptual framework for measuring business performance in construction: An empirical evaluation. *Construction Management and Economics*, *23*(5), 495–507. doi:10.1080/0144619042000301401

Battini, F., Agostini, A., Boulamanti, A. K., Giuntoli, J., & Amaducci, S. (2014). Mitigating the environmental impacts of milk production via anaerobic digestion of manure: Case study of a dairy farm in the Po Valley. *The Science of the Total Environment*, *481*, 196–208. doi:10.1016/j.scitotenv.2014.02.038 PMID:24598150

Battisti, M., & Perry, M. (2011). Walking the talk? Environmental responsibility from the perspective of small-business owners. *Corporate Social Responsibility and Environmental Management*, *18*(3), 172–185. doi:10.1002/csr.266

Baum, J. R., & Locke, E. A. (2004). The Relationship of Entrepreneurial Traits, Skill, and Motivation to Subsequent Venture Growth. *The Journal of Applied Psychology*, *89*(4), 587–598. doi:10.1037/0021-9010.89.4.587 PMID:15327346

Beck, N., & Katz, J. N. (1995). What to do (and not to do) with time-series cross-section data. *The American Political Science Review*, *89*(3), 634–647. doi:10.2307/2082979

Belchior, R., Vasconcelos, A., Guerreiro, S., & Correia, M. P. (2022). A Survey on Blockchain Interoperability: Past, Present, and Future Trends. *ACM Computing Surveys*, *54*(8), 1–41. doi:10.1145/3471140

Ben Moussa, F. (2019). The Influence of Internal Corporate Governance on Bank Credit Risk: An Empirical Analysis for Tunisia. *Global Business Review*, *20*(3), 640–667. doi:10.1177/0972150919837078

Benbasat, I., Goldstein, D. K., & Mead, M. (1987). The case research strategy in studies of information systems. *Management Information Systems Quarterly, 11*(3), 369–386. doi:10.2307/248684

Berger, A. N., & Udell, G. F. (2006). A more complete conceptual framework for SME finance. *Journal of Banking & Finance, 30*(11), 2945–2966. doi:10.1016/j.jbankfin.2006.05.008

Besser, T. L. (1999). Community involvement and the perception of success among small business operators in small towns. *Journal of Small Business Management, 37*(4), 16–30.

Bessire, D. (1999). Définir la performance. *Comptabilité Contrôle Audit, 5*(2), 127–150. doi:10.3917/cca.052.0127

Biondi, V., Frey, M., & Iraldo, F. (2000). Environmental management systems and SMEs. *Greener Management International, 2000*(29), 55–69. doi:10.9774/GLEAF.3062.2000.sp.00007

Bley, K., Leyh, C., & Schäffer, T. (2016). Digitization of German enterprises in the production sector-Do they know how “digitized” they are? *Twenty-second Americas Conference on Information Systems.*

Blowfield, M., Visser, W., & Livesey, F. (2008, September). Sustainability innovation: mapping the territory. In *Corporate Responsibility Research Conference*, Cambridge University Press.

BNM. (2010). *“Guidelines on the Governance of Shariah Committee for the Islamic Financial Institutions”, Islamic Banking and Takaful Department, RH/GL/012-1.* Bank Negara Malaysia-Central Bank of Malaysia.

BNM. (2010). *“Shariah Governance Framework for Islamic Financial Institutions”, Islamic Banking and Takaful Department, RH/GL/012-23.* Bank Negara Malaysia-Central Bank of Malaysia.

BNM. (2013). *“Guidelines on Corporate Governance for Licensed Islamic Banks (GP1-i)”, Islamic Banking and Takaful Department, RH/GL/002-1.* Bank Negara Malaysia-Central Bank of Malaysia.

BNM. (2015). *“Guidelines on Financial Reporting for Licensed Islamic Banks”, Islamic Banking and Takaful Department, RH/GL/002-2.* Bank Negara Malaysia-Central Bank of Malaysia.

Bogner, E., Voelklein, T., Schroedel, O., & Franke, J. (2016). Study based analysis on the current digitalization degree in the manufacturing industry in Germany. *Procedia CIRP, 57*, 14–19. doi:10.1016/j.procir.2016.11.004

Bouckaert, G., & Halligan, J. (2008). *Managing performance, International comparison.* Routledge.

Bouquin, H. (2004). Le contrôle de gestion. Presses Universitaires de France, Collection Gestion, 6ème édition, Paris.

Bourguignon, A. (1997). *Sous les pavés, la plage... ou les multiples fonctions du vocabulaire comptable: Exemple la performance.* Comptabilité Contrôle Audit.

Bourguignon, A. (2000). *Performance et contrôle de gestion. Encyclopédie de Comptabilité, Contrôle de gestion et Audit*. Ed. Economica.

Bourkhis, K., & Nabi, M. S. (2013). Islamic and conventional banks' soundness during the 2007–2008 financial crisis. *Review of Financial Economics*, *22*(2), 68–77. doi:10.1016/j.rfe.2013.01.001

Boussaada, R. (2012). *L'impact De La Gouvernance Bancaire Et De La Relation Bancaire Sur Le Risque De Crédit: Cas Des Banques Tunisiennes* [Ph.D. thesis]. University Montesquieu-University Tunis.

Bowen, H. (1953). *Social Responsibilities of the Businessman*. Harper & Brothers.

Brettel, M., Friederichsen, N., Keller, M., & Rosenberg, M. (2017). How virtualization, decentralization and network building change the manufacturing landscape: An industry 4.0 perspective. *FormaMente, 12*.

Buallay, A. (2019). Corporate governance, Sharia'ah governance and performance: A crosscountry comparison in MENA region. *International Journal of Islamic and Middle Eastern Finance and Management*, *12*(2), 216–235. doi:10.1108/IMEFM-07-2017-0172

Bukair, A. A., & Abdul Rahman, A. (2015). Bank performance and board of directors attributes by Islamic banks. *International Journal of Islamic and Middle Eastern Finance and Management*, *8*(3), 291–309. doi:10.1108/IMEFM-10-2013-0111

Callens, I., & Tyteca, D. (1999). Towards indicators of sustainable development for firms - A productive efficiency perspective. *Ecological Economics*, *28*(1), 41–53. doi:10.1016/S0921-8009(98)00035-4

Cantele, S., & Zardini, A. (2018). Is sustainability a competitive advantage for small businesses? An empirical analysis of possible mediators in the sustainability–financial performance relationship. *Journal of Cleaner Production*, *182*, 166–176. doi:10.1016/j.jclepro.2018.02.016

Capron, M. and Quairel-Lanoizelee, F. (2004). *Mythes et réalités de l'entreprise responsable.* La Découverte.

Cardoni, A., Zanin, F., Corazza, G., & Paradisi, A. (2020). Knowledge management and performance measurement systems for SMEs' economic sustainability. *Sustainability*, *12*(7), 2594. doi:10.3390u12072594

Carroll, A. B. (1979). A three dimensional conceptual model of corporate social performance. *Academy of Management Review*, *4*(4), 97–505. doi:10.2307/257850

Carroll, A. B. (1999). Corporate Social Responsibility. Evolution of a definitional construct. *Business & Society*, *38*(3), 268–295. doi:10.1177/000765039903800303

Carvalho, R. M. D. C. (2017). *Industry 4.0–Is Portugal prepared for the future?* [Doctoral dissertation]. The School of Technology and Management of the Polytechnic Institute of Leiria, Portugal.

Cassar, G. (2007). *Money, money, money? A longitudinal investigation of entrepreneur career reasons, growth preferences and achieved growth* (Vol. 19). Entrepreneurship & Regional Development, Taylor & Francis Journals.

Castelnau, P., & Noël, C. (2004). *Engagement pour un développement durable et performance des entreprises: Le cas français, Actes des journées La performance: de la mesure à l'action.* CERMAT.

Chan, A. P. C., Scott, D., & Chan, A. P. L. (2004). Factors affecting the success of a construction project. *Journal of Construction Engineering and Management, 130*(1), 153–155. doi:10.1061/(ASCE)0733-9364(2004)130:1(153)

Chaum, D. L. (1982). *Computer systems established, maintained and trusted by mutually suspicious groups* [Unpublished doctoral dissertation]. Department of Computer Sciences, The University of California, Berkeley, CA.

Chen, C. (2010). *System and method for automatically generating systematic reviews of a scientific field.* US Patent US20110295903A1.

Chen, C. (2004). Searching for intellectual turning points: Progressive Knowledge Domain Visualization. *Proceedings of the National Academy of Sciences of the United States of America, 101*(Suppl.), 5303–5310. doi:10.1073/pnas.0307513100 PMID:14724295

Chen, C. (2006). CiteSpace II: Detecting and visualizing emerging trends and transient patterns in scientific literature. *Journal of the American Society for Information Science and Technology, 57*(3), 359–377. doi:10.1002/asi.20317

Chen, C. (2016). *CiteSpace: A Practical Guide for Mapping Scientific Literature.* Nova Science Publishers.

Chen, C. (2017). Science mapping: A systematic review of the literature. *Journal of Data and Information Science, 2*(2), 1–40. doi:10.1515/jdis-2017-0006

Chen, C. (2020). A Glimpse of the First Eight Months of the COVID-19 Literature on Microsoft Academic Graph. *Frontiers in Research Metrics and Analytics, 5*, 607286. doi:10.3389/frma.2020.607286 PMID:33870064

Chen, C. X., Lu, H., & Sougiannis, T. (2012). The agency problem, corporate governance, and the asymmetrical behavior of selling, general, and administrative costs. *Contemporary Accounting Research, 29*(1), 252–282. doi:10.1111/j.1911-3846.2011.01094.x

Chen, C., Ibekwe-SanJuan, F., & Hou, J. (2010). The structure and dynamics of co-citation clusters: A multiple-perspective co-citation analysis. *Journal of the American Society for Information Science and Technology, 61*(7), 1386–1409. doi:10.1002/asi.21309

Chen, C., & Song, M. (2019). Visualizing a field of research: A methodology of systematic scientometric reviews. *Public Library of Science ONE, 14*(10), e0223994. doi:10.1371/journal.pone.0223994 PMID:31671124

Cherrafi, A., Garza-Reyes, J. A., Kumar, V., Mishra, N., Ghobadian, A., & Elfezazi, S. (2018). Lean, green practices and process innovation: A model for green supply chain performance. *International Journal of Production Economics*, *206*, 79–92. doi:10.1016/j.ijpe.2018.09.031

Chidinma Maduekwe, C., & Kamala, P. (2016). Performance measurement by small and medium enterprises in Cape Metropolis, South Africa. *Problems and Perspectives in Management*, *14*(2), 46–55. doi:10.21511/ppm.14(2).2016.05

Choi, D., & Gray, E. (2008). The venture development processes of sustainable entrepreneurs. *Management Research News*, *31*(8), 558–569. doi:10.1108/01409170810892127

Christmann, P. (2000). Effects of "Best practices" Of environmental management on cost advantage: The role of complementary assets. *Academy of Management Journal*, *43*(4), 663–680. doi:10.2307/1556360

Ciftci, I. E., Tatoglu, G., Demirbag, W. M., & Zaim, S. (2019). Corporate governance and firm performance in emerging markets: Evidence from Turkey. *International Business Review*, *28*(1), 90–103. doi:10.1016/j.ibusrev.2018.08.004

Čihák, M., & Hesse, H. (2010). Islamic Banks and Financial Stability: An Empirical Analysis. *Journal of Financial Services Research*, *38*(2-3), 95–113. doi:10.100710693-010-0089-0

CIMA. (2020). Accounting for sustainable development performance. *Research Executive Summaries Series*, *2*(15). https://www.cimaglobal.com

Cliff, J. (1998). Does one size fit all? Exploring the relationship between attitudes towards growth, gender and business size. *Journal of Business Venturing*, *13*(5), 523–542. doi:10.1016/S0883-9026(97)00071-2

Cohan, B. and al. (2006). Toward a sustainable conceptualization of dependent variables in entrepreneurship research. *Business Strategy and the Environment*, 17.

Cox, R. F., Issa, R. R. A., & Ahrens, D. (2003). Management's perception of key performance indicators for construction. *Journal of Construction Engineering and Management*, *129*(2), 142–151. doi:10.1061/(ASCE)0733-9364(2003)129:2(142)

D'Amboise, G., & Bakanibona, A. (1990). La planification dans les PME: une synthèse de résultats empiriques: conclusions et recommandations. *Revue internationale P.M. E (Norwalk, Conn.)*, *3*(2), 147–166.

Dai, J., & Vasarhelyi, M. A. (2017). Toward blockchain-based accounting and assurance. *Journal of Information Processing Systems*, *31*(3), 5–21.

Daily News. (2021a). *Egypt announces tax exemptions to boost economic growth*. https://dailynewsegypt.com/2021/12/13

Daily News. (2021b). *Simplified tax system could be applied to SMEs: Egypt's Finance Minister*. https://dailynewsegypt.com

Dalenogare, L. S., Benitez, G. B., Ayala, N. F., & Frank, A. G. (2018). The expected contribution of Industry 4.0 technologies for industrial performance. *International Journal of Production Economics*, *204*, 383–394. doi:10.1016/j.ijpe.2018.08.019

Daly, S., & Frikha, M. (2015). Corporate governance: What about Islamic banks? *International Journal of Financial Services Management*, *8*(1), 18–41. doi:10.1504/IJFSM.2015.066567

Daly, S., & Frikha, M. (2015). Corporate governance: What about Islamic banks? *International Journal of FinancialServices Management*, *8*(1), 18–41.

Davis, L. (1966). The design of jobs. *Industrial Relations*, *6*(1), 21–45. doi:10.1111/j.1468-232X.1966.tb00833.x

Demerens, F., & Paré, J. L. (2011). *Quel enseignement de la finance entrepreneuriale? Une proposition pragmatique* (Vol. 24). Revue Internationale PME.

Dengiz, O. (2017). Endüstri 4.0: Üretimde kavram ve algı devrimi [Industry 4.0: A revolution of concepts and perceptions]. *Makina Tasarım ve İmalat Dergisi/Journal of Machine Design and Manufacturing, 15*(1), 38-45.

Dhouibi, R., & Mamoghli, C. (2013). Determinants of voluntary disclosure in Tunisian Bank's reports. *Research Journal of Finance and Accounting*, *4*(5), 80–94.

Díaz-García, C., González-Moreno, Á., & Sáez-Martínez, F. J. (2015). Eco-innovation: Insights from a literature review. *Innovation*, *17*(1), 6–23. doi:10.1080/14479338.2015.1011060

Dick, M., Wagner, E., & Pernsteiner, H. (2021). Founder-Controlled Family Firms, Overconfidence, and Corporate Social Responsibility Engagement: Evidence From Survey Data. *Family Business Review*, *34*(1), 71–92. doi:10.1177/0894486520918724

DN. (2022). *EIB announces supporting Egypt's green, sustainable projects*. https://dailynewsegypt.com/2022/07/07/eib-announces-supporting-egypts-green-sustainable-projects/

Doluca, H., Wagner, M., & Block, J. (2018). Sustainability and environmental behaviour in family firms: A longitudinal analysis of environment-related activities, innovation and performance. *Business Strategy and the Environment*, *27*(1), 152–172. doi:10.1002/bse.1998

Douhou, A., & Berland, N. (2007). *Mesure de la performance globale des entreprises*. Congrès de l'Association Francophone de Comptabilité.

Drexhage, J., & Murphy, D. (2012). *Sustainable Development: From Brundtland to Rio 2012*. International Institute for Sustainable Development (IISD), United Nations. https://www.e-education.psu.edu/emsc302/sites

Dutta, G., Kumar, R., Sindhwani, R., & Singh, R. K. (2021). Digitalization priorities of quality control processes for SMEs: A conceptual study in perspective of Industry 4.0 adoption. *Journal of Intelligent Manufacturing*, *32*(6), 1–20. doi:10.100710845-021-01783-2

Ebert, C., & Duarte, C. H. C. (2018). Digital Transformation. *IEEE Software, 35*(4), 16–21. doi:10.1109/MS.2018.2801537

Eggers, F. (2020). Masters of disasters? Challenges and opportunities for SMEs in times of crisis. *Journal of Business Research, 116*, 199–208. doi:10.1016/j.jbusres.2020.05.025 PMID:32501306

Ehrenberg, A. (1991). *Le Culte de la performance*. Calmann-Lévy.

Eisenhardt, K. M., & Graebner, M. E. (2007). Theory building from cases: Opportunities and challenges. *Academy of Management Journal, 50*(1), 25–32. doi:10.5465/amj.2007.24160888

Eissa, N. (2020). Egypt within the Sustainable Development Goals One and Two of the United Nations: Overview and Recommendations Thereof. *Research in World Economy*. https://www.researchgate.net/publication/344977238

El Baz, J., Laguir, I., Marais, M., & Staglianò, R. (2016). Influence of national institutions on the corporate social responsibility practices of small-and medium-sized enterprises in the food-processing industry: Differences between France and Morocco. *Journal of Business Ethics, 134*(1), 117–133. doi:10.100710551-014-2417-z

El Kington, J. (1997). *The triple Bottom Line: sustainability's accountants in Russo M. V. (2008), Environmental Management: Reading and cases* (2nd ed.). Sage.

El Saady, R. (2021). *The Role of SMEs in Mediterranean Economies: The Egyptian Experience*. https://www.iemed.org/wp-content/uploads/2021/02/The-Role-of-SMEs-in-Mediterranean-Economies-The-Egyptian-Experience.pdf

Elhaj, M. A., Muhamed, N. A., & Ramli, N. M. (2018). The effects of board attributes on Sukuk rating. *International Journal of Islamic and Middle Eastern Finance and Management, 11*(2), 312–330. doi:10.1108/IMEFM-03-2017-0057

El-Kassar, A. N., & Singh, S. K. (2019). Green innovation and organizational performance: The influence of big data and the moderating role of management commitment and HR practices. *Technological Forecasting and Social Change, 144*, 483–498. doi:10.1016/j.techfore.2017.12.016

Elyasiani, E., & Jia, J. (2010). Distribution of institutional ownership and corporate firm performance. *Journal of Banking & Finance, 34*(3), 606–620. doi:10.1016/j.jbankfin.2009.08.018

Emerton. (2012). *What Makes an Exceptional Independent Non Executive Director?* The Korn/Ferry Institute.

Enterprise. (2019). *Egypt gov't decides on tax reductions for SMEs*. https://enterprise.press/stories/2019/04/03/egypt-govt-decides-on-tax-reductions-for-smes

European Bank. (2022). *Egypt Country Strategy 2022-2027*. https://www.ebrd.com/documents/strategy-and-policy-coordination/egypt-country-strategy.pdf

European Commission (2021) *EU's Next Long-Term Budget & NextGenerationEU: Key Facts and Figures*. EC. https://ec.europa.eu/info/publications/eus-next-long-term-budget-nextgenerationeu-key-facts-and-figures_en

European Commission. (2020). EU budget: European Commission welcomes agreement on €1.8 trillion package to help build greener, more digital and more resilient. *Europe*.

European Commission. (2022). *Internal Market, Industry, Entrepreneurship and SMEs*. https://ec.europa.eu/growth/smes/sme-strategy/taxation-and-smes_en

Ezeldin, A. S., & Sharara, L. M. (2006). Neural Networks for Estimating the Productivity of Concreting Activities. *Journal of Construction Engineering and Management*, *132*(6), 650–656. doi:10.1061/(ASCE)0733-9364(2006)132:6(650)

Ezziadi, A., & Chachdi, A. (2021). Using of the Circularity Indicators in the Financial Communication of Listed Companies in the Construction Industry, *Journal of Economics. Finance and Management Studies*, *4*(6), 766–771.

Ezziadi, A., & Ouhadi, S. (2016). Les perceptions de la performance des PME marocaines. *Economie et société*, 16.

Fama, E. F. (1980). Agency problems and the theory of the firm. *Journal of Political Economy*, *88*(2), 288–307. doi:10.1086/260866

Fama, E. F., & Jensen, M. C. (1983). Separation of ownership and control. *The Journal of Law & Economics*, *26*(2), 301–325. doi:10.1086/467037

Fanning, K., & Centers, D. P. (2016). Blockchain and its coming impact on financial services. *Journal of Corporate Accounting & Finance*, *27*(5), 53–57. doi:10.1002/jcaf.22179

Farag, H., Mallin, C., & Ow-Yong, K. (2014). Corporate social responsibility and financial performance in Islamic banks. *Journal of Economic Behavior & Organization*, *103*, 25–38.

Fassin, Y. (2008). SMEs and the fallacy of formalising CSR. *Business Ethics: a European Review*, *17*(4), 364–378. doi:10.1111/j.1467-8608.2008.00540.x

Ferreira, A., & Otley, D. (2009). The design and use of performance management systems: An extended framework for analysis. *Management Accounting Research*, *20*(4), 263–282. doi:10.1016/j.mar.2009.07.003

Field, L., Lowry, M., & Mkrtchyan, A. (2013). Are busy boards detrimental? *Journal of Financial Economics*, *109*(1), 63–82. doi:10.1016/j.jfineco.2013.02.004

Fořt, J., & Černý, R. (2020). Transition to circular economy in the construction industry: Environmental aspects of waste brick recycling scenarios. *Waste Management (New York, N.Y.)*, *118*, 510–520. doi:10.1016/j.wasman.2020.09.004 PMID:32980730

Freeman, R. E. (2010). *Strategic management: A stakeholder approach*. Cambridge university press. doi:10.1017/CBO9781139192675

Freeman, R. E., Dmytriyev, S. D., & Phillips, R. A. (2021). Stakeholder theory and the resource-based view of the firm. *Journal of Management, 47*(7), 1757–1770. doi:10.1177/0149206321993576

Freeman, R. E., Phillips, R., & Sisodia, R. (2020). Tensions in stakeholder theory. *Business & Society, 59*(2), 213–231. doi:10.1177/0007650318773750

Friedman, A. L., & Miles, S. (2002). SMEs and the environment: Evaluating dissemination routes and handholding levels. *Business Strategy and the Environment, 11*(5), 324–341. doi:10.1002/bse.335

FY22. (2021). *Unlocking Egypt's Potential for Poverty Reduction and Inclusive Growth.* https://documents1.worldbank.org/curated/en/407981634140851775

Gabarret, I. & Vedel, B. (2012). Pour une nouvelle approche de la motivation entrepreneurial. *Congrès international francophone en Entrepreneuriat.* PME.

Gadenne, D. L., Kennedy, J., & McKeiver, C.Gadenne and al. (2009). An Empirical Study of Environmental Awareness and Practices in SMEs. *Journal of Business Ethics, 84*(1), 45–63. doi:10.100710551-008-9672-9

Gauzente, C. (2000). Mesurer la performance des entreprises en l'absence d'indicateurs objectifs: Quelle validité? Analyse de la pertinence de certains indicateurs. *Revue Finance Contrôle Stratégie, 3*(2), 145–165.

Germain, C. and Trébucq, S. (2004). *La performance globale de l'entreprise et son pilotage: quelques réflexions.* Semaine sociale Lamy.

Gets, D., & Petersen, T. (2005). Growth and profit-oriented entrepreneurship among family business owners in the tourism and hospitality industry. *Hospital Management, 24*(2), 219–242. doi:10.1016/j.ijhm.2004.06.007

Ghaemi, S., Rouhani, S., Belchior, R., Cruz, R., Khazaei, H., & Musílek, P. (2021). *A Pub-Sub Architecture to Promote Blockchain Interoperability.* ArXiv, abs/2101.12331.

Ghayad, R. (2008). Corporate governance and the global performance of Islamic banks. *Humanomics, 24*(3), 207–216. doi:10.1108/08288660810899368

Ghisetti, C., & Rennings, K. (2014). Environmental innovations and profitability: How does it pay to be green? An empirical analysis on the German innovation survey. *Journal of Cleaner Production, 75*, 106–117. doi:10.1016/j.jclepro.2014.03.097

Ginena, K., & Hamid, A. (2015). *Foundations of Shariah Governance of Islamic Banks.* Edition Wiley. doi:10.1002/9781119053507

Gioia, D. A., Corley, K. G., & Hamilton, A. L. (2013). Seeking qualitative rigor in inductive research: Notes on the Gioia methodology. *Organizational Research Methods, 16*(1), 15–31. doi:10.1177/1094428112452151

Giordino, D., & Crocco, E. (2022). Sustainable Development: A New Frontier for SMEs. In *Management Strategies for Sustainability, New Knowledge Innovation, and Personalized Products and Services* (pp. 68–93). IGI Global. doi:10.4018/978-1-7998-7793-6.ch003

Glachant M., Vicarelli M. et Vincent F., (2004), Management environnemental: Une enquête auprès de 270 Etablissements Industriels Français. Rapport pour *l'ADEME et l'OCDE.*

Gomez, F. (2001). Financing investment. *The American Economic Review*, 91.

Gong, L. (2021). Microbank's supply chain financial service model for small and micro enterprises. *Banker*, *6*, 123–124.

Grassa, R. (2013). Shariah supervisory system in Islamic financial institutions: New issues and challenges: a comparative analysis between Southeast Asia models and GCC models. *Humanomics*, *29*(4), 333–348. doi:10.1108/H-01-2013-0001

Grassa, R., & Matoussi, H. (2014). Corporate Governance Of Islamic Banks: A Comparative Study Between GCC And Southeast Asia Countries. *International Journal of Islamic and Middle Eastern Finance and Management*, *7*(3), 346–362. doi:10.1108/IMEFM-01-2013-0001

Guenoun, M. (2009), *Le Management de la performance publique locale: Etude de l'utilisation des outils de gestion dans deux organisations intercommunales* [Thèse de doctorat en Sciences de Gestion, Université de Paul Cézanne, Marseille, France].

Gujarati, D. (1995). *Basic Econometrics*. McGraw Hill.

Günaydın, D. (2018). Türkiye'de dördüncü sanayi devrimini beklerken: Çerkezköy Organize Sanayi Bölgesi'nde bir araştırma [While waiting for fourth industrial revolution in Turkey: A case study in Çerkezköy Organized Industrial Zone]. *Istanbul Management Journal*, *29*(85), 73–106.

Guo, L., Liu, Q., Shi, K., Gao, Y., Luo, J., & Chen, J. (2021). A blockchain-driven electronic contract management system for commodity procurement in electronic power industry. *IEEE Access: Practical Innovations, Open Solutions*, *9*, 9473–9480. doi:10.1109/ACCESS.2021.3049562

Gürlek, M., & Tuna, M. (2018). Reinforcing competitive advantage through green organizational culture and green innovation. *Service Industries Journal*, *38*(7-8), 467–491. doi:10.1080/02642069.2017.1402889

Haber, S., & Stornetta, W. S. (1991). How to time-stamp a digital document. *Journal of Cryptology*, *3*(2), 99–111. doi:10.1007/BF00196791

Haddad, A., & Bouri, A. (2022). *The impact of Shariah Advisory Board characteristics on the financial performance of Islamic banks*. Cogent Economics & Finance. doi:10.1080/23322039.2022.2062911

Hakimi, A., Rachdi, H., Ben Selma Mokni, R., & Hssini, H. (2018). Do board characteristics affect bank performance? Evidence from the Bahrain Islamic banks. *Journal of Islamic Accounting and Business Research*, *9*(2), 251–272. doi:10.1108/JIABR-06-2015-0029

Halila, F. (2007). Networks as a means of supporting the adoption of organizational innovations in SMEs: The case of environmental management systems (EMSs) based on ISO 14001. *Corporate Social Responsibility and Environmental Management*, *14*(3), 167–181. doi:10.1002/csr.127

Hamdi, F. M., & Zarai, M. A. (2014). Corporate Governance Practices and Earnings Management in Islamic Banking Institutions. *Research Journal of Finance and Accounting*, *5*(9), 81–96.

Hammer, J., & Pivo, G. (2016). The Triple Bottom Line and Sustainable Economic Development Theory and Practice. *Economic Development Quarterly*, *31*(1), 25–36.

Hamza, H. (2013). Shariah governance in Islamic banks: Effectiveness and supervision model. *International Journal of Islamic and Middle Eastern Finance and Management*, *6*(3), 226–237. doi:10.1108/IMEFM-02-2013-0021

Haniffa, R. M., & Cooke, T. E. (2002). Culture, Corporate Governance andDisclosure in Malaysian Corporations. *Abacus*, *38*(3), 317–349. doi:10.1111/1467-6281.00112

Haribowo, I., Putri, Z. E., & Yulianti, Y. (2021). Corporate Governance and Financial Stability of Islamic Banks in Asia. *Journal of Asian Finance, Economics and Business*, *8*(12), 353–361.

Haridan, N. M., Hassan, A. F. S., & Karbhari, Y. (2018). Governance, religious assurance and Islamic banks: Do Shariah boards effectively serve? *The Journal of Management and Governance*, *22*(4), 1015–1043. doi:10.100710997-018-9418-8

Hashi, S. (2017). *Role of Small & Medium Enterprises in Economic Development*. https://www.linkedin.com/pulse

Hassan, M.K., Sanchez, B., & Safa, M.F. (2013). Impact of financial liberalization and foreign bank entry on Islamic banking performance. *International Journal of Islamic and Middle Eastern Finance and Management*, *6*(1), 7-42.

Hassan, A., & Chachi, A. (2008). Corporate Governance of the Islamic Financial Services Industry in Brunei Darussalam. *Journal of Islamic Economics, Banking and Finance*, *4*(1), 1–21.

Hawkamah. (2011). *Policy Brief On Corporate Governance For Islamic Banks And Financial Institutions In The Middle East And North Africa Region*. Hawkamah, The Institute for Corporate Governance.

Henriette, E., Feki, M., & Boughzala, I. (2015). The shape of digital transformation: A systematic literature review. *MCIS 2015 Proceedings, 10*, 431-443.

Hermundsdottir, F., & Aspelund, A. (2021). Sustainability innovations and firm competitiveness: A review. *Journal of Cleaner Production*, *280*, 124715. doi:10.1016/j.jclepro.2020.124715

Hinings, B., Gegenhuber, T., & Greenwood, R. (2018). Digital innovation and transformation: An institutional perspective. *Information and Organization*, *28*(1), 52–61. doi:10.1016/j.infoandorg.2018.02.004

Hojnik, J., & Ruzzier, M. (2016). The driving forces of process eco-innovation and its impact on performance: Insights from Slovenia. *Journal of Cleaner Production*, *133*, 812–825. doi:10.1016/j.jclepro.2016.06.002

Holden, E., Linnerud, K., & Banister, D. (2014). Sustainable development: Our Common Future revisited. *Global Environmental Change*, *26*, 130–139. doi:10.1016/j.gloenvcha.2014.04.006

Holm-Nielsen, J. B. (2009). Seadi tA, Oleskowicz-Popiel P. *Bioresource Technology*, *100*, 5478–5484. doi:10.1016/j.biortech.2008.12.046 PMID:19217772

Hou, Y., Velthof, G. L., Case, S. D. C., Oelofse, M., Grignani, C., Balsari, P., Zavattaro, L., Gioelli, F., Bernal, M. P., Fangueiro, D., Trindade, H., Jensen, L. S., & Oenema, O. (2018). Stakeholder perceptions of manure treatment technologies in Denmark, Italy, the Netherlands and Spain. *Journal of Cleaner Production*, *172*, 1620–1630. doi:10.1016/j.jclepro.2016.10.162

Hu, L. (2020). *Analysis of micro-credit business of WeBank* [Master's thesis]. Hebei University.

Hu, B., & Fan, Y. (2021). Internet joint lending: Theoretical logic, potential problems and regulatory directions. *Journal of Wuhan University*, (03), 131–142. doi:10.14086/j.cnki.wujss.2021.03.013

Hu, F. (2020). The role and potential of blockchain to advance sustainable development. *Journal of Sustainable Development Economics*, *5*, 59–61.

Hussain, N., Rigoni, U., & Cavezzali, E. (2018). Does it pay to be sustainable? Looking inside the black box of the relationship between sustainability performance and financial performance. *Corporate Social Responsibility and Environmental Management*, *25*(6), 1198–1211. doi:10.1002/csr.1631

Ibrahim, S. H. B. M., Wirman, A., Alrazi, B., Nor, M. N. B. M., & Pramono, S. (2012). *Alternative Disclosure & Performance Measures For Islamic Banks*. Working Paper, International Islamic University Malaysia.

ICLEL. (2015). *The importance of all Sustainable Development Goals (SDGs) for cities and communities*. https://www.local2030.org/library/234

IFSB. (2006). Guiding Principles On Corporate Governance For Institutions Offering Only Islamic Financial Services (Excluding Islamic Insurance (Takaful) Institutions And Islamic Mutual Funds). Islamic Financial Services Board.

IFSB. (2009). *Guiding Principles On Shariah Governance Systems For Institutions Offering Islamic Financial Services*. Islamic Financial Services Board.

Ikram, M., Zhang, Q., Sroufe, R., & Ferasso, M. (2021). Contribution of certification bodies and sustainability standards to sustainable development goals: An integrated grey systems approach. *Sustainable Production and Consumption*, *28*, 326–345. doi:10.1016/j.spc.2021.05.019

ILO Monitor. (2021). Covid-19 and the world of work, (7th ed.): Updated estimates and analysis. International Labor Organization.

Imaobong, N., Felix, A., Linus, E., & Stella, O. (2022). Taxation Practices and the Survival of Small and Medium-Sized Enterprises (SMEs). *Universal Journal of Accounting and Finance, 10*(2), 399-410. https://www.hrpub.org/download/20220228/UJAF4-12225594.pdf

IMF. (2006). *Financial Soundness Indicators*. International Monetary Fund.

IMF. (2006). *Financial Stability Indicators*. International Monetary Fund.

Inna, M., & Alex, P. (2017). The role of accounting in sustainable development. *Accounting and Financial Control, 1*(2). https://www.businessperspectives.org/index.php/journals?controller=pdfview&task=download&item_id=9472, 5/2/2022.

Institut, IMANOR (2020). Guide développement durable dans la construction: Rôles des normes pour une meilleure assimilation des principes et pratiques de développement durable dans la construction. IMANOR.

Ittner, C. D., & Larcker, D. F. (1998). Are nonfinancial measures leading indicators of financial performance? An analysis of customer satisfaction. *Journal of Accounting Research, 36*, 1. doi:10.2307/2491304

Iturriaga, F. J. L., & Rodríguez, I. M. (2014). Boards of directors and firm performance: The effect of multipleDirectorships. *Revista Española de Financiación y Contabilidad, 43*(2), 177–192. doi:10.1080/02102412.2014.913909

Jamali, D., Zanhour, M., & Keshishian, T. (2009). Peculiar strengths and relational attributes of SMEs in the context of CSR. *Journal of Business Ethics, 87*(3), 355–377. doi:10.100710551-008-9925-7

Javaid, M., Haleem, A., Singh, R. P., Rab, S., & Suman, R. (2021). Upgrading the manufacturing sector via applications of Industrial Internet of Things (IIoT). *Sensors International, 2*, 100129. doi:10.1016/j.sintl.2021.100129

Jayashree, S., Hassan Reza, M. N., Malarvizhi, C. A. N., Maheswari, H., Hosseini, Z., & Kasim, A. (2021). The Impact of Technological Innovation on Industry 4.0 Implementation and Sustainability: An Empirical Study on Malaysian Small and Medium Sized Enterprises. *Sustainability, 13*(18), 10115. doi:10.3390u131810115

Jenkins, H. (2006). Small Business Champions for Corporate Social Responsibility. *Journal of Business Ethics, 67*(3), 241–256. doi:10.100710551-006-9182-6

Jensen, M. C. (1993). The modern industrial revolution, exit and the failure of internal control systems. *The Journal of Finance, 48*(3), 831–880. doi:10.1111/j.1540-6261.1993.tb04022.x

Jensen, M. C., & Meckling, W. H. (1976). Theory of the firm: Managerial behavior, agency cost and ownership structure. *Journal of Financial Economics, 3*(4), 305–360. doi:10.1016/0304-405X(76)90026-X

Jimenez, R. M., Hernández-Ortiz, M. J., & Cabrera Fernández, A. I. (2020). Gender diversity influence on board effectiveness and business performance. *Corporate Governance*, *20*(2), 307–323. doi:10.1108/CG-07-2019-0206

Johnson, H. (1971). *Business in contemporary society: Framework and issues*. Wadsworth.

Journeault, M., Perron, A., & Vallières, L. (2021). The collaborative roles of stakeholders in supporting the adoption of sustainability in SMEs. *Journal of Environmental Management*, *287*, 112349. doi:10.1016/j.jenvman.2021.112349 PMID:33735683

Julien, P. A., & Marchensay, M. (1996). *L'entrepreneuriat*. Economica.

Junaid, M. (2022). Effects of sustainable supply chain integration on green innovation and firm performance. *Sustainable Production and Consumption*, *30*, 145–157.

Kachkar, O., & Yilmaz, M.K. (2022). How diverse are Shariah supervisory boards of Islamic banks? A global empirical survey. *International Journal of Ethics and Systems*. . doi:10.1108/IJOES-10-2021-0195

Kamali, M., & Hewage, K. (2017). Development of performance criteria for sustainability evaluation of modular versus conventional construction methods. *Journal of Cleaner Production*, *142*(4).

Karabacak, N., & Aras, N. (2017). Kobi'lerin malzeme aktarma ve depolama sistemlerine yönelik Endüstri 4.0 uygulamalarında karşılaşılan güçlükler ve çözüm önerileri [Challenges in Industry 4.0 applications and solutions to material handling and storage systems of SMEs]. *Makina Tasarım ve İmalat Dergisi/Journal of Machine Design and Manufacturing*, *17*(2), 39-45.

Karakuş, G., & Güneş, K. (2021). An Action Research to Identify Problems Experienced in the ERP System Installation Process in SMEs: Sample of an SMEs Operating in Turkey. In Handbook of Research on Recent Perspectives on Management, International Trade, and Logistics (pp. 352-372). IGI Global. doi:10.4018/978-1-7998-5886-7.ch019

Kasi, B. R., & Mahmood, N. (2019). Composition and Working of the Sharia Supervisory Boards in Bahrain's Islamic Banks. *Economy*, *6*(2), 76–81. doi:10.20448/journal.502.2019.62.76.81

Kasim, N., Htay, S. N. N., & Salman, S. A. (2013). Conceptual Framework for Shariah Corporate Governance with Special Focus on Islamic Capital Market in Malaysia. *International Journal of Trade, Economics and Finance*, *4*(5), 336–339. doi:10.7763/IJTEF.2013.V4.312

Kennedy, P. (1998). *A guide to econometrics*. Blackwell.

Kennedy, P. (2008). *A Guide to Econometrics*. Blackwell.

Kennerley, M., & Neely, A. (2003). Measuring performance in a changing Business Environment. *International Journal of Operations & Production Management*, *23*(2), 23. doi:10.1108/01443570310458465

Kerr, I. R. (2006). Leadership strategies for sustainable SME operation. *Business Strategy and the Environment*, *15*(1), 30–39. doi:10.1002/bse.451

Khalil, A., & Chihi, S. (2020b). Would meetings between the Board of Directors and the Shariah Supervisory Board affect the financial performance of Islamic banks? *Journal of the International Academy for Case Studies*, *26*(6), 1-7.

Khalil, A., & Chihi, S. (2020c). Does the Shariah Board structure influence the financial performance of Islamic banks? *Journal of the International Academy for Case Studies*, *26*(6), 1-7.

Khalil, A., & Chihi, S. (2020c). Would foreign directors and women directors affect the financial performance of Islamic banking? *Journal of the International Academy for Case Studies*, *26*(6), 1-5.

Khalil, A., & Chihi, S. (2020d). Does the Shariah Board structure influence the financial performance of Islamic banks? *Journal of the International Academy for Case Studies*, *26*(6), 1-7.

Khalil, A. (2020). Relationship between the Shariah Council and the Board of Directors and its effect on the financial soundness of Islamic banks. *Asian Journal of Accounting and Finance*, *2*(4), 1–10.

Khalil, A. (2021). The impact of the Board of Directors and the Shariah Board on the financial soundness of Islamic banks. *Journal of Islamic Accounting and Business Research*, *12*(5), 646–660. doi:10.1108/JIABR-01-2019-0011

Khalil, A., & Ben Slimene, I. (2021). Financial Soundness of Islamic banks: Does the Structure of the Board of Directors Matter? *Corporate Governance*, *21*(7), 1393–1415. doi:10.1108/CG-06-2020-0237

Khalil, A., & Chihi, S. (2020a). Do board characteristics affect the financial soundness of Islamic banks. *African Scientific Journal*, *3*(2), 85–102.

Khalil, A., & Chihi, S. (2020a). Do board characteristics affect the financial stability of Islamic banks. *African Scientific Journal*, *3*(2), 85–102.

Khalil, A., & Taktak, N. B. (2020). The impact of the Shariah Board's characteristics on the financial soundness of Islamic banks. *Journal of Islamic Accounting and Business Research*, *11*(9), 1807–1825. doi:10.1108/JIABR-08-2018-0127

Khan, M. H., Fraz, A., Hassan, A., & Abedifar, P. (2019). *Board Gender Diversity, Risk taking and Performance: Evidence from Dual Banking Systems.* Working Papers in Responsible Banking and Finance, No.19-003, pp.1-35.

Khan, S.A., Piprani, A.Z., & Yu, Z. (2022). Digital technology and circular economy practices: future of supply chains. *Operations Management Research*, 1-13.

Khlif, W. (1998). *La Conception et la Mesure de Performance dans l'Industrie Hôtelière: Cas de Trois Entreprises Tunisienne, In la Gestion des Entreprises: Contextes et Performances, Actes du Colloques Organisé le 28, 29 et 30 Novembre 1996 par la Faculté des Sciences Economiques et de Gestion de Sfax.* Centre de Publication Universitaire.

Khorshid, A. (2009). Understanding Derivatives within Islamic Finance. In A. Khorshid (Ed.), *Euromoney Encyclopedia of Islamic Finance. Euromoney Books.*

Kibler, K. M., Reinhart, D., Hawkins, C., Motlagh, A. M., & Wright, J. (2018). Food waste and the food-energy-water nexus: A review of food waste management alternatives. *Waste Management (New York, N.Y.), 74*, 52–62. doi:10.1016/j.wasman.2018.01.014 PMID:29366796

Kiveu, M. N., Namusonge, M., & Muathe, S. (2019). Effect of innovation on firm competitiveness: The case of manufacturing SMEs in Nairobi County, Kenya. International. *Journal of Business Innovation and Research, 18*(3), 307–327. doi:10.1504/IJBIR.2019.098251

Klarin, T. (2018). The Concept of Sustainable Development: From its Beginning to the Contemporary Issues. *Zagreb International Review of Economics and Business, 21*(1), 67-94. https://www.researchgate.net/publication/326164068

Kusi-Sarpong, S., Gupta, H., & Sarkis, J. (2019). A supply chain sustainability innovation framework and evaluation methodology. *International Journal of Production Research, 57*(7), 1990–2008. doi:10.1080/00207543.2018.1518607

Kuzma, E., Padilha, L. S., Sehnem, S., Julkovski, D. J., & Roman, D. J. (2020). The relationship between innovation and sustainability: A meta-analytic study. *Journal of Cleaner Production, 259*, 120745. doi:10.1016/j.jclepro.2020.120745

Labaronne, D. (1998). Les lenteurs de la privatisation en Europe de l'Est: Une conséquence de la stratégie d'enracinement des managers. *Revue d'Économie Politique, 108*(5), 671–689.

Lahouirich, M. W. (2021). De la performance financière et la performance globale: Un panorama multidimensionnel et des approches complémentaires, (2nd ed.). *Colloque International Gouvernance. Entrepreneuriat et Performance.*

Lahouirich, M.W. (2022), Impact of family shareholding on firm's performance: Cas of listed companies in Casablanca stock exchange. *International Review of Management and Computer, 1.*

Lahouirich, M.W. (2022). From financial performance to sustainable development: A great evolution and an endless debate. *Financial Markets, Institutions and Risks (FMIR), 6.*

Lahouirich, M. W and al. (2017). Autour de la performance, de l'évaluation au pilotage: Une revue de littérature, *3ème Colloque International de Recherche en Economie & Gestion.*

Lassoued, M. (2018). Corporate governance and financial stability in Islamic banking. *Managerial Finance, 44*(5), 524–539. doi:10.1108/MF-12-2016-0370

Lebas, M. J. (1995). Performance Measurement and Performance Management. *International Journal of Production Economics, 41*(1-3), 23–35. doi:10.1016/0925-5273(95)00081-X

LeCornu, M. and al. (1996). The small entreprise financial objective function. *Journal of Small Business Management*, 34.

Lee, J., Jun, S., Chang, T. W., & Park, J. (2017). A smartness assessment framework for smart factories using analytic network process. *Sustainability, 9*(5), 794. doi:10.3390u9050794

Lepoutre, J., & Heene, A. (2006). Investigating the Impact of Firm Size on Small Business Social Responsibility: A Critical Review. *Journal of Business Ethics*, *67*(3), 257–273. doi:10.100710551-006-9183-5

Le, T. T., & Ikram, M. (2022). Do sustainability innovation and firm competitiveness help improve firm performance? Evidence from the SME sector in vietnam. *Sustainable Production and Consumption*, *29*, 588–599. doi:10.1016/j.spc.2021.11.008

Leyh, C., Bley, K., Schäffer, T., & Forstenhäusler, S. (2016, September). SIMMI 4.0-a maturity model for classifying the enterprise-wide it and software landscape focusing on Industry 4.0. In 2016 federated conference on computer science and information systems (fedcsis) (pp. 1297-1302). IEEE.

Lim, C. S., & Mohamed, M. Z. (1999). Criteria of project success: An exploratory re-examination. *International Journal of Project Management*, *17*(4), 243–248. doi:10.1016/S0263-7863(98)00040-4

Li, Y., Zhao, J., Krooneman, J., & Euverink, G. J. W. (2021). Strategies to boost anaerobic digestion performance of cow manure: Laboratory achievements and their full-scale application potential. *The Science of the Total Environment*, *755*, 142940. doi:10.1016/j.scitotenv.2020.142940 PMID:33348487

Lloréns Montes, F. J., Verdú Jover, A., & Miguel Molina Fernández, L. (2003). Factors affecting the relationship between total quality management and organizational performance. *International Journal of Quality & Reliability Management*, *20*(2), 189–209. doi:10.1108/02656710310456617

Long, Y., Zhang, J., & Ai, R. (2019). Blockchain technology-based supply s chain financial system optimization research. *Southwest Finance*, *1*, 72–79.

Lorino, P. (2001). *Le balanced scorecard revisité: Dynamique stratégique et pilotage de performance, exemple d'une entreprise énergétique.* Actes du 22ème congrès de l'A.F.C., Metz.

Lorino, P. (2003). *Méthodes et pratiques de la performance*. Collection Références.

Luo, Y., & Hou, Y. (2016). Development strategies and policy regulation of China's Internet banks - A case study based on Wezuo Bank and Online Business Bank. *Modern Economic Exploration*, (07), 42–46. doi:10.13891/j.cnki.mer.2016.07.009

Magdalina, Z. (2021). *Adapting and Mitigating Environmental, Social, and Governance Risk in Business*. IGI Global.

Maged, H., & El Gareib, A. (2021). Entrepreneurship and SMEs Sustainable Development through Business Incubators: The case of Oman. *Scientific Journal for Financial and Commercial Studies and Researches, 2*(2). https://cfdj.journals.ekb.eg/article_146717_f954e2090a386a0118533a70313459eb.pdf

Mahler. (2020). *Lives and Livelihoods: Estimates of the Global Mortality and Poverty Effects of the COVID-19 Pandemic. Policy [Research Working Paper; No. 9277].* World Bank.

Mahmoud, H. (2021). *Sustainable Development Practices of Small and Medium-Sized Enterprises: A Case Study of Egypt* [PhD thesis]. Arab Academy for science, Technology & Maritime Transport (AASTMT). https://www.researchgate.net/publication/35406138

Maignan, I. (2001). Consumers' perceptions of Corporate Social Responsibilities: A Cross-Cultural Comparison. *Journal of Business Ethics*, *30*(1), 57–72. doi:10.1023/A:1006433928640

Ma, L., Chen, X., Zhou, J., & Aldieri, L. (2022). Strategic Management Accounting in Small and Medium-Sized Enterprises in Emerging Countries and Markets: A Case Study from China. *Economies*, *10*(4), 74. doi:10.3390/economies10040074

Maletič, M., Gomišček, B., & Maletič, D. (2021). The missing link: Sustainability innovation practices, non-financial performance outcomes and economic performance. *Management Research Review*, *44*(11), 1457–1477. doi:10.1108/MRR-09-2020-0562

Malsa, N., Vyas, V., Gautam, J., Shaw, R. N., & Ghosh, A. (2021). *Framework and Smart Contract for Blockchain Enabled Certificate Verification System Using Robotics*. Machine Learning for Robotics Applications. doi:10.1007/978-981-16-0598-7_10

Mans-Kemp, N., Viviers, S., & Collins, S. (2018). Exploring the causes and consequences of director overboardedness in an emerging market. *International Journal of Disclosure and Governance*, *15*(2), 210–220. doi:10.105741310-018-0048-9

Mans-Kemp, N., Viviers, S., & Weir, J. (2020). Investigating the extent and impact of director overboardedness using a comprehensive measure. *Corporate Governance: The International Journal of Business in Society*, *20*(5), 821–836. doi:10.1108/CG-07-2019-0234

Maranon, E., Salter, A. M., Castrillon, L., Heaven, S., & Fernández-Nava, Y. (2011). Reducing the environmental impact of methane emissions from dairy farms by anaerobic digestion of cattle waste. *Waste Management (New York, N.Y.)*, *31*(8), 1745–1751. doi:10.1016/j.wasman.2011.03.015 PMID:21504844

Marchesnay, M. (1991). *Économie d'entreprise*. Eyrolles.

Marmuse C. (1997). In Ed. Economica (Ed.), Performance in SIMON Y. & JOFFRE P. (sous la direction de): Encyclopédie de Gestion, 2, (pp. 2194–2207).

Marsden, C. (2000). The New Corporate Citizenship of Big Business: Part of the Solution to Sustainability? *Business and Society Review*, *105*(1), 9–25.

Marston, C. L., & Shrives, P. J. (1991). The use of disclosure indices in accounting research: A review article. *The British Accounting Review*, *23*(3), 195–210. doi:10.1016/0890-8389(91)90080-L

Masulis, R. W., Wang, C., & Xie, F. (2012). Globalizing the boardroom-The effects of foreign directors on corporate governance and firm performance. *Journal of Accounting and Economics*, *53*(3), 527–554. doi:10.1016/j.jacceco.2011.12.003

Mathrani, S., Mathrani, A., & Viehland, D. (2013). Using enterprise systems to realize digital business strategies. *Journal of Enterprise Information Management*, *26*(4), 363–386. doi:10.1108/JEIM-01-2012-0003

Mensah, J., & Ricart, S. (2022, March 2). 2019, "Sustainable development: Meaning, history, principles, pillars, and implications for human action: Literature review. *Cogent Social Sciences*, *5*(1), 1653531. doi:10.1080/23311886.2019.1653531

Metin, S. (2019). *İşletmelerin Dijital Dönüşüm (Endüstri 4.0) Farkındalık ve Algı Düzeyinin Değerlendirilmesi: Elazığ OSB Örneği* [Assessment of Businesses Awareness and Perception Level of Digital Transformation (Industry 4.0): The Case of Elazığ OIZ] [PhD Thesis]. Firat University Social Sciences Institute Technology and Information Management, Elazığ, Türkiye.

Meyssonnier, F. (2015). Quel contrôle de gestion pour les start-ups? *Comptabilité Contrôle Audit*, *21*, 33–61.

Ministère de l'économie et des finances. (2020). *Tableau de bord Sectoriel de l'année 2019.* Ministère de l'économie et des finances.

Ministère délégué chargé de l'environnement. (2016), *Plan sectoriel « Eco-Construction et bâtiment durable* . MDCE.

Ministry of Housing and Urban policy. (2020). *Immobilier 2020: Eléments de prospective.* Ministry of Housing and Urban policy. http://www.mhpv.gov.ma/?page_id=1168

Min, Z., Sawang, S., & Kivits, R. (2021). Proposing Circular Economy Ecosystem for Chinese SMEs: A Systematic Review. *International Journal of Environmental Research and Public Health*, *18*(5), 18. doi:10.3390/ijerph18052395 PMID:33804522

Mittal, S., Khan, M. A., Romero, D., & Wuest, T. (2018). A critical review of smart manufacturing & Industry 4.0 maturity models: Implications for small and medium-sized enterprises (SMEs). *Journal of Manufacturing Systems*, *49*, 194–214. doi:10.1016/j.jmsy.2018.10.005

Mohieldin, M. (2022). Financing Sustainable Development in Egypt. In *Conference Management Section Economic and Social Commission for Western Asia (ESCWA).* A League of Arab States Publication. https://mped.gov.eg/AdminPanel/sharedFiles/9d6b07e2-80fd-4f8a-b13a-8485a773f406

Mohiuddin, M., Al Azad, M. S., Ahmed, S., Ed-Dafali, S., & Reza, M. N. H. (2022). *Evolution of Industry 4.0 and Its Implications for International Business.* . doi:10.5772/intechopen.101764

Momaya, K. S. (2019). The past and the future of competitiveness research: A review in an emerging context of innovation and EMNEs. *International Journal of Global Business and Competitiveness*, *14*(1), 1–10. doi:10.100742943-019-00002-3

Moneim, D. A. (2021). *Egypt's central bank approves new facilities for MSMEs*. Ahram Online. https://english.ahram.org.eg/NewsContent/3/12/404632/Business/Economy/Egypt%E2%80%99s-central-bank-approves-new-facilities-for-M.aspx

Morris, M., Miyasaki, N. N., Watters, C. E., & Coombes, S. M. (2006). The dilemma of growth: Uinderstanding venture size choice of women entrepreneurs. *Journal of Small Business Management*, *44*(2), 221–244. doi:10.1111/j.1540-627X.2006.00165.x

Morsing, M., & Spence, L. J. (2019). Corporate social responsibility (CSR) communication and small and medium sized enterprises: The governmentality dilemma of explicit and implicit CSR communication. *Human Relations*, *72*(12), 1920–1947. doi:10.1177/0018726718804306

Muhammad, R., Annuar, H. A., Taufik, M., & Nugraheni, P. (2021). *The influence of the SSB's characteristics toward Sharia compliance of Islamic banks*. Cogent Business & Management. doi:10.1080/23311975.2021.1929033

Muller, P., Caliandro, C., Peycheva, V., Gagliardi, D., Marzocchi, C., Ramlogan, R., & Cox, D. (2015). *Annual report on European SMEs 2014/2015: SMEs start hiring again*. European Commission.

Muneeza, A., & Hassan, R. (2014). Shariah corporate governance: The need for a special governance code. *Corporate Governance*, *14*(1), 120–129. doi:10.1108/CG-02-2011-0015

Murillo, D., & Lozano, J. (2006). SMEs and CSR: An Approach to CSR in their own words. *Journal of Business Ethics*, *67*(3), 227–240. doi:10.100710551-006-9181-7

Nakamoto, S. (2008). *Bitcoin: a peer-to-peer electronic cash system*. https://bitcoin.org/bitcoin.pdf

Nandi, M. L., Nandi, S., Moya, H., & Kaynak, H. (2020). Blockchain technology-enabled supply chain systems and supply chain performance: A resource-based view. *Supply Chain Management*, *25*(6), 841–862. doi:10.1108/SCM-12-2019-0444

Nathan, S., & Ribière, V. (2007). From Knowledge To Wisdom: The Case Of Corporate Governance In Islamic Banking. *The Journal of Information and Knowledge Management Systems*, *37*(4), 471-483.

Nivyintizo S. (1995), *Déterminants de performance dans le secteur du bâtiment et travaux publics: le cas des entreprises de construction du Burundi*. Mémoire de maîtrise, Université du Québec à Chicoutimi.

Nomran, N. M., Haron, R., & Hassan, R. (2018). Shariah supervisory board characteristics effects on Islamic banks' performance: Evidence from Malaysia. *International Journal of Bank Marketing*, *36*(2), 290–304. doi:10.1108/IJBM-12-2016-0197

OECD. (2020). OECD Investment Policy Reviews: Egypt 2020. *Assessment and Recommendations*. https://www.oecd-ilibrary.org/sites/9f9c589a-en

Ola, B., & Henrik, S. (2013). The United Nations Conference on Sustainable Development: Forty Years in the Making. *Environment and Planning C Government and Policy, 31*(6), 971-987. https://www.researchgate.net/publication/277683928 doi:10.1068/c12287

Ondua, B.V. (2008). *Stratégies de développement durable dans les PME: Une étude exploratoire auprès des PME camerounaises*. Communication présentée au CIFEPME 9, Belgique.

Otley, D. (1999). Performance management: A framework for management control systems research. *Management Accounting Research*, *10*(4), 363–382. doi:10.1006/mare.1999.0115

Oud, R. E., & Amedjar, A. (2016). Analyse comparative des normes comptables appliquées à la finance participative – Cas de la Mourabaha. *International Journal of Innovation and Applied Studies*, *15*(4), 812–821.

Özdemir, M. (2010). Nitel veri analizi: Sosyal bilimlerde yöntembilim sorunsalı üzerine bir çalışma [Qualitative data analysis: A study on methodology problem in social sciences]. *Eskişehir Osmangazi Üniversitesi Sosyal Bilimler Dergisi/Eskişehir Osmangazi University Journal of Social Sciences*, *11*(1), 323–343.

Oztemel, E., & Gursev, S. (2020). Literature review of Industry 4.0 and related technologies. *Journal of Intelligent Manufacturing*, *31*(1), 127–182. doi:10.100710845-018-1433-8

Paré, J. L., & Rédis, J. (2011). Réorienter la recherche en finance entrepreneuriale. Gestion 2000, 28.

Parthiban, P., & Goh, M. (2011). An integrated model for performance management of manufacturing units. *Benchmarking*, *18*(2), 261–281. doi:10.1108/14635771111121702

Pathan, S., & Faff, R. (2013). Does board structure in banks really affect their performance. *Journal of Banking & Finance*, *37*(5), 1573–1589. doi:10.1016/j.jbankfin.2012.12.016

Pesqueux, Y. (2004). *La notion de performance globale, 5ème forum internationale sur La Performance Globale de l'Entreprise*. Université Tunis Carthage.

Peters, G. W., & Panayi, E. (2015). Understanding modern banking ledgers through blockchain technologies: future of transaction processing and smart contracts on the Internet of money. Springer International Publishing.

Pilkington, M. (2016). Blockchain technology: principles and applications. In F. Xavier Olleros & M. Zhegu (Eds.), *Research Handbook on Digital Transformations* (p. 225). doi:10.4337/9781784717766.00019

Pinkston, T. S., & Carroll, A. B. (1996). A retrospective examination of CSR orientations: Have they changed? *Journal of Business Ethics*, *15*(2), 199–206. doi:10.1007/BF00705587

Porter, M. E. (1992). Capital disadvantage: America's Failing Capital Investment System. *Harvard Business Review*, *76*, 65–82. PMID:10121317

Poza, F. and T. Messer (2001). Spousal leadership and continuity in the family firm, *Family Business Review*, *14*(1), pp. 25-36.

Pranata, M. W., & Laela, S. F. (2020). Board characteristics, good corporate governance and maqashid performance in Islamic banking. *Journal of Islamic Monetary Economics and Finance*, *6*(2), 1–24. doi:10.21098/jimf.v6i2.1189

Prause, M. (2019). Challenges of industry 4.0 technology adoption for SMEs: The case of Japan. *Sustainability*, *11*(20), 5807. doi:10.3390u11205807

Prowses, S. (1997). The Corporate Governance System In Banking: What Do We Know? *BNL Quarterly Review*, (Special issue), 11–40.

PwC. (2016). *Global Industry 4.0 Survey. Industry 4.0: Building the Digital Enterprise 2016.* Available online: https://www.pwc.com/gx/en/industries/industries-4.0/landing-page/industry-4.0-building-yourdigitalenterprise-april-2016.pdf

PWC. (2018). *Innovation et BTP: la transformation du secteur est en marche*. PWC. www.pwc.fr

Qasim, Y. (2020). Z-Score Application for Jordanian Islamic Banks. *Journal of Public Administration and Governance*, *10*(1), 289–297. doi:10.5296/jpag.v10i1.16335

Quttainah, M. A. (2012). *Four Essays on the Impact of Shari'ah (Islamic Law) as an Institutional Governance Mechanism on Organizational Performance and Managerial Behavior* [Ph.D. Thesis]. Institute Rensselaer Polytechnic.

Quttainah, M. A. (2012). *Four Essays on the Impact of Shari'ah (Islamic Law) as an Institutional Governance Mechanism on Organizational Performance and Managerial Behavior* [PhD Thesis]. Institute Rensselaer Polytechnic.

Rachdi, H. (2014). The role of banking governance in financial and ethical profitability: The case of Malaysian Islamic Banks. *Journal of Islamic Economics, Banking and Finance*, *10*(3), 14–28. doi:10.12816/0025950

Rafindaa, A., Rafindab, A., Witiastutia, R. S., Surosob, A., & Trinugroho, I. (2018). Board diversity, risk and sustainability of Bank Performance: Evidence from India. *Journal of Security And Sustainability Issues*, *7*(4), 793–806. doi:10.9770/jssi.2018.7.4(15)

Ramly, Z., Datuk, N., & Nordin, M. H. (2018). Shariah Supervision Board, Board Independence, Risk Committee and Risk-taking of Islamic Banks in Malaysia. *International Journal of Economics and Financial Issues*, *8*(4), 290–300.

Rammal, H. G. (2006). The Importance Of Shariah Supervision In Islamic Financial Institutions. *Corporate Ownership and Control*, *3*(3), 204–208. doi:10.22495/cocv3i3c1p5

Rauter, R., Globocnik, D., Perl-Vorbach, E., & Baumgartner, R. J. (2019). Open innovation and its effects on economic and sustainability innovation performance. *Journal of Innovation & Knowledge*, *4*(4), 226–233. doi:10.1016/j.jik.2018.03.004

Raymond, L., Marchand, M., St-Pierre, J., Cadieux, L., & Labelle, F. (2013). Dimensions of small business performance from the owner-manager's perspective: A reconceptualization and empirical validation. *Entrepreneurship and Regional Development*, *25*(5-6), 468–499. doi:10.1080/08985626.2013.782344

Rédis, J. (2009). *Finance entrepreneuriale, L'Harmattan.* Collection De Boeck.

Rédis, J., & Paré, J. (2007). *Qu'est-ce que la finance entrepreneuriale? Séminaire de finance entrepreneuriale Advancia – Institut pour la recherche CDC – CDC Entreprises, 25 septembre 2007*. Advancia-Négocia.

Rehman Khan, S. A., Yu, Z., Sarwat, S., Godil, D. I., Amin, S., & Shujaat, S. S. (2021). The role of block chain technology in circular economy practices to improve organisational performance. *International Journal of Logistics Research and Applications*, *25*(4-5), 605–622. doi:10.1080/13675567.2021.1872512

Reijonen, H. & Komppula, R. (2007). Perception of success and its effect on small firm performance. *Journal of Small Business Entreprise Development, 14*.

Revell, A., & Rutherfoord, R. (2003). UK environmental policy and the small firm: Broadening the focus. *Business Strategy and the Environment*, *12*(1), 26–35. doi:10.1002/bse.347

Revell, A., Stokes, D., & Chen, H. (2010). Small businesses and the environment: Turning over a new leaf? *Business Strategy and the Environment*, *19*(5), 273–288.

Reynaud, E. (2003). *Développement durable et entreprise: vers une relation symbiotique, Journée AIMS, Atelier développement durable*. ESSCA Angers.

Russo, A., & Tencati, A. (2009). Formal vs. Informal CSR strategies: Evidence from Italian Micro, Small, Medium-sized, and Large Firms. *Journal of Business Ethics*, *85*(S2), 339–353. doi:10.100710551-008-9736-x

Sachs, S., & Kujala, J. (2021). *Stakeholder engagement in management studies: Current and future debates*. Oxford Research Encyclopedia of Business and Management.

Sadeq H. (2013), Les programmes d'appui à la PME. Publications de l'IRES, p. 32

Saeed, M. B., & Saeed, S. K. (2018). Characteristics of Shariah Supervisory Board, Corporate Governance Mechanisms and Efficiency of Islamic Banks: Evidence from Listed Banks in Asia. *Journal of Islamic Business and Management*, *8*(1), 116–138.

Salgado M. (2013). *La performance: une dimension fondamentale pour l'évaluation des entreprises et des organisations*. hal-00842219

Sardi, A., Sorano, E., Garengo, P., & Ferraris, A. (2020). The role of HRM in the innovation of performance measurement and management systems: A multiple case study in SMEs. *Employee Relations: The International Journal*, *43*(2), 589–606. doi:10.1108/ER-03-2020-0101

Sarvari, P. A., Ustundag, A., Cevikcan, E., Kaya, I., & Cebi, S. (2018). Technology roadmap for Industry 4.0. In *Industry 4.0: Managing the digital transformation* (pp. 95–103). Springer. doi:10.1007/978-3-319-57870-5_5

Savitz, A. (2013). *Talent, Transformation, and the Triple Bottom Line: How Companies Can Leverage Human Resources to Achieve Sustainable Growth*. John Wiley & Sons.

Savitz, A. W. (2013). *The Triple Bottom Line: How Today's Best-Run Companies Are Achieving Economic, Social and Environmental Success - and How You Can Too*. John Wiley & Sons.

Schulte, M. A. (2016). *Digital transformation in the manufacturing industry, Industry 4.0: From Vision to Reality*. IDC White Paper.

Schumacher, A., Erol, S., & Sihn, W. (2016). A maturity model for assessing Industry 4.0 readiness and maturity of manufacturing enterprises. *Procedia CIRP*, *52*, 161–166. doi:10.1016/j.procir.2016.07.040

Schwab, K. (2016), *The fourth industrial revolution*. World Economic Forum, Geneva, Switzerland.

Schwertner, K. (2017). Digital transformation of business. *Trakia Journal of Sciences*, *15*(1, Suppl.1), 388–393. doi:10.15547/tjs.2017.s.01.065

Šelih, J. (2007). Environmental management systems and construction SMES: A case study for Slovenia. *Journal of Civil Engineering and Management*, *13*(3), 217–226. doi:10.3846/13923730.2007.9636440

Sergeeva, A., Huysman, M., Soekijad, M., & van den Hooff, B. (2017). Through the eyes of others: How onlookers shape the use of technology at work. *Management Information Systems Quarterly*, *41*(4), 1153–1178. doi:10.25300/MISQ/2017/41.4.07

Sert, E. (2020), *Dijital Dönüşümde Endüstri 4.0 Değer Zinciri Temel Faaliyetler Analizi: Otomotiv Sektörü için Model Önerisi* [Industrial 4.0 value chain primary activities model analysis in digital transformation: Proposal fort he automotive sector] [PhD Thesis]. İstanbul Üniversitesi, Sosyal Bilimler Enstitüsü, İşletme Anabilim Dalı, İstanbul/Istanbul University, Institute of Social Sciences, Department of Business Administration, Türkiye.

Shachaf, P. (2008). Cultural diversity and information and communication technology impacts on global virtual teams: An exploratory study. *Information & Management*, *45*(2), 131–142. doi:10.1016/j.im.2007.12.003

Shih, J. C. (2015). Development of Anaerobic Digestion of Animal Waste: From Laboratory, Research and Commercial Farms to a Value-Added New Product. In Anaerobic Biotechnology: Environmental Protection and Resource Recovery (pp. 339-352).

Shin, J., Kim, C., & Yang, H. (2018). The effect of sustainability as innovation objectives on innovation efficiency. *Sustainability*, *10*(6), 1966. doi:10.3390u10061966

Shobhalata, U., & Sakkarnaikar, F. S. (2015). From Stockholm to Rio to Rio+20: Green Economy and the Road Ahead. *American International Journal of Research in Humanities, Arts and Social Sciences*. http://iasir.net/AIJRHASSpapers

Sloan, K., Klingenberg, B., & Rider, C. (2013). Towards sustainability: Examining the drivers and change process within SMEs. *Journal of Management and Sustainability*, *3*(2), 19. doi:10.5539/jms.v3n2p19

Smith, A. (2000), Small firms and the environment: Factors that influence small and medium sized entreprises environmental behaviour. *Small and medium-sized entreprises and the environment*.

Spence, L. J. (2015). (in press). Small business social responsibility: Expanding core CSR theory'. *Business & Society*. doi:10.1177/0007650314523256

Spence, L. J., & Lozano, J. (2000). Communicating About ethics with small firms: Experiences from the U.K. and Spain. *Journal of Business Ethics*, *27*(1/2), 43–53. doi:10.1023/A:1006417425446

Spence, L., & Rutherfoord, R. (2001). Social Responsibility, profit maximization and the small firm owner-manager. *Journal of Small Business and Enterprise Development*, *8*(2), 126–139. doi:10.1108/EUM0000000006818

Spence, M. (2007). *Développement durable et PME: Une étude exploratoire des déterminants de leur engagement* (Vol. 20). Revue Internationale PME.

Stekelorum, R. (2020). The roles of SMEs in implementing CSR in supply chains: A systematic literature review. *International Journal of Logistics Research and Applications*, *23*(3), 228–253. doi:10.1080/13675567.2019.1679101

Stiglitz, J. (2009). The measurement of economic performance and social progress revisited: Reflections and overview. *Sciences Po Publications, 33*.

St-Perre, J. & Cadieux, L. (2011), La conception de la performance: Quels liens avec le profil entrepreneurial des propriétaires dirigeants de PME?, *Revue de l'entrepreneuriat, 10.*

St-Pierre, J. (2012), *Configuration de capacités stratégiques et performance des PME: Une étude exploratoire de l'influence de l'environnement national.* CIFEPME, Brest, France.

St-Pierre, J., & Cadieux, L. (2011). La conception de la performance: Quels liens avec le profil entrepreneurial des propriétaires dirigeants de PME? *Revue de l'Entrepreneuriat*, *10*, 33–52.

Sufian, F. (2006). Size and Returns to Scale of the Islamic Banking Industry in Malaysia: Foreign Versus Domestic Banks. *IIUM Journal of Economics and Management*, *14*(2), 147–175.

Sufian, F. (2010). Does foreign presence foster Islamic banks' performance? Empirical evidence from Malaysia. *Journal of Islamic Accounting and Business Research*, *1*(2), 128–147. doi:10.1108/17590811011086723

Sufian, F., & Abdul Majid, M. (2008). Bank Ownership, Characteristics, and Performance: A Comparative Analysis of Domestic and Foreign Islamic Banks in Malaysia. *J.KAU: Islamic Econ.*, *21*(2), 3–37.

Sun, W., Dedahanov, A. T., Shin, H. Y., & Li, W. P. (2021). Using extended complexity theory to test SMEs' adoption of Blockchain-based loan system. *PLoS One*, *16*(2), 16. doi:10.1371/journal.pone.0245964 PMID:33544745

Sun, Y., Chen, Y., Li, D., Lu, H., Li, B., Liu, C., & Lu, W. (2021). The research of source-load transaction mechanism based on blockchain. *IOP Conference Series. Earth and Environmental Science*, *675*(1), 675. doi:10.1088/1755-1315/675/1/012142

Tang, X. (2022). New Schemes for Investment in of Small and Medium-Sized Enterprises of China: Role of Access to Finance, Innovation, and Sustainability. *Frontiers in Psychology*, *13*, 13. doi:10.3389/fpsyg.2022.857193 PMID:35558710

Tang, Y. J. (2021). An overview of commercial banks' credit risk management and the difficulty of financing for small and medium-sized enterprises. *Business News*, *12*, 73–74.

Tan, Y. (2021). The dilemma and the way out of the regulation of the abuse of market dominance by Internet platforms. *Research on the Rule of Law*, *4*, 110–123. doi:10.16224/j.cnki.cn33-1343/d.20210701.004

Tazilah, M. D. A. K., & Abdul Rahman, R. (2014). Risk Management and Corporate Governance Characteristics in the Malaysian Islamic Financial Institutions. *Research Journal of Finance and Accounting*, *5*(12), 116–128.

Thanh, T. L., Huan, N. Q., & Hong, T. T. T. (2021). Effects of corporate social responsibility on SMEs' performance in emerging market. *Cogent Business & Management*, *8*(1), 1878978. doi: 10.1080/23311975.2021.1878978

The Global Reporting Initiative (GRI) (2001). *Guidelines for sustainability reporting*. GRI.

TOBB. (2020), *Türkiye'nin KOBİ'leri / Turkey's SMEs*. https://www.tobb.org.tr/KobiArastirma/Documents/TOBB_T%C3%BCrkiyenin%20KOBIleri%20B%C3%BClteni.pdf

Toor, S.-R., & Ogunlana, S. O. (2008). Critical COMs of success in large-scale construction projects: Evidence from Thailand construction industry. *International Journal of Project Management*, *26*(4), 420–430. doi:10.1016/j.ijproman.2007.08.003

Toor, S.-R., & Ogunlana, S. O. (2010). Beyond the 'iron triangle': Stakeholder perception of key performance indicators (KPIs) for large-scale public sector development projects. *International Journal of Project Management*, *28*(3), 228–236. doi:10.1016/j.ijproman.2009.05.005

Trappey, A. J., Trappey, C. V., Govindarajan, U. H., Chuang, A. C., & Sun, J. J. (2017). A review of essential standards and patent landscapes for the Internet of Things: A key enabler for Industry 4.0. *Advanced Engineering Informatics*, *33*, 208–229. doi:10.1016/j.aei.2016.11.007

Tripathi, K. K., & Jha, K. N. (2018). An empirical study on performance measurement factors for construction organizations. *KSCE Journal of Civil Engineering*, *22*(4), 1052–1066. doi:10.100712205-017-1892-z

Tripathi, K.K., & Jha, K.N. (2018). Determining success factors for a construction organization: A structural equation modeling approach. *Journal of Management Engineering*, *34*(1), 1–15.

Ujunwa, A. (2012). Board characteristics and the financial performance of Nigerian quoted firms. *Corporate Governance*, *12*(5), 656–674. doi:10.1108/14720701211275587

Ukko, J., Nasiri, M., Saunila, M., & Rantala, T. (2019). Sustainability strategy as a moderator in the relationship between digital business strategy and financial performance. *Journal of Cleaner Production*, *236*, 117626. doi:10.1016/j.jclepro.2019.117626

Ullah, S., Khokhar, Z.A., Tanveer, N., Khan, M.W., Shabbir, G., & Ahmed, A. (2014). *Shariah Governance Framework For Islamic Banking Institutions*. Islamic Banking Department, State Bank of Pakistan.

Ulrich, L. (2000). Small and medium-sized enterprises – delimitation and the European definition in the area of industrial business. *European Business Review, 12*(5), 261–264. doi:10.1108/09555340010373537

United Nations Environment Programme. (2021). *Global Status report for building and construction.*

Valentinov, V., & Chia, R. (2022). Stakeholder theory: A process-ontological perspective. *Business Ethics, the Environment & Responsibility, 31*(3), 762-776.

Verma, V., Bisht, P., & Joshi, S. (2022). Sustainable Supply chain Systems of Food and Beverages SMEs in developing countries: Theoretical perspective. *Journal of Decision Analytics and Intelligent Computing, 2*(1), 36–52. doi:10.31181/jdaic10011062022v

Vives, A. (2006). Social and Environmental Responsibility in Small and Medium Enterprises in Latin America. *Journal of Corporate Citizenship, 21*(21), 39–50. doi:10.9774/GLEAF.4700.2006.sp.00006

Vo, L. C. (2011). Corporate social responsibility and SMEs: A literature review and agenda for future research. *Problems and Perspectives in Management*, 9(4), 89–97.

Vrchota, J., Volek, T., & Novotná, M. (2019). Factors Introducing Industry 4.0 to SMES. *Soc. Sci., 8*(5), 130. doi:10.3390ocsci8050130

Walcott, H. F. (1994). *Transforming qualitative data: Description, analysis and interpretation.* SAGE Publications.

Walker, E., & Brown, A. (2004). What success factors are important to small business owners? *International Small Business Journal, 22*(6), 577–594. doi:10.1177/0266242604047411

Wan, J. (2018). *Countermeasures for the characteristic development of Qianhai WeBank in Shenzhen* [Master's thesis]. Hebei University.

Wang, R., Lin, Z., & Luo, H. (2019). Blockchain, bank credit and SME financing. *Quality & Quantity, 53*(3), 1127–1140. doi:10.100711135-018-0806-6

Wang, W., & Wang, Y. (2016). Integrated Innovation Theory: Theory Exploration of a Complex System. *Management & Engineering*, (23), 228.

Wang, X., & Huang, J. (2006). The relationships between key stakeholders ' project performance and project success: Perceptions of Chinese construction supervising engineers. *International Journal of Project Management, 24*(3), 253–260. doi:10.1016/j.ijproman.2005.11.006

Westhead, P., & Wright, M. (1999). Portfolio and serial founders located in rural and urban area. *Regional Studies, 33*(2).

Wiklund, J., & Shepherd, D. (2005). Entrepreneurial orientation and small business performance: A configurational approach. *Journal of Business Venturing, 20*(1), 71–91. doi:10.1016/j.jbusvent.2004.01.001

Wong, P. F., Chia, F. C., Kiu, M. S., & Lou, E. C. (2020). *Potential integration of blockchain technology into smart sustainable city (SSC) developments: A systematic review*. Smart and Sustainable Built Environment.

Wood, D. J. (1991). Corporate social performance revisited. *Academy of Management Review*, *16*(4), 691. doi:10.2307/258977

World Commission on Environment and Development. (1987). Our Common Future, United Nations. WCED.

Worthington, I., Ram, M., Boyal, H., & Shah, M. (2008). Researching the Drivers of Socially Responsible Purchasing: A Cross-National Study of Supplier Diversity Initiatives. *Journal of Business Ethics*, *79*(3), 319–331. doi:10.100710551-007-9400-x

WTO (World Trade Organization). (2021). *World Trade Report 2016: Economic resilience and trade*. https://www.wto.org/english/res_e/booksp_e/wtr21_e/00_wtr21_e.pdf

Xavier, A. F., Naveiro, R. M., Aoussat, A., & Reyes, T. (2017). Systematic literature review of eco-innovation models: Opportunities and recommendations for future research. *Journal of Cleaner Production*, *149*, 1278–1302. doi:10.1016/j.jclepro.2017.02.145

Xie, W. S. (2022). Study on Enterprise Financial Risk Prevention and Early Warning System Based on Blockchain Technology. *Mobile Information Systems*, *2022*(1), 5–10. doi:10.1155/2022/4435296

Yang, H., Zhang, W., Xi, X., Liu, Y., & Zhai, T. (2020). Block Research on the game of supply chain finance based on accounts receivable model in a chain environment. *Mathematical Practice and Understanding*, *13*, 313–320.

Yang, J. (2021). China's small and medium-sized enterprise financing dilemma and countermeasures research. *Economist*, *11*, 288–290.

Yar, S., & Ahmed, S. Y. (2020). Impact of Board Gender Diversity on The Financial Performance of Conventional and Islamic Banks – An Evidence from Pakistan. *MPRA*, (98798), 1–28.

Yermack, D. (2017). Corporate governance and blockchains. *Review of Finance*, *21*(1), 7–31.

Yin, R. (2018). *Case Study Research: Design and Methods* (6th ed.). Sage.

Yin, R. K. (2018). *Case Study Research and Applications: Design and Methods* (6th ed.). SAGE.

Yu, P., Yu, M., & Sampat, M. (2022g). Smart Management for Digital Transformation in China. In B. Barbosa, S. Filipe, & C. Santos (Eds.), Handbook of Research on Smart Management for Digital Transformation (pp. 411-438). IGI Global. doi:10.4018/978-1-7998-9008-9.ch019

Yu, P., Chen, D., & Ahuja, A. (2022a). Smart and Sustainable Economy: How COVID-19 Has Acted as a Catalyst for China's Digital Transformation. In S. Kautish & G. Kaur (Eds.), *AI-Enabled Agile Internet of Things for Sustainable FinTech Ecosystems* (pp. 106–146). IGI Global. doi:10.4018/978-1-6684-4176-3.ch006

Yu, P., Gong, R., & Sampat, M. (2022b). Blockchain Technology in China's Digital Economy: Balancing Regulation and Innovation. In P. Tehrani (Ed.), *Regulatory Aspects of Artificial Intelligence on Blockchain* (pp. 132–157). IGI Global. doi:10.4018/978-1-7998-7927-5.ch007

Yu, P., Gu, H., Zhao, Y., & Ahuja, A. (2022c). Digital Transformation Driven by Internet Data Center: Case Studies on China. In D. Piaggesi, H. Landazuri, & B. Jia (Eds.), *Cases on Applying Knowledge Economy Principles for Economic Growth in Developing Nations* (pp. 203–230). IGI Global. doi:10.4018/978-1-7998-8417-0.ch011

Yu, P., Jiao, A., & Sampat, M. (2022d). The Effect of Chinese Green Transformation on Competitiveness and the Environment. In P. Ordóñez de Pablos, X. Zhang, & M. Almunawar (Eds.), *Handbook of Research on Green, Circular, and Digital Economies as Tools for Recovery and Sustainability* (pp. 257–279). IGI Global. doi:10.4018/978-1-7998-9664-7.ch014

Yu, P., Liu, Z., Hanes, E., & Mumtaz, J. (2022e). Integration of IoT and Blockchain for Smart and Secured Supply Chain Management: Case Studies of China. In S. Goyal, N. Pradeep, P. Shukla, M. Ghonge, & R. Ravi (Eds.), *Utilizing Blockchain Technologies in Manufacturing and Logistics Management* (pp. 179–207). IGI Global. doi:10.4018/978-1-7998-8697-6.ch010

Yu, P., Lu, S., Hanes, E., & Chen, Y. (2022f). The Role of Blockchain Technology in Harnessing the Sustainability of Chinese Digital Finance. In P. Swarnalatha & S. Prabu (Eds.), *Blockchain Technologies for Sustainable Development in Smart Cities* (pp. 155–186). IGI Global. doi:10.4018/978-1-7998-9274-8.ch009

Yusoff, T., Wahab, S. A., Latiff, A. S., Osman, S. I., Zawawi, N. F., & Fazal, S. A. (2018). Sustainable growth in SMEs: A review from the Malaysian perspective. *Journal of Management and Sustainability*, *8*(3), 43. doi:10.5539/jms.v8n3p43

Zainol, Z., Shaari, R., & Muhamad Ali, H. (2008). A Comparative Analysis of Bankers' Perceptions on Islamic Banking. *International Journal of Business and Management*, *3*(4), 157–168.

Zapata, M. L., Berrah, L., & Tabourot, L. (2020, August). Towards the Definition of an Impact Level Factor of SME Features Over Digital Transformation. In *IFIP International Conference on Advances in Production Management Systems* (pp. 123-130). Springer.

Zefeng, M., Gang, Z., Xiaorui, X., Yongmin, S., & Junjiao, H. (2018). The extension of the Porter hypothesis: Can the role of environmental regulation on economic development be affected by other dimensional regulations? *Journal of Cleaner Production*, *203*, 933–942. doi:10.1016/j.jclepro.2018.08.332

Zepeda, R. (2013). Enhancing Islamic Finance through Risk Benchmarking. *The Capco Institute Journal of Financial Transformation*, *38*, 16–36.

Zhang, L. (2021). The role of SME business administration in promoting economic development. *China Small and Medium Enterprises*, *5*, 142–143.

Zhou, L., Qiu, X., Liu, J., & Chen, W. (2020). Research on FinTech innovation to serve small and micro enterprises' financing - a survey based on 840 small and micro enterprises in FinTech pilot areas. *Southwest Finance*, *10*, 24–35.

Zhu, Y. (2019). *R&D input, innovation output and firm performance* [Master's thesis]. Zhongnan University of Economics and Law. https://kns.cnki.net/KCMS/detail/detail.aspx?dbname=CMFD202002&filename=1019862670.nh

Zouari, S. Z., & Taktak, N. B. (2014). Ownership structure and financial performance in Islamic banks: Does bank ownership matter? *International Journal of Islamic and Middle Eastern Finance and Management*, *7*(2), 146–160. doi:10.1108/IMEFM-01-2013-0002

Related References

To continue our tradition of advancing information science and technology research, we have compiled a list of recommended IGI Global readings. These references will provide additional information and guidance to further enrich your knowledge and assist you with your own research and future publications.

Abdul Razak, R., & Mansor, N. A. (2021). Instagram Influencers in Social Media-Induced Tourism: Rethinking Tourist Trust Towards Tourism Destination. In M. Dinis, L. Bonixe, S. Lamy, & Z. Breda (Eds.), *Impact of New Media in Tourism* (pp. 135-144). IGI Global. https://doi.org/10.4018/978-1-7998-7095-1.ch009

Abir, T., & Khan, M. Y. (2022). Importance of ICT Advancement and Culture of Adaptation in the Tourism and Hospitality Industry for Developing Countries. In C. Ramos, S. Quinteiro, & A. Gonçalves (Eds.), *ICT as Innovator Between Tourism and Culture* (pp. 30–41). IGI Global. https://doi.org/10.4018/978-1-7998-8165-0.ch003

Abtahi, M. S., Behboudi, L., & Hasanabad, H. M. (2017). Factors Affecting Internet Advertising Adoption in Ad Agencies. *International Journal of Innovation in the Digital Economy*, *8*(4), 18–29. doi:10.4018/IJIDE.2017100102

Afenyo-Agbe, E., & Mensah, I. (2022). Principles, Benefits, and Barriers to Community-Based Tourism: Implications for Management. In I. Mensah & E. Afenyo-Agbe (Eds.), *Prospects and Challenges of Community-Based Tourism and Changing Demographics* (pp. 1–29). IGI Global. doi:10.4018/978-1-7998-7335-8.ch001

Agbo, V. M. (2022). Distributive Justice Issues in Community-Based Tourism. In I. Mensah & E. Afenyo-Agbe (Eds.), *Prospects and Challenges of Community-Based Tourism and Changing Demographics* (pp. 107–129). IGI Global. https://doi.org/10.4018/978-1-7998-7335-8.ch005

Agrawal, S. (2017). The Impact of Emerging Technologies and Social Media on Different Business(es): Marketing and Management. In O. Rishi & A. Sharma (Eds.), *Maximizing Business Performance and Efficiency Through Intelligent Systems* (pp. 37–49). Hershey, PA: IGI Global. doi:10.4018/978-1-5225-2234-8.ch002

Ahmad, A., & Johari, S. (2022). Georgetown as a Gastronomy Tourism Destination: Visitor Awareness Towards Revisit Intention of Nasi Kandar Restaurant. In M. Valeri (Ed.), *New Governance and Management in Touristic Destinations* (pp. 71–83). IGI Global. https://doi.org/10.4018/978-1-6684-3889-3.ch005

Alkhatib, G., & Bayouq, S. T. (2021). A TAM-Based Model of Technological Factors Affecting Use of E-Tourism. *International Journal of Tourism and Hospitality Management in the Digital Age*, *5*(2), 50–67. https://doi.org/10.4018/IJTHMDA.20210701.oa1

Altinay Ozdemir, M. (2021). Virtual Reality (VR) and Augmented Reality (AR) Technologies for Accessibility and Marketing in the Tourism Industry. In C. Eusébio, L. Teixeira, & M. Carneiro (Eds.), *ICT Tools and Applications for Accessible Tourism* (pp. 277-301). IGI Global. https://doi.org/10.4018/978-1-7998-6428-8.ch013

Anantharaman, R. N., Rajeswari, K. S., Angusamy, A., & Kuppusamy, J. (2017). Role of Self-Efficacy and Collective Efficacy as Moderators of Occupational Stress Among Software Development Professionals. *International Journal of Human Capital and Information Technology Professionals*, *8*(2), 45–58. doi:10.4018/IJHCITP.2017040103

Aninze, F., El-Gohary, H., & Hussain, J. (2018). The Role of Microfinance to Empower Women: The Case of Developing Countries. *International Journal of Customer Relationship Marketing and Management*, *9*(1), 54–78. doi:10.4018/IJCRMM.2018010104

Antosova, G., Sabogal-Salamanca, M., & Krizova, E. (2021). Human Capital in Tourism: A Practical Model of Endogenous and Exogenous Territorial Tourism Planning in Bahía Solano, Colombia. In V. Costa, A. Moura, & M. Mira (Eds.), *Handbook of Research on Human Capital and People Management in the Tourism Industry* (pp. 282–302). IGI Global. https://doi.org/10.4018/978-1-7998-4318-4.ch014

Arsenijević, O. M., Orčić, D., & Kastratović, E. (2017). Development of an Optimization Tool for Intangibles in SMEs: A Case Study from Serbia with a Pilot Research in the Prestige by Milka Company. In M. Vemić (Ed.), *Optimal Management Strategies in Small and Medium Enterprises* (pp. 320–347). Hershey, PA: IGI Global. doi:10.4018/978-1-5225-1949-2.ch015

Aryanto, V. D., Wismantoro, Y., & Widyatmoko, K. (2018). Implementing Eco-Innovation by Utilizing the Internet to Enhance Firm's Marketing Performance: Study of Green Batik Small and Medium Enterprises in Indonesia. *International Journal of E-Business Research, 14*(1), 21–36. doi:10.4018/IJEBR.2018010102

Asero, V., & Billi, S. (2022). New Perspective of Networking in the DMO Model. In M. Valeri (Ed.), *New Governance and Management in Touristic Destinations* (pp. 105–118). IGI Global. https://doi.org/10.4018/978-1-6684-3889-3.ch007

Atiku, S. O., & Fields, Z. (2017). Multicultural Orientations for 21st Century Global Leadership. In N. Baporikar (Ed.), *Management Education for Global Leadership* (pp. 28–51). Hershey, PA: IGI Global. doi:10.4018/978-1-5225-1013-0.ch002

Atiku, S. O., & Fields, Z. (2018). Organisational Learning Dimensions and Talent Retention Strategies for the Service Industries. In N. Baporikar (Ed.), *Global Practices in Knowledge Management for Societal and Organizational Development* (pp. 358–381). Hershey, PA: IGI Global. doi:10.4018/978-1-5225-3009-1.ch017

Atsa'am, D. D., & Kuset Bodur, E. (2021). Pattern Mining on How Organizational Tenure Affects the Psychological Capital of Employees Within the Hospitality and Tourism Industry: Linking Employees' Organizational Tenure With PsyCap. *International Journal of Tourism and Hospitality Management in the Digital Age, 5*(2), 17–28. https://doi.org/10.4018/IJTHMDA.2021070102

Ávila, L., & Teixeira, L. (2018). The Main Concepts Behind the Dematerialization of Business Processes. In M. Khosrow-Pour, D.B.A. (Ed.), Encyclopedia of Information Science and Technology, Fourth Edition (pp. 888-898). Hershey, PA: IGI Global. https://doi.org/ doi:10.4018/978-1-5225-2255-3.ch076

Ayorekire, J., Mugizi, F., Obua, J., & Ampaire, G. (2022). Community-Based Tourism and Local People's Perceptions Towards Conservation: The Case of Queen Elizabeth Conservation Area, Uganda. In I. Mensah & E. Afenyo-Agbe (Eds.), *Prospects and Challenges of Community-Based Tourism and Changing Demographics* (pp. 56–82). IGI Global. https://doi.org/10.4018/978-1-7998-7335-8.ch003

Baleiro, R. (2022). Tourist Literature and the Architecture of Travel in Olga Tokarczuk and Patti Smith. In R. Baleiro & R. Pereira (Eds.), *Global Perspectives on Literary Tourism and Film-Induced Tourism* (pp. 202-216). IGI Global. https://doi.org/10.4018/978-1-7998-8262-6.ch011

Barat, S. (2021). Looking at the Future of Medical Tourism in Asia. *International Journal of Tourism and Hospitality Management in the Digital Age, 5*(1), 19–33. https://doi.org/10.4018/IJTHMDA.2021010102

Barbosa, C. A., Magalhães, M., & Nunes, M. R. (2021). Travel Instagramability: A Way of Choosing a Destination? In M. Dinis, L. Bonixe, S. Lamy, & Z. Breda (Eds.), *Impact of New Media in Tourism* (pp. 173-190). IGI Global. https://doi.org/10.4018/978-1-7998-7095-1.ch011

Bari, M. W., & Khan, Q. (2021). Pakistan as a Destination of Religious Tourism. In E. Alaverdov & M. Bari (Eds.), *Global Development of Religious Tourism* (pp. 1-10). IGI Global. https://doi.org/10.4018/978-1-7998-5792-1.ch001

Bartens, Y., Chunpir, H. I., Schulte, F., & Voß, S. (2017). Business/IT Alignment in Two-Sided Markets: A COBIT 5 Analysis for Media Streaming Business Models. In S. De Haes & W. Van Grembergen (Eds.), *Strategic IT Governance and Alignment in Business Settings* (pp. 82–111). Hershey, PA: IGI Global. doi:10.4018/978-1-5225-0861-8.ch004

Bashayreh, A. M. (2018). Organizational Culture and Organizational Performance. In W. Lee & F. Sabetzadeh (Eds.), *Contemporary Knowledge and Systems Science* (pp. 50–69). Hershey, PA: IGI Global. doi:10.4018/978-1-5225-5655-8.ch003

Bechthold, L., Lude, M., & Prügl, R. (2021). Crisis Favors the Prepared Firm: How Organizational Ambidexterity Relates to Perceptions of Organizational Resilience. In A. Zehrer, G. Glowka, K. Schwaiger, & V. Ranacher-Lackner (Eds.), *Resiliency Models and Addressing Future Risks for Family Firms in the Tourism Industry* (pp. 178–205). IGI Global. https://doi.org/10.4018/978-1-7998-7352-5.ch008

Bedford, D. A. (2018). Sustainable Knowledge Management Strategies: Aligning Business Capabilities and Knowledge Management Goals. In N. Baporikar (Ed.), *Global Practices in Knowledge Management for Societal and Organizational Development* (pp. 46–73). Hershey, PA: IGI Global. doi:10.4018/978-1-5225-3009-1.ch003

Bekjanov, D., & Matyusupov, B. (2021). Influence of Innovative Processes in the Competitiveness of Tourist Destination. In J. Soares (Ed.), *Innovation and Entrepreneurial Opportunities in Community Tourism* (pp. 243–263). IGI Global. https://doi.org/10.4018/978-1-7998-4855-4.ch014

Bharwani, S., & Musunuri, D. (2018). Reflection as a Process From Theory to Practice. In M. Khosrow-Pour, D.B.A. (Ed.), Encyclopedia of Information Science and Technology, Fourth Edition (pp. 1529-1539). Hershey, PA: IGI Global. doi:10.4018/978-1-5225-2255-3.ch132

Bhatt, G. D., Wang, Z., & Rodger, J. A. (2017). Information Systems Capabilities and Their Effects on Competitive Advantages: A Study of Chinese Companies. *Information Resources Management Journal*, *30*(3), 41–57. doi:10.4018/IRMJ.2017070103

Bhushan, M., & Yadav, A. (2017). Concept of Cloud Computing in ESB. In R. Bhadoria, N. Chaudhari, G. Tomar, & S. Singh (Eds.), *Exploring Enterprise Service Bus in the Service-Oriented Architecture Paradigm* (pp. 116–127). Hershey, PA: IGI Global. doi:10.4018/978-1-5225-2157-0.ch008

Bhushan, S. (2017). System Dynamics Base-Model of Humanitarian Supply Chain (HSCM) in Disaster Prone Eco-Communities of India: A Discussion on Simulation and Scenario Results. *International Journal of System Dynamics Applications*, *6*(3), 20–37. doi:10.4018/IJSDA.2017070102

Binder, D., & Miller, J. W. (2021). A Generations' Perspective on Employer Branding in Tourism. In V. Costa, A. Moura, & M. Mira (Eds.), *Handbook of Research on Human Capital and People Management in the Tourism Industry* (pp. 152–174). IGI Global. https://doi.org/10.4018/978-1-7998-4318-4.ch008

Birch Freeman, A. A., Mensah, I., & Antwi, K. B. (2022). Smiling vs. Frowning Faces: Community Participation for Sustainable Tourism in Ghanaian Communities. In I. Mensah & E. Afenyo-Agbe (Eds.), *Prospects and Challenges of Community-Based Tourism and Changing Demographics* (pp. 83–106). IGI Global. https://doi.org/10.4018/978-1-7998-7335-8.ch004

Biswas, A., & De, A. K. (2017). On Development of a Fuzzy Stochastic Programming Model with Its Application to Business Management. In S. Trivedi, S. Dey, A. Kumar, & T. Panda (Eds.), *Handbook of Research on Advanced Data Mining Techniques and Applications for Business Intelligence* (pp. 353–378). Hershey, PA: IGI Global. doi:10.4018/978-1-5225-2031-3.ch021

Boragnio, A., & Faracce Macia, C. (2021). "Taking Care of Yourself at Home": Use of E-Commerce About Food and Care During the COVID-19 Pandemic in the City of Buenos Aires. In M. Korstanje (Ed.), *Socio-Economic Effects and Recovery Efforts for the Rental Industry: Post-COVID-19 Strategies* (pp. 45–71). IGI Global. https://doi.org/10.4018/978-1-7998-7287-0.ch003

Borges, V. D. (2021). Happiness: The Basis for Public Policy in Tourism. In A. Perinotto, V. Mayer, & J. Soares (Eds.), *Rebuilding and Restructuring the Tourism Industry: Infusion of Happiness and Quality of Life* (pp. 1–25). IGI Global. https://doi.org/10.4018/978-1-7998-7239-9.ch001

Bücker, J., & Ernste, K. (2018). Use of Brand Heroes in Strategic Reputation Management: The Case of Bacardi, Adidas, and Daimler. In A. Erdemir (Ed.), *Reputation Management Techniques in Public Relations* (pp. 126–150). Hershey, PA: IGI Global. doi:10.4018/978-1-5225-3619-2.ch007

Buluk Eşitti, B. (2021). COVID-19 and Alternative Tourism: New Destinations and New Tourism Products. In M. Demir, A. Dalgıç, & F. Ergen (Eds.), *Handbook of Research on the Impacts and Implications of COVID-19 on the Tourism Industry* (pp. 786–805). IGI Global. https://doi.org/10.4018/978-1-7998-8231-2.ch038

Bureš, V. (2018). Industry 4.0 From the Systems Engineering Perspective: Alternative Holistic Framework Development. In R. Brunet-Thornton & F. Martinez (Eds.), *Analyzing the Impacts of Industry 4.0 in Modern Business Environments* (pp. 199–223). Hershey, PA: IGI Global. doi:10.4018/978-1-5225-3468-6.ch011

Buzady, Z. (2017). Resolving the Magic Cube of Effective Case Teaching: Benchmarking Case Teaching Practices in Emerging Markets – Insights from the Central European University Business School, Hungary. In D. Latusek (Ed.), *Case Studies as a Teaching Tool in Management Education* (pp. 79–103). Hershey, PA: IGI Global. doi:10.4018/978-1-5225-0770-3.ch005

Camillo, A. (2021). *Legal Matters, Risk Management, and Risk Prevention: From Forming a Business to Legal Representation*. IGI Global. doi:10.4018/978-1-7998-4342-9.ch004

Căpusneanu, S., & Topor, D. I. (2018). Business Ethics and Cost Management in SMEs: Theories of Business Ethics and Cost Management Ethos. In I. Oncioiu (Ed.), *Ethics and Decision-Making for Sustainable Business Practices* (pp. 109–127). Hershey, PA: IGI Global. doi:10.4018/978-1-5225-3773-1.ch007

Chan, R. L., Mo, P. L., & Moon, K. K. (2018). Strategic and Tactical Measures in Managing Enterprise Risks: A Study of the Textile and Apparel Industry. In K. Strang, M. Korstanje, & N. Vajjhala (Eds.), *Research, Practices, and Innovations in Global Risk and Contingency Management* (pp. 1–19). Hershey, PA: IGI Global. doi:10.4018/978-1-5225-4754-9.ch001

Charlier, S. D., Burke-Smalley, L. A., & Fisher, S. L. (2018). Undergraduate Programs in the U.S: A Contextual and Content-Based Analysis. In J. Mendy (Ed.), *Teaching Human Resources and Organizational Behavior at the College Level* (pp. 26–57). Hershey, PA: IGI Global. doi:10.4018/978-1-5225-2820-3.ch002

Chumillas, J., Güell, M., & Quer, P. (2022). The Use of ICT in Tourist and Educational Literary Routes: The Role of the Guide. In C. Ramos, S. Quinteiro, & A. Gonçalves (Eds.), *ICT as Innovator Between Tourism and Culture* (pp. 15–29). IGI Global. https://doi.org/10.4018/978-1-7998-8165-0.ch002

Dahlberg, T., Kivijärvi, H., & Saarinen, T. (2017). IT Investment Consistency and Other Factors Influencing the Success of IT Performance. In S. De Haes & W. Van Grembergen (Eds.), *Strategic IT Governance and Alignment in Business Settings* (pp. 176–208). Hershey, PA: IGI Global. doi:10.4018/978-1-5225-0861-8.ch007

Damnjanović, A. M. (2017). Knowledge Management Optimization through IT and E-Business Utilization: A Qualitative Study on Serbian SMEs. In M. Vemić (Ed.), *Optimal Management Strategies in Small and Medium Enterprises* (pp. 249–267). Hershey, PA: IGI Global. doi:10.4018/978-1-5225-1949-2.ch012

Daneshpour, H. (2017). Integrating Sustainable Development into Project Portfolio Management through Application of Open Innovation. In M. Vemić (Ed.), *Optimal Management Strategies in Small and Medium Enterprises* (pp. 370–387). Hershey, PA: IGI Global. doi:10.4018/978-1-5225-1949-2.ch017

Daniel, A. D., & Reis de Castro, V. (2018). Entrepreneurship Education: How to Measure the Impact on Nascent Entrepreneurs. In A. Carrizo Moreira, J. Guilherme Leitão Dantas, & F. Manuel Valente (Eds.), *Nascent Entrepreneurship and Successful New Venture Creation* (pp. 85–110). Hershey, PA: IGI Global. doi:10.4018/978-1-5225-2936-1.ch004

David, R., Swami, B. N., & Tangirala, S. (2018). Ethics Impact on Knowledge Management in Organizational Development: A Case Study. In N. Baporikar (Ed.), *Global Practices in Knowledge Management for Societal and Organizational Development* (pp. 19–45). Hershey, PA: IGI Global. doi:10.4018/978-1-5225-3009-1.ch002

De Uña-Álvarez, E., & Villarino-Pérez, M. (2022). Fostering Ecocultural Resources, Identity, and Tourism in Inland Territories (Galicia, NW Spain). In G. Fernandes (Ed.), *Challenges and New Opportunities for Tourism in Inland Territories: Ecocultural Resources and Sustainable Initiatives* (pp. 1-16). IGI Global. https://doi.org/10.4018/978-1-7998-7339-6.ch001

Delias, P., & Lakiotaki, K. (2018). Discovering Process Horizontal Boundaries to Facilitate Process Comprehension. *International Journal of Operations Research and Information Systems*, *9*(2), 1–31. doi:10.4018/IJORIS.2018040101

Denholm, J., & Lee-Davies, L. (2018). Success Factors for Games in Business and Project Management. In *Enhancing Education and Training Initiatives Through Serious Games* (pp. 34–68). Hershey, PA: IGI Global. doi:10.4018/978-1-5225-3689-5.ch002

Deshpande, M. (2017). Best Practices in Management Institutions for Global Leadership: Policy Aspects. In N. Baporikar (Ed.), *Management Education for Global Leadership* (pp. 1–27). Hershey, PA: IGI Global. doi:10.4018/978-1-5225-1013-0.ch001

Deshpande, M. (2018). Policy Perspectives for SMEs Knowledge Management. In N. Baporikar (Ed.), *Knowledge Integration Strategies for Entrepreneurship and Sustainability* (pp. 23–46). Hershey, PA: IGI Global. doi:10.4018/978-1-5225-5115-7.ch002

Dezdar, S. (2017). ERP Implementation Projects in Asian Countries: A Comparative Study on Iran and China. *International Journal of Information Technology Project Management*, *8*(3), 52–68. doi:10.4018/IJITPM.2017070104

Domingos, D., Respício, A., & Martinho, R. (2017). Reliability of IoT-Aware BPMN Healthcare Processes. In C. Reis & M. Maximiano (Eds.), *Internet of Things and Advanced Application in Healthcare* (pp. 214–248). Hershey, PA: IGI Global. doi:10.4018/978-1-5225-1820-4.ch008

Dosumu, O., Hussain, J., & El-Gohary, H. (2017). An Exploratory Study of the Impact of Government Policies on the Development of Small and Medium Enterprises in Developing Countries: The Case of Nigeria. *International Journal of Customer Relationship Marketing and Management*, *8*(4), 51–62. doi:10.4018/IJCRMM.2017100104

Durst, S., Bruns, G., & Edvardsson, I. R. (2017). Retaining Knowledge in Smaller Building and Construction Firms. *International Journal of Knowledge and Systems Science*, *8*(3), 1–12. doi:10.4018/IJKSS.2017070101

Edvardsson, I. R., & Durst, S. (2017). Outsourcing, Knowledge, and Learning: A Critical Review. *International Journal of Knowledge-Based Organizations*, *7*(2), 13–26. doi:10.4018/IJKBO.2017040102

Edwards, J. S. (2018). Integrating Knowledge Management and Business Processes. In M. Khosrow-Pour, D.B.A. (Ed.), Encyclopedia of Information Science and Technology, Fourth Edition (pp. 5046-5055). Hershey, PA: IGI Global. doi:10.4018/978-1-5225-2255-3.ch437

Eichelberger, S., & Peters, M. (2021). Family Firm Management in Turbulent Times: Opportunities for Responsible Tourism. In A. Zehrer, G. Glowka, K. Schwaiger, & V. Ranacher-Lackner (Eds.), *Resiliency Models and Addressing Future Risks for Family Firms in the Tourism Industry* (pp. 103–124). IGI Global. https://doi.org/10.4018/978-1-7998-7352-5.ch005

Eide, D., Hjalager, A., & Hansen, M. (2022). Innovative Certifications in Adventure Tourism: Attributes and Diffusion. In R. Augusto Costa, F. Brandão, Z. Breda, & C. Costa (Eds.), *Planning and Managing the Experience Economy in Tourism* (pp. 161-175). IGI Global. https://doi.org/10.4018/978-1-7998-8775-1.ch009

Ejiogu, A. O. (2018). Economics of Farm Management. In *Agricultural Finance and Opportunities for Investment and Expansion* (pp. 56–72). Hershey, PA: IGI Global. doi:10.4018/978-1-5225-3059-6.ch003

Ekanem, I., & Abiade, G. E. (2018). Factors Influencing the Use of E-Commerce by Small Enterprises in Nigeria. *International Journal of ICT Research in Africa and the Middle East*, *7*(1), 37–53. doi:10.4018/IJICTRAME.2018010103

Ekanem, I., & Alrossais, L. A. (2017). Succession Challenges Facing Family Businesses in Saudi Arabia. In P. Zgheib (Ed.), *Entrepreneurship and Business Innovation in the Middle East* (pp. 122–146). Hershey, PA: IGI Global. doi:10.4018/978-1-5225-2066-5.ch007

El Faquih, L., & Fredj, M. (2017). Ontology-Based Framework for Quality in Configurable Process Models. *Journal of Electronic Commerce in Organizations*, *15*(2), 48–60. doi:10.4018/JECO.2017040104

Faisal, M. N., & Talib, F. (2017). Building Ambidextrous Supply Chains in SMEs: How to Tackle the Barriers? *International Journal of Information Systems and Supply Chain Management*, *10*(4), 80–100. doi:10.4018/IJISSCM.2017100105

Fernandes, T. M., Gomes, J., & Romão, M. (2017). Investments in E-Government: A Benefit Management Case Study. *International Journal of Electronic Government Research*, *13*(3), 1–17. doi:10.4018/IJEGR.2017070101

Figueira, L. M., Honrado, G. R., & Dionísio, M. S. (2021). Human Capital Management in the Tourism Industry in Portugal. In V. Costa, A. Moura, & M. Mira (Eds.), *Handbook of Research on Human Capital and People Management in the Tourism Industry* (pp. 1–19). IGI Global. doi:10.4018/978-1-7998-4318-4.ch001

Gao, S. S., Oreal, S., & Zhang, J. (2018). Contemporary Financial Risk Management Perceptions and Practices of Small-Sized Chinese Businesses. In I. Management Association (Ed.), Global Business Expansion: Concepts, Methodologies, Tools, and Applications (pp. 917-931). Hershey, PA: IGI Global. doi:10.4018/978-1-5225-5481-3.ch041

Garg, R., & Berning, S. C. (2017). Indigenous Chinese Management Philosophies: Key Concepts and Relevance for Modern Chinese Firms. In B. Christiansen & G. Koc (Eds.), *Transcontinental Strategies for Industrial Development and Economic Growth* (pp. 43–57). Hershey, PA: IGI Global. doi:10.4018/978-1-5225-2160-0.ch003

Gencer, Y. G. (2017). Supply Chain Management in Retailing Business. In U. Akkucuk (Ed.), *Ethics and Sustainability in Global Supply Chain Management* (pp. 197–210). Hershey, PA: IGI Global. doi:10.4018/978-1-5225-2036-8.ch011

Gera, R., Arora, S., & Malik, S. (2021). Emotional Labor in the Tourism Industry: Strategies, Antecedents, and Outcomes. In V. Costa, A. Moura, & M. Mira (Eds.), *Handbook of Research on Human Capital and People Management in the Tourism Industry* (pp. 73–91). IGI Global. https://doi.org/10.4018/978-1-7998-4318-4.ch004

Giacosa, E. (2018). The Increasing of the Regional Development Thanks to the Luxury Business Innovation. In L. Carvalho (Ed.), *Handbook of Research on Entrepreneurial Ecosystems and Social Dynamics in a Globalized World* (pp. 260–273). Hershey, PA: IGI Global. doi:10.4018/978-1-5225-3525-6.ch011

Glowka, G., Tusch, M., & Zehrer, A. (2021). The Risk Perception of Family Business Owner-Manager in the Tourism Industry: A Qualitative Comparison of the Intra-Firm Senior and Junior Generation. In A. Zehrer, G. Glowka, K. Schwaiger, & V. Ranacher-Lackner (Eds.), *Resiliency Models and Addressing Future Risks for Family Firms in the Tourism Industry* (pp. 126–153). IGI Global. https://doi.org/10.4018/978-1-7998-7352-5.ch006

Glykas, M., & George, J. (2017). Quality and Process Management Systems in the UAE Maritime Industry. *International Journal of Productivity Management and Assessment Technologies*, *5*(1), 20–39. doi:10.4018/IJPMAT.2017010102

Glykas, M., Valiris, G., Kokkinaki, A., & Koutsoukou, Z. (2018). Banking Business Process Management Implementation. *International Journal of Productivity Management and Assessment Technologies*, *6*(1), 50–69. doi:10.4018/IJPMAT.2018010104

Gomes, J., & Romão, M. (2017). The Balanced Scorecard: Keeping Updated and Aligned with Today's Business Trends. *International Journal of Productivity Management and Assessment Technologies*, *5*(2), 1–15. doi:10.4018/IJPMAT.2017070101

Gomes, J., & Romão, M. (2017). Aligning Information Systems and Technology with Benefit Management and Balanced Scorecard. In S. De Haes & W. Van Grembergen (Eds.), *Strategic IT Governance and Alignment in Business Settings* (pp. 112–131). Hershey, PA: IGI Global. doi:10.4018/978-1-5225-0861-8.ch005

Goyal, A. (2021). Communicating and Building Destination Brands With New Media. In M. Dinis, L. Bonixe, S. Lamy, & Z. Breda (Eds.), *Impact of New Media in Tourism* (pp. 1-20). IGI Global. https://doi.org/10.4018/978-1-7998-7095-1.ch001

Grefen, P., & Turetken, O. (2017). Advanced Business Process Management in Networked E-Business Scenarios. *International Journal of E-Business Research, 13*(4), 70–104. doi:10.4018/IJEBR.2017100105

Guasca, M., Van Broeck, A. M., & Vanneste, D. (2021). Tourism and the Social Reintegration of Colombian Ex-Combatants. In J. da Silva, Z. Breda, & F. Carbone (Eds.), *Role and Impact of Tourism in Peacebuilding and Conflict Transformation* (pp. 66-86). IGI Global. https://doi.org/10.4018/978-1-7998-5053-3.ch005

Haider, A., & Saetang, S. (2017). Strategic IT Alignment in Service Sector. In S. Rozenes & Y. Cohen (Eds.), *Handbook of Research on Strategic Alliances and Value Co-Creation in the Service Industry* (pp. 231–258). Hershey, PA: IGI Global. doi:10.4018/978-1-5225-2084-9.ch012

Hajilari, A. B., Ghadaksaz, M., & Fasghandis, G. S. (2017). Assessing Organizational Readiness for Implementing ERP System Using Fuzzy Expert System Approach. *International Journal of Enterprise Information Systems, 13*(1), 67–85. doi:10.4018/IJEIS.2017010105

Haldorai, A., Ramu, A., & Murugan, S. (2018). Social Aware Cognitive Radio Networks: Effectiveness of Social Networks as a Strategic Tool for Organizational Business Management. In H. Bansal, G. Shrivastava, G. Nguyen, & L. Stanciu (Eds.), *Social Network Analytics for Contemporary Business Organizations* (pp. 188–202). Hershey, PA: IGI Global. doi:10.4018/978-1-5225-5097-6.ch010

Hall, O. P. Jr. (2017). Social Media Driven Management Education. *International Journal of Knowledge-Based Organizations, 7*(2), 43–59. doi:10.4018/IJKBO.2017040104

Hanifah, H., Halim, H. A., Ahmad, N. H., & Vafaei-Zadeh, A. (2017). Innovation Culture as a Mediator Between Specific Human Capital and Innovation Performance Among Bumiputera SMEs in Malaysia. In N. Ahmad, T. Ramayah, H. Halim, & S. Rahman (Eds.), *Handbook of Research on Small and Medium Enterprises in Developing Countries* (pp. 261–279). Hershey, PA: IGI Global. doi:10.4018/978-1-5225-2165-5.ch012

Hartlieb, S., & Silvius, G. (2017). Handling Uncertainty in Project Management and Business Development: Similarities and Differences. In Y. Raydugin (Ed.), *Handbook of Research on Leveraging Risk and Uncertainties for Effective Project Management* (pp. 337–362). Hershey, PA: IGI Global. doi:10.4018/978-1-5225-1790-0.ch016

Hass, K. B. (2017). Living on the Edge: Managing Project Complexity. In Y. Raydugin (Ed.), *Handbook of Research on Leveraging Risk and Uncertainties for Effective Project Management* (pp. 177–201). Hershey, PA: IGI Global. doi:10.4018/978-1-5225-1790-0.ch009

Hawking, P., & Carmine Sellitto, C. (2017). Developing an Effective Strategy for Organizational Business Intelligence. In M. Tavana (Ed.), *Enterprise Information Systems and the Digitalization of Business Functions* (pp. 222–237). Hershey, PA: IGI Global. doi:10.4018/978-1-5225-2382-6.ch010

Hawking, P., & Sellitto, C. (2017). A Fast-Moving Consumer Goods Company and Business Intelligence Strategy Development. *International Journal of Enterprise Information Systems*, *13*(2), 22–33. doi:10.4018/IJEIS.2017040102

Hawking, P., & Sellitto, C. (2017). Business Intelligence Strategy: Two Case Studies. *International Journal of Business Intelligence Research*, *8*(2), 17–30. doi:10.4018/IJBIR.2017070102

Hee, W. J., Jalleh, G., Lai, H., & Lin, C. (2017). E-Commerce and IT Projects: Evaluation and Management Issues in Australian and Taiwanese Hospitals. *International Journal of Public Health Management and Ethics*, *2*(1), 69–90. doi:10.4018/IJPHME.2017010104

Hernandez, A. A. (2018). Exploring the Factors to Green IT Adoption of SMEs in the Philippines. *Journal of Cases on Information Technology*, *20*(2), 49–66. doi:10.4018/JCIT.2018040104

Hollman, A., Bickford, S., & Hollman, T. (2017). Cyber InSecurity: A Post-Mortem Attempt to Assess Cyber Problems from IT and Business Management Perspectives. *Journal of Cases on Information Technology*, *19*(3), 42–70. doi:10.4018/JCIT.2017070104

Ibrahim, F., & Zainin, N. M. (2021). Exploring the Technological Impacts: The Case of Museums in Brunei Darussalam. *International Journal of Tourism and Hospitality Management in the Digital Age*, *5*(1), 1–18. https://doi.org/10.4018/IJTHMDA.2021010101

Igbinakhase, I. (2017). Responsible and Sustainable Management Practices in Developing and Developed Business Environments. In Z. Fields (Ed.), *Collective Creativity for Responsible and Sustainable Business Practice* (pp. 180–207). Hershey, PA: IGI Global. doi:10.4018/978-1-5225-1823-5.ch010

Iwata, J. J., & Hoskins, R. G. (2017). Managing Indigenous Knowledge in Tanzania: A Business Perspective. In P. Jain & N. Mnjama (Eds.), *Managing Knowledge Resources and Records in Modern Organizations* (pp. 198–214). Hershey, PA: IGI Global. doi:10.4018/978-1-5225-1965-2.ch012

Jain, P. (2017). Ethical and Legal Issues in Knowledge Management Life-Cycle in Business. In P. Jain & N. Mnjama (Eds.), *Managing Knowledge Resources and Records in Modern Organizations* (pp. 82–101). Hershey, PA: IGI Global. doi:10.4018/978-1-5225-1965-2.ch006

James, S., & Hauli, E. (2017). Holistic Management Education at Tanzanian Rural Development Planning Institute. In N. Baporikar (Ed.), *Management Education for Global Leadership* (pp. 112–136). Hershey, PA: IGI Global. doi:10.4018/978-1-5225-1013-0.ch006

Janošková, M., Csikósová, A., & Čulková, K. (2018). Measurement of Company Performance as Part of Its Strategic Management. In R. Leon (Ed.), *Managerial Strategies for Business Sustainability During Turbulent Times* (pp. 309–335). Hershey, PA: IGI Global. doi:10.4018/978-1-5225-2716-9.ch017

Jean-Vasile, A., & Alecu, A. (2017). Theoretical and Practical Approaches in Understanding the Influences of Cost-Productivity-Profit Trinomial in Contemporary Enterprises. In A. Jean Vasile & D. Nicolò (Eds.), *Sustainable Entrepreneurship and Investments in the Green Economy* (pp. 28–62). Hershey, PA: IGI Global. doi:10.4018/978-1-5225-2075-7.ch002

Joia, L. A., & Correia, J. C. (2018). CIO Competencies From the IT Professional Perspective: Insights From Brazil. *Journal of Global Information Management*, *26*(2), 74–103. doi:10.4018/JGIM.2018040104

Juma, A., & Mzera, N. (2017). Knowledge Management and Records Management and Competitive Advantage in Business. In P. Jain & N. Mnjama (Eds.), *Managing Knowledge Resources and Records in Modern Organizations* (pp. 15–28). Hershey, PA: IGI Global. doi:10.4018/978-1-5225-1965-2.ch002

K., I., & A, V. (2018). Monitoring and Auditing in the Cloud. In K. Munir (Ed.), *Cloud Computing Technologies for Green Enterprises* (pp. 318-350). Hershey, PA: IGI Global. https://doi.org/ doi:10.4018/978-1-5225-3038-1.ch013

Kabra, G., Ghosh, V., & Ramesh, A. (2018). Enterprise Integrated Business Process Management and Business Intelligence Framework for Business Process Sustainability. In A. Paul, D. Bhattacharyya, & S. Anand (Eds.), *Green Initiatives for Business Sustainability and Value Creation* (pp. 228–238). Hershey, PA: IGI Global. doi:10.4018/978-1-5225-2662-9.ch010

Kaoud, M. (2017). Investigation of Customer Knowledge Management: A Case Study Research. *International Journal of Service Science, Management, Engineering, and Technology*, *8*(2), 12–22. doi:10.4018/IJSSMET.2017040102

Katuu, S. (2018). A Comparative Assessment of Enterprise Content Management Maturity Models. In N. Gwangwava & M. Mutingi (Eds.), *E-Manufacturing and E-Service Strategies in Contemporary Organizations* (pp. 93–118). Hershey, PA: IGI Global. doi:10.4018/978-1-5225-3628-4.ch005

Khan, M. Y., & Abir, T. (2022). The Role of Social Media Marketing in the Tourism and Hospitality Industry: A Conceptual Study on Bangladesh. In C. Ramos, S. Quinteiro, & A. Gonçalves (Eds.), *ICT as Innovator Between Tourism and Culture* (pp. 213–229). IGI Global. https://doi.org/10.4018/978-1-7998-8165-0.ch013

Kinnunen, S., Ylä-Kujala, A., Marttonen-Arola, S., Kärri, T., & Baglee, D. (2018). Internet of Things in Asset Management: Insights from Industrial Professionals and Academia. *International Journal of Service Science, Management, Engineering, and Technology*, *9*(2), 104–119. doi:10.4018/IJSSMET.2018040105

Klein, A. Z., Sabino de Freitas, A., Machado, L., Freitas, J. C. Jr, Graziola, P. G. Jr, & Schlemmer, E. (2017). Virtual Worlds Applications for Management Education. In L. Tomei (Ed.), *Exploring the New Era of Technology-Infused Education* (pp. 279–299). Hershey, PA: IGI Global. doi:10.4018/978-1-5225-1709-2.ch017

Kővári, E., Saleh, M., & Steinbachné Hajmásy, G. (2022). The Impact of Corporate Digital Responsibility (CDR) on Internal Stakeholders' Satisfaction in Hungarian Upscale Hotels. In M. Valeri (Ed.), *New Governance and Management in Touristic Destinations* (pp. 35–51). IGI Global. https://doi.org/10.4018/978-1-6684-3889-3.ch003

Kożuch, B., & Jabłoński, A. (2017). Adopting the Concept of Business Models in Public Management. In M. Lewandowski & B. Kożuch (Eds.), *Public Sector Entrepreneurship and the Integration of Innovative Business Models* (pp. 10–46). Hershey, PA: IGI Global. doi:10.4018/978-1-5225-2215-7.ch002

Kumar, J., Adhikary, A., & Jha, A. (2017). Small Active Investors' Perceptions and Preferences Towards Tax Saving Mutual Fund Schemes in Eastern India: An Empirical Note. *International Journal of Asian Business and Information Management*, *8*(2), 35–45. doi:10.4018/IJABIM.2017040103

Latusi, S., & Fissore, M. (2021). Pilgrimage Routes to Happiness: Comparing the Camino de Santiago and Via Francigena. In A. Perinotto, V. Mayer, & J. Soares (Eds.), *Rebuilding and Restructuring the Tourism Industry: Infusion of Happiness and Quality of Life* (pp. 157–182). IGI Global. https://doi.org/10.4018/978-1-7998-7239-9.ch008

Lavassani, K. M., & Movahedi, B. (2017). Applications Driven Information Systems: Beyond Networks toward Business Ecosystems. *International Journal of Innovation in the Digital Economy*, *8*(1), 61–75. doi:10.4018/IJIDE.2017010104

Lazzareschi, V. H., & Brito, M. S. (2017). Strategic Information Management: Proposal of Business Project Model. In G. Jamil, A. Soares, & C. Pessoa (Eds.), *Handbook of Research on Information Management for Effective Logistics and Supply Chains* (pp. 59–88). Hershey, PA: IGI Global. doi:10.4018/978-1-5225-0973-8.ch004

Lechuga Sancho, M. P., & Martín Navarro, A. (2022). Evolution of the Literature on Social Responsibility in the Tourism Sector: A Systematic Literature Review. In G. Fernandes (Ed.), *Challenges and New Opportunities for Tourism in Inland Territories: Ecocultural Resources and Sustainable Initiatives* (pp. 169–186). IGI Global. https://doi.org/10.4018/978-1-7998-7339-6.ch010

Lederer, M., Kurz, M., & Lazarov, P. (2017). Usage and Suitability of Methods for Strategic Business Process Initiatives: A Multi Case Study Research. *International Journal of Productivity Management and Assessment Technologies*, *5*(1), 40–51. doi:10.4018/IJPMAT.2017010103

Lee, I. (2017). A Social Enterprise Business Model and a Case Study of Pacific Community Ventures (PCV). In V. Potocan, M. Üngan, & Z. Nedelko (Eds.), *Handbook of Research on Managerial Solutions in Non-Profit Organizations* (pp. 182–204). Hershey, PA: IGI Global. doi:10.4018/978-1-5225-0731-4.ch009

Leon, L. A., Seal, K. C., Przasnyski, Z. H., & Wiedenman, I. (2017). Skills and Competencies Required for Jobs in Business Analytics: A Content Analysis of Job Advertisements Using Text Mining. *International Journal of Business Intelligence Research*, *8*(1), 1–25. doi:10.4018/IJBIR.2017010101

Levy, C. L., & Elias, N. I. (2017). SOHO Users' Perceptions of Reliability and Continuity of Cloud-Based Services. In M. Moore (Ed.), *Cybersecurity Breaches and Issues Surrounding Online Threat Protection* (pp. 248–287). Hershey, PA: IGI Global. doi:10.4018/978-1-5225-1941-6.ch011

Levy, M. (2018). Change Management Serving Knowledge Management and Organizational Development: Reflections and Review. In N. Baporikar (Ed.), *Global Practices in Knowledge Management for Societal and Organizational Development* (pp. 256–270). Hershey, PA: IGI Global. doi:10.4018/978-1-5225-3009-1.ch012

Lewandowski, M. (2017). Public Organizations and Business Model Innovation: The Role of Public Service Design. In M. Lewandowski & B. Kożuch (Eds.), *Public Sector Entrepreneurship and the Integration of Innovative Business Models* (pp. 47–72). Hershey, PA: IGI Global. doi:10.4018/978-1-5225-2215-7.ch003

Lhannaoui, H., Kabbaj, M. I., & Bakkoury, Z. (2017). A Survey of Risk-Aware Business Process Modelling. *International Journal of Risk and Contingency Management*, *6*(3), 14–26. doi:10.4018/IJRCM.2017070102

Li, J., Sun, W., Jiang, W., Yang, H., & Zhang, L. (2017). How the Nature of Exogenous Shocks and Crises Impact Company Performance?: The Effects of Industry Characteristics. *International Journal of Risk and Contingency Management*, *6*(4), 40–55. doi:10.4018/IJRCM.2017100103

Lopez-Fernandez, M., Perez-Perez, M., Serrano-Bedia, A., & Cobo-Gonzalez, A. (2021). Small and Medium Tourism Enterprise Survival in Times of Crisis: “El Capricho de Gaudí. In D. Toubes & N. Araújo-Vila (Eds.), *Risk, Crisis, and Disaster Management in Small and Medium-Sized Tourism Enterprises* (pp. 103–129). IGI Global. doi:10.4018/978-1-7998-6996-2.ch005

Mahajan, A., Maidullah, S., & Hossain, M. R. (2022). Experience Toward Smart Tour Guide Apps in Travelling: An Analysis of Users' Reviews on Audio Odigos and Trip My Way. In R. Augusto Costa, F. Brandão, Z. Breda, & C. Costa (Eds.), *Planning and Managing the Experience Economy in Tourism* (pp. 255-273). IGI Global. https://doi.org/10.4018/978-1-7998-8775-1.ch014

Malega, P. (2017). Small and Medium Enterprises in the Slovak Republic: Status and Competitiveness of SMEs in the Global Markets and Possibilities of Optimization. In M. Vemić (Ed.), *Optimal Management Strategies in Small and Medium Enterprises* (pp. 102–124). Hershey, PA: IGI Global. doi:10.4018/978-1-5225-1949-2.ch006

Malewska, K. M. (2017). Intuition in Decision-Making on the Example of a Non-Profit Organization. In V. Potocan, M. Üngan, & Z. Nedelko (Eds.), *Handbook of Research on Managerial Solutions in Non-Profit Organizations* (pp. 378–399). Hershey, PA: IGI Global. doi:10.4018/978-1-5225-0731-4.ch018

Maroofi, F. (2017). Entrepreneurial Orientation and Organizational Learning Ability Analysis for Innovation and Firm Performance. In N. Baporikar (Ed.), *Innovation and Shifting Perspectives in Management Education* (pp. 144–165). Hershey, PA: IGI Global. doi:10.4018/978-1-5225-1019-2.ch007

Marques, M., Moleiro, D., Brito, T. M., & Marques, T. (2021). Customer Relationship Management as an Important Relationship Marketing Tool: The Case of the Hospitality Industry in Estoril Coast. In M. Dinis, L. Bonixe, S. Lamy, & Z. Breda (Eds.), Impact of New Media in Tourism (pp. 39-56). IGI Global. https://doi.org/doi:10.4018/978-1-7998-7095-1.ch003

Martins, P. V., & Zacarias, M. (2017). A Web-based Tool for Business Process Improvement. *International Journal of Web Portals*, *9*(2), 68–84. doi:10.4018/IJWP.2017070104

Matthies, B., & Coners, A. (2017). Exploring the Conceptual Nature of e-Business Projects. *Journal of Electronic Commerce in Organizations*, *15*(3), 33–63. doi:10.4018/JECO.2017070103

Mayer, V. F., Fraga, C. C., & Silva, L. C. (2021). Contributions of Neurosciences to Studies of Well-Being in Tourism. In A. Perinotto, V. Mayer, & J. Soares (Eds.), *Rebuilding and Restructuring the Tourism Industry: Infusion of Happiness and Quality of Life* (pp. 108–128). IGI Global. https://doi.org/10.4018/978-1-7998-7239-9.ch006

McKee, J. (2018). Architecture as a Tool to Solve Business Planning Problems. In M. Khosrow-Pour, D.B.A. (Ed.), Encyclopedia of Information Science and Technology, Fourth Edition (pp. 573-586). Hershey, PA: IGI Global. doi:10.4018/978-1-5225-2255-3.ch050

McMurray, A. J., Cross, J., & Caponecchia, C. (2018). The Risk Management Profession in Australia: Business Continuity Plan Practices. In N. Bajgoric (Ed.), *Always-On Enterprise Information Systems for Modern Organizations* (pp. 112–129). Hershey, PA: IGI Global. doi:10.4018/978-1-5225-3704-5.ch006

Meddah, I. H., & Belkadi, K. (2018). Mining Patterns Using Business Process Management. In R. Hamou (Ed.), *Handbook of Research on Biomimicry in Information Retrieval and Knowledge Management* (pp. 78–89). Hershey, PA: IGI Global. doi:10.4018/978-1-5225-3004-6.ch005

Melian, A. G., & Camprubí, R. (2021). The Accessibility of Museum Websites: The Case of Barcelona. In C. Eusébio, L. Teixeira, & M. Carneiro (Eds.), *ICT Tools and Applications for Accessible Tourism* (pp. 234–255). IGI Global. https://doi.org/10.4018/978-1-7998-6428-8.ch011

Mendes, L. (2017). TQM and Knowledge Management: An Integrated Approach Towards Tacit Knowledge Management. In D. Jaziri-Bouagina & G. Jamil (Eds.), *Handbook of Research on Tacit Knowledge Management for Organizational Success* (pp. 236–263). Hershey, PA: IGI Global. doi:10.4018/978-1-5225-2394-9.ch009

Menezes, V. D., & Cavagnaro, E. (2021). Communicating Sustainable Initiatives in the Hotel Industry: The Case of the Hotel Jakarta Amsterdam. In F. Brandão, Z. Breda, R. Costa, & C. Costa (Eds.), *Handbook of Research on the Role of Tourism in Achieving Sustainable Development Goals* (pp. 224-234). IGI Global. https://doi.org/10.4018/978-1-7998-5691-7.ch013

Menezes, V. D., & Cavagnaro, E. (2021). Communicating Sustainable Initiatives in the Hotel Industry: The Case of the Hotel Jakarta Amsterdam. In F. Brandão, Z. Breda, R. Costa, & C. Costa (Eds.), *Handbook of Research on the Role of Tourism in Achieving Sustainable Development Goals* (pp. 224-234). IGI Global. https://doi.org/10.4018/978-1-7998-5691-7.ch013

Mitas, O., Bastiaansen, M., & Boode, W. (2022). If You're Happy, I'm Happy: Emotion Contagion at a Tourist Information Center. In R. Augusto Costa, F. Brandão, Z. Breda, & C. Costa (Eds.), *Planning and Managing the Experience Economy in Tourism* (pp. 122-140). IGI Global. https://doi.org/10.4018/978-1-7998-8775-1.ch007

Mnjama, N. M. (2017). Preservation of Recorded Information in Public and Private Sector Organizations. In P. Jain & N. Mnjama (Eds.), *Managing Knowledge Resources and Records in Modern Organizations* (pp. 149–167). Hershey, PA: IGI Global. doi:10.4018/978-1-5225-1965-2.ch009

Mokoqama, M., & Fields, Z. (2017). Principles of Responsible Management Education (PRME): Call for Responsible Management Education. In Z. Fields (Ed.), *Collective Creativity for Responsible and Sustainable Business Practice* (pp. 229–241). Hershey, PA: IGI Global. doi:10.4018/978-1-5225-1823-5.ch012

Monteiro, A., Lopes, S., & Carbone, F. (2021). Academic Mobility: Bridging Tourism and Peace Education. In J. da Silva, Z. Breda, & F. Carbone (Eds.), *Role and Impact of Tourism in Peacebuilding and Conflict Transformation* (pp. 275-301). IGI Global. https://doi.org/10.4018/978-1-7998-5053-3.ch016

Muniapan, B. (2017). Philosophy and Management: The Relevance of Vedanta in Management. In P. Ordóñez de Pablos (Ed.), *Managerial Strategies and Solutions for Business Success in Asia* (pp. 124–139). Hershey, PA: IGI Global. doi:10.4018/978-1-5225-1886-0.ch007

Murad, S. E., & Dowaji, S. (2017). Using Value-Based Approach for Managing Cloud-Based Services. In A. Turuk, B. Sahoo, & S. Addya (Eds.), *Resource Management and Efficiency in Cloud Computing Environments* (pp. 33–60). Hershey, PA: IGI Global. doi:10.4018/978-1-5225-1721-4.ch002

Mutahar, A. M., Daud, N. M., Thurasamy, R., Isaac, O., & Abdulsalam, R. (2018). The Mediating of Perceived Usefulness and Perceived Ease of Use: The Case of Mobile Banking in Yemen. *International Journal of Technology Diffusion*, *9*(2), 21–40. doi:10.4018/IJTD.2018040102

Naidoo, V. (2017). E-Learning and Management Education at African Universities. In N. Baporikar (Ed.), *Management Education for Global Leadership* (pp. 181–201). Hershey, PA: IGI Global. doi:10.4018/978-1-5225-1013-0.ch009

Naidoo, V., & Igbinakhase, I. (2018). Opportunities and Challenges of Knowledge Retention in SMEs. In N. Baporikar (Ed.), *Knowledge Integration Strategies for Entrepreneurship and Sustainability* (pp. 70–94). Hershey, PA: IGI Global. doi:10.4018/978-1-5225-5115-7.ch004

Naumov, N., & Costandachi, G. (2021). Creativity and Entrepreneurship: Gastronomic Tourism in Mexico. In J. Soares (Ed.), *Innovation and Entrepreneurial Opportunities in Community Tourism* (pp. 90–108). IGI Global. https://doi.org/10.4018/978-1-7998-4855-4.ch006

Nayak, S., & Prabhu, N. (2017). Paradigm Shift in Management Education: Need for a Cross Functional Perspective. In N. Baporikar (Ed.), *Management Education for Global Leadership* (pp. 241–255). Hershey, PA: IGI Global. doi:10.4018/978-1-5225-1013-0.ch012

Nedelko, Z., & Potocan, V. (2017). Management Solutions in Non-Profit Organizations: Case of Slovenia. In V. Potocan, M. Üngan, & Z. Nedelko (Eds.), *Handbook of Research on Managerial Solutions in Non-Profit Organizations* (pp. 1–22). Hershey, PA: IGI Global. doi:10.4018/978-1-5225-0731-4.ch001

Nedelko, Z., & Potocan, V. (2017). Priority of Management Tools Utilization among Managers: International Comparison. In V. Wang (Ed.), *Encyclopedia of Strategic Leadership and Management* (pp. 1083–1094). Hershey, PA: IGI Global. doi:10.4018/978-1-5225-1049-9.ch075

Nedelko, Z., Raudeliūnienė, J., & Črešnar, R. (2018). Knowledge Dynamics in Supply Chain Management. In N. Baporikar (Ed.), *Knowledge Integration Strategies for Entrepreneurship and Sustainability* (pp. 150–166). Hershey, PA: IGI Global. doi:10.4018/978-1-5225-5115-7.ch008

Nguyen, H. T., & Hipsher, S. A. (2018). Innovation and Creativity Used by Private Sector Firms in a Resources-Constrained Environment. In S. Hipsher (Ed.), *Examining the Private Sector's Role in Wealth Creation and Poverty Reduction* (pp. 219–238). Hershey, PA: IGI Global. doi:10.4018/978-1-5225-3117-3.ch010

Obicci, P. A. (2017). Risk Sharing in a Partnership. In *Risk Management Strategies in Public-Private Partnerships* (pp. 115–152). Hershey, PA: IGI Global. doi:10.4018/978-1-5225-2503-5.ch004

Obidallah, W. J., & Raahemi, B. (2017). Managing Changes in Service Oriented Virtual Organizations: A Structural and Procedural Framework to Facilitate the Process of Change. *Journal of Electronic Commerce in Organizations*, *15*(1), 59–83. doi:10.4018/JECO.2017010104

Ojo, O. (2017). Impact of Innovation on the Entrepreneurial Success in Selected Business Enterprises in South-West Nigeria. *International Journal of Innovation in the Digital Economy*, *8*(2), 29–38. doi:10.4018/IJIDE.2017040103

Okdinawati, L., Simatupang, T. M., & Sunitiyoso, Y. (2017). Multi-Agent Reinforcement Learning for Value Co-Creation of Collaborative Transportation Management (CTM). *International Journal of Information Systems and Supply Chain Management*, *10*(3), 84–95. doi:10.4018/IJISSCM.2017070105

Olivera, V. A., & Carrillo, I. M. (2021). Organizational Culture: A Key Element for the Development of Mexican Micro and Small Tourist Companies. In J. Soares (Ed.), *Innovation and Entrepreneurial Opportunities in Community Tourism* (pp. 227–242). IGI Global. doi:10.4018/978-1-7998-4855-4.ch013

Ossorio, M. (2022). Corporate Museum Experiences in Enogastronomic Tourism. In R. Augusto Costa, F. Brandão, Z. Breda, & C. Costa (Eds.), Planning and Managing the Experience Economy in Tourism (pp. 107-121). IGI Global. https://doi.org/doi:10.4018/978-1-7998-8775-1.ch006

Ossorio, M. (2022). Enogastronomic Tourism in Times of Pandemic. In G. Fernandes (Ed.), *Challenges and New Opportunities for Tourism in Inland Territories: Ecocultural Resources and Sustainable Initiatives* (pp. 241–255). IGI Global. https://doi.org/10.4018/978-1-7998-7339-6.ch014

Özekici, Y. K. (2022). ICT as an Acculturative Agent and Its Role in the Tourism Context: Introduction, Acculturation Theory, Progress of the Acculturation Theory in Extant Literature. In C. Ramos, S. Quinteiro, & A. Gonçalves (Eds.), *ICT as Innovator Between Tourism and Culture* (pp. 42–66). IGI Global. https://doi.org/10.4018/978-1-7998-8165-0.ch004

Pal, K. (2018). Building High Quality Big Data-Based Applications in Supply Chains. In A. Kumar & S. Saurav (Eds.), *Supply Chain Management Strategies and Risk Assessment in Retail Environments* (pp. 1–24). Hershey, PA: IGI Global. doi:10.4018/978-1-5225-3056-5.ch001

Palos-Sanchez, P. R., & Correia, M. B. (2018). Perspectives of the Adoption of Cloud Computing in the Tourism Sector. In J. Rodrigues, C. Ramos, P. Cardoso, & C. Henriques (Eds.), *Handbook of Research on Technological Developments for Cultural Heritage and eTourism Applications* (pp. 377–400). Hershey, PA: IGI Global. doi:10.4018/978-1-5225-2927-9.ch018

Papadopoulou, G. (2021). Promoting Gender Equality and Women Empowerment in the Tourism Sector. In F. Brandão, Z. Breda, R. Costa, & C. Costa (Eds.), Handbook of Research on the Role of Tourism in Achieving Sustainable Development Goals (pp. 152-174). IGI Global. https://doi.org/ doi:10.4018/978-1-7998-5691-7.ch009

Papp-Váry, Á. F., & Tóth, T. Z. (2022). Analysis of Budapest as a Film Tourism Destination. In R. Baleiro & R. Pereira (Eds.), *Global Perspectives on Literary Tourism and Film-Induced Tourism* (pp. 257-279). IGI Global. https://doi.org/10.4018/978-1-7998-8262-6.ch014

Patiño, B. E. (2017). New Generation Management by Convergence and Individual Identity: A Systemic and Human-Oriented Approach. In N. Baporikar (Ed.), *Innovation and Shifting Perspectives in Management Education* (pp. 119–143). Hershey, PA: IGI Global. doi:10.4018/978-1-5225-1019-2.ch006

Patro, C. S. (2021). Digital Tourism: Influence of E-Marketing Technology. In M. Dinis, L. Bonixe, S. Lamy, & Z. Breda (Eds.), *Impact of New Media in Tourism* (pp. 234-254). IGI Global. https://doi.org/10.4018/978-1-7998-7095-1.ch014

Pawliczek, A., & Rössler, M. (2017). Knowledge of Management Tools and Systems in SMEs: Knowledge Transfer in Management. In A. Bencsik (Ed.), *Knowledge Management Initiatives and Strategies in Small and Medium Enterprises* (pp. 180–203). Hershey, PA: IGI Global. doi:10.4018/978-1-5225-1642-2.ch009

Pejic-Bach, M., Omazic, M. A., Aleksic, A., & Zoroja, J. (2018). Knowledge-Based Decision Making: A Multi-Case Analysis. In R. Leon (Ed.), *Managerial Strategies for Business Sustainability During Turbulent Times* (pp. 160–184). Hershey, PA: IGI Global. doi:10.4018/978-1-5225-2716-9.ch009

Perano, M., Hysa, X., & Calabrese, M. (2018). Strategic Planning, Cultural Context, and Business Continuity Management: Business Cases in the City of Shkoder. In A. Presenza & L. Sheehan (Eds.), *Geopolitics and Strategic Management in the Global Economy* (pp. 57–77). Hershey, PA: IGI Global. doi:10.4018/978-1-5225-2673-5.ch004

Pereira, R., Mira da Silva, M., & Lapão, L. V. (2017). IT Governance Maturity Patterns in Portuguese Healthcare. In S. De Haes & W. Van Grembergen (Eds.), *Strategic IT Governance and Alignment in Business Settings* (pp. 24–52). Hershey, PA: IGI Global. doi:10.4018/978-1-5225-0861-8.ch002

Pérez-Uribe, R. I., Torres, D. A., Jurado, S. P., & Prada, D. M. (2018). Cloud Tools for the Development of Project Management in SMEs. In R. Perez-Uribe, C. Salcedo-Perez, & D. Ocampo-Guzman (Eds.), *Handbook of Research on Intrapreneurship and Organizational Sustainability in SMEs* (pp. 95–120). Hershey, PA: IGI Global. doi:10.4018/978-1-5225-3543-0.ch005

Petrisor, I., & Cozmiuc, D. (2017). Global Supply Chain Management Organization at Siemens in the Advent of Industry 4.0. In L. Saglietto & C. Cezanne (Eds.), *Global Intermediation and Logistics Service Providers* (pp. 123–142). Hershey, PA: IGI Global. doi:10.4018/978-1-5225-2133-4.ch007

Pierce, J. M., Velliaris, D. M., & Edwards, J. (2017). A Living Case Study: A Journey Not a Destination. In N. Silton (Ed.), *Exploring the Benefits of Creativity in Education, Media, and the Arts* (pp. 158–178). Hershey, PA: IGI Global. doi:10.4018/978-1-5225-0504-4.ch008

Pipia, S., & Pipia, S. (2021). Challenges of Religious Tourism in the Conflict Region: An Example of Jerusalem. In E. Alaverdov & M. Bari (Eds.), *Global Development of Religious Tourism* (pp. 135-148). IGI Global. https://doi.org/10.4018/978-1-7998-5792-1.ch009

Poulaki, P., Kritikos, A., Vasilakis, N., & Valeri, M. (2022). The Contribution of Female Creativity to the Development of Gastronomic Tourism in Greece: The Case of the Island of Naxos in the South Aegean Region. In M. Valeri (Ed.), *New Governance and Management in Touristic Destinations* (pp. 246–258). IGI Global. https://doi.org/10.4018/978-1-6684-3889-3.ch015

Radosavljevic, M., & Andjelkovic, A. (2017). Multi-Criteria Decision Making Approach for Choosing Business Process for the Improvement: Upgrading of the Six Sigma Methodology. In J. Stanković, P. Delias, S. Marinković, & S. Rochhia (Eds.), *Tools and Techniques for Economic Decision Analysis* (pp. 225–247). Hershey, PA: IGI Global. doi:10.4018/978-1-5225-0959-2.ch011

Radovic, V. M. (2017). Corporate Sustainability and Responsibility and Disaster Risk Reduction: A Serbian Overview. In M. Camilleri (Ed.), *CSR 2.0 and the New Era of Corporate Citizenship* (pp. 147–164). Hershey, PA: IGI Global. doi:10.4018/978-1-5225-1842-6.ch008

Raghunath, K. M., Devi, S. L., & Patro, C. S. (2018). Impact of Risk Assessment Models on Risk Factors: A Holistic Outlook. In K. Strang, M. Korstanje, & N. Vajjhala (Eds.), *Research, Practices, and Innovations in Global Risk and Contingency Management* (pp. 134–153). Hershey, PA: IGI Global. doi:10.4018/978-1-5225-4754-9.ch008

Raman, A., & Goyal, D. P. (2017). Extending IMPLEMENT Framework for Enterprise Information Systems Implementation to Information System Innovation. In M. Tavana (Ed.), *Enterprise Information Systems and the Digitalization of Business Functions* (pp. 137–177). Hershey, PA: IGI Global. doi:10.4018/978-1-5225-2382-6.ch007

Rao, Y., & Zhang, Y. (2017). The Construction and Development of Academic Library Digital Special Subject Databases. In L. Ruan, Q. Zhu, & Y. Ye (Eds.), *Academic Library Development and Administration in China* (pp. 163–183). Hershey, PA: IGI Global. doi:10.4018/978-1-5225-0550-1.ch010

Ravasan, A. Z., Mohammadi, M. M., & Hamidi, H. (2018). An Investigation Into the Critical Success Factors of Implementing Information Technology Service Management Frameworks. In K. Jakobs (Ed.), *Corporate and Global Standardization Initiatives in Contemporary Society* (pp. 200–218). Hershey, PA: IGI Global. doi:10.4018/978-1-5225-5320-5.ch009

Rezaie, S., Mirabedini, S. J., & Abtahi, A. (2018). Designing a Model for Implementation of Business Intelligence in the Banking Industry. *International Journal of Enterprise Information Systems, 14*(1), 77–103. doi:10.4018/IJEIS.2018010105

Richards, V., Matthews, N., Williams, O. J., & Khan, Z. (2021). The Challenges of Accessible Tourism Information Systems for Tourists With Vision Impairment: Sensory Communications Beyond the Screen. In C. Eusébio, L. Teixeira, & M. Carneiro (Eds.), *ICT Tools and Applications for Accessible Tourism* (pp. 26–54). IGI Global. https://doi.org/10.4018/978-1-7998-6428-8.ch002

Rodrigues de Souza Neto, V., & Marques, O. (2021). Rural Tourism Fostering Welfare Through Sustainable Development: A Conceptual Approach. In A. Perinotto, V. Mayer, & J. Soares (Eds.), *Rebuilding and Restructuring the Tourism Industry: Infusion of Happiness and Quality of Life* (pp. 38–57). IGI Global. https://doi.org/10.4018/978-1-7998-7239-9.ch003

Romano, L., Grimaldi, R., & Colasuonno, F. S. (2017). Demand Management as a Success Factor in Project Portfolio Management. In L. Romano (Ed.), *Project Portfolio Management Strategies for Effective Organizational Operations* (pp. 202–219). Hershey, PA: IGI Global. doi:10.4018/978-1-5225-2151-8.ch008

Rubio-Escuderos, L., & García-Andreu, H. (2021). Competitiveness Factors of Accessible Tourism E-Travel Agencies. In C. Eusébio, L. Teixeira, & M. Carneiro (Eds.), *ICT Tools and Applications for Accessible Tourism* (pp. 196–217). IGI Global. https://doi.org/10.4018/978-1-7998-6428-8.ch009

Rucci, A. C., Porto, N., Darcy, S., & Becka, L. (2021). Smart and Accessible Cities?: Not Always – The Case for Accessible Tourism Initiatives in Buenos Aries and Sydney. In C. Eusébio, L. Teixeira, & M. Carneiro (Eds.), *ICT Tools and Applications for Accessible Tourism* (pp. 115–145). IGI Global. https://doi.org/10.4018/978-1-7998-6428-8.ch006

Ruhi, U. (2018). Towards an Interdisciplinary Socio-Technical Definition of Virtual Communities. In M. Khosrow-Pour, D.B.A. (Ed.), Encyclopedia of Information Science and Technology, Fourth Edition (pp. 4278-4295). Hershey, PA: IGI Global. doi:10.4018/978-1-5225-2255-3.ch371

Ryan, L., Catena, M., Ros, P., & Stephens, S. (2021). Designing Entrepreneurial Ecosystems to Support Resource Management in the Tourism Industry. In V. Costa, A. Moura, & M. Mira (Eds.), *Handbook of Research on Human Capital and People Management in the Tourism Industry* (pp. 265–281). IGI Global. https://doi.org/10.4018/978-1-7998-4318-4.ch013

Sabuncu, I. (2021). Understanding Tourist Perceptions and Expectations During Pandemic Through Social Media Big Data. In M. Demir, A. Dalgıç, & F. Ergen (Eds.), *Handbook of Research on the Impacts and Implications of COVID-19 on the Tourism Industry* (pp. 330–350). IGI Global. https://doi.org/10.4018/978-1-7998-8231-2.ch016

Safari, M. R., & Jiang, Q. (2018). The Theory and Practice of IT Governance Maturity and Strategies Alignment: Evidence From Banking Industry. *Journal of Global Information Management*, *26*(2), 127–146. doi:10.4018/JGIM.2018040106

Sahoo, J., Pati, B., & Mohanty, B. (2017). Knowledge Management as an Academic Discipline: An Assessment. In B. Gunjal (Ed.), *Managing Knowledge and Scholarly Assets in Academic Libraries* (pp. 99–126). Hershey, PA: IGI Global. doi:10.4018/978-1-5225-1741-2.ch005

Saini, D. (2017). Relevance of Teaching Values and Ethics in Management Education. In N. Baporikar (Ed.), *Management Education for Global Leadership* (pp. 90–111). Hershey, PA: IGI Global. doi:10.4018/978-1-5225-1013-0.ch005

Sambhanthan, A. (2017). Assessing and Benchmarking Sustainability in Organisations: An Integrated Conceptual Model. *International Journal of Systems and Service-Oriented Engineering*, *7*(4), 22–43. doi:10.4018/IJSSOE.2017100102

Sambhanthan, A., & Potdar, V. (2017). A Study of the Parameters Impacting Sustainability in Information Technology Organizations. *International Journal of Knowledge-Based Organizations*, *7*(3), 27–39. doi:10.4018/IJKBO.2017070103

Sánchez-Fernández, M. D., & Manríquez, M. R. (2018). The Entrepreneurial Spirit Based on Social Values: The Digital Generation. In P. Isaias & L. Carvalho (Eds.), *User Innovation and the Entrepreneurship Phenomenon in the Digital Economy* (pp. 173–193). Hershey, PA: IGI Global. doi:10.4018/978-1-5225-2826-5.ch009

Sanchez-Ruiz, L., & Blanco, B. (2017). Process Management for SMEs: Barriers, Enablers, and Benefits. In M. Vemić (Ed.), *Optimal Management Strategies in Small and Medium Enterprises* (pp. 293–319). Hershey, PA: IGI Global. doi:10.4018/978-1-5225-1949-2.ch014

Sanz, L. F., Gómez-Pérez, J., & Castillo-Martinez, A. (2018). Analysis of the European ICT Competence Frameworks. In V. Ahuja & S. Rathore (Eds.), *Multidisciplinary Perspectives on Human Capital and Information Technology Professionals* (pp. 225–245). Hershey, PA: IGI Global. doi:10.4018/978-1-5225-5297-0.ch012

Sarvepalli, A., & Godin, J. (2017). Business Process Management in the Classroom. *Journal of Cases on Information Technology*, *19*(2), 17–28. doi:10.4018/JCIT.2017040102

Saxena, G. G., & Saxena, A. (2021). Host Community Role in Medical Tourism Development. In M. Singh & S. Kumaran (Eds.), *Growth of the Medical Tourism Industry and Its Impact on Society: Emerging Research and Opportunities* (pp. 105–127). IGI Global. https://doi.org/10.4018/978-1-7998-3427-4.ch006

Saygili, E. E., Ozturkoglu, Y., & Kocakulah, M. C. (2017). End Users' Perceptions of Critical Success Factors in ERP Applications. *International Journal of Enterprise Information Systems*, *13*(4), 58–75. doi:10.4018/IJEIS.2017100104

Saygili, E. E., & Saygili, A. T. (2017). Contemporary Issues in Enterprise Information Systems: A Critical Review of CSFs in ERP Implementations. In M. Tavana (Ed.), *Enterprise Information Systems and the Digitalization of Business Functions* (pp. 120–136). Hershey, PA: IGI Global. doi:10.4018/978-1-5225-2382-6.ch006

Schwaiger, K. M., & Zehrer, A. (2021). The COVID-19 Pandemic and Organizational Resilience in Hospitality Family Firms: A Qualitative Approach. In A. Zehrer, G. Glowka, K. Schwaiger, & V. Ranacher-Lackner (Eds.), *Resiliency Models and Addressing Future Risks for Family Firms in the Tourism Industry* (pp. 32–49). IGI Global. https://doi.org/10.4018/978-1-7998-7352-5.ch002

Scott, N., & Campos, A. C. (2022). Cognitive Science of Tourism Experiences. In R. Augusto Costa, F. Brandão, Z. Breda, & C. Costa (Eds.), Planning and Managing the Experience Economy in Tourism (pp. 1-21). IGI Global. https://doi.org/ doi:10.4018/978-1-7998-8775-1.ch001

Seidenstricker, S., & Antonino, A. (2018). Business Model Innovation-Oriented Technology Management for Emergent Technologies. In M. Khosrow-Pour, D.B.A. (Ed.), Encyclopedia of Information Science and Technology, Fourth Edition (pp. 4560-4569). Hershey, PA: IGI Global. doi:10.4018/978-1-5225-2255-3.ch396

Selvi, M. S. (2021). Changes in Tourism Sales and Marketing Post COVID-19. In M. Demir, A. Dalgıç, & F. Ergen (Eds.), *Handbook of Research on the Impacts and Implications of COVID-19 on the Tourism Industry* (pp. 437–460). IGI Global. doi:10.4018/978-1-7998-8231-2.ch021

Senaratne, S., & Gunarathne, A. D. (2017). Excellence Perspective for Management Education from a Global Accountants' Hub in Asia. In N. Baporikar (Ed.), *Management Education for Global Leadership* (pp. 158–180). Hershey, PA: IGI Global. doi:10.4018/978-1-5225-1013-0.ch008

Sensuse, D. I., & Cahyaningsih, E. (2018). Knowledge Management Models: A Summative Review. *International Journal of Information Systems in the Service Sector*, *10*(1), 71–100. doi:10.4018/IJISSS.2018010105

Seth, M., Goyal, D., & Kiran, R. (2017). Diminution of Impediments in Implementation of Supply Chain Management Information System for Enhancing its Effectiveness in Indian Automobile Industry. *Journal of Global Information Management*, *25*(3), 1–20. doi:10.4018/JGIM.2017070101

Seyal, A. H., & Rahman, M. N. (2017). Investigating Impact of Inter-Organizational Factors in Measuring ERP Systems Success: Bruneian Perspectives. In M. Tavana (Ed.), *Enterprise Information Systems and the Digitalization of Business Functions* (pp. 178–204). Hershey, PA: IGI Global. doi:10.4018/978-1-5225-2382-6.ch008

Shaqrah, A. A. (2018). Analyzing Business Intelligence Systems Based on 7s Model of McKinsey. *International Journal of Business Intelligence Research*, *9*(1), 53–63. doi:10.4018/IJBIR.2018010104

Sharma, A. J. (2017). Enhancing Sustainability through Experiential Learning in Management Education. In N. Baporikar (Ed.), *Management Education for Global Leadership* (pp. 256–274). Hershey, PA: IGI Global. doi:10.4018/978-1-5225-1013-0.ch013

Shetty, K. P. (2017). Responsible Global Leadership: Ethical Challenges in Management Education. In N. Baporikar (Ed.), *Innovation and Shifting Perspectives in Management Education* (pp. 194–223). Hershey, PA: IGI Global. doi:10.4018/978-1-5225-1019-2.ch009

Sinthupundaja, J., & Kohda, Y. (2017). Effects of Corporate Social Responsibility and Creating Shared Value on Sustainability. *International Journal of Sustainable Entrepreneurship and Corporate Social Responsibility*, *2*(1), 27–38. doi:10.4018/IJSECSR.2017010103

Škarica, I., & Hrgović, A. V. (2018). Implementation of Total Quality Management Principles in Public Health Institutes in the Republic of Croatia. *International Journal of Productivity Management and Assessment Technologies*, *6*(1), 1–16. doi:10.4018/IJPMAT.2018010101

Skokic, V. (2021). How Small Hotel Owners Practice Resilience: Longitudinal Study Among Small Family Hotels in Croatia. In A. Zehrer, G. Glowka, K. Schwaiger, & V. Ranacher-Lackner (Eds.), *Resiliency Models and Addressing Future Risks for Family Firms in the Tourism Industry* (pp. 50–73). IGI Global. doi:10.4018/978-1-7998-7352-5.ch003

Smuts, H., Kotzé, P., Van der Merwe, A., & Loock, M. (2017). Framework for Managing Shared Knowledge in an Information Systems Outsourcing Context. *International Journal of Knowledge Management*, *13*(4), 1–30. doi:10.4018/IJKM.2017100101

Sousa, M. J., Cruz, R., Dias, I., & Caracol, C. (2017). Information Management Systems in the Supply Chain. In G. Jamil, A. Soares, & C. Pessoa (Eds.), *Handbook of Research on Information Management for Effective Logistics and Supply Chains* (pp. 469–485). Hershey, PA: IGI Global. doi:10.4018/978-1-5225-0973-8.ch025

Spremic, M., Turulja, L., & Bajgoric, N. (2018). Two Approaches in Assessing Business Continuity Management Attitudes in the Organizational Context. In N. Bajgoric (Ed.), *Always-On Enterprise Information Systems for Modern Organizations* (pp. 159–183). Hershey, PA: IGI Global. doi:10.4018/978-1-5225-3704-5.ch008

Steenkamp, A. L. (2018). Some Insights in Computer Science and Information Technology. In *Examining the Changing Role of Supervision in Doctoral Research Projects: Emerging Research and Opportunities* (pp. 113–133). Hershey, PA: IGI Global. doi:10.4018/978-1-5225-2610-0.ch005

Stipanović, C., Rudan, E., & Zubović, V. (2022). Reaching the New Tourist Through Creativity: Sustainable Development Challenges in Croatian Coastal Towns. In M. Valeri (Ed.), *New Governance and Management in Touristic Destinations* (pp. 231–245). IGI Global. https://doi.org/10.4018/978-1-6684-3889-3.ch014

Tabach, A., & Croteau, A. (2017). Configurations of Information Technology Governance Practices and Business Unit Performance. *International Journal of IT/Business Alignment and Governance*, *8*(2), 1–27. doi:10.4018/IJITBAG.2017070101

Talaue, G. M., & Iqbal, T. (2017). Assessment of e-Business Mode of Selected Private Universities in the Philippines and Pakistan. *International Journal of Online Marketing*, *7*(4), 63–77. doi:10.4018/IJOM.2017100105

Tam, G. C. (2017). Project Manager Sustainability Competence. In *Managerial Strategies and Green Solutions for Project Sustainability* (pp. 178–207). Hershey, PA: IGI Global. doi:10.4018/978-1-5225-2371-0.ch008

Tambo, T. (2018). Fashion Retail Innovation: About Context, Antecedents, and Outcome in Technological Change Projects. In I. Management Association (Ed.), Fashion and Textiles: Breakthroughs in Research and Practice (pp. 233-260). Hershey, PA: IGI Global. https://doi.org/ doi:10.4018/978-1-5225-3432-7.ch010

Tantau, A. D., & Frăţilă, L. C. (2018). Information and Management System for Renewable Energy Business. In *Entrepreneurship and Business Development in the Renewable Energy Sector* (pp. 200–244). Hershey, PA: IGI Global. doi:10.4018/978-1-5225-3625-3.ch006

Teixeira, N., Pardal, P. N., & Rafael, B. G. (2018). Internationalization, Financial Performance, and Organizational Challenges: A Success Case in Portugal. In L. Carvalho (Ed.), *Handbook of Research on Entrepreneurial Ecosystems and Social Dynamics in a Globalized World* (pp. 379–423). Hershey, PA: IGI Global. doi:10.4018/978-1-5225-3525-6.ch017

Teixeira, P., Teixeira, L., Eusébio, C., Silva, S., & Teixeira, A. (2021). The Impact of ICTs on Accessible Tourism: Evidence Based on a Systematic Literature Review. In C. Eusébio, L. Teixeira, & M. Carneiro (Eds.), *ICT Tools and Applications for Accessible Tourism* (pp. 1–25). IGI Global. doi:10.4018/978-1-7998-6428-8.ch001

Trad, A., & Kalpić, D. (2018). The Business Transformation Framework, Agile Project and Change Management. In M. Khosrow-Pour, D.B.A. (Ed.), Encyclopedia of Information Science and Technology, Fourth Edition (pp. 620-635). Hershey, PA: IGI Global. https://doi.org/ doi:10.4018/978-1-5225-2255-3.ch054

Trad, A., & Kalpić, D. (2018). The Business Transformation and Enterprise Architecture Framework: The Financial Engineering E-Risk Management and E-Law Integration. In B. Sergi, F. Fidanoski, M. Ziolo, & V. Naumovski (Eds.), *Regaining Global Stability After the Financial Crisis* (pp. 46–65). Hershey, PA: IGI Global. doi:10.4018/978-1-5225-4026-7.ch003

Trengereid, V. (2022). Conditions of Network Engagement: The Quest for a Common Good. In R. Augusto Costa, F. Brandão, Z. Breda, & C. Costa (Eds.), *Planning and Managing the Experience Economy in Tourism* (pp. 69-84). IGI Global. https://doi.org/10.4018/978-1-7998-8775-1.ch004

Turulja, L., & Bajgoric, N. (2018). Business Continuity and Information Systems: A Systematic Literature Review. In N. Bajgoric (Ed.), *Always-On Enterprise Information Systems for Modern Organizations* (pp. 60–87). Hershey, PA: IGI Global. doi:10.4018/978-1-5225-3704-5.ch004

Vargas-Hernández, J. G. (2017). Professional Integrity in Business Management Education. In N. Baporikar (Ed.), *Management Education for Global Leadership* (pp. 70–89). Hershey, PA: IGI Global. doi:10.4018/978-1-5225-1013-0.ch004

Varnacı Uzun, F. (2021). The Destination Preferences of Foreign Tourists During the COVID-19 Pandemic and Attitudes Towards: Marmaris, Turkey. In M. Demir, A. Dalgıç, & F. Ergen (Eds.), *Handbook of Research on the Impacts and Implications of COVID-19 on the Tourism Industry* (pp. 285–306). IGI Global. https://doi.org/10.4018/978-1-7998-8231-2.ch014

Vasista, T. G., & AlAbdullatif, A. M. (2017). Role of Electronic Customer Relationship Management in Demand Chain Management: A Predictive Analytic Approach. *International Journal of Information Systems and Supply Chain Management, 10*(1), 53–67. doi:10.4018/IJISSCM.2017010104

Vieru, D., & Bourdeau, S. (2017). Survival in the Digital Era: A Digital Competence-Based Multi-Case Study in the Canadian SME Clothing Industry. *International Journal of Social and Organizational Dynamics in IT*, *6*(1), 17–34. doi:10.4018/IJSODIT.2017010102

Vijayan, G., & Kamarulzaman, N. H. (2017). An Introduction to Sustainable Supply Chain Management and Business Implications. In M. Khan, M. Hussain, & M. Ajmal (Eds.), *Green Supply Chain Management for Sustainable Business Practice* (pp. 27–50). Hershey, PA: IGI Global. doi:10.4018/978-1-5225-0635-5.ch002

Vlachvei, A., & Notta, O. (2017). Firm Competitiveness: Theories, Evidence, and Measurement. In A. Vlachvei, O. Notta, K. Karantininis, & N. Tsounis (Eds.), *Factors Affecting Firm Competitiveness and Performance in the Modern Business World* (pp. 1–42). Hershey, PA: IGI Global. doi:10.4018/978-1-5225-0843-4.ch001

Wang, C., Schofield, M., Li, X., & Ou, X. (2017). Do Chinese Students in Public and Private Higher Education Institutes Perform at Different Level in One of the Leadership Skills: Critical Thinking?: An Exploratory Comparison. In V. Wang (Ed.), *Encyclopedia of Strategic Leadership and Management* (pp. 160–181). Hershey, PA: IGI Global. doi:10.4018/978-1-5225-1049-9.ch013

Wang, J. (2017). Multi-Agent based Production Management Decision System Modelling for the Textile Enterprise. *Journal of Global Information Management, 25*(4), 1–15. doi:10.4018/JGIM.2017100101

Wiedemann, A., & Gewald, H. (2017). Examining Cross-Domain Alignment: The Correlation of Business Strategy, IT Management, and IT Business Value. *International Journal of IT/Business Alignment and Governance, 8*(1), 17–31. doi:10.4018/IJITBAG.2017010102

Wolf, R., & Thiel, M. (2018). Advancing Global Business Ethics in China: Reducing Poverty Through Human and Social Welfare. In S. Hipsher (Ed.), *Examining the Private Sector's Role in Wealth Creation and Poverty Reduction* (pp. 67–84). Hershey, PA: IGI Global. doi:10.4018/978-1-5225-3117-3.ch004

Yablonsky, S. (2018). Innovation Platforms: Data and Analytics Platforms. In *Multi-Sided Platforms (MSPs) and Sharing Strategies in the Digital Economy: Emerging Research and Opportunities* (pp. 72–95). Hershey, PA: IGI Global. doi:10.4018/978-1-5225-5457-8.ch003

Yaşar, B. (2021). The Impact of COVID-19 on Volatility of Tourism Stocks: Evidence From BIST Tourism Index. In M. Demir, A. Dalgıç, & F. Ergen (Eds.), *Handbook of Research on the Impacts and Implications of COVID-19 on the Tourism Industry* (pp. 23–44). IGI Global. https://doi.org/10.4018/978-1-7998-8231-2.ch002

Yusoff, A., Ahmad, N. H., & Halim, H. A. (2017). Agropreneurship among Gen Y in Malaysia: The Role of Academic Institutions. In N. Ahmad, T. Ramayah, H. Halim, & S. Rahman (Eds.), *Handbook of Research on Small and Medium Enterprises in Developing Countries* (pp. 23–47). Hershey, PA: IGI Global. doi:10.4018/978-1-5225-2165-5.ch002

Zacher, D., & Pechlaner, H. (2021). Resilience as an Opportunity Approach: Challenges and Perspectives for Private Sector Participation on a Community Level. In A. Zehrer, G. Glowka, K. Schwaiger, & V. Ranacher-Lackner (Eds.), *Resiliency Models and Addressing Future Risks for Family Firms in the Tourism Industry* (pp. 75–102). IGI Global. https://doi.org/10.4018/978-1-7998-7352-5.ch004

Zanin, F., Comuzzi, E., & Costantini, A. (2018). The Effect of Business Strategy and Stock Market Listing on the Use of Risk Assessment Tools. In *Management Control Systems in Complex Settings: Emerging Research and Opportunities* (pp. 145–168). Hershey, PA: IGI Global. doi:10.4018/978-1-5225-3987-2.ch007

Zgheib, P. W. (2017). Corporate Innovation and Intrapreneurship in the Middle East. In P. Zgheib (Ed.), *Entrepreneurship and Business Innovation in the Middle East* (pp. 37–56). Hershey, PA: IGI Global. doi:10.4018/978-1-5225-2066-5.ch003

About the Contributors

Naima Bentouir, PhD in finance and business management, is assistant professor at Ain Temouchent University.

Aziza Chachdi is an assistant professor at the Polydisciplinary Faculty Sidi Bennour, University of Chouaîb Doukkali, El Jadida.

Abdelali Ezziadi, born in Marrakech in 1989, is an assistant professor at Polydisciplinary Faculty of Sidi Bennour, Chouaib Doukkali University. His research interests are in the areas of management control, public governance, and SI and project management. He has published his work in research publications including Journal of Economics, Finance And Management Studies and Springer.

Yao Ge is an independent researcher. His research interests include FinTech, Chinese business and FashionTech.

Güzide Karakuş is an Assistant Professor at Necmettin Erbakan University, department of Aviation Management. He holds a bachelor's degree in Industrial Engineering from Kocaeli University (1999) and an MBA degree from Gebze Institute of Technology. (2002). She completed her PhD in Production Management and Marketing at Selçuk Universitiy 2014. Prior joining academia, she worked in consulting about quality management systems, CE marking and project management. She works and teaches Innovation Management, Technology Management, Project Management, Quality Management, Sustainable Operations Management, Supply Chain Management, both undergraduate and graduate level.

Mohamed Wadie Lahouirich, born in Marrakech in 1990, studied at the National School of Commerce and Management of Cadi Ayyad University, option Financial and Accounting Management. Top of his class, he showed a strong interest in research and pedagogy, thus encouraging him to continue his studies to obtain a doctorate in Management Sciences from the same university. Mohamed Wadie began an atypical professional career reconciling between science and experience, which allowed him to evolve quickly in both worlds, private and public sectors. His passion for teaching and research as well as his vocation to reconcile fieldwork and pedagogy have enabled him to provide training in several establishments. Currently, Mohamed Wadie is a Professor at the Chouaib Doukkali University of El Jadida.

Khaled Mohamed Mahmoud is assistant professor of accounting at the International Higher Institute for Languages and Translation and has a PhD of Accounting and Auditing from Ainshams University.

Kudzai Mandizvidza is an Economic Development professional who over time has worked in vast, multidisciplinary areas involving, Economic Research and Quantitative Analysis, Consultancy and Training, Agricultural Investment Management, Rural Economic Development, Agricultural Marketing, Project Management and Education. He holds amongst other qualifications, a Master of Science in Agricultural Economics degree, as well as a Bachelor of Agribusiness Management degree. Kudzai has also worked with seasoned, multi- cultural and international researchers, at both academic and professional levels. He has contributed to the body of knowledge through publications, conference papers, desk studies, sector analysis, along with international investment reports.

Hesham Mohamed is assistant professor of accounting at the International Higher Institute for Languages and Translation and has a Ph.D. of Accounting and Auditing from Helwan University.

Mujeeb Saif Mohsen Al-Absy is Assistant Professor at Department of Accounting and Financial Sciences, College of Administrative and Financial Sciences, Gulf University, Kingdom of Bahrain.

James Mulli is the President and Academic Dean of the European Business University. He lectures in Blockchain Technologies, post-graduate Corporate Finance & Business Statistics, and Managerial Accounting. He worked as a Portfolio Manager for the Soros Fund Management's Quantum Industrial Partners and holds a Doctorate and Masters degree from Saint Johns University, New York, and an MBA from New Hampshire Plymouth State University with specialization in Investment and Finance. Dr. Mulli is an international educator, and educational technology consultant with a keen interest in looking over the horizon at how technology is shaping the world. His search for trends in emerging technologies allows him to be an educator who applies skills to help students thrive. He is the founder of European Business University of Luxembourg, both non-for-profit educational providers whose initiative is to support existing Institutions in developing e-learning. His belief is that education is the silver bullet for development and through existing expertise and support infrastructure, EBU can provide the needed "jump-start" to institutions in Europe, Africa, Asia and beyond.

Poshan (Sam) Yu is a Lecturer in Accounting and Finance in the International Cooperative Education Program of Soochow University (China). He is also an External Professor of FinTech and Finance at SKEMA Business School (China), a Visiting Professor at Krirk University (Thailand) and a Visiting Researcher at the Australian Studies Centre of Shanghai University (China). Sam leads FasterCapital (Dubai, UAE) as a Regional Partner (China) and serves as a Startup Mentor for AIC RAISE (Coimbatore, India). His research interests include financial technology, regulatory technology, public-private partnerships, mergers and acquisitions, private equity, venture capital, start-ups, intellectual property, art finance, and China's "One Belt One Road" policy.

Index

A

Adverse Selection 53, 84

B

Blockchain 52-54, 56-57, 59-65, 67-69, 71, 73-84, 182
Board of Directors 18, 20-21, 26-27, 29-30, 48, 116

C

Chinese Market 52-53, 59, 78
Chinese Policies 53, 65-67, 69, 71
CiteSpace 61, 63-64, 80
Concept of Sustainable Development 2-3, 16, 131, 134, 136
Construction 58, 65, 119, 130-141, 143-148, 167
Corporate Governance 18, 21, 24-34, 44-49, 83, 125
Corporate Social Responsibility (CSR) 110-111, 129
Cost Centre 109
Credit 8, 13, 15, 34, 45, 52-53, 55-56, 65, 69, 74-75, 77-78, 82, 84
Credit Rationing 53, 84
Cryptocurrency 84

D

Data Silos 57, 84
Decentralized Public Ledger 52-53, 84
Digital Transformation 83, 179-182, 186-188, 193-194, 197-205
Digitalization 66, 182, 186, 188, 193, 196, 201

E

Enterprise Resource Management (ERP) 205
Entrepreneurial dynamic 164, 169
Entrepreneurial finance 157
Entrepreneurial motivations 149, 151
Environmental Impact 87, 90, 94-95, 107, 109, 114
Environmental Performance 87, 94, 109

F

Financial Innovation 52
Financial performance 1, 21, 30, 32, 36-37, 46, 48, 50, 89-90, 92-93, 100, 103, 106, 108, 124, 135, 138, 149-151, 153, 155-156, 159, 164-165, 168-169, 171-172, 174-175
Financial Stability 18, 20-22, 24-26, 29-30, 33-39, 41, 43, 45-48, 86, 88, 96, 99-101
Firm Competitiveness 88-90, 101, 105-107
Firm Performance 26, 28-30, 84, 86-89, 100, 107, 146, 176

G

Gender 21, 30, 32, 36, 47-48, 50, 91, 174
Global performance 46, 162-163
Grasping the Big and Releasing the Small

57, 84

H

Hashing Algorithms 54, 84

I

ICO 71, 84
Importance of Sustainable Development 1-2
Industry 4.0 179-183, 185-193, 195, 197-204, 206
Islamic Banking 18, 20-21, 25, 27, 29-38, 41, 44, 46-49
Islamic Banks 18, 20-25, 27-36, 39, 41, 43-50

M

Manufacturing Enterprises 204
Merkle Trees 54, 85

N

non-family companies 124

P

Panel Data 18, 22, 27, 33, 45
Performance 1-2, 4-5, 8, 15, 20-21, 26-32, 36-37, 45-50, 76, 81-82, 84, 86-90, 92-94, 97-98, 100-109, 113, 116-117, 121, 124, 128, 130-138, 144-149, 151-159, 161-165, 168, 170-177, 182, 197-198, 201
Performance Management 130-133, 135-136, 144-147, 172, 197
Profit Centre 97, 109

R

Resilience 86, 99, 101, 204

S

Small and Meduim Entreprises (SME) 15, 52, 58, 77, 83, 109, 129, 131, 134, 138, 140, 146
SME family 112, 117
Sustainability Innovation 86-90, 93-94, 97-103, 106-107, 109
Sustainable Development 1-5, 9-11, 13-17, 20-21, 34-35, 37, 41, 52-53, 78, 81, 83, 91, 105-106, 116, 130-131, 133-134, 136, 143, 149-151, 153, 158-159, 162-164, 170, 172-173, 175, 205
Sustainable Management 109, 137, 140-141
Sustainable performance 131, 152

T

Timestamps 85

Recommended Reference Books

IGI Global's reference books are available in three unique pricing formats:
Print Only, E-Book Only, or Print + E-Book.

Order direct through IGI Global's Online Bookstore at **www.igi-global.com** or through your preferred provider.

ISBN: 9781799887096
EISBN: 9781799887119
© 2022; 413 pp.
List Price: US$ **250**

ISBN: 9781799874157
EISBN: 9781799874164
© 2022; 334 pp.
List Price: US$ **240**

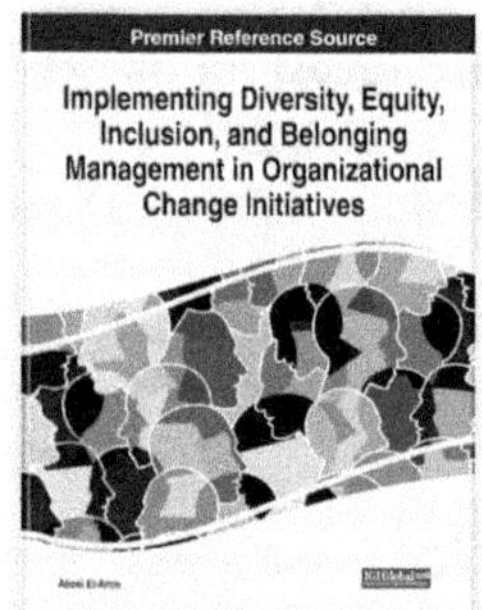

ISBN: 9781668440230
EISBN: 9781668440254
© 2022; 320 pp.
List Price: US$ **215**

ISBN: 9781799889502
EISBN: 9781799889526
© 2022; 263 pp.
List Price: US$ **240**

ISBN: 9781799885283
EISBN: 9781799885306
© 2022; 587 pp.
List Price: US$ **360**

ISBN: 9781668455906
EISBN: 9781668455913
© 2022; 2,235 pp.
List Price: US$ **1,865**

Do you want to stay current on the latest research trends, product announcements, news, and special offers?
Join IGI Global's mailing list to receive customized recommendations, exclusive discounts, and more.
Sign up at: **www.igi-global.com/newsletters.**

Publisher of Timely, Peer-Reviewed Inclusive Research Since 1988

IGI Global
PUBLISHER of TIMELY KNOWLEDGE

www.igi-global.com Sign up at www.igi-global.com/newsletters facebook.com/igiglobal twitter.com/igiglobal

www.ingramcontent.com/pod-product-compliance
Lightning Source LLC
LaVergne TN
LVHW061538290926
849162LV00004B/841

* 9 7 8 1 6 6 8 4 4 8 3 4 2 *